False
Economies

False Economies

THE STRANGEST, LEAST SUCCESSFUL AND MOST AUDACIOUS FINANCIAL FOLLIES, PLANS AND CRAZES OF ALL TIME

S. D. TUCKER

AMBERLEY

S. D. Tucker is the author of *Space Oddities*, *Great British Eccentrics* and *Forgotten Science*. He writes a regular column in the *Fortean Times*.

First published 2018

Amberley Publishing
The Hill, Stroud
Gloucestershire, GL5 4EP

www.amberley-books.com

British Library Cataloguing in Publication Data.
A catalogue record for this book is available from the British Library.

ISBN 978 1 4456 7234 2 (paperback)
ISBN 978 1 4456 7235 9 (ebook)

Typeset in 10pt on 12pt Sabon.
Typesetting and Origination by Amberley Publishing.
Printed in the UK.

Contents

A crank? Yes, I'm a crank; a little device that causes revolutions!

E. F. Schumacher, economist

*A bank is a place that will lend you money if
you can prove that you don't need it.*

Bob Hope, comedian

The safest place of deposit is in the pants of the people.

Thomas Jefferson, US Founding Father

88.2 per cent of all statistics are made up on the spot.

Vic Reeves, comedian

Introduction
An Expert Dismissal

Beware of false prophets, which come to you in sheep's clothing, but inwardly they are ravening wolves.

Matthew 7:15

On the evening of 3 June 2016, during the build-up to the great European referendum vote, then Justice Secretary Michael Gove made one of the most famous political statements of modern times during a live Sky News television debate. 'People in this country have had enough of experts,' he said.[1] Indeed we had – and the precise experts he was talking about were economists.

When it came to Brexit, the vast majority of the profession had warned the public, in increasingly doom-laden tones, that a vote for Britain to leave the EU would lead to a sudden and sharp financial decline. All kinds of disasters would befall our foolish island immediately, it was said, and any number of punitive fiscal measures would have to be taken. The Chancellor at the time, George Osborne, warned he would have no option but to present the country with a special Emergency Budget, filled with swingeing tax hikes and punitive spending cuts in a desperate attempt to keep Britain from simply crawling into the nearest ditch and dying like a lame dog. An alphabet soup of supposedly impartial transnational financial organisations predicted that the British economy would instantly fall off a cliff, followed moments later by a wave of terrified investors, eager to end it all on the rocks below. As it was … nothing much happened. The pound lost some of its value, and then stabilised – at a level which was actually of benefit to some British firms who relied on making exports. The FTSE 100 also declined in value, only to recover and then surpass its original pre-referendum rating; as I write, it stands at a record high. Of course, economic matters being what they are, perhaps you are reading these words in five or ten years' time and reduced to eating wallpaper like at Stalingrad. Maybe you will even feel compelled to eat this book. Some economists and financial institutions have since recalibrated their models for post-Brexit Britain, and now claim that our destruction will come in a drip-drip fashion rather than in a sudden flood akin to the 1929 Wall Street Crash, which does rather smack of an exercise in institutional face-saving. The fact is that these people, these alleged experts, promised us *immediate* calamity, and, no doubt to the great displeasure of Remoaners like Mr Osborne, it never came. Why?

When he made his comment about Britain having had enough of experts, Michael Gove was interrupted mid-sentence by his interlocutor. What Gove had *intended* to say was not a volley aimed at experts in general, but something along the lines of 'People in this country have had enough of experts from organisations with acronyms saying that they know what is best and getting it consistently wrong.'[2] Whoever could he have had in mind? Consider the IMF. Initially, the International Monetary Fund took the line that, in the long term, investment and trade with the UK would slowly decline if Brexit really took place. Then, as the polls narrowed as referendum day on 23 June closed in, they began to change their tune; less than a week before polling stations opened, the IMF released a report cautioning that a Leave vote would immediately send the UK sliding into a long recession, with a potential 5.5 per cent slashed from our GDP. This followed on from an assessment made in mid-May by the IMF's managing director, Christine Lagarde, that the IMF had looked into the issue most thoroughly, concluding that there wasn't 'anything positive to say about a Brexit vote'. Lagarde predicted panic among investors, increased borrowing costs, a stock market crash, and very probably plagues of locusts and the immediate death of all first-borns. Suspicious critics pointed out that the IMF's advice at such a time was highly useful to its friends within the British government, whose official position was to recommend staying in the EU. Largade, however, denied it: 'We are not doing this out of politics; that is not how the IMF works.' Really? Their latest forecasts are that Brexit will prove merely a 'mild negative' for the British economy, with growth still occurring but at a somewhat 'tepid' rate, which is a little less alarmist than Lagarde's original claim that Brexit would be 'pretty bad to very, very bad' for the UK. Now, the IMF claim to have a 'fairly optimistic' view of how our EU exit will go, but don't expect this to be their final *volte-face* on the subject.[3]

The Bank of England, too, predicted Armageddon in the event of a Leave vote. The Bank's Governor, Mark Carney, had claimed before the referendum that the organisation's negative conclusion here was 'not a political opinion, it is an economic opinion – it's a judgement, a judgement based on analysis.' If so, then both the judgement and the analysis were wildly skewed. Following the Leave vote, Carney came out before the cameras and reassuringly told the world that the fundamentals of the British economy were all still perfectly sound, and there was no need for any alarm. To reassure foreign investors and shore up the economy further, he announced that the Bank of England would be introducing various financial stabilisation measures such as a halving of interest rates and the printing of more money via quantitative easing, which soon helped stabilise the markets. In predicting sudden decline prior to the Brexit vote itself, it seems that the Bank had completely neglected to take into account the likely effect of the numerous financial stabilisation tools which it itself possessed; in forecasting doom, it was as though the Bank was forgetting somehow that it would obviously step in and try to head off any such immediate collapse by *using* those same tools. In January 2017, the Bank's Chief Economist, Andy Haldane, admitted his organisation had been wrong, saying it was 'almost as though the referendum had not taken place', in the sense that the British economy was more-or-less where it had been prior to the Leave vote. Rather than sliding into recession, the economy had actually *grown* a little. The whole profession of economic forecasting, Haldane said, was now 'to some degree in crisis' because it had failed singularly to predict the global economic crash of 2007/08, and had then wrongly forecast profound trouble for Britain in the direct light of Brexit. He compared economic fortune-tellers like himself to the BBC weather forecaster Michael Fish, who had infamously failed to anticipate the Great Storm of 1987, which had caused rather more chaos and destruction across Britain than Brexit initially did. The economic models used by institutions such as the Bank of England, Haldane implied, had been 'rather narrow and rather fragile' and, evidently, didn't work all that well.[4]

It's the Economy, Stupid!

Some commentators have suggested the problem was slightly different, however, with the real issue being that men like Carney and Haldane were simply stuck in a London-centric Remain bubble, and refused to even countenance the possibility that 'Brexit' and 'Meltdown' might not necessarily be synonyms, as such a vote went against everything they stood for. This was the opinion of one of the Bank of England's former governors, Mervyn King. Lord King spoke in February 2017 of how politicians and economists' deeply patronising and sanctimonious attitudes towards the referendum had made a Leave vote in his view 'inevitable'. In a speech at the London School of Economics (LSE), King noted how big the gap between his friends who lived in London and those who lived elsewhere was, with those who dwelled in the capital telling him things such as 'If you even contemplate voting for Brexit, you must be either ignorant, uneducated, stupid or racist.' To which Lord King's response was: 'I'm none of those, and I resent being described in those terms.' Other people across the land also resented being described in such terms, Lord King theorised, making them all the more likely to raise two fingers towards their alleged 'betters' and refuse to vote the way they were being told to do so by an entire class of lofty-sounding persons who clearly held them in utter contempt.

All economists and financial institutions get things wrong sometimes; the future cannot be anything like 100 per cent accurately predicted, particularly with so complex a thing as the world economy. Investment advice always comes with the legal caveat that investors may see the value of their portfolio go up as well as down. Honest mistakes and errors of judgement inevitably occur in an uncertain world, and utterly unforeseeable events occur all the time, so we shouldn't demonise economists too much; they sometimes get things right, too! However, what many economists *do* deserve criticism for are some of the apparent reasons *why* they have been getting so many things so very wrong of late. As Lord King implied, some of them simply wanted Brexit to fail, and so just convinced themselves that it would, and straight away, too. Because most of the London-based financial and political elite were so blasé about the presumed fact that Remain would win the referendum vote, they probably never even thought their forecasts of woe would end up being tested in real-world conditions, so felt they could effectively say anything they liked upon the matter. You can see this in some of the highly dubious *post hoc* reasoning economists and financial bodies have engaged in following the disappointing failure of Britain to suddenly turn into the Weimar Republic overnight following the Brexit victory.

Hallowe'en Horror Show

Possibly the most risible excuses emerged from the giant global investment bank Morgan Stanley, who in January 2017 admitted that they were 'eating humble pie' after forecasting an immediate nosedive in the post-referendum British economy. Rather than consumer spending going down, as they thought, it actually rose. Why the mistake? Well, despite being financial experts, they somehow failed to foresee that the Bank of England would step in to try and stabilise the markets – as, indeed, did the Bank of England itself. Then, there were the conveniently generic 'special factors' which they had apparently failed to take into account, a rather random jumble of phenomena plucked from airy nothing, including 'the growth of Hallowe'en as a major consumer event in the UK', something that had been going on for about thirty years. Best of all was their lucid assessment that 'More than half the electorate who voted, voted Brexit', and that being on the winning side led these happy Brexiteers to feel such elation that they went out on a consumer spending spree, buying up entire warehouses worth of Union Jacks and those hideous purple ties with yellow pound-signs on them that UKIP sell. Just think about that statement for a moment: 'More than half the electorate who voted, voted Brexit'. Well of course they did! How would it have been possible for the Leave side to win if they hadn't got more than half of the vote? That Morgan Stanley apparently didn't realise that, if Brexit won, more than 50 per cent of persons would have had to vote for it doesn't bode well for their economists' powers of mathematical analysis. The idea that Morgan Stanley employees were unaware of things such as the prior existence of Hallowe'en or the way that a referendum works is simply not plausible. Surely they made up these 'explanations' for their failed forecast because the true reason they foresaw swift Brexit disaster was that they, like most such institutions, were suffering from a bad case of pro-EU groupthink. Indeed, at one point in the official report Morgan Stanley released about all this, it was admitted that that the bank was 'unconvinced by its own argument' about why we escaped an instant 'Brecession'.[5]

When confronted with such dishonesty and scaremongering, you can certainly see how the general public might get the impression that many economists are making it up as they go along, largely for ideological reasons. Indeed, if you look at the history of the whole field of economics itself, you will quickly find that it is a surprisingly recent invention; the generally agreed beginnings of the kind of economics we know and love today came only in 1776, with the publication of the Scottish Enlightenment thinker Adam Smith's (1723–90) ground-breaking text *An Inquiry into the Nature and Causes of the Wealth of Nations*. The very term 'economy', at least when used in the modern sense, is an invention of the late 1800s and early 1900s. At the dawn of the twentieth century, the US government employed only one man who had the word 'economic' in his job title – and his task was to study birds, not money, being a so-called 'economic ornithologist', who tracked avian numbers, distribution and general well-being. A mere forty years later, the US National Bureau of Economic Research employed 5,000 economists, few of whom would have known a sparrow from a starling. The great god GDP (Gross Domestic Product – the sum-total value of all goods and services any given nation produces over the course of a single year) seems like a concept we should have had a rough idea of for centuries, but it was only properly formulated by the Russian-American economist Simon Kuznets (1901–85) in the 1930s. When people said 'the economy' prior to the Second World War, they basically just meant 'society and business' in a general sense, they didn't imagine that a definitive monetary figure could be placed upon the value of their entire nation, or that all could be known to the Eye of the Economist as to the Eye of God.[6] There would be some who might still like to argue along these lines.

False Profits

Before we truly begin, I feel as if I should attempt to win the approval of the admirably sceptical Mr Gove by admitting that I am not by any means an expert myself, having zero academic background or training in economics. However, most of this book deals with economic and monetary ideas which are so insane as to make the idea that Hallowe'en has saved Britain from penury sound positively mainstream. You don't need to have spent five years at the London School of Economics to be able to work out that the claims of someone to have taken financial advice from an alien Economics Minister or from the conjured transgender ghost of Margaret Thatcher are unlikely to be true, nor to be able to deduce that a man who equates the optimum level of flow of money into an economy with the optimum level of flow of sperm through his own testicles is probably just a bit suspect. The rest of this book mainly focuses upon such deluded notions as that the stock exchange is secretly controlled by vampires, or that cash can very easily be replaced by metaphorical potatoes, ideas which any fool can see are as dodgy as a nine-bob note. Some of those who have made such proposals were genuine, mainstream economists, while others were just fringe nutters. A fair proportion of the theorists and activists described in this book are quite clearly profoundly disturbed, and I don't just mean George Osborne.

What is interesting, though, is that some of them have gained thousands – occasionally even millions – of followers, despite the fact their ideas are so obviously, demonstrably loony and unworkable. The appeal of such notions, clearly, is not primarily logical, but much more emotional, moral, quasi-religious or ideological in nature. Witness the enthusiasm of the Corbynista wing of the modern-day Labour Party for the failed socialist economic experiment in Venezuela; the reality of mass poverty and food shortages in that utterly ruined land is staring them in the face, but still they cannot see it, any more than people like Christine Lagarde and George Osborne were capable of seeing that an event like Brexit might not necessarily lead to immediate and irreversible financial collapse back in 2016. Whether on the Left or the Right (or that peculiar mixture of the two we now denote by the term 'liberal'), it is probably your pre-existing political beliefs which will largely determine what your economic beliefs are, not the actual evidence or reality *per se*. But what happens when your pre-existing beliefs are even more deluded than those of men like Comrade Corbyn are? What if, rather than having a long-standing commitment towards nationalising industry, or increasing public spending to unaffordable levels, you have a long-standing commitment towards belief in benign alien beings who wish to abolish all Earth-money, or possess an unshakeable conviction that Jewish wizards are busily conjuring up gold from their anuses in an evil attempt to enslave mankind within the usurious bonds of debt forever? What if you believe in werewolves and think that money should, all things considered, resemble such creatures somehow? What if you suppose that the global economy is in severe danger of farting itself to death any day now? What kind of bizarre economic programmes for the supposed advancement or salvation of humanity will you come up with then? This book will give you a clue.

As the world continues to suffer the long-term after-effects of the 2007/08 global financial crash, could such ideas, or ones of equal lunacy, take hold of men's minds once more? If you think that the answer is a definite 'no', then you just haven't been paying enough attention to the news lately ...

Unsound as a Pound

Ezra Pound, Vegetable-Money, Social Credit and Other Great Follies of the Great Depression

Money is gold, and nothing else
                                              J. P. Morgan, banker

The forgotten history of how a ranting fascist poet tried to get Mussolini to replace cold, hard cash with a new currency based upon imaginary potatoes – and the wide variety of strange Depression-era schemes connected to the idea, from incredible shrinking money to a mad Major's Social Credit.

Parents who work in unusual places should be very careful about whether or not to participate in the annual ritual of 'Bring Your Child to Work Day'. Homer Pound (1858–1942), the father of the celebrated Modernist American poet – and rather less celebrated ranting fascist madman – Ezra Loomis Pound (1885–1972) was one such man. Homer worked as an assayer for the US Mint in Philadelphia from 1889 to 1928, therefore making money by, literally, making money. One day, Homer decided to take his son along to the Mint building to see what went on there. The most striking sight of the trip for young Ezra was being taken down to see the gigantic basement vaults, where four million silver dollars lay around in great heaps on the floor, being carelessly shovelled up into giant counting machines by bare-chested workmen armed with oversized spades. It was as if it had snowed silver, or as if the coins were simply huge piles of horse manure, which had to be quickly bagged up and disposed of somehow. The sight of a genuine fortune being treated like mere dung made a great impression upon the young boy, and laid in him the seeds of an idea – that all money based on the supply of precious metals was really nothing but shiny trash, with no inherent worth whatsoever. As Pound described in 1962:

> The government offices were more informal then ... you could be taken
> around in the smelting room and see the gold piled up in the safe. You were

offered a large bag of gold and told you could have it if you could take it away with you. You couldn't lift it ... [One day] they recounted all the silver dollars, four million dollars in silver. All the bags had rotted in these enormous vaults, and they were heaving it into the counting machines with shovels bigger than coal shovels. This spectacle of coin being shovelled around like it was litter – these fellows naked to the waist shovelling it around in the gas-flares – things like that strike your imagination.[1]

Pound's formative years of the 1890s were a time of great economic controversy in the United States. Back then, the idea of the 'Gold Standard' ruled, which held that the amount of money in circulation in the world economy should be strictly pegged back to the amount of global gold reserves held by governments and their Treasuries, with the value of each currency unit such as pound or dollar being defined as representing a fixed weight of precious metal; in short, the idea that money itself was a direct symbolic expression of gold, a relationship between signifier and signified which was painted as inherently natural. Nowadays, we have 'floating' currencies, or 'fiat money', which can be printed at will by governments if they so desire, irrespective of how much gold reserves they possess, and which derives its value not from any inherent quality within itself, but by comparison with other competing currencies on the international exchange market. You never hear of the British pound being worth an ounce of gold, for instance, but 1.3 US dollars, 1.15 Euros or 140 Japanese yen. In the 1890s, though, gold was king. Simultaneously, however, there was a boom in US silver-mining taking place, with certain monetary theorists demanding these new hoards of shiny metal be minted into spendable coins, but official policy was to refuse; endlessly pumping out more and more silver dollars would devalue the American currency, the Mint said, leading to hyperinflation. If such a thing were allowed to take place, then the value of any debt already incurred by either individuals or governments would find itself greatly reduced, leading to creditors being out of pocket.

The Democrat Party's William Jennings Bryan (1860–1925) took advantage of the situation and twice ran for President on the slogan 'Thou shalt not crucify mankind on a cross of gold!', but failed to win the race for the White House in either 1896 or 1900. What the silver-bugs wanted was a 'bimetallic' currency, whose value was based upon a combination of both gold *and* silver; this would allow many more dollars to be printed and minted, as the amount of the two metals stored in the US Treasury would obviously be higher than the amount simply of gold. More dollars meant more coins and bills for people to spend and so more inflation, which in turn meant cheaper debts for those who already owed them. Congress disagreed, and in 1900 passed the Gold Standard Act, officially confirming gold as being the *only* metal upon which the value of the dollar could be based. The situation seemed ridiculous;

here were large numbers of people, being deliberately kept under a massive debt burden – and why? Simply so the already bloated loan sharks of the country could continue feasting on the poor. That, at least, is how the young Ezra Pound viewed the matter; and it was the kind of opinion he would go on holding throughout the rest of his adult life.[2]

Spuds for Goods

Although his only true qualifications lay in literature – he had studied for an unfinished degree course in English, from which he was summarily ejected after insulting his boring lecturers to their faces – Pound's childhood experiences led him to consider himself to be an expert economic theoriser, to such an extent that he once wrote to the US presidential wannabe Senator Huey Long (1893–1935), offering to be his 'Sekkertary of Treasury' should he ever gain power, which he didn't, because someone shot him.[3] Pound thought himself an economist of such genius that he had no need of any paper qualifications in the subject; like paper money, they were worthless things. If he was going to be a true poet, he needed to write, not study under boring, dust-dry professors; and if he was going to be a famous economist, then he needed to think up some new economic theories, not waste his time writing essays about those of others. Fortunately, embarking upon a life as a poet is a sure-fire way to experience the distressing economic effects of poverty for oneself, and his subsequent school of monetary thought could be best considered as a means of alleviating such penury – if not for himself,

Ezra Pound, who ranted about the alleged connections which existed between Jews, moneylending, gold and anal sex; and, indeed, about the connection between cash-flow and the contents of his own testicles. (Courtesy of the Library of Congress)

then for his fellow hand-to-mouth scribblers. 'Only the artist,' Pound once wrote, 'has succeeded in detaching the idea of work from the idea of profit.'[4] But having said that, surely a genius had to scrape by somehow?

In 1927, Pound won an annual poetry award from a high-brow literary magazine called *The Dial*, worth some $2,000 – a large figure at the time. He invested this at a rate of 5 per cent interest, took from this sum what little he needed to live off, and donated the rest to other writers whose needs were greater than his own. Living in England and Europe from 1908 onwards, and moving to Italy in 1924, where he considered a life of poverty to be more 'decent and honourable' than in the Anglo-Saxon lands, Pound obsessively made contact with a large number of European poets and novelists of notable talent whose earning potential was nonetheless virtually nil. An undoubtedly generous man, among those he showered with gifts of currency were future staples of the English Literature curriculum James Joyce (1882–1941) and T. S. Eliot (1888–1965), and his largesse was not limited only to cash. He would buy meals for those gifted writers he considered to be under-fed, and even donate these rag-clad figures items of clothing – up to and including his own used underpants. In Europe, Pound was disgusted by the news that an old manuscript of Edgar Allen Poe's (1809–49) had recently been sold to a collector for the then-absurd sum of $20,000. During his lifetime Poe himself, now seen as the undisputed literary master of American Gothic, had been largely unrecognised and forced to live in poverty, with riches flooding his way only after death when they were of no use to him, and it seemed as if the same fate might await Joyce and Eliot, too. Clearly, when such literary titans were in dire need of another man's used underwear while fat-cat big-city loan sharks could just sit there in their mansions all day watching the dollars roll in, something was rotten at the heart of the world's financial system. Therefore, Pound sat down to write a series of so-called 'Money Pamphlets', one of which asked *What Is Money For?*, with Pound's conclusion being that cash's only true purpose was 'for getting the country's food and goods justly distributed.'[5] The problem, of course, was that food and goods were *not* currently being justly distributed, with some men rich and others poor, and producers of worthwhile things such as great literature being paid less than producers of non-worthwhile things like cheap and vulgar advertising. Pound's solution to this state of affairs was simple, yet undeniably original – to replace money with vegetables.

Sadly this was not a literal proposition, but a metaphorical one. Pound wished to create a special new kind of currency, which has since been dubbed 'vegetable-money' by the American cultural critic Lewis Hyde, in a classic 1983 essay. This vegetable-money would be 'no more durable than potatoes', and thus be vegetable-like only in an imaginary sense. Rich men, Pound said, were able to hoard their coinage in giant vaults so full of gold and silver they could swim around in them all day long like Scrooge McDuck, if they wanted to. Therefore, by replacing such old-fashioned 'money-wealth' with a brand-new form of 'potato-wealth', whose value rotted away quite quickly, week by week, Pound felt he would force the rich to spend their money before it grew worthless, instead of keeping it all hidden away inside banks, thus spreading their wealth around more fairly. The natural purpose of growing a potato is to eat it; then, it is recycled out onto the land as compost, when the potato-eater relieves him or herself in the fields, making new potatoes grow out of the result. In such a way, the vegetable-coin is also 'eaten' when spent, and then recycled or reincarnated anew as the useful item or service purchased; the person who receives this potato-coin then also has to spend/eat it quickly, taking a figurative crap in a cash register, and thus went Pound's virtuous new circle of economic life. Also, before they rotted, Pound hoped that rich people would try to invest their 'potatoes' in the creation of a form of goods which were so durable, they would last forever – namely, classic works of art, such as the immortal poems and paintings commissioned by the likes of the Medici and Sforza families of Italy centuries beforehand, thus bringing about a new, second Renaissance, in which Joyce and Eliot would receive money by the bucket-load, thus allowing them to concentrate upon their writing, rather than having to take up ordinary day jobs just to keep the roof over their heads. Even though most mainstream economists dismissed his ideas as crazy – 'wot these bastards lack is a little intelligence', he wrote angrily at the time – Pound had supreme confidence in them himself.[6] The next step was to try to get them enacted; and, with that in mind, Ezra Pound decided that it was about time he paid a visit upon Italy's new fascist dictator, *Il Duce* himself ...

Tea with Mussolini

Pound thought Benito Mussolini (1883–1945) might be sympathetic towards his ideals because, under fascist economic models, the State tended to have complete control over significant sectors of industrial and monetary policy. Mussolini sought to transform Italy into what is known as an 'autarky'; that is, a more-or-less self-sufficient economy, free from the chains of the international money markets. Pound came to worship Mussolini as a great monetary theorist and man of action, who saw with a gimlet eye precisely what was wrong with the corrupt global finance system. So it was that Pound increasingly began to agitate for a head-to-head meeting to discuss such pressing matters as the fate of the Italian cork industry, an audience which, after ten months of pleading, was reluctantly granted by *Il Duce* on 30 January 1933. Here, Pound gifted Mussolini a copy of some of his early *Cantos*, a long and ultimately unfinished series of poems written on and off between 1917 and 1969, and dealing with the history and cultural decline of the world from ancient times to the present day.

When Mussolini received this volume, together with a typescript of Pound's economic plans, he made a polite comment to the effect that it all looked very interesting ('*è divertente*'). Instead of realising that Mussolini was simply being courteous, Pound took this statement literally, and concluded that Mussolini agreed with his basic financial outlook, and had perhaps even read his *Cantos* beforehand.

Encouraged by such imagined positivity, Pound then sat down and bombarded Benito with a series of pre-prepared queries upon economic matters which, ever the optimist, he would later combine into an 'official' questionnaire and send out to various prominent world figures such as US President Franklin D. Roosevelt (1882–1945) and the top banker James Warburg (1896–1969), seriously expecting them to fill it in and post it back to him, ASAP. By Pound's own account, Mussolini's only response to being asked things such as whether he thought taxes would soon no longer be necessary, or if the very notion of State debt was now outdated, as Pound did, was to grunt vaguely in a way which probably indicated little other than noncommittal boredom. Pound, however, felt the great man's grunts were a sign of him absorbing all this valuable new information, and walked away delighted he had been given a fair hearing and convinced his theories now stood a real chance of being implemented throughout the land. Mussolini, for his own part, no doubt closed the door on his strange visitor and tossed his economic typescript and copy of the *Cantos* straight into the nearest dustbin.[7] Had Mussolini ever actually bothered to read any of Pound's verses,

Little Mussolini in full flow. Perhaps in this picture he had lost it after listening to Ezra Pound's time-wasting explanation of why it was he should replace the Italian *lira* with a new currency based upon metaphorical potatoes. (Courtesy of the Library of Congress)

though, then he may have been surprised to discover that, unlike the work of most poets, they contained many lines relating to fiscal matters. Consider the following stanza, taken from *Canto XCVII* which Pound intended as a learned literary commentary upon a textbook he had once read called *The History of Monetary Systems*:

> £.s.d. as from Caracalla,
> Venice, Florence, Amalfi maintained 12 to 1 ratio,
> One gold against that in silver.

But what precise ratio existed between money and poetry in Pound's work? Sometimes it could seem almost 1:1. One literary critic has described Pound's ideal economic system as one in which 'each coin [is] weighed and measured as precisely as the individual syllables of prosody or the orderly rhythms of revenue, the ratios of gold and silver [in coinage] maintaining the pure proportions of music or grammar.'[8] The poet's grandfather Thaddeus, once the proud owner of the largest sawmill in the world, had corresponded with his bank manager in verse, and Pound did not see why he should abandon the old family tradition. Recalling the dominance which the Gold Standard had possessed during his youth, before its abandonment during the inter-war years as a result of the Great Depression, Pound considered the worlds of finance and poetry to be fundamentally linked. His father's specific job at the US Mint had involved assaying gold and silver to see whether it was real or mere worthless *iron pyrites* (fool's gold), and Pound told in a 1962 interview of how the test for whether silver-samples were genuine or not involved exposing it to some kind of 'cloudy solution' and then seeing how the silver reacted with it. According to Pound, 'the accuracy of the eye in measuring the thickness of the cloud [and thus the genuineness of the silver] is an aesthetic perception, like the critical sense', something which he compared 'by analogy to the habit of testing verbal manifestations' – or, to put it another way, the art of sussing out whether specific lines and images of poetry were any good or not.[9]

Dead Letters

Pound had been part of a literary movement known as 'Imagism', whose central tenet was 'go in fear of abstractions', and which called for 'direct treatment of the thing' being written about.[10] Around 1912, Pound came into contact with the writings of Ernest Fenollosa (1853–1908), an American professor who had taught in Japan, where he had become an expert on Chinese and Japanese calligraphy. Pound was greatly taken with Fenollosa's essay *The Chinese Written Character as a Medium of Poetry*, which discussed the fact that in China and Japan, rather than making use of a letter-based alphabet, as in the West, ideograms were used instead. Ideograms are a sort of 'picture-writing'. Rather than writing out the word 'man' letter by letter, for example, the Chinese would use the following ideogram, which (in Fenollosa's view, at least) is supposed to look like the lower half of a sort of stick-figure person, with two legs and the beginning of a torso, walking forwards:

For Pound such ideograms were marvellous things as, unlike the wholly abstract depiction of the word 'man' formed up by the letters 'M-A-N' in our alphabet, the Chinese stick-figure ideogram directly embodies the thing it is supposed to represent. The relationship between symbol (the ideogram) and the thing it is supposed to symbolise (an actual real-life human) is direct and tangible, rather like the relationship between a poetic phrase and the thing it was supposed to represent in an Imagist poem. Because of this direct relationship, Fenollosa proposed oriental ideograms were somehow alive, being units of living energy filled with the accumulated history of their own existence not only as ideograms, but as the natural, pre-existing things they were meant to embody. The real, living man and his corresponding ideogram were somehow one unified whole, like the Imagist poet's words and the things he wrote of. Furthermore, many abstract ideograms were composed of parts of other, more concrete, ideograms, thus rooting such words more directly in the natural world. The Chinese ideogram for 'red', for example, contained truncated parts of other ideograms meaning 'rose', 'rust', 'cherry' and 'flamingo' … or at least it did according to Professor Fenollosa. In fact, much of his research was pure wishful thinking, but it was a brand of linguistic romance which greatly appealed to Ezra Pound, who began incorporating ideograms into his poetry, thinking them sacred sigils. Like a fortune-teller interpreting tea leaves, Pound would spend hours staring at Chinese dictionaries, hoping that, because symbol was said to correspond naturally with object, the true meanings of each ideogram would just automatically come to him, in a revelation. According to Alec Marsh, of the Ezra Pound Society, Chinese ideograms 'gradually became the bearer of Pound's ethics' as, to him, they came direct from a time when mankind had existed more in harmony with Nature, carrying the ancient, sacred energy of this age into what he saw as the corrupt and fallen modern world in which he unfortunately lived.[11]

Clashing Symbols

The worst sin of modernity for Pound (who, like several Modernists, paradoxically hated many manifestations of the contemporary world) was the way in which symbol and referent had increasingly become separated from one another. Pound felt there were two diametrically opposed forces at work within history, one which severed the natural unity between man and the world, and one which strengthened it. In the ancient pagan word of old, Pound saw evidence of primitive cults whose members had drawn an innate link between the fertility of man and the fertility of the crops, seeing the latter as dependent upon the former. Their rituals and bucolic way of life emphasised this purity and ensured all was well, as in Eden. In the modern world, however, a sinister force was at work which 'destroys every clearly delineated symbol, dragging man into a maze of abstract arguments, destroying not one but every religion.'[12] We could see this separation between man and Nature not only in the disgustingly abstract letters of the Western alphabet but, even more strikingly, within the world of finance. Most standard elements of the Western economic system were considered by Pound to be unnatural lies. Debt, for example, was 'a mere artifice to facilitate keeping accounts' which had 'no counterpart in Nature or life'.[13] Money itself was equally artificial, a fake 'common denominator' made up 'FOR THE SAKE OF ACCOUNTING, so as not to send bookkeepers crazy with columns of twelve cows, [or] nine locomotives'.[14] Sometimes, Pound even flirted with the idea of abolishing all coinage and returning to a primitive barter economy instead: 'It is unjust that a man who has a cow and another who has a plough cannot exchange [them] without leave of a third who has metal.'[15] Modern corporations, too, were naught but legal abstractions, being run by boards of directors who were personally legally immune from the irresponsible actions those corporations then undertook; specifically, Pound despised the Franco-German armaments manufacturer Schneider-Creusot, which, he said, had slyly supplied munitions to both sides during the First World War. Apparently, wars existed purely in order to get nations in debt to such transnational firms, and to the equally rootless and unnatural international bankers who lent them the money to buy their weapons in the first place.[16]

The most unnatural economic lie of all, however, related to gold. Here, the difference between object and symbol had been twisted out of all recognition. According to Pound, 'For a long time now, the Gold Standard has not, in fact, existed; what has existed has been a *False-Gold* Standard.'[17] The system of the Gold Standard, we will remember, was based upon the notion that there was a direct relationship between money, in the form of notes and coins, and the amount of physical gold reserves kept safely locked away in places such as Fort Knox and the vaults of the Bank of England. This latter establishment, however, had been the birth of a great evil, for in 1694 a prospectus had been written for potential investors by one of the Bank's founders, William Paterson (1658–1719), to the effect that 'The Bank hath benefit on the interest on all moneys which it creates out of nothing.'

This quote was actually apocryphal, but Pound thought it was definitely true in spirit, and began obsessively repeating it within his poems and prose.[18] If Paterson's alleged quote stood true, then how could it be that there really was some kind of direct relation between gold and its symbol, money? If banks could indeed create money 'out of nothing', then cash clearly wasn't based directly upon gold supplies, was it? It seemed to Pound as if financiers simply wanted to pretend that money was based upon gold as part of some vile international conspiracy intended to maintain the value of the debts they were owed. By artificially limiting the money supply by pegging back the amount of dollars, pounds and francs in circulation, the vampire-squids could keep on sucking the people dry by denying them access to adequate funds, thus forcing them to take out more loans, at ever-higher interest rates, from their fraudulent institutions.

But if money was not genuinely related to the amount of gold present in the world, then what *was* it based upon? For Pound, the answer was simple – grass. Grass and sheep, tomatoes and potatoes, wheat and corn; the bounties of the natural world God had been pleased to provide us with. In one of his Money Pamphlets, *Social Credit: An Impact*, Pound spoke of his ideal financial institution being the *Banca Monte dei Paschi* of Siena. The world's oldest surviving bank, it was founded in 1472 and then expanded its operations in 1624 when Fernando II de' Medici (1610–1670), Grand Duke of Tuscany, underwrote its capital with the aim of securing for the city the

William Paterson, one of the founders of the Bank of England, an apparently profoundly evil man who Ezra Pound claimed was behind a long-running global conspiracy to fraudulently conjure up money from nowhere, in order to enslave the world forever. (Public domain)

To Ezra Pound, the Jewish Hell Bankers were rather like alchemists, manufacturing gold from thin air (or from within their pregnant anuses) via black magic. (Courtesy of the Rijksmuseum)

revenue from the *paschi*, the sheep-grazing meadows that then surrounded Siena. The bank's business model did include lending, but, at an annual rate of 5.5 per cent, all such loans were directly tied back to the estimated annual increase in the number of Siena's sheep, the flock generally growing by about 5 per cent per annum. All of the bank's excess profits, after wages and overheads were taken into account, Fernando then had distributed to local hospitals and programmes of public works, rather than between fat-cat executives and shareholders as today. Such an admirable economic model, wrote Pound, was 'the very basis of solid banking' because the availability of credit for lending rests not upon blatant frauds like the Gold Standard, but instead '*in ultimate* upon the ABUNDANCE OF NATURE, on the growing grass that can nourish the living sheep.' Hence, we should really have some kind of a Grass Standard or Sheep Standard, not a Gold one. Because the *Banca Monte dei Paschi* was based upon such woolly (in a good sense) natural foundations, wrote Pound, it had endured down the centuries in a way which its more avaricious rivals had not: 'You can open an account there tomorrow.'[19]

This is still true today ... but it nearly wasn't. In 1995, upon the order of the Italian Treasury, the venerable institution was split into two arms, one of which was supposed to continue the charitable and cultural functions begun by Fernando, the other of which existed purely to make money. In 1999, the Banca was listed for the first time on the Italian Stock Exchange, and embarked upon a programme of relentless commercial expansion, with the predictable result that it ended up overreaching itself, sustaining massive losses, and having to be bailed out by the State. There are still fears that the Banca's stores of bad debt may prove to be unmanageable, especially if there is another global economic crisis as in 2007/08 – and, if so, then say goodbye to 500 years of history. Sometimes it pays not to follow the financial herd.[20]

Golden Fleeced

Foolishly, Pound's beloved Banca appears in recent years to have become one of the 'Hell Banks' he so often castigated in his writings, engaging in abstract and incomprehensible financial manoeuvres involving things like derivatives markets and hedge funds, whatever they might be when they're at home. For Pound, the malign consequences of such greedy abstraction are not purely financial, however, they are also cultural. Consider the way in which the Catholic Church itself had sometimes become corrupted by the evil example of high finance, as when they first began selling indulgences (forgiveness for sins) during the 1200s; the Church claimed it had access to a 'Treasury of Merit', a form of accumulated moral capital created by the good deeds of Jesus and the saints. If you had committed a sin yourself, you could 'borrow' some morality from this alleged treasury, for a reasonable fee, and use it to gain forgiveness from that great banker in the sky. That is to say, you could rent good karma.[21] Was nothing now sacred?

For Pound, easily the worst Hell Bank of the Italian Renaissance was the *Banca S. Giorgio*, a 'pitiless company of Genoese creditors' which had, sadly, since become 'the model bank among bankers'. Its money-grabbing ways had not only ruined many individual debtors, but also the cultural life of Genoa itself where, unlike in Siena, 'the arts did not flourish … Cities a tenth of her size have left more durable treasure.'[22] The problem with such Hell Banks' business model was that gold could not breed, whereas living assets like sheep could. Unless a bank happened to own a gold-mine, then its gold reserves were unlikely to substantially increase, whereas the sheep of the fields grew larger in number every year. The sheep and the grass they ate, as endlessly renewable financial resources, were thus the original 'durable treasure' upon which the later creation of great Renaissance paintings and poems like those of Siena were ultimately based. Indeed, Pound was moved to classify all goods available for sale into three different categories. There were 'transient goods', or things which rotted and faded away quickly, like fruit and vegetables, 'durable goods', such as well-built houses, walls and roads, and 'permanent goods', like great artworks. The initial category of transient goods, however, was split down further into two; as well as positive transients, like food, there were negative transients, such as 'jerry-built houses, fake art [and] pseudo-books'. It was always possible to turn a quick profit on selling trash literature or cheap flats that would fall down on their occupants, and under an economic system dominated by Hell Banks, this is precisely what would happen. An economy based upon the 'durable treasure' of Nature's bounty, however, would produce an outlook among the citizenry which would result in the production of great, Sistine Chapel-style masterpieces.[23] Bemoaning the sin of usury (lending out money at excessive rates of interest) as a cancer that ate away at the soul of any civilisation greedy or imprudent enough to allow it to take root, in his book *Guide to Kulchur* Pound suggested that, one day, 'finer and future critics of art will be able to tell from the quality of a painting the degree of tolerance or intolerance of usury extant in the age and milieu that produced it.'[24] Had Pound lived to see the work of such present-day ultra-rich artists as Damien Hirst and Jeff Koons, I think we can guess what conclusions he may have drawn.

Economic models like that of the hated Genoese Hell Bank were fundamentally unnatural because they were based solely upon creating credit magically out of finite and sterile stores of gold. The problem with basing your system of credit on gold, Pound explained to readers of his Money Pamphlet *Gold and Work*, was that gold, unlike sheep (or, as here, poultry) does not have sex or go to the toilet:

> Gold is durable, but does not reproduce itself – not even if you put two bits of it together, one shaped like a cock, the other like a hen. It is absurd to speak of it as bearing fruit or yielding interest. Gold does not germinate like grain … Metal is durable, but it does not reproduce itself. If you sow gold you will not be able to reap a harvest many times greater than the gold you sowed. The vegetable leads a more or less autonomous existence, but its natural reproductiveness can be increased by cultivation. The animal gives to and takes from the vegetable world: manure in exchange for food. Fascinated by the lustre of a metal, man has made it into chains. Then he invented something against Nature, a false representation in the mineral world of laws which apply only to animals and vegetables … The durability of metal gives it certain advantages not possessed by potatoes or tomatoes. Anyone who has a stock of metal can keep it until conditions are most favourable for exchanging it against less durable goods … It should be remembered that the soil does not require monetary compensation for the wealth extracted from it. With her wonderful efficiency Nature sees to it that the circulation of material capital and its fruits is maintained, and that what comes out of the soil goes back into the soil with majestic rhythm, despite human interference.[25]

The Root of All Evil

In an increasingly usury-dominated world like the one Pound felt he lived in, however, transient goods of little real worth would proliferate endlessly and so destroy the vitality of the human spirit; instead of durable goods, which had once been made with love and care by individual human craftsmen, cheap and shoddy tat was now rolling off the world's mechanised factory production lines like there was no tomorrow. As one of Pound's biographers put it, 'Usura is the rot induced when short-sighted greed feeds on the public good, making for shoddy goods, adulterated food, the neglect of permanent values for fleeting sensations and short-term profit.'[26] If goods and services were made and provided only with profit in mind, then the social bonds within society would become purely transactional, rather than based upon any lingering idea of a shared community of feeling, leaving that same society utterly hollow, dead and doomed.[27] In these lines taken from his famous and quite majestic *Canto XLV*, Pound illustrated precisely what a culture (if such it could still be called) whose economy was based wholly upon usury would look like:

> *With usura hath no man a house of good stone*
> *each block cut smooth and well fitting*
> *that design might cover their face ...*
> *no picture is made to endure nor to live with*
> *but it is made to sell and sell quickly*
> *with usura, sin against nature,*
> *is thy bread ever more of stale rags*
> *is thy bread dry as paper ...*

Ironically, the images of barrenness caused by usury in this Canto do nothing but multiply. Reading the rest of the poem, craftsmen and artisans are left unemployed, with their tools and skills alike rusting away, the bounty of art and design wither on the vine, the young man is unable to afford his courting and the young bridegroom to have a child, even the sheep in the fields 'bringeth no gain with usura', for usury is quite simply 'CONTRA NATURUM', 'Against Nature'. The poem ends with some skeletal corpses propped up at a table, unable to enjoy the fresh banquet laid out before them. Money-worship and excessive debt have ruined everything, banished the creative spirit of the Renaissance, made civilisation a desert and called it peace. Pound provided a note to *Canto XLV*, in which he defined usury as being: 'A charge for the use of purchasing power, levied without regard to production; often without regard to the possibilities of production.' What he meant was that the Hell Banks, by giving easy credit to all comers, lent out money which did not actually exist. Unlike the sound credit provided by the Bank of Siena, which was based upon the natural production of tangible sheep-based goods like wool and meat, the Bank of Genoa and its imitators doled out credit based upon the risible fantasy of their gold reserves somehow managing to have sex with one another and getting pregnant. Production of baby gold ingots is clearly not possible, whereas production of baby lambs is, so the usurers were peddling a blatant lie. The Hell Banks' only purpose was to get people in debt, and the scarcer that gold-backed money initially was, the less cash people would have to fund their everyday needs. Therefore, they would come looking to the Hell Banks seeking easy, fictional credit, which would gladly be given them at rates of excessively high interest. Then, when their victims prove unable to pay, the usurers claim their newly bankrupt debtors' tangible assets in the form of their homes, farms and businesses, and the whole horrible cycle starts itself anew – because, being penniless, the debtors will need to borrow from the moneylenders once more, thus effectively being handed back a liquid portion of their previous assets, like houses, and being charged a fee for the privilege, in interest.[28]

Pound's thought here has an internal contradiction, in that he blames Hell Banks on the one hand for producing and distributing too much money, to get people into debt, and then also blames them for not producing enough money, to keep the value of those same debts artificially high. Presumably, he viewed Hell Bankers as deliberately oscillating between these two extremes to keep people forever in their clutches – but, in order to be able to maintain this story, he had to become selective in his use of evidence. For instance, far from the Satanic Bank of England just conjuring vast sums of banknotes out of nowhere, as William Paterson's 'The Bank hath benefit on the interest on all moneys which it creates out of nothing' quote implied, the organisation had for centuries religiously followed Sir Isaac Newton's (1643–1727) immutable formula that an ounce of gold should be worth precisely £3 17s 10½d, something he had developed during his time as Master of the Royal Mint between 1699 and 1727. So committed was the Bank of England to maintaining this value that, from the mid-1890s until the First World War, the worth of all the gold in the Treasury was actually *higher* than the face value of all the British banknotes then in circulation; far from making money out of nothing, the London Hell Bank was really printing less than it should have been, according to Gold Standard rules. This would have kept the value of debts stable and high, but would not have facilitated the distribution of excessive fictional cash to ensnare debtors.[29] Or, in simple terms, Ezra Pound was factually incorrect in many of his assertions – as we shall see when he starts ranting on about the hitherto obscure connections between bullion and bumming.

The Same Circle of Hell

Lending money without regard for capacity for production of natural things like wool was, to Pound, roughly akin to having anal sex and expecting to get pregnant. Oddly, this idea had been adapted from old teachings of the Catholic Church, the sermons of whose priests must once have been much more interesting than they usually are today. As Pound put it, 'Usury and sodomy the Church condemned as a pair, to one Hell, for the same one reason, that they are both against natural increase.'[30] Pound found evidence for this linkage in the *Divine Comedy* of Dante Alighieri (1265–1321), where usurers and sodomites are placed together within the same innermost Seventh Circle of Hell, on the grounds that both forms of buggering mankind were deemed equally unnatural. The usurers Pound so despised were characterised by him as inveterate perverts, who spent all day sodomising one another senseless before going off to work at the Hell Banks, where they happily issued their customers with bum notes. (By the way, a 2014 study found that 6 per cent of British banknotes contain similar levels of *E. coli* bacteria to the average toilet, so maybe some money really is born straight out of bankers' backsides – this was reported under superb headlines such as 'Don't Put Your Money Where Your Mouth Is' at the time.[31])

Initially, such notions seem amusing. Unfortunately, we must face the fact that when Pound used the word 'usurers', what he really meant was 'Jews'. There was an undeniable strain of overt anti-Semitism present within Ezra Pound, which found expression in the numerous war-time propaganda radio broadcasts he made upon behalf of his hero Mussolini, given unpleasant titles such as *The Big Jew*, or in newspaper articles he penned with headings like *The Jew: Disease Incarnate*. In this latter work, Pound condemned the Jews as living embodiments of venereal disease, maladies which they caught and then spread on to others through their continual acts of anal penetration; Jews, he said, were 'the gonorrhoeal elements' behind the scams of international finance, and 'the syphilis' of the poor cursed nations they inhabited. Rotting society from within, like prostate cancer in human form, the Jews had totally corrupted the British Empire, he said, coming to pull all its financial and political strings to the extent that MPs in London had now 'outjewed the Jew' in their vile money-worship and subservience towards the evil Bank of England.

Pound felt that the newspapers were really 'Jewspapers' controlled by Jewish media barons who used them to suppress the truth, and subscribed to a delusional view of history in which Jews had been secretly responsible for everything from the assassination of Abraham Lincoln (1809–65) to the outbreak of the First World War. Indeed, Pound believed that war itself had become nothing more than a sinister scam perpetrated by the Jewish bankers and 'gombeen-men' (Irish slang for con-artists) whom he claimed ran the world from behind the scenes on behalf of Jew-riddled firms such as Schneider-Creusot.[32]

The absurd slander that Jews control all the world's banks stems ultimately from the fact that ever since the Catholic Church's Third Lateran Council in 1179, usury had been officially classified as a sin. So serious a sin was it that come the Council of Vienna of 1311–12, for a Christian even to *argue* that it was not a sin was defined as being a sin. Usurers were denied communion, sacraments and Christian burial. Specific biblical precedent for this comes from Exodus 22:25, where Jehovah states: 'If thou lend money to any of my people … thou shalt not be to him as an usurer.' But Christians still needed credit, and so a convenient loophole was found; invite Jews into European cities, quarantine them in ghettos, persuade them to lend Christian folk their money, label them sinners for doing so, and then let them all rot in Hades forever. It's what Jesus would have wanted, had He not actually been a Jew Himself. In fact, there was a famous example of Jesus disapproving of usury in the Bible too, namely the day he went all Incredible Hulk and stormed into the Temple in Jerusalem, overturning the tables of the Jewish moneylenders. The moral of this tale is often confused as being that money has no place in religion. This is mistaken. Within the outer court of Jewish temples at the time, various necessary items were available for purchase by pilgrims. Because pilgrims often came from afar, they needed their money converting into local currency to buy things. The moneylenders that Jesus confronted and called 'a den of thieves' were actually the biblical equivalent of one of those rip-off *bureau de change* outlets you see in airports, offering bad deals on transforming pounds into Euros. This Jesus defined as being disguised usury, and this is why he began attacking furniture, not because the bankers were operating within holy grounds *per se*.[33] So, if even the normally meek and mild-mannered Lamb of God had once taken matters into his own hands like Dirty Harry smashing up a branch of Cash Converters, why shouldn't other concerned individuals like Ezra Pound attack greedy Jews too, if only verbally?

Albrecht Dürer's depiction of Jesus Christ, a very violent man, going on the rampage against the moneylenders in the Temple. (Courtesy of the Metropolitan Museum of Art)

False Protocols

Pound's descent into anti-Semitism began around 1934, when one of his friends sent him an American fascist magazine called *Liberation!* as a joke. Unfortunately, as Pound read through it, he began to take its absurd claims about rich Jewish bankers starting off the US Civil War with a seriousness they did not deserve. By 1940, Pound was in thrall to the most widely read anti-Semitic document of all time, the notorious *Protocols of the Elders of Zion*. A known forgery, the *Protocols* purport to record the details of a secret meeting held by the world's most prominent Jews at which they laid out their sinister plans for global domination via infiltration of the world's governments, media empires and financial organisations – and then, rather stupidly, wrote them all down, thus giving people prior warning.[34] Weirdly, Pound knew the *Protocols* were a fake, but with typical twisted logic used this fact to argue they were actually genuine in nature. As Pound put it in one of his war-time radio broadcasts, 'Certainly [the *Protocols*] are a forgery, and that is the one proof we have of their authenticity.' How did Pound work that one out? Because 'the Jews have worked with forged documents for the past twenty-four hundred years, namely ever since they have had any documents whatsoever.' Oh, right. The most significant element of the Jews' equally fake/real plan was as follows: 'We shall surround our government with a whole world of economists. That is the reason why economic sciences form ... Around us again will be a whole constellation of bankers, industrialists, capitalists and ... millionaires, because in substance everything will be settled by the question of figures.'[35] Thus, the rotten state of the modern, war-torn world was really a reflection of the rotten state of the economic model the sneaky Jews had imposed down upon us from above.

However, the greatest crime was how the sinister Zionist gombeen-men had used their control over the world's banks to completely sever the natural relationship between symbol and referent in terms of money, after the wicked model of the Satanic Bank of Genoa. 'The false system of bookkeeping' was, Pound said, an outgrowth of Jewish 'code-worship', or the way in which Jews slavishly obeyed their false religion's petty rules and regulations, such as not eating pork, instead of living life in harmony with Nature and God, as the old fertility cults had supposedly once done.[36] Another age-old stereotype relating to the Jews is that they were all Satanists or black magicians of some kind, something which led Pound to libel the Jews and their British allies in Parliament and the City of London as having created 'a species of monetary Black Mass' through which they had succeeded in 'endowing money with properties of a quasi-religious nature' which allowed it to shift shape and give the false impression of spontaneously reproducing itself in the shape of goods and services even in spite of its true rectal barrenness. The Jews and their anal allies had been allowed to claim that a kind of 'energy' lay inherent within a coin or banknote, akin to 'the divine quality of consecrated bread' without which no goods or services could possibly ever be allowed to exist. This, though, was nothing but a gigantic Jewish lie: 'a half-*lira* piece has never created the cigarette or the piece of chocolate that … issues from the slot machine.' Coins did not make the crops grow; Nature did. Banknotes did not make us our daily bread; bakers did. The true basis of wealth was therefore not money at all, but the bounty of God and the constant efforts of human labour. Jewish claims that the 'energy' which created our food, clothes and consumer goods lay within the money supply itself were pure financial witchcraft, a kind of alchemy. We had been duped into seeing the Jewish Black Mass as reality, when in fact it was the Devil's illusion. The only hope for humanity to combat this process of 'Satanic transubstantiation', said Pound, was to defy Jewish bamboozlement and restore the link between symbol and referent once more in terms of national currency, just as Fenollosa's Chinese had done with their ideograms.[37]

Just the Ticket!

The best way to do this, Pound argued, was to redefine money not as money *per se*, but as a 'general sort of ticket'. The main difference between a ten-dollar bill and a theatre ticket or a train ticket was that theatre tickets couldn't get you a seat on a train, nor train tickets a seat within a theatre, but a ten-dollar bill could get you either – or, indeed, something completely different, as *Monty Python* used to say. However, another distinction lay in the fact that a train ticket was what Pound termed a 'measured ticket'. If you bought a ticket from London to Brighton, then that ticket would always get you between those two locations, and those two locations would always remain the same number of miles apart, as the precise distance measured out by the very concept of a mile would remain forever constant. However, with dollar bills, or 'money tickets', as Pound dubbed them, the situation was different because 'a money ticket, under a corrupt system, wobbles' as prices of goods change and inflation eats away at the contents of your wallet. Also, the cost of goods and services in one part of the country might be different from the cost of the very same things in another part of the country, whereas the measurement of a mile would always remain the same wherever you were.

The solution was for national governments to take complete fiscal control and determine stable and precise 'measurements' for a single dollar, pound or franc: 'The US Government has the right to say a dollar is one wheat-bushel thick, it is one serge-foot long, it is ten gallons of petrol wide.' If a dollar was indeed ten gallons of petrol wide, then one would get you the same amount of gas in rural Alabama as it would in Washington DC; a twelve-inch ruler would always be twelve inches long, and a dollar would always be ten gallons wide. Once a national government had firmly established the most 'just' measurement value of the money ticket by regulating the price of goods and services, its next job would be to ensure these tickets were distributed properly, so everybody had enough for their own personal needs. 'The country's money is a mass of tickets for getting the country's food and goods justly distributed,' said Pound, but at the moment there were 'not enough tickets moving about among the WHOLE people to BUY what they need – EVEN when the goods are there on the counter or going to rot on the wharves.' The answer was for governments to abolish private banking, begin printing new money on a mass scale and then simply give it away to its citizens, including in the form of non-interest-bearing loans for those who wanted to do useful things, thus abolishing poverty forever. This might sound a bit like the Jewish Hell Bankers conjuring new money from nowhere, but this was not the case: 'For a professor to tell you that the country cannot do this, that or the other, because it lacks money is as black and foetid a lie, as grovelling and imbecile, as it would be to say it cannot build roads because it has no kilometres.'[38]

The 'rascals', 'bastards' and 'mental abortions' who ran the banks and the Jewspapers didn't want the public to know that money was really a measured ticket, however, being content to keep on conning the people into accepting the current Jewish-controlled system of 'demoliberal usurocracy' for 'as long as dung stinks'. The Jews had within their pay various 'hired professors' who deliberately mis-taught economics to the young at university, paid academic quislings who cruelly tricked their students into believing that the financial system of Genoa was superior to that of Siena out of sheer 'dog-like contempt for the wellbeing of all mankind'. Jewish usury, explained Pound, was 'the cancer of the world, which only the surgeon's knife of fascism can cut out of the life of the nations.'[39] But, when a nation's professors deliberately misrepresented the surgeon's knife as a dangerous stiletto, then what chance did the young have of seeing through the tangled web of lies? Pound's opinion of academia was not high; having been expelled from his English Literature course for insulting his own dust-dry tutors, he went on to pen pamphlets referring to such appalling people as mere 'agglomerates of protoplasm' and 'soft, incompetent, low-voiced nonentities' who 'bleat that money is just false teeth, metal and spectacle frames', vile falsehoods which negatively affected 'the vitality, the whole health of a nation'. Through their control of the media and universities, prominent Jewish banking families like the Rothschilds had transformed the world's Presidents and Prime Ministers into nothing but 'hypnotised rabbits', with Washington now an intellectual 'dung-hill' in which wrong-headed, Jew-taught economists spent all their time 'bleating of universals to avoid concrete, immediate fact', tricking politicians into being unable to see the truth about money being an easily printable ticket, pure and simple. Softened up by the Jew-duped economists into paying attention to Jewish 'war-profiteers and gun-bastards', Western leaders had been fooled into trying to alleviate the effects of the Jewish-engineered Great Depression by going to war against the heroic fascist nations of Germany and Italy who had seen through the entire Zionist con-trick and bravely tried to stand up and bring an end to it all.[40]

Not the Many, But the Jew

Because a widespread rumour had arisen that Mayer Amel Rothschild (1744–1812), the founder of the premier Jewish banking dynasty, had allegedly once boasted 'Give me control of a nation's money supply, and I care not who makes its laws!' it was easy for Pound to maintain paranoid rubbish like this.[41] The Bank of Rothschild spanned the entirety of Western Europe, and was for much of the nineteenth century the biggest beast on Planet Finance. Through mastery of the bond market, and an ability to use their continental connections to get Treasury gold safely across the Channel and into the Duke of Wellington's military war-chests, the Rothschilds had helped fund Britain's victory during the Napoleonic Wars, something which should have turned them into heroes – instead, they became the ultimate bond villains of their day. In order to defeat Napoleon, London had been forced to get herself into immense debt. Scapegoats were needed and, despite their indispensable service to the Crown, the so-called 'Bonapartes of Finance' proved convenient patsies. Rumours spread that the Rothschilds owned a magical Hebrew talisman which accounted for their financial success, and so began the pernicious legend that the Jewish-Satanist Rothschilds control all the world's banks – a legend which still has its thick-headed adherents today. The Bank of Rothschild began to be depicted as nothing less than a gigantic Jewish octopus, the stretch of whose malevolent tentacles knew no limit. In particular, the Rothschilds were accused of secretly starting off more wars to gain further valuable government debts by funding them. But they were damned if they did, and damned if they didn't; by *failing* to agree to back the South financially during the American Civil War, for example, the Rothschilds inadvertently caused sympathisers with the Confederate cause to blame the Jews for their defeat.[42] The overall impression you get is that, whatever the nature of your own financial or political misfortunes, it was best to just blame the omnipotent octopus for it.

Clearly, Ezra Pound had many previous models to copy when it came to anti-Semitic slander. For example, in his 1944 Money Pamphlet *America, Roosevelt and the Causes of the Present War*, Pound was quite explicit that, contrary to popular belief, the Second World War 'was not caused by any caprice on Mussolini's part, nor on Hitler's.' Rather than having anything to do with the Nazi invasion of Poland, the conflict was simply part of the age-old 'secular war between … the usurocracy and whomever does an honest day's work with his own brain or hands.' The question of who had started the Second World War was really but a minor sub-plot within the much wider 'great whodunit of money', with Pound playing the role of Poirot and all the evidence pointing towards the murderer saluting the Star of David with a raised tentacle. Even if President Roosevelt had *appeared* to send America into war against the Axis Powers, this was in fact a mere illusion, with the President's true puppetmasters being the Jewish bankers; FDR, said Pound, was nothing but 'a malignant tumour, not autonomous, not self-created, but an unclean exponent of something less circumscribed than his own evil personal existence; a magistrate with legally limited jurisdiction, a perjurer, not fully aware of what he does, why he does it, or where it leads to.'[43] The hypnotised rabbit Roosevelt (or 'Jewsfeldt' and 'Stinky Roosenstein' as Pound childishly called him[44]) may have thought he was fighting for freedom, but in reality he was inadvertently battling to maintain the West's financial enslavement, and to continue the mesmeric illusion that money was money, rather than a disguised train ticket. This was all really quite unsurprising, as Pound claimed to have uncovered evidence that the United States had been secretly 'sold to the Rothschilds in 1863'.

Other Allied leaders such as Winston Churchill (1874–1965) had also been hypnotised into fighting fascism, due to the fact that the Jews and the Bank of England had surreptitiously gained control of the *Times Literary Supplement* and branches of W. H. Smith up and down Britain in order to encourage people to waste their time reading undemanding Agatha Christie murder mysteries instead of proper books like Pound's, which exposed the limitless monetary crimes of the Jews. Shockingly, such evil ephemera involving much-loved but ultimately harmful figures like Sherlock Holmes, Father Brown and Miss Marple had even now reached the fascist nations themselves, as part of the Jews' global campaign to instil a kind of false consciousness among the

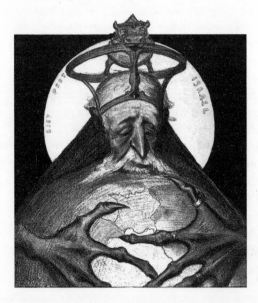

A malicious 1898 cartoon showing one of the Rothschilds holding the entire globe within his greedy grasp; a variant of the paranoid idea that a giant Jewish octopus secretly ruled the world. (*Le Rire*, 16 April 1898)

A 1904 cartoon by Udo J. Keppler, showing the massive US corporation Standard Oil as a giant octopus controlling American politics; not only Jews were libelled by this common motif, therefore. (Courtesy of the Library of Congress)

populace: 'In Italy, as elsewhere, crime fiction has served to distract attention from the great underlying crime, the crime of the usurocratic system itself.' By reading Satanic Jewish filth like *Murder on the Orient Express* instead of fine, wholesome educational tomes like *Mein Kampf* or *The Protocols of the Elders of Zion*, the people of Europe were being infected with 'the English disease' by the publishing and media wings of the Rothschild Bank of England, thus gaining 'a pathological disposition to believe the fantastic tales put out from London and disseminated gratis by indigenous simpletons' who wrote columns in the continental Press. This bizarre literary conspiracy even extended towards the publishers of dictionaries, within which no clear definition of the word 'money' could anywhere be found. All lexicographers had to do was print a sentence along the lines of 'MONEY: A form of measured ticket to be used to enable the fair distribution of goods and services to those who need them', but nowhere had these not-so harmless drudges done so. According to Pound, this was because 'as long as the word "money" is not clearly defined ... to all the peoples of the world, they will go blindly to war with each other, never knowing the reason why.' It was in the interests of those 'stinking dregs of humanity', the Jewish bankers, to maintain the false 'mirage of money' in this way so that they could go on owning us forever.[45]

An Honest Dollar

One way in which the 'mirage of money' could be dispelled would be to link cash back directly to the concept of labour and the time spent performing it. 'Against every hour's work,' proposed Pound, there should be 'an hour's certificate', or 'an hour-dollar for an hour-work'.[46] If symbol and referent were reunited in this way, as with Chinese ideograms, then it would be impossible for the Jewish gombeen-men to keep on tricking the people; knowing that their dollar represented an hour's work and was ten gallons of petrol wide, the world's workers would begin to view cash as something concrete rather than abstract in nature, and thus more directly comprehensible. Once the dollar or pound had become a solid, specific thing again, the Jewish hypnotists would get found out and overthrown, with the public refusing to 'lick the boots of bloated financiers or the syphilitics of the market-place' ever again.[47] To Pound it was obvious that 'All value [of money] comes from labour; wheat from ploughing, chestnuts from being picked up', not from the Jewish witchcraft of gold having anal sex with itself. However, there was more to the matter than this. As he pointed out, 'a lot of WORK has already been done by men (mostly inventors, well-diggers, constructors of factory-plant, etc.) now DEAD and who therefore cannot eat and wear clothes.' Dead people had worked very hard for our benefit, argued Pound, accumulating millions of hour dollars down the years which represented a kind of 'Social Credit' whose value could surely be distributed to currently living people as 'a bonus over and above their wage-packet'.[48]

Because of the past efforts of the industrious dead, Pound viewed the problem of production of goods as having been solved, an opinion Mussolini also shared.[49] Clearly, with all the factories and farms that had been established down the years by dead people, it was perfectly possible for enough food and clothing to be made to satisfy the needs of all living citizens. The problem was that the Jews and greedy industrialists had conspired together to ensure that these necessary goods could not simply be distributed to those who needed them. To do this, they had invented the false concept of 'overproduction', which held that it was possible to produce an unnecessary glut of some specific product, for example shoes, which could then not be shifted on the marketplace. But why could they not be shifted? Even during periods of overproduction of shoes, there were still many poor folk who could have done with a new pair. 'Nature habitually overproduces,' Pound explained. 'Chestnuts go to waste on the mountainside, and it has never yet caused a world crisis.'[50] The real problem, as laid out by Pound in his 1933 book *ABC of Economics*, was not overproduction, but under-distribution. There were enough shoes for everyone to have a brand-new pair, but not enough money tickets in circulation for them to be able to buy them. One possible solution lay in wholesale reform of the working day. Instead of some people working all the hours God sent while others sat idle, Pound proposed that it would be better for those currently employed to accept a large drop in their hours worked per day, so that the jobless could share their jobs and get some money too.[51] If the value of the hour dollar was fixed forever at a fair level by the government, and measured so many gallons of petrol wide, or so many loaves of bread tall, then those workers who would experience a drop in their hours would still be able to enjoy an acceptable standard of living, while also gaining many free hours of leisure, which could be filled far more profitably and enjoyably than by standing around pushing buttons on a production line:

> Let the man work four hours for pay, and if he still wants to work after that let him work as any artist or poet works, let him embellish his home or his garden, or stretch his legs in some form of exercise, or crook his back over a pool table, or sit on his rump and smoke ... [As a poet] I know, not from theory but from practice, that you can live infinitely better with a very little money and a lot of spare time, than with more money and less time. Time is not money, but it is almost everything else.[52]

Due to the so-called 'Cultural Inheritance' of inventions and infrastructure from the dead, there was no longer any need to have such a long working day. Just as sheep will naturally keep on growing wool on their backs while the indolent shepherd just lazes about on the sun-kissed hillside for most of the time idly watching them, so modern dynamos will go on producing electricity with minimal human input. Under such circumstances, said Pound, it would be 'as idiotic to expect members of a civilised ... community to go on working eight hours a day as it would be to expect ... the poulterer to sit on his hens' eggs.'[53] Overwork and joblessness, according to this outlook, were two sides of the same coin. When it came to unemployment, said Pound, 'I am an expert. I have lived nearly all my life ... among the unemployed' as had many of the starving young artists and writers he had set out to help down the years.[54] Unlike certain people on the Left, Pound knew that taxing the rich was not a realistic solution to this impasse, as 'The rich man's pocket happens to be a mere pipe and not an inexhaustible upspringing fountain.'[55] Instead, Central Banks should bite the bullet and print as much money as people needed to buy things with, and then let citizens work enough hours each for them to earn these tickets. Mainstream economists might argue that such a plan would lead to disaster, but mainstream economics was, of course, a fake modern Jewish invention; as Pound said, 'An economic library in 1800 could have been packed in a trunk.'[56] 'We artists have known this for a long time, and laughed,' explained Pound, taking poverty 'as our punishment for being artists', but now more and more ordinary people were beginning to realise that the money supply was inadequate and needed to be increased, too.[57]

Who's Been Debasing My Porridge?

Economists may have said that simply printing endless money would lead to runaway inflation, but Pound argued that not enough money being printed led instead to a kind of constipation. By transforming finance into some gigantic monetary anus, the perverted Jews and Jew-like industrialists had created a somewhat dyspeptic situation wherein the anal passage of commerce had become bunged up with bad dung, as there were more goods in existence than could be plopped out of the economic bum-pipe and sold on to the public, as they didn't have enough banknotes to be able to buy them all with.[58] On the other hand, sometimes the Jews did indeed cause too much money to be printed in order to trick people into seeking easy credit, something Pound viewed as being equivalent to excessive masturbation.

Like many an autodidact, Pound had weird theories about everything under the sun, not just money and poetry; for example, he had developed certain very peculiar ideas about his own sperm. When closely examining the quality of his 'liquid solution' following ejaculation in order to see how good it was, just like his dad testing silver at the US Mint, Pound noticed that, if he produced such emissions too often, they would come out all thin and runny, like watery milk. Leave it too long between ejaculations, however, and you could paste your wallpaper with it. The solution was to adopt a middle path and keep the sperm at the 'right consistency', just like Goldilocks' porridge, by leaving the correct amount of time for testicular recovery between climaxes, not too long and not too short, in order to achieve the optimum 'balance of ejector and retentive media'. As for ejaculation, so for poetry; spilling too much ink on the page, day after day, would lead to thin gruel indeed being produced, like the work of Kate Tempest. Leaving it too long between poems, however, would lead to your pen getting all blocked up with dried ink-blobs. The hoarding of sperm or of ink was just as bad for you, then, as was spraying it around everywhere willy-nilly like a leaky hosepipe. And it was exactly the same with the world's money supply, too. Jewish sins like usury made the cum curdle in a civilisation's balls as young men were unable to take wives due to being in debt, as in *Canto XLV*, while excessive Jewish conjuring of money gave a society a bad case of the runs, debasing the currency and turning banknotes into mere toilet paper like the worthless hyperinflated Reichsmarks of Weimar Germany, through an excess of quantitative squeezing. What was needed was not too little money in circulation, argued Pound, nor too much, but just the right amount – the world didn't need a Gold Standard, so much as a Goldilocks Standard.[59]

However, of the two evils, too much money in circulation and too little, the former was doubtless the lesser. Surely monetary inflation was better than monetary constipation, of either the anal or testicular variety? In fact, for Pound there was good inflation and bad inflation. Bad inflation was when the Jews artificially lowered the worth of money by conjuring it out of nowhere within their Hell Banks, whereas good inflation was when central government began printing more money tickets to spread around properly so that everything which was produced could actually be bought. If you had

a theatre with 500 seats one year, but expanded it to seat 1,000 customers
the next year because it kept on getting sold out, then it would make no
sense to keep on only issuing 500 tickets per performance; obviously, you
would double the number of tickets issued, thus equating supply with
demand. To do otherwise would lead to severe constipation at the box office.
It was exactly the same with industrial production. If that doubled from one
year to the next, then so too should the supply of money tickets, argued
Pound; it was only if you printed the monetary equivalent of 2,000 tickets
for a 1,000-seat theatre that inflation was a bad thing. Any economist who
thought otherwise was 'a saphead'.[60] As a further benefit, if the government
constantly printed out a steady supply of new hour-dollars and gave them to
everyone who ever did any work for the State, from the loftiest Senator to
the humblest road sweeper, then there would be no need to bother citizens to
pay taxes for the upkeep of public services, as the money to fund them would
just be manufactured by the Treasury on the spot. There would never be any
need for government austerity in Pound-Land.[61] Admittedly, such financial
reform would play havoc with all those rich fat-cat speculators who get
their kicks by gambling in stocks and shares on Wall Street, but if it was
excitement such Jewish plutocrats wanted in their lives, said Pound, then 'it
would be much better' from the general public's viewpoint 'if they were to
kill themselves racing motor-boats' instead.[62] Money should be conceived
of as a 'public convenience', not a 'private bonanza',[63] concluded the by
now rabid anti-Semite, and if any constipated Jewish economists disagreed
with him, well then – they should go and invest in a poorly made speedboat
immediately.

Ecumenical Economics

Many of Pound's ideas sound cuckoo, and it probably would not surprise many
readers to learn that, following Italy's defeat in 1945, Pound was captured by
American forces and spent the next decade or so locked up in a mental home.
But does this *necessarily* mean he was insane? There was more debate about
whether or not Pound was truly mad than for anyone since Hamlet, Prince of
Denmark; some thought he really was nutty, others that he just preferred to
pretend to be so to avoid a prison sentence (or worse) on grounds of treason,
and yet others claimed the American authorities had simply labelled him loony
because they were unable to comprehend the fact that one of their own citizens
was able to hold views so wholly at variance with mainstream public opinion.
However, far from being his own unique creation, Pound's apparently mad
economic ideas were in fact personal adaptations of the plans of several other
(slightly) more respectable persons – including two Popes!

While Christ's kingdom was, famously, not of this world, several of His
earthly representatives have seen fit to stick their nose into economic matters

nonetheless. Pound was favourably disposed towards the economic aspects of something called Canon Law, or *jus canonicum*, the body of laws and regulations once enforced across Europe by the medieval Church. The first modern Western legal system, Canon Law recognised the benefits of commerce and the creation and spread of wealth, but taught that there were other, greater principles which stood above such things. For example, there was the idea of the 'Just Price' developed by St Thomas Aquinas (1225–74), Catholicism's greatest theologian. In his thirteenth-century *Summa Theologiae*, Aquinas had broadened the traditional prohibition against usury out to apply to merchants as well, whom he said had no business raising the price of goods which they already held, should demand for them suddenly increase – for example a builders' merchant hiking up the cost of his bricks following an earthquake, an early form of what we now call 'surge pricing'. According to Aquinas, such behaviour was commercial usury, as the merchant was getting something extra in terms of profit in return for no extra work; in Pound's terms, the usurer and the greedy merchant were performing that old black magic of making gold anally breed. The solution, said Aquinas, was to introduce the idea of a Just Price, meaning the original reasonable price the merchant would have sold his items on for before there was any spike in demand, a sum which covered his costs, then made a little extra profit for him to live off.[64] In modern times, the idea of the Just Price has now been replaced by impersonal laws of supply and demand – you'll pay more for a lolly-ice in summer than in winter, or for a family holiday outside of term-time – and nobody thinks anything much of the fact.

However, in separating our economies from the ancient precepts of Canon Law, were modern Westerners separating themselves from the basic moral and religious precepts underlying reality at the same time? This was the view of Pope Leo XIII (1810–1903), who on 15 May 1891 issued his encyclical *Rerum novarum* ('of revolutionary change'), which attempted to address the rapid growth of capitalism and Communism. Leo criticised the excesses of both unfettered *laissez faire* capitalism and revolutionary socialism, seeking a kind of 'third path' between the two. From a Right-wing perspective, it supported the institution of private property, criticising those who would seek to seize it as thieves, while at the same time adopting a somewhat Left-wing position of encouraging working men to form into unions, just so long as their demands were reasonable and their methods non-violent. Ideally, employers, workers and unions were to pull together for the greater good of society, instead of for their own selfish ends; acrimonious strikes were not the way forward. Nonetheless, the State had its limits, and should not interfere with the traditional life of the family, the ultimate building block of civilisation. Pursuit of profit over all else was yet another kind of usury, Leo taught, with corporate greed being a contravention of the biblical injunction not to covet thy neighbour's ox, house, fields, ass and suchlike. On the other hand, some degree of economic inequality was simply a natural fact of life, and Left-wing attempts to promote absolute equality for all would actually just end up dragging everyone down to a lower level, in a kind of parity of misery.

Class conflict was therefore a mistake; the different classes needed one another if society was going to function. As Leo said, 'capital cannot do without labour, nor labour without capital'. Nonetheless, it was clearly the case that many workers at the time were being exploited, in conditions of 'misery and wretchedness', and Leo called for them to be given a Just Wage to go with a Just Price, demanded an end to child labour and excessively dangerous working conditions, and encouraged unions to ensure that their members be given enough time off to worship God. It was only through the labour of the workers that companies and nations grew rich, so it was the reciprocal responsibility of industrialists and governments to ensure their people had access to enough clothing, food and shelter – these things existed, so they should be distributed fairly to the people, as Ezra Pound later argued. Claiming that trade unions had specific biblical precedents, Leo called for them to be modified in their outlook nonetheless, hoping for some kind of restoration of the old medieval guild system, in which associations of specific craftsmen and merchants – guilds of tailors, say, or stonemasons – had bound themselves together and regulated and promoted their own trades for mutual economic, social, technological and spiritual benefit.[65]

Encyclical Economics

Rerum novarum was a much-discussed document, and on 15 May 1931, precisely forty years after it had been issued, Pope Pius XI (1857–1939) issued his own response, entitled *Quadragesimo anno*, or 'in the fortieth year'. Pius' encyclical mostly endorsed and reiterated the wise conclusions of Leo XIII, but also added some further ideas of his own – including, it would appear, a specific blessing for the economic programmes of fascist Italy. Essentially, Pius encouraged the development of a tripartite structure to society in which government, labour and industry worked together in the name of something greater – the State itself. He seems to have envisaged a form of subsidiarity in which giant multinational companies were, wherever possible, replaced by smaller concerns modelled upon a more human scale, where employees and employers united within a shared interest, perhaps with the ordinary labour force receiving a share of company profits in the form of dividends, or having some say in management of the factories in which they worked. Jeremy Corbyn would have loved it! While all such organisations would ultimately work together for the greater good, thereby eliminating the 'poison spring' of 'the errors of individualist economic teaching', the State would not interfere in their day-to-day running too closely, merely steer them towards the general direction in which it wanted everyone to be travelling. These various privately owned enterprises, Pius proposed, would fulfil a 'subsidiary function' within the State, being somewhat independent from it, so that men might be free, but nonetheless participating within a greater national collective, so that the country and its population as a whole might be strong and cohesive.

In short, a nation's economic life must be *directed*, but not *enslaved* by State control, with 'economic life again subjected to and governed by a true and effective directing principle', as it had been under the rule of the medieval Church. The sense of national unity thereby achieved would not be a form of inescapable and all-encompassing social imprisonment, as under Communism, but an imitation of the natural, divine unity to be found within the Holy Trinity. Again, Pius called for some modern-day guild system to be established, a system he saw as being closely approached by the social reforms of Mussolini. In such an arrangement, rather than being judged according to their income or wealth, 'men may have their place not according to the position each has in the labour market, but according to the respective social functions which each performs.' While Pius doesn't specifically mention *Il Duce* or fascism by name, it is clear what sort of thing he is referring to. He asks 'that God bless' such systems, and that 'all men of good will' should work to see them more fully implemented. The true dictatorship in economic affairs, said Pius, was 'being most forcibly exercised by those who, since they hold the money and completely control it, control credit also and rule the lending of money ... [who] regulate the flow, so to speak, of the life-blood whereby the entire economic system lives, and have so firmly in their grasp the soul, as it were, of economic life that no one can breathe against their will.' Condemning the 'accursed internationalism of finance ... whose country is where profit is', Pius asks if there might not be a better way of doing things.[66] As we have seen already, the Popes were not the only ones to be asking themselves such questions, or using such language, at around this time.

Distributing Justice?

Writings like *Rerum novarum* led to the development of an economic philosophy called Distributism, a school to which Pound's economics are often said broadly to belong. Distributism's two main promoters were also men of letters, namely the English novelist, essayist, playwright and poet G. K. Chesterton (1874–1936) and Hilaire Belloc (1870–1953), an Anglo-French writer, poet, historian and one-time Salford MP. As the creator of Father Brown, Chesterton may well have been partly responsible for flooding the market with yet more diabolically distracting detective novels, but his strong Catholic beliefs led him to team up with his fellow Catholic Belloc to try to devise a new, more non-materialist model of economics that would help put the teachings of Leo XIII into action. The plan of 'Chesterbelloc', as the pair were dubbed, had a misleading name in 'Distributism'. This sounds as if it should be a form of socialism, in which the welfare state distributes things such as money, food and shelter. However, surprisingly for the author of *Cautionary Tales for Children*, which famously advised toddlers to 'hold on to nurse for fear of something worse', Hilaire Belloc was not a great fan of the nanny state, nor of those who wished to hold onto its comforting yet infantilising apron strings forever. Both Chesterton and Belloc despised the rise of the modern, increasingly powerful and centralised *Servile State*, as Belloc called it in the title of a 1912 book, and wished to see a virtual end to the concept of 'free' (meaning paid for by other people's taxes) welfare altogether.

Instead, what they both wanted to see distributed among the people was the means of production. This sounds like a Marxist ideal, but it was not. Marxists desired to seize the means of production – factories, land, farms, machinery and industrial infrastructure – from private owners and then distribute them among the proletariat in the limited sense that they would be nationalised in the people's name, while the high-up Commissars actually ran them all. For Chesterbelloc, the situation was quite different; rather than outlawing the very notion of private property, as in Communism, they preferred the idea of seeing it shared more widely among the people. In *Rerum novarum*, Leo XIII had spoken of the need to ensure that workers had access to 'that [form of] justice which is called *distributive*', and this was how Chesterbelloc chose to interpret the term. Leo had spoken of his hope that 'property will ... become more equitably divided' because 'If working people can be encouraged to look forward to obtaining a share in the land, the consequence will be that the gulf between vast wealth and sheer poverty will be bridged over, and the respective classes will be brought nearer to one another.' G. K. Chesterton and Hilaire Belloc agreed. In no sense did they wish to seize existing landowners' and industrialists' property, as in the Soviet Union, but they did wish to see governments introduce policies to encourage the spread of homeownership among the masses, and enable the self-employed and those who ran workers' co-operatives, family businesses and small farms to flourish. The problem with capitalism as perceived by Distributism, it might be said, was that there were not enough capitalists; most ordinary workers, unlike their rich bosses, had little or no money other than weekly wages, and didn't own capital resources such as land, tools or machinery either. Neither man called for revolution, only gradual change, and sought not to inhabit utopia, only a *somewhat* better society. Being Catholics, Chesterbelloc knew full well that man was not built to inhabit Paradise prior to death.

Even though the movement attracted many followers during the inter-war years, Chesterbelloc were quite pessimistic about what Distributism could actually achieve; neither man really expected to fully succeed in their aims. 'We are only attempting to change the general tone of society,' wrote Belloc, 'and restore property as a commonly present, not a universal, institution.' Unlike the Servile State of socialism, which had unrealistic aspirations towards all-encompassing flawlessness, the Distributist State, being based upon Catholicism, knew that such an aim was impossible. 'There can be no perfection about it,' said Belloc, 'it must remain incomplete; nor could there be a better proof that the attempt is a human one, consonant to human nature.' Unlike in the fraudulent socialist promise of a shining New Jerusalem, Belloc admitted that, under his plans, there would still be 'many comparatively poor, and some comparatively rich', as well as 'presumably … some portion of dispossessed', as it was a historical commonplace that, sadly, the poor are always with us. All he hoped for was that 'Property, and its accompaniment, Economic Freedom, will be the [general] mark of society as a whole'. Refusing to promise impossible things is not always popular with the voting public, however, and Distributism never really caught on among the wider British political class. Nonetheless, the Distributists helped place moral pressure on governments to do things like break up large monopolies in the public interest, and facilitate increased homeownership, so it is not as if they had no victories. Possessing only limited aims, however, and with a realistically limited faith in the perfectibility of human nature and society, this is perhaps the best Chesterbelloc could have really expected.

Milking It

Essentially, Distributism was a development of the principle of subsidiarity, as preached by Pope Pius. Large-scale organisations, be they massive State-owned monopolies, or gigantic international corporations, were profoundly dehumanising forces, thought Chesterbelloc. They may well have been efficient in a financial and business sense, but they were not necessarily any good for the people who had to work in them. It seemed that society was being organised for the well-being of the economy, rather than the other way around; rather like today, in fact. You didn't have to be a Catholic to be a Distributist – Chesterbelloc had no wish to create a Christian theocracy – but it certainly helped. Many Distributists were former radical socialists, who saw in the movement a gentler and more humane way of improving the lot of the proletariat than fostering a Red Revolution, but such people must have been slightly puzzled by statements such as the following, taken from Chesterton's 1910 political tract *What's Wrong With the World*:

> Property is merely the art of democracy. It means that every man should have something that he can shape in his own image, as he is shaped in the image of Heaven [i.e. God]. But because he is not God, but only a graven

46

image of God, his self-expression must deal with limits; properly with limits that are strict and even small.[67]

Today, Christian aid groups who try to promote economic development in the Third World have coined memorable little slogans along the lines of 'Give a man a fish and you feed him for a day; give a man a net and you feed him for a lifetime' (or until the net breaks). Chesterton penned a similar slogan to promote Distributism, 'Three Acres and a Cow', which was more-or-less all he thought the average landowning person should need to live off; instead of giving a man a welfare state dole cheque to buy milk with, why not encourage him to milk his own cow instead? Naturally, this proposition is open to some obvious criticism. Adhering to the idea that small is beautiful in agriculture and industry means that you forgo the very real benefits of large economies of scale. Chesterbelloc might have dreamed of a future similar to the pre-Industrial Revolution past, where individual artisans made individual products with their own hands, but any pot or plate made in such a labour-intensive way is bound to cost the consumer more than its mass-produced equivalent, a thousand of which pop neatly off the production line in the same time it takes the independent potter to make and glaze a single one. A Distributist economy, it may be argued, simply isn't very efficient. Also, you can tell that Chesterton himself had never spent much time labouring on a farm, if he seriously thought that making an acceptable living from 'Three Acres and Cow' would involve anything other than masses of backbreaking drudgery, something which would be even worse if, as he suggested, some people might like to pursue such activities *in their spare time* away from another job. You can just imagine a self-employed plumber or mechanic (both professions Chesterton imagined flourishing under his model) coming home from a full day's labour and then having to go out and milk the cow himself if he fancies a quick drink, rather than simply opening the refrigerator.

Some Distributists, anticipating the later arguments of the Austro-Hungarian economic historian Karl Polanyi (1886–1964), liked to claim that capitalist societies had artificially legislated a proletariat into being, in order to provide cheap factory fodder for industrialists. Once upon a time, this argument goes, the English peasant had been able to collect firewood from forests *gratis*, catch hares, fish and birds for free dinners, and maintain small strips of land for cultivating personal supplies of crops, as allotment fans like jam-making Jeremy Corbyn do today. Around the time of the Industrial Revolution, however, many of these things became illegal, with gathering firewood redefined as theft from landowners, and shooting or trapping game transformed into poaching. Many Distributists suspected these legal 'innovations' were really intended to make the poor starve and shiver, thus giving them no option but to seek employment at a pittance in the new factories of the day. Chesterbelloc's ilk wished to reverse this process and give the people back their land and their ancient rights, a noble cause indeed if their assessment of history was correct. Unfortunately, an alternative way of interpreting employment patterns within the early Industrial Revolution, as espoused by the likes of Ludwig von Mises (1881–1973), a leading light of the pro-free market 'Austrian School' of economics, was that many of the people who went to work in factories actually *wanted* to work in them, and that gaining such employment, with the regular wages that came with it, led to all kinds of improvements in health, nutrition, lifespan and standards of living. According to the Austrian School, the population of Britain boomed following the Industrial Revolution because, with more jobs to go around, a larger population of poor people who otherwise simply would have starved was enabled to get enough food with their (admittedly pitiful) wages to survive.[68]

A Woman's Place is in the Home

To be fair, Chesterbelloc were always quite clear that their primary arguments for reforming the economy were not first and foremost economic in nature. By going back towards a more traditional way of life, they hoped to lead men into enjoying a closer relationship with God, or at least with what they saw as being the permanent human values in life, not the artificial ones of industrial modernity. Primarily, the leading Distributists wished to restore the idea of the family unit to its former prominence, a prominence they saw as under threat from growing consumerism and money-worship. Nowadays we tend to think of the Left as encouraging the break-up of the traditional nuclear family, through the liberalisation of divorce laws, denigration of (non-gay) marriage, abandonment of the stigma surrounding single-parenthood and the beatification of homosexuality, but Chesterbelloc lived long before Labour Home Secretary 'Woy' Jenkins (1920–2003) set all this in motion with his 'liberalising' reforms of the 1960s, and felt that unfettered *laissez faire* capitalism of the kind now more associated with the post-Thatcherite Right was the real problem in relation to increasing social incoherence.

From today's perspective, the family unit of Chesterbelloc's day looks enviably rock-solid, but both men – rather like Ezra Pound – believed that any nation's social model and the corresponding economic model it chose to pursue were inherently linked, with the one reflecting and influencing the other. G. K. Chesterton viewed the modern West as a profoundly disjointed place, full of too many specialists whose knowledge was so narrowly focused that they couldn't understand one another, with not enough generalists like himself who could slot different subjects together into a more coherent bigger picture. Like Michael Gove, Chesterton had had enough of experts who only ever pursued their own narrow goals to the detriment of wider society as a whole. For example, there was the issue of women going out to work instead of remaining in the home looking after the children and doing the housework, something which was increasingly occurring in the years following the First World War, when women had been emancipated to work in munitions factories and suchlike. The specialist economist, seeing this situation only from his own narrow standpoint, would call this an unalloyed positive, because more women in work meant an increase in GDP and boosted tax-take for the Treasury. The generalist Chesterton, however, was able to argue that this was not a wholly positive development, as women going out to work helped fragment the family, depriving young children of essential elements of maternal love.

For Chesterton, such economic 'specialists' were better deserving of the name 'heretics', because their teachings went against all the accumulated wisdom of mankind that was once honoured under the name 'tradition'. The very word 'economy' is derived from a Greek term meaning something like 'household management', and more fundamentally from the Greek word for 'home', *oikos*. By the early Edwardian age, though, the English term 'economy' – which was still then a new one – had come to refer to the direct opposite of the home, being used to describe the machinations and operations of international capital. Unless you lived in a flat above your own cornershop or something, then your *oikos* was definitively not the realm of the woefully misnamed *oik*onomy. Capitalism and socialism had separated craft and creativity from the home, feminism had separated women from the home, school had separated children from the home and filled their heads with 'progressive' nonsense, and the need for men to go out to work in factories all the time had separated men from the home, too. Distributists like Chesterbelloc wanted to restore the *oikos* to its rightful place at the centre of the *oik*onomy, because this would restore dignity to mankind, and bring him back closer to God, where he belonged. The false deity of the marketplace should be dispelled from the hearthside, because the family unit was the most important human institution in existence, not the stock exchange, which by comparison was wholly insignificant. 'There is nothing queerer today than the importance [given to] unimportant things,' the paradox-loving Chesterton once wrote. 'Except, of course, the unimportance [given to] important things.'

Chesterbelloc shared a rather romantic image of the independent worker, who, freed from the shackles of the production line or the clerk's office, would spend much of his new-found free time not only bothering cattle, but also engaging in acts of creativity around the home, whether that be reading great books of the past or writing new ones of the future, painting, making artisanal furniture, or simply engaging in bouts of deep thought. Creativity, Chesterbelloc decreed, was a God-like quality, God being the Creator of the

Heavens and the Earth, and a private home or farm of one's own should provide men with the complete freedom necessary to pursue such activities. These ideas then fed back into Pope Pius' doctrine of subsidiarity, as a society based around the individual family and privately owned homestead, instead of the tempting but poisonous collectivist liquor of the emergent welfare state, would be one in which small, independent, localised ways of life endured, making the nation strong and able to weather all storms; people who have deep roots are not as easily buffeted by the harsh winds of history and economic and demographic change. If a family raised its children properly, with the mother back in the home where she belonged, then the generations became like one single large extended kindred living on throughout time, linking each cohort tightly to previous and future ones, an image previously advanced by the great Anglo-Irish Tory MP-cum-philosopher Edmund Burke (1729–97). Was such an ideal – a 'democracy of the dead', as Chesterton had it – not worth rather more than mere gold?[69]

At first glance the economic ideas of Chesterbelloc and Ezra Pound might not seem to have an excessive amount in common, but actually they had numerous crossovers. For one thing, Distributism favoured banking reform, and robustly condemned the practice of usury – sometimes to the point of anti-Semitism, of which both halves of the Chesterbelloc double-act were often (somewhat justly) accused. The profit-making function of banks, in which they lent out money on interest, was to be abolished under Distributist dogma; this would have had obvious appeal to Pound. Also, Distributists favoured the elimination of trade unions, to be replaced with a kind of traditional guild system – another distinct echo of *Rerum novarum*, and an acknowledged desire of Pound's, too. There is also the fact that the rival Social Credit movement, with which Pound was seriously obsessed, as we shall soon see, was essentially Distributist in nature, albeit with money, rather than land, being the thing which was supposed to be shared out in order to save the proles from Servile State control. Personally, as a deeply conservative man myself, I also rather like the idea of Distributism; with the emphasis purely upon the word *idea*. A peculiar mixture of broad realism and specific fantasy, as for how well it would actually work in practice, I have scant optimism. I just have no especial desire to tug on a cow's udders every night, no matter how close the experience makes me feel towards Christ.

Fascist Finance

If Ezra Pound wanted the world's prevailing economic model to be influenced by the teachings of the Catholics and the Vatican, then he had to acknowledge that, in terms of temporal power, Italy these days was ruled not by the Pope but by *Il Duce*; fortunately, as we have seen, Pound was something of a fan. In any case, the fascist economic principles of Mussolini's

Italy also drew upon the teachings of Popes Pius and Leo.[70] In 1944, Pound wrote: 'My efforts during the last ten years … have been directed towards establishing a correlation between fascist economics and the economics of Canon Law,'[71] and the existence of such a correlation was no delusion. Why else would Pope Pius have blessed it in all but name? Pound's true love of the economics of Benito Mussolini and Adolf Hitler (1889–1945), however, seemed based upon the fact that, under fascism, the State controlled almost every aspect of its citizens' lives – something which, paradoxically, he saw as lending them more freedom.

It seems to have been forgotten that fascism started out as an avowedly Left-wing philosophy. Nowadays, the very term has become so over-used by Lefty Millie Tant-style critics and protestors (who are themselves arguably more fascist than the people they censure) that it has become essentially meaningless. Fascism, in fact, grew directly from out of the trade union movement, which explains why the likes of Arthur Scargill and Len McCluskey are such horrible Little Hitlers. The word *fascio*, from which *fascism* is derived, means 'bundle', as in a bundle of twigs or rods. A bundle of twigs bound tightly together into one solid whole is much stronger than any easily snapped individual twig, something which has a direct parallel with the idea of an individual factory worker being more easily exploited by the vicious boss class than he would be if he bundled himself together with others for his own protection. One Italian word for a union is a *fascio*, and it was in Italy where fascism first truly began, under Mussolini. A correspondent of the not notably Right-wing leader of the Russian Revolution V. I. Lenin (1870–1924), Mussolini first made a name for himself while living in exile in Switzerland from 1900, where he penned various radical Left-wing tracts, after which he returned to Italy and became editor of the socialist organ *Class War*. Eventually, Mussolini became familiar with the writings of Georges Sorel (1847–1922), a Far Left proponent of a movement known as Syndicalism, which proposed that a country should be ruled not by politicians as such, but by groups of radical trade unions. Mussolini's (ostensible) split with the Left came with the outbreak of the First World War which, unlike many of his old socialist pals, he supported. In order to discredit him for taking this position, the Italian Left adopted the standard smear tactic of painting him as a Right-winger, even though he wasn't. Mussolini was still a socialist but, rather than being an international socialist, he became a *national* socialist. Recognising that nationalism clearly existed among the ordinary working people, even though their supposed intellectual champions among the Marxist elite claimed it didn't (spot the parallels with today …), Mussolini saw no good reason why he should not acknowledge and exploit this fact. Mussolini might have been on the Right-wing end of the Left-wing spectrum, but he was still Left-wing.[72]

A nation needs to be bound together – like rods in a *fascio*, you might say – and, once he came to power in 1922, Mussolini set about doing so. Besides claiming to be a living embodiment of the spirit of ancient Rome, encouraging people to call him 'The Boss' and rallying them around dubious military adventures in places like Libya and Ethiopia, *Il Duce* also began laying the economic foundations for something called the Italian Corporate State. Corporatism, essentially, is a form of disguised nationalisation of industry. The term is derived from the Latin *corpus*, meaning 'body'; just as Popes Leo and Pius had taught, society as a whole was meant to be imagined as a human body, with its various constituent parts, such as industries, armies and governments, all working together in the national interest, thus eliminating class conflict forever. As St Paul put it in 1 Corinthians 12:25: 'There should be no schism in the body, but the members [limbs and organs] should have the same care for one another' – thus proving that Mussolini really did have God on his side. In short, every person and organisation would be in*corporated* into the *corpus*. There would be no escaping this fate but, just so long as a factory was working for the good of the body as a whole, it would be left alone to do its own thing – at least in theory. Just as your spleen very rarely complains to your lungs about the way they are going about their job, just so long as they are still pumping air around, so the State wasn't supposed to complain to arms manufacturers about their precise working methods just so long as they were still pumping out tanks and aircraft at the desired rate.

Corporate Interests

Again, this idea was greatly based upon the teachings of Georges Sorel and his Syndicalist movement. Sorel's major 1908 work *Reflections on Violence* urged workers to bind themselves together into violent mobs called 'syndicates', seize control of factories, ports and other such infrastructure, and take the place of the ruling politicians in a kind of dictatorship of the proletariat. Another Frenchman, Professor Léon Duguit (1859–1928), added to such ideas with his notion of *solidarité sociale*, or 'social solidarity', which further developed the thought that units of workers were akin to the organs in a human body. Around the same time, the British economist G. D. H. Cole (1889–1959) was developing his idea of 'Guild Socialism' in which, as the Popes had recommended, a variant of the ancient guild system would be resurrected, replacing the current model of trade unionism. Another source for Italian fascism's use of the word 'Corporatism' was the *corporazioni delle arti e dei mestieri*, the old term for medieval guilds of Italian artists and craftsmen. Tie all these twigs together and buttress them with a glue of extremely strong nationalist sentiment, and you had the basis for the future Italian Corporate State.

Ultimately, a form of guild system was indeed implemented in Italy, in which groups representing various fields of industry and commerce – including one for 'professional men and artists' – sat within a pseudo-democratic national chamber, where they reputedly had the ability to influence national policy. This had the effect of making not only those who sat in the chamber, but also the ordinary workers and employers whom they represented, complicit within Mussolini's dictatorship. Nonetheless, Ezra Pound still thought that his interests would be better represented by the head of the Artists' Guild than under the Jew-bought Congresses and Parliaments of America and Britain. While the new fascist state was supposed (in theory) to recognise the rights of the individual where possible, it was not, like the Anglo-Saxon capitalist lands, supposed to be based upon the active fetishisation of the individual above all else. In the economy of fascist Italy, liberty was best thought of as a *method*, not a *principle*; when it worked best, allow it, and when it failed, destroy. Wherever they were in conflict, the interests of the State were to be placed above those of the individual on the grounds that the nation was not simply a random aggregation of transient residents, but a kind of living entity, within which the dead and the living communed.[73] As Mussolini himself once put it, sounding weirdly like Edmund Burke:

> For us fascists, the State is not merely a guardian, preoccupied solely with the duty of assuring the personal safety of its citizens ... It is also the custodian and transmitter of the spirit of the people as it has grown up through the centuries in language, in customs, and in faith. And the State is not only a living embodiment of the present, it is also linked with the past and with the future, and thus transcending the brief limits of individual life, it represents the immanent spirit of the nation.[74]

In short, the economy was supposed to serve society, not society serve the economy, which Pound thought was rather a good thing, especially when expressed in Mussolini's poetic terms. To him, an economy serving society meant a return to the less usurious values of Renaissance Siena, not a government which ordered its factories to abandon their usual output and start making artillery, as actually happened. Although Pound preferred *Il Duce* to *der Führer*, the Nazis too had their own native form of Corporatism, termed *Gleichschaltung*, or 'co-ordination'; the word 'Nazi' was a German-language contraction of the Party's full name, the National *Socialist* German Workers' Party. When it came to nationalism and race, the Nazis were as Right-wing as you can get; but when it came to economics and organisational matters of State, their policies were pure Left-wing interventionism. If the characteristic feature of Right-wing political philosophy is a belief in a small State, and that of Left-wing political philosophy belief in a large State, then what did that make Mussolini and Hitler?[75] Mussolini's famous slogan 'Everything in the State, nothing outside the State, nothing against the State' now sounds rather totalitarian – but *Il Duce* meant it to be. The word 'totalitarian' is now a synonym for the kind of horrific, unfree regime we can see operating in such benighted lands as North Korea, Saudi Arabia and Islington North. However, the term was actually coined by Mussolini to describe his own period of rule in Italy, and he meant it in a *positive* way! According to one modern description, Mussolini's totalitarian Italy was intended to become a society 'where everybody belonged, where everyone was taken care of, where everything was inside the State and nothing was outside, where truly no child was left behind.'[76] That is, an all-inclusive Scandinavian-style welfare state – albeit a violent, muscular and militarised welfare state gone horribly wrong, which persecuted, oppressed and imprisoned those who dared criticise how it operated. (Draw your own conclusions about the soft totalitarianism of modern day political correctness here – this itself being a term first invented by the rather less than tolerant Soviets.[77])

The Lies that Bind

Ezra Pound did not discern the dark side of the *Duce*. To him, the *fascio*, which was displayed on as many Italian buildings as the swastika was in Germany, was not a threatening image, but an economically reassuring one. For Pound, it stood as the ultimate symbol of what he called 'the increment of association', or the notion that a group of people working together as one could perform wonders which were impossible for the individualistic Jew-like man of capitalism to perform alone. This increment of association, said Pound, 'is affirmed in every *fascio* clamped onto a public building, in every bundle of rods set up as a symbol.'[78] To Pound the *fascio* was a comforting sign that The Boss had created a society in which, once more, the gap between symbol and referent created by the Jews had been completely wiped away. In the words of one literary critic, Pound's conception of Mussolini's Corporate State was as 'a kind of totalitarian plenum [all-encompassing body] which institutes an absolute continuum among the signs of the natural, political and economic world, thus guaranteeing both the order of representation and the representation of order.'

The *fascio* was not a false symbol, like the US Stars and Stripes or British Union Jack, because, in Italy, the people really were (forcibly!) united together as one, unlike in the Jew-dominated pseudo-democracies, with the State acting like a supposedly benign totalitarian Big Brother, looking after their interests – so long as the State's interests and the people's interests coincided, that is. No longer could Jewish wizards conjure *lira* from Hell; the reign of the Bank of Siena had been symbolically restored by *Il Duce*, who, as Pound had recommended, issued people with newly printed money tickets in return for honest toil performed for the State, such as building roads and draining swamps. For Pound, the value of the Italian *lira* was 'based on the word of the *Duce*', something which was 'for me a much more secure basis than other people's gold'.[79] When Mussolini needed more money, he would never have gone to the Jews, begging them to make it for him with their magic spells. Instead, when in 1935 Italy was facing economic sanctions following his illegal invasion of Ethiopia, Mussolini, in his guise as husband of the nation, made a public plea to the women of Italy to donate their gold wedding rings to him, so he could melt them down and restock his Treasury; more than 250,000 wives in Rome alone did so, pledging their love to the swaggering figure of Big Boy Benito and not their real partners.[80] At last, someone had found a practical, non-Jewish way to make gold reproduce! No wonder Ezra Pound loved hm.

As Easy as A + B

Fascist and Catholic economics were not Pound's only influences, however, nor were they even the initial ones. In 1917, Pound learned of the 'Social Credit' teachings of Major C. H. Douglas (1879–1952), an Anglo-Scottish engineer of original – if in later life somewhat unsound – mind, and soon became one of his most prominent converts. Both Douglas and Pound wrote for the literary weekly *The New Age*, whose editor, A. R. Orage (1873–1934), introduced them in the name of promoting alternative thought. The main basis of Douglas' theory was summed up in the so-called 'A + B Theorem', which he devised while working at Farnborough's Royal Aircraft Factory during the First World War. Here, Douglas was given the task of sorting out the factory's accounting books which had gotten into 'a certain amount of muddle'. Having no prior economic interests or training, Douglas decided to apply the technical logic of his engineering career to balancing the books rather than using any recognised accountancy methods, thus leading him to make some original (that is to say, totally mistaken[81]) observations.

While examining the factory's accounts, he noticed, or *thought* he noticed, that the total value of weekly wages and dividends given out to workers (A) was always lower than the weekly cost of actually making the factory's products (B), when you considered the need for expenditure on tools, raw materials, transport, rent and other such inevitable costs of doing business. Presuming that the value of A, the workers' wages, must always be lower than B, the cost of manufacture, Douglas concluded that the purchasing power of any nation's workers could, by definition, never be able to maintain pace with the total price of goods placed on sale in shops. In other words, there was always more on sale than could be bought, as the cost of making things was larger than the wages workers received to buy them with, which should have led to total economic disaster, through overproduction. Thus far, manufacturing companies in leading nations like Britain had temporarily got around this problem by taking out bank loans secured against the presumed value of future production, and by dumping surplus products for sale abroad, but this short-term dodge could not last forever. Eventually, things would get so bad that the only way out of the impasse was for the industrialised nations to go to war, thus leading to a massive demand for aeroplanes, guns, warships and tanks, to be bought by the government, thus staving off bankruptcy in heavy industry – hence, it would appear, the outbreak of the First World War. 'Peace is economic war; war is economic peace!' was one of the main slogans of the Social Credit movement Douglas later founded. Given Pound's own acerbic ideas about the perfidy of arms manufacturers like Schneider-Creusot, it is little wonder he became a convert to Douglas' cause.

Bad Credit

Many of Pound's ideas were derived from Douglas' teachings, which the Major promulgated worldwide, from Japan to New Zealand, while operating a Social Credit Secretariat from his regional powerbase in Liverpool, picking up many acolytes as he did so. Like Pound, Douglas also didn't trust the Gold Standard, and wished to remove power from private banks, giving legal permission to print and distribute banknotes exclusively to the State, considering money to be nothing but a kind of generalised ticket, just as Pound said. The problem of actually creating enough goods to go around had been solved by mass production, said Douglas, anticipating Mussolini's similar conclusion, now all that remained to be fixed was their means of effective distribution. Maintaining the correct rate of monetary flow throughout an economy was truly another sort of engineering problem, like getting water to flow through pipes properly, or designing an efficient way to keep traffic moving on a motorway; so, engineers should really take control of the global economy, not economists, as this latter class of inferior being, having less logical minds, were prone to bouts of womanish 'emotional irrelevancy'. Compare such opinions back to Pound's whimsies about the connection between the correct level of monetary flow and the correct level of sperm pumping through his own testicles, and you can see yet another link between the two men. Another parallel lies in their shared belief that most loans given out by the usurers who controlled the banking system were issued in completely fictional, made-up money, and intended to enslave those who were foolish or desperate enough to sign up to them. In a speech given to the King of Norway in Oslo on 14 February 1935, later published as the pamphlet *Money and the Price System*, the Major explained his views thus:

> The method by which the banker makes money is ingenious, and consists very largely of bookkeeping ... Every bank-loan creates a [fictional] deposit

[in the borrower's bank account] ... All but 0.7 of 1 per cent ... in Great Britain ... [of all] money transactions ... are in the form of 'bank credit', which is actually manufactured by the banking system and is claimed by the banking system as its own property ... some of us ... are still hypnotised into thinking that money is real wealth ... money is not real wealth ... The whole economic and financial system in its present form stands or falls by the contention that the price system is self-liquidating, that is to say, that no matter what price is charged for an article, there is always sufficient money distributed through the production of that or other articles [for consumers] to buy the article and therefore there is nothing inherent in the system ... to prevent the process going on indefinitely. This belief is not true ... the world as a whole is consistently getting further and further into debt ... it is obvious that the price system demands [of the public] more purchasing power than is available ... [meaning that individuals, businesses and governments have to endlessly borrow money to keep on paying for things] ... In the year 1694, the Bank of England was formed ... [to create money out of nothing; because of such institutions] in the 17th century ... the world debt ... increased 47 per cent ... By the end of the 18th century the world debt had increased by 466 per cent and by the end of the 19th century the world debt, public and private, had increased by 12,000 per cent.

The basic purpose of this sinister scheme was for the financiers to create cumulative debts so massive they could never be fully paid off, thus giving the banks a permanent source of income as governments were forced to increase the tax burden on their helpless citizens to try to service the ballooning national debt. If you're looking for a significant source for Ezra Pound's hatred of the Rothschild Bank of England, then look no further than this speech. However, while the future of mankind stood in the balance, all was not yet lost. The 'perfectly simple' cure for this appalling situation, Douglas informed his audience, was for those self-same government debtors to 'create money at the rate at which debt is created ... if you create money even at the astronomical rate at which debts are being created, you can apply the money so created to the liquidation of the debt, and both money and debt will go out of existence at the same time,' a process which, he optimistically argued, 'can be carried on indefinitely' with no ill effects whatsoever.[82]

We Are Forever in Your Debt, Mr Douglas

You may think that paying for imaginary debts by creating a never-ending supply of equally imaginary money might destroy the value of a nation's currency, making it next to worthless via hyperinflation, but this would be to approach the matter from the wrong perspective. Instead of being based on the possession of gold reserves or backed up by fake loans from Hell Banks, the true value of a nation's wealth for Douglas, as for Pound, was directly linked back to the productive capacity of its people in terms of agriculture and industry. Douglas was also the source of Pound's idea that the accumulated labour of the dead had built up a store of so-called 'Cultural Inheritance' and 'Social Credit' for their descendants in terms of inventions, cultivated farmlands, factories and infrastructure. The Major argued that the continued value of this Social Credit to the modern economy could easily be divided out and distributed to a country's living people today in a free, no-strings-attached monthly benefits cheque called the 'National Dividend', hailed as 'the logical successor to the wage'. (This scheme was also the logical predecessor to the contemporary fantasy of the 'Citizens' Wage', or 'Universal Basic Income'; the completely impractical and unaffordable idea, growing in popularity across the increasingly delusional post-2007/08 crash world, that governments should pay each and every one of their citizens, even millionaires, a free monthly fee for sitting around and doing absolutely nothing all day long, should they wish to do so.)

Furthermore, in tribute to Canon Law, Douglas also proposed the creation of a new Just Price system. Douglas said when a product was placed on sale in a shop, the consumer should pay only the cost-price for it, rather than an additional charge on top to give the producer and vendor any profit. If a pair of shoes cost £1.00 to manufacture, then £1.00 is what the consumer would pay. Wouldn't this send shops and factories into insolvency? No. Imagine that, under the current system, a £1.00 pair of shoes actually costs £1.50 to the shopper, with 25p going to the manufacturer and 25p to the shop, thus making business worth their while. Under Douglas' Just Price system, each would still get their 25p, but from the government, not the ordinary consumer, who would only have to pay the cost-price of £1.00. Either the customer would pay £1.50 in the shop, get a receipt and then reclaim the difference from their local bank, who would then shovel up such receipts and post them off to the Treasury to be reimbursed, or customers would pay the reduced price in the stores themselves, with the sellers and manufacturers later reclaiming their profit direct from the national Exchequer. As for how the State was supposed to pay for such limitless subsidy, Douglas again suggested they should just crank up the Royal Mint's presses and churn out endless amounts of new money tickets.

So, we can see that Pound was not in fact a lone loon; C. H. Douglas won interest from a number of persons associated with the arts, with poets, writers and actors as varied as T. S. Eliot, Charlie Chaplin and Aldous Huxley all expressing curiosity about what he had to say. Given the problems such people often have earning money during the early phases of their careers, as repeatedly bemoaned by Pound in his writings, perhaps it is no wonder Douglas' promise of free National Dividend money for all won praise from those penniless *artistes* who saw in it a means to prevent themselves from starving in a garret. Some sympathetic authors even went so far as to write utopian sci-fi novels about a future world in which the Major's ideas had been successfully adopted, given hopeful titles such as *Asses in Clover*. Among the non-literary public the Social Credit movement was also somewhat successful, winning thousands of adherents all across the British Empire, especially in Canada where in 1935 a Social Credit Party actually came to power. The Canadians offered Douglas the opportunity to move across the Atlantic and become their Minister of Finance, but he politely declined. Ezra Pound, however, was not quite so shy. When he heard about Douglas' refusal to serve, he contacted the Canadian Social Crediteers himself, and eagerly offered his own services for the job. This time, it was the Canadians' turn to proffer a polite refusal.

Social Credit is often said to be yet another Distributist movement at heart, as Major Douglas always said his main aim was to distribute not land and property to individual citizens, as with Chesterbelloc's version of the idea, but freedom. Secure in the knowledge of their entitlement to a National Dividend, workers under a Douglasite model would have some measure of independence from both Servile State and overbearing captains of industry, as having such a guaranteed income would mean they were much freer than they are today to turn down unsuitable employment, to refuse to move to distant parts of the country upon the whims of the boss class, or to voice criticism without being instantly thrown out onto the street. Douglas hoped that workers would ultimately feel confident enough to demand lower hours and use their new-found leisure time to develop their latent capacity for independent thought, thereby evolving almost into a new species whose 'capacities are likely to take new forms of which we have so far little conception'. Admittedly, all this *did* sound a bit like taking a dole from the welfare state, an evil Communist institution which, like all good Distributists, Douglas hated with a passion, but never mind; for Douglas, Social Credit made Parliament and big business much weaker, and the little guy much stronger. As the problem of industrial production had been entirely solved, and yet many people were still poor enough to be forced to go without certain necessary goods which clearly existed in the factory warehouses, Douglas came to the ultimate conclusion that society as a whole was nothing less than a gigantic fiscal conspiracy designed to enrich certain greedy persons at the expense of the economic enslavement of others.[83] And who, precisely, were these greedy persons? Oh yes, *them* again …

World War Jew

A further aspect of the Social Credit movement which Ezra Pound found very much to his tastes was its obvious anti-Semitism. Because neither Major

Douglas nor his disciples ever specifically advocated any Nazi-style political programme of barring Jews from certain occupations, curtailing their rights of worship, banning them from inter-marriage, confiscating their assets or gassing them in death camps, the Social Credit movement is sometimes said by historians not to have truly been anti-Semitic in nature. This is a rather naïve assessment. While Douglas may have claimed to abhor 'Jew-baiting', and (at least in his more generous moments) to have regarded most ordinary Jews as being mere innocent dupes who were being cynically exploited by the 'bigger' Jews whom he saw as secretly running the world, his works are in fact full of bizarre diatribes and nefarious accusations against Judaism in general, some of which are so absurd as to be comical. For example, did you know that, contrary to natural expectations, Adolf Hitler himself was actually a Jew? Douglas set out to prove that the German Führer was actually the grandson of an illegitimate daughter of one of the Rothschilds, who was simply *pretending* to persecute the Jews throughout the Third Reich, in order to trick England into allowing itself to be flooded with fake Jewish 'refugees', who were in fact fully trained spies, primed to destroy the British Empire from within. The real purpose of the Second World War, it transpired, was to act as a platform to allow the Jews and their chief ally the Anti-Christ to launch a Third World War before the other one had even ended, thus allowing them to conquer the globe once Britain and her colonies had been bankrupted through the pressure of endless conflict. Once this had been done, an 'alien culture' could then be imposed across the ruined Empire and all its Dominions by the Jewish bankers and war financiers, thus turning the once-proud Anglo-Saxon race into the eternal slaves of the Mammon-Zionist axis. Other prominent Nazis were really Jews in disguise, too; Douglas swore blind that Admiral Canaris (1887–1945), head of the German secret service, was really named Moses Meyerbeer.

To Douglas, all forms of Left-wing collectivism (including fascism) were nothing but Jewish schemes to steal English people's sacred property rights from under their feet. Any nationalisation of British industry or mineral deposits such as coal-mines was really enforced Zionisation, Douglas argued, and he even went so far as to claim that the slaughter of cattle by the Ministry of Agriculture following outbreaks of foot-and-mouth disease were part of a joint Jewish-Communist plot to bankrupt independent farmers and seize their land. The list of organisations who were in on this evil scheme was as bewildering as it was unlikely; the Nazis, the Bank of England, the Japanese Empire, the Russian Communists, the US Federal Reserve, the Freemasons, the original writers of the Old Testament and even the London School of Economics were really all secret Jewish front organisations, according to Major Douglas. Jews, Douglas said, were 'the most undesirable Orientals the world has produced', real-life Fu Manchus who had crucified Jesus because his basic philosophy was in accordance with traditional British ideas of the freedom of the individual, and who now held disturbing levels of influence even within the Church of England. Like Pound, Douglas admitted that the *Protocols of the Elders of Zion* was, in narrow terms, a fake – but argued that it still expressed the same basic tricks that the Jewish bankers and media moguls were up to nonetheless, and so was really true after all, even though it wasn't. As this suggests, the Mad Major was of a somewhat paranoid mindset, to say the least, and towards the end of his life he ended up being consigned to a mental hospital and labelled certifiably insane. One contemporary critic accused Douglas of having a 'highly developed persecution complex' which led him to see 'a "financier" [re: Jew] with a false beard watching him from behind every bush', which doesn't sound like too much of an exaggeration. Given all this, if you read between the lines, it appears that Douglas' entire scheme to destroy the evils unleashed by the A + B Theorem and implement an early Citizens' Wage was really an attempt to set the people free from the wicked hyper-Jews, a bunch of vampiric monetary occultists whom he felt were seeking to imprison them forever in chains of debt and usury. But despite all this, remember, Major Douglas didn't actually believe in 'Jew-baiting' himself.[84]

Douglas' views upon such matters could be somewhat inconsistent and, to the uninitiated, many of his speeches and writings might just sound as if they were criticising bankers in general, as the word 'Jews' did not always specifically appear within them. At other times, the situation could be quite different; his opinions seemed to shift around confusingly. For example, far from always thinking that Adolf Hitler was a Jew, in May 1939, a few months before war between Britain and Germany finally broke out, Douglas' propaganda journal *The Social Crediter* was carrying a front-page 'LETTER TO HERR HITLER' on its front cover, in which the Major begged to bring to the attention of Hitler's 'eminent self' a guaranteed way of ensuring peace. A copy of the letter in question had supposedly been delivered to Hitler by one of Douglas' most trusted contacts, and claimed that, contrary to all apparent evidence, there was actually no real difference between the political ideologies of the Allies of Britain and France, and the Axis powers of Germany and Italy, these rival power blocs being but 'artificially created antagonists'. According to Douglas, the major European powers' political policies 'proceed from the fundamental assumption … that full employment of their populations is the test of success.' However, said the Major, this notion was utterly false. Pursuit of full employment had led Europe's governments to massively increase their production of tanks and warplanes to keep people in jobs in factories like the one he had once worked in at Farnborough. This strategy, though, was simply a plot upon behalf of 'the Jewish Financial System', intended to enrich the rootless international financiers even though it would inevitably 'destroy civilisation in Europe' once the well-equipped armies of Axis and Allies went to war. If only Hitler would make a close study of Douglas' writings and reverse his Jewish-inspired policy of guaranteeing full employment through munitions manufacturing, then 'not President Roosevelt, but yourself, would be recognised as the representative of all those [liberal humanitarian] values which are cherished equally in the so-called democracies' of the world. Hitler must have been rather upset at being accused of running an inherently 'Jewish' economic policy throughout the Third Reich, however, and didn't reply to Douglas' letter; maybe he had heard about Mussolini's own meeting with another rogue Social Crediteer over in Rome, and thought better of the idea.[85]

Abstract Thought

One aspect of Douglas' anti-Semitism which struck a particular chord with Ezra Pound was the Scotsman's claim that Judaism was based upon inherently abstract, and therefore profoundly evil, principles. Just as Pound had declared war upon verbal abstractionism when helping launch the Imagist movement, so Major Douglas had declared war upon the monetary branch of the very same enemy when launching his own Social Credit crusade. As a qualified engineer, Douglas prided himself upon being a practically minded sort of fellow, and in a 1937 speech later published in pamphlet form as *The Policy of a Philosophy*, explained how the Jews had systematically pushed Britain away from a concrete basis for underpinning its way of life and towards a much more intangible one. Douglas traced back the etymological history of the word 'religion', finding it was derived ultimately from the Latin word *religare*, meaning 'to bind back'. What was religion supposed to bind its followers back towards, though? Towards reality. Increasingly, however, Britain was drifting away from that sensible principle. 'This country, which is allegedly a Christian country, is probably the greatest exponent of abstractionism as a national policy in the world today,' Douglas told his audience. Every aspect of our way of governance, from the administration of our penal system to our preferred methods of doing business, 'actually have no relationship whatever to Christianity, or anything which could be remotely related to it,' Douglas said. The rot had set in during 1656, when Oliver Cromwell (1599–1658) had imprudently allowed the Jews, sensibly expelled during 1290 by Edward I (1239–1307), back into the country. The Jews, inevitably, had then cynically exploited Cromwell's naïve generosity and conspired to transform Britain's political and financial system into something much more hellishly abstract, thus binding back the nation's underlying philosophy not to the true reality of things as revealed by Christ, but to the false non-reality of things as espoused by Judaism.

The end result was that, by Douglas' day, Britain's entire national governance was based purely upon a typical Jewish reliance upon 'the adulation of money', which was nothing but 'an abstraction ... a thing of no value whatever'. In this way, the Jews had imposed false values in place of true ones, and that, explained Douglas, 'is abstractionism ... giving to a thing [or person] qualities that it does not possess.' 'I believe the whole philosophy of the modern world is essentially unreal,' he declared, being nothing but 'an orgy of calculated delusions'. In a way, we were all now living within a kind of giant Jewish hologram. As an engineer, Douglas knew that you had to build small-scale models of structures before you actually built them, to test whether your paper blueprints really stood up to the actual laws of physics or not; basing our whole Empire upon the vile abstractions of Jewish money-worship was akin to building a bridge off the top of your head and then being surprised when it fell down. Social Credit, however, was different. Douglas urged his acolytes to enter local politics and set up small-scale regional Social Credit programmes of their own to prove in actual everyday reality that his ideas really worked, in a manner equivalent to an architect building a small model bridge. Once armed with this initial proof-of-concept, Douglas proclaimed, it would become apparent that Social Credit was *not* a mere clever theory, but instead 'the policy of a philosophy'. Unlike the incomprehensible and fundamentally holographic theories of Jewish high finance, his creed of Social Credit was, Douglas believed, based upon a genuine 'glimpse [of] a portion of reality', akin to that experienced by mystics in their religious visions. What he sought with his own economic model, therefore, was nothing less than a 'right science of metaphysics ... something which is just as much in the [true] nature of things as gravity is in regard to physics'.[86]

In another of his speeches, delivered in 1936 in Westminster and entitled *The Approach to Reality*, Douglas laid out further variations on this theme. If our current economic system was based upon reality, he asked, then how come the world was thought to be rich the day before the Wall Street Crash, and in a state of destitution the day after? All the goods, homes, property, land, food, gold, factories, infrastructure, jewels and banknotes which had existed twenty-four hours previously still existed; it was just a jumble of abstract numbers on the stock exchange which had collapsed, not concrete reality.

People should have just ignored this wholly irrelevant and unimportant event and gone on precisely as they had before, and everything would have been fine. However, this was not to be, because the forces of Jewish capitalism had brainwashed the people. Money and stock prices were pure illusions, yet it seemed they ruled our globe. 'To imagine that we are born into the world to be governed by something not inherent in the cosmos is one of the most astonishing pieces of hypnotism that has ever affected the world,' Douglas told his audience; would it not be better if society was ruled by something non-fictional instead, like the Word of Christ?[87]

Unholy Cows

Douglas' entertaining essay *Money: A Historical Survey*, delivered as a speech to student members of the Conservative Party in 1936, contained a full account of how, in his opinion, the very notion of abstract, non-physical 'bank money' had developed in the first place. His apparent aim was to get these young Tory Boys to reverse the 'alien' policies which modern Conservative and Labour MPs alike were pushing through Parliament by convincing these possible future politicians of the evils of abstractionism. Money, he told his audience, had once been embodied exclusively in the form of cows. As with the wool-producing sheep of the Bank of Siena, during ancient times the main basis of wealth had been entirely natural, and based upon the idea of possession of herds. Men with lots of cows were rich; men with no cows were poor. This was the immutable law of the prehistoric economy. However, while cow-rich, the owner of a large herd might nonetheless still be fodder-poor. If he didn't have enough fodder, how could he feed his cows? To answer this need, the wandering fodder merchant emerged, marching from place to place selling feed. But how could the merchant get paid if there was no such thing as money? Naturally, he was paid in cows. This caused a further problem, as it often proved inconvenient for the successful fodder merchant to take long lines of cows around with him everywhere he went, like some bovine Pied Piper. Therefore, the cow owner gave him a leather disc to take away, imprinted with a picture of the head of a cow. This leather disc became the first money; should the fodder merchant wish to buy something from somebody else, he could hand across his cow-disc and pay for it that way. Then, the third party who he had just bought something from could visit the rich herd owner in his turn, hand over his leather disc, and claim a cow of his own. ('Capital' and 'cattle' come from the same Latin word *caput*, meaning 'head', as in 'head of cattle', so Douglas' idea may have possessed some truth.[88])

If only things had stayed this way, everything would have been fine, but as the centuries rolled on humanity began to replace cows with gold as the main underlying basis for its wealth. Rich men would hand their gold over to goldsmiths to make coins and jewellery from it. This gold being valuable, the goldsmiths made themselves huge safes which were impenetrable to thieves. When the rich men saw this, they asked the goldsmiths to keep their gold coins inside such vaults on a permanent basis, seeing this as safer than storing them in their own homes. As proof of deposit, the goldsmiths gave their rich customers receipts saying 'upon production of this voucher, you can reclaim your 100 gold coins'. These were the basis of the first banknotes; if the rich man wanted to buy himself a new castle, he just handed over the receipt to the person he was buying it from rather than going to the bother of riding back to the vault and drawing out all his gold. Unfortunately, corrupt goldsmiths saw an easy opportunity for fraud. If somebody deposited 100 gold coins in his safe, and was unlikely to want to draw them all back out at once, then why not issue the depositor with one receipt worth 100 coins, and himself with another one worth fifty? Then, he could spend his own fake note on luxuries and make himself rich. From a deposit of only 100 gold coins, the criminal goldsmith had conjured up banknotes worth 150 gold sovereigns. Just so long as all his clients didn't come along and take out all of their coins at the same time – something which would be incredibly unlikely to occur – then the goldsmith could keep such a cunning scam going forever. It was the very first Hell Bank!

This procedure sounded positively criminal, but was precisely what modern bankers still do today, Douglas told his audience. If you examine a £20 banknote, the reader will observe that, signed in the name of the serving Chief Cashier of the Bank of England, it says 'I promise to pay the bearer on demand the sum of £20'. Traditionally, this meant that you could, at least in theory, walk into the Bank of England with a £20 note and demand £20 worth of its gold reserves in return, in the form of gold sovereigns. If everybody did this at once, the Bank would immediately collapse, because of course nowadays it ignores Isaac Newton's wisdom of old and prints notes to a far greater value than the amount of gold it actually possesses within its vaults. To counter this remote possibility, however, the Bank of England had since outdone even the crooked pre-medieval goldsmiths by no longer guaranteeing to give bearers of its notes their alleged value in gold at all; instead, if you hand over your £20 note to the cashier and demand you be given its value back in real money today, all you will get back in return is a funny look and another banknote of the exact same denomination. In this way, said Douglas, the national currency had been utterly divorced from the true source of wealth, which was Nature. It would have been far more right-minded for London's biggest Hell Bank to have handed you over £20 worth of a cow to take away and eat in return for your note, but by now all was mere Jewish abstractionism. It was as if, said Douglas, a railway company, with its tracks, trains, employees and infrastructure, had been subjected to a hostile takeover by its own ticket office, who were now randomly printing billions of tickets when there were only a few dozen actual seats per carriage, and expecting this not to cause any problems the next day when all of the ticket bearers turned up at the station. 'The history of money,' Douglas could only conclude, 'is one long history of fraud.' To call money a real thing was to mistake a ticket for a train, and paper tickets without a locomotive would get a man absolutely nowhere.[89]

Taxing His Patience

Taxation was another abstract Jewish con. In 1936, Douglas travelled to Belfast to deliver a speech called *Dictatorship by Taxation* to his Northern

Irish followers, in which he claimed quite truthfully that 'taxation is legalised robbery' on behalf of the Servile State. Perhaps rather less truthfully (or maybe not, it depends how paranoid you are) Douglas then went on to claim that, as a result of his spreading this seditious wisdom to his disciples up and down the kingdom, he had been pestered by the taxman peering closely into his affairs in an attempt to shut him up, a nefarious 'method of inflicting punishment without trial' because of all the time, money and legal fees it had eaten up. At the insistence of certain 'anonymous individuals', Douglas had been endlessly harassed by small bowler-hatted Men from the Ministry, which he knew from his alleged contacts with 'the more hidden side of politics' was a standard tactic on behalf of the Deep State intended to ruin the lives of those who threatened their interests. These incidents worried the Major, who saw in the 'frankly unintelligible' minutiae of the British tax system a deliberate attempt to tie ordinary citizens up in knots, being perpetrated by 'the oligarchy which rules us at present'. Instead of stealing our money in the shape of tax, the government should really be giving us free money in the shape of the National Dividend, Douglas argued; the whole system had been wilfully turned upside-down, thus embodying the old saying that *Demon est Deus inversus*, or 'the Devil is God upside-down', as he put it in another 1936 companion speech, *The Tragedy of Human Effort*.

What, precisely, was the nature of this tragedy? To Douglas, it lay in the conclusion of an unnamed economic historian he had been reading that 'in 1495 the [average] labourer was able to maintain himself in a standard of living considerably higher, relative to his age' than that of the average present-day worker with only fifty days' labour per annum. Nowadays, however, people had to slave away all year long, with this complete waste of workers' valuable time being the deliberate creation of 'the financial octopus' which had been allowed to enslave us by the thuggish 'men of gangster mentality, whose proper place is in a borstal' who ran the British Empire. The chief task of the octopus' 'slimy tentacles' was to reach into our wallets and steal our money through excessive taxes. Douglas had evidently been reading his Hilaire Belloc, criticising the Servile State for its socialistic scheme of robbing us of our own wealth and then using it to bribe us back with, tying us to its overly centralised welfare state apron strings forever. The poor were not poor because the rich were rich, Douglas argued, explaining that if you soaked the wealthy to the extent they would no longer be able to buy Rolls-Royces, all that would happen would be the rapid closure of the Rolls-Royce factory. Anyway, most taxation only went to service annual interest payments on the National Debt, which was ballooning further every year. This allowed the international bankers to make politicians dance to their tune by escalating ordinary people's taxes. Then, the citizenry would fall into ever deeper debt too, enriching the Hell Banks further.

The main problem, once again, was that taxes had been allowed to become utterly abstract in nature. The original tithe that was demanded by the Catholic Church during the days of Canon Law was a fair and concrete tax, 'genuine and justifiable' in its nature, as it demanded only that people pay the clergy 10 per cent of the value of their agricultural products, once grown and sold. This represented a solid tax on solid wealth, which truly existed in the form of food. A farmer could easily just grow a bit more than he would otherwise have needed and use this to pay the tithe, with no loss to his standard of living. Now, however, farmers in Britain were being persecuted with taxes placed upon their *land*, not their *produce*, which took no account of how well the crops had grown that year. If you had a lot of land but most of your harvest failed, you'd still have to cough up a sum based not upon how much your land had *actually* produced, but on a notional estimate of how much it *could* have produced, in theory – yet another tyrannical Jewish abstraction. 'The farmer does not grow money, he grows produce,' Douglas raged, but HMRC wasn't listening. While everyone could see that the modern taxation system was a miserable and unjust failure, it had been made so inchoate and intangible that it was now virtually impossible to fight back against. After all, 'you cannot fight robbery, you can only fight robbers; you cannot fight malaria, you can only destroy mosquitoes.' What was needed was to compel the amorphous forces of international capitalism and international Communism (two sides of the same counterfeit coin, to Douglas) to assume concrete human form – that concrete human form, sadly, being some unholy cross between Shylock, Karl Marx, Count Dracula and the Wandering Jew.[90]

Britons Ever, Ever, Ever Shall Be Slaves

As Social Credit sought to bind its followers back to the underlying reality of God's universe through its teachings, did this make it more akin to a disguised religious cult than an ordinary economic reform movement? The fact that Douglas considered Social Credit to be nothing less than a form of 'practical Christianity' in action suggests so. Douglas' future economic paradise was not meant to be some hard-line Christian theocracy – he would even let ordinary common-or-garden Jews live in it, just so long as they weren't Hell Bankers or tentacled cephalopods in disguise – but it would certainly be modelled upon certain core Christian principles, at least as the Major saw them. Douglas believed that the transcendent writ of Canon Law ran through the universe, with Jesus Christ as its physical embodiment – compare this with the way Social Credit was supposed to be based upon underlying cosmic principles which would then be physically manifested on Earth through local politics, like the bridge manifesting the blueprint. I'm not saying Douglas thought he was Christ, but there was an unspoken parallel. His idea of giving free money away to idlers in the form of the National Dividend, for example, was supposed to be a real-life, visible version of the otherwise abstract Christian principle of salvation through unearned grace; just as Jesus died on the cross to save you from Hell even if you're an appalling sinner totally undeserving of such a favour, so Major Douglas would step in and save you from penury even if you were a parasitic workshy fop – or, yet more generously, *even if you were Jewish*.[91]

Douglas believed the constitution of any Social Credit-based society should be considered a living spiritual organism, based upon three basic principles in imitation of the Holy Trinity of God, Christ and Holy Ghost, an idea also touched upon by Popes Leo and Pius. As Douglas explained in his simultaneously wise and yet in places also deeply alarming 1947 speech *Realistic Constitutionalism*, the traditional tripartite constitutional separation of powers between King, Lords and Commons within Britain was the only thing which had kept us from total slavery to international finance down the years, with our greatest periods of national glory coinciding with those same periods when this three-way structure had worked at its best, when the national will and God's will were operating in union, thus guaranteeing our success on the world stage. The British constitution had not been deliberately *created* all in one go, Douglas correctly perceived, it had simply *grown* in a natural, unplanned way, over the course of our history, in pragmatic response to actual historical events and needs. This meant that, like flowers in a garden, it had bloomed in accordance with the natural rules underlying God's universe, rather than being organised artificially at the whim of mankind, like fake plastic flowers arranged in a vase. 'The real British constitution ... is an *organism*' said Douglas, but 'The Russian constitution ... is an *organisation*.' As the laws of God were more perfect than the laws of man, this meant that organic constitutions which had grown up accidentally to resemble the structure of the Holy Trinity like Britain's were far more humane than those of the Communists, which had been written all in one go around a conference table by self-styled 'intellectuals' in the name of abstract Jewish nostrums like 'equality' and 'social justice', all of which meant different things to different people. Such misguided 'materialism' was really nothing more than a form of 'black magic', which was presently causing a 'spiritual short-circuit' among the British people.

In my view, Douglas had here identified a genuine social evil; witness the way that Britain today has been forced to abandon the cumulative wisdom of our ancestors as represented by English Common Law and submit instead to the shysterish vagaries of transnational Human Rights legislation, for instance, which is often so hazy and abstract in nature that it allows judges to become activists instead of mere impartial arbiters, effectively empowering them to invent new and frequently absurd interpretations of such deliberately flexible 'laws' on the spot. Douglas may have been severely deluded in blaming the Jews for creating such lamentable trends, but he was way ahead of his time in spotting how much of the traditional British way of life was about to come under assault as the twentieth century progressed. Douglas taught that we were now living in a society in which the power of the House of Commons outweighed that of King and Lords by an excessive degree, as if the Holy Spirit had gotten above himself one day and locked Jesus and God in a prison cell on bread-and-water rations, pending a show trial. Instead of the Divine Right of Kings, we now had 'the Divine Right of Parliament' Douglas moaned, with MPs and unelected bureaucrats of all persuasions busily undermining our cherished Common Law traditions by pumping out legislation at a truly colossal rate, impinging upon citizens' historic rights ever more with each passing day. Instead of trying to implement the Kingdom of God on Earth, Parliament was now trying to implement the Kingdom of Man, a misguided Communist-aping path, which would ultimately enslave us all and lead to Britain's 'final eclipse'. Left and Right alike were equally guilty of such crimes. All political parties could now be bought – Douglas claimed he had once been offered full control of the Liberals for a mere £250,000, but he didn't have the cash on him at the time[92] – so none of them were truly independent from the forces of rootless international capital any more. The traditional vitality of the British constitution was being 'insidiously sapped by the Dark Forces that knew its strength', Douglas warned.

Unqualified Majority Voting

For Douglas, the best way for the workers to throw off their chains and prevent the future rise of 'the secular materialistic totalitarian State' was to replace the current method of electoral dictatorship with something much more limited in nature, a paradoxical restriction of democracy in order to increase it. The standard aphorism of *vox populi, vox dei*, or 'the voice of the people is the voice of God' should be reformulated as *vox populi, vox diaboli*, or 'the voice of the people is the voice of Satan'. Modern ideas about one-man, one-vote were demonic alien imports, Douglas told his 1947 audience, foreign 'weeds' that were busily 'choking' Britain's natural and organic constitution, destroying our links with the wisdom of our past. These non-native socialist forces were waging a kind of culture war against the British people, who were themselves being 'obliterated by cross-breeding with inferior stock'. It is, Douglas said, 'an established fact that the general level of intelligence in this country is declining, and is lowest in those strata of society which produce large families, have probably the largest admixture of alien stock, and have predominant voting power under present conditions,' thus presumably accounting for the 1945 Labour landslide. 'It ought to be clear to any unprejudiced individual that a majority is *always* wrong,' he said, not necessarily in terms of what it ultimately wants from life (a more just society), but in terms of the specific methods it thinks would be best to achieve such an aim (for example, through socialism). The entire system of secret ballots was therefore to be abolished, not only because most voters were cross-bred morons, but also on account of its allegedly 'Jewish' nature; after all, had not Barabbas been freed, and Our Lord Jesus Christ crucified, upon the basis of an anonymous show of hands from a baying Jewish mob before Pontius Pilate? 'The merry game of voting yourself benefits at the expense of your neighbour must stop,' Douglas argued. If you wanted more money for public services, then you should damn well pay for them yourself, not expect the man next door to do so; under a non-secret ballot, only those who had voted in favour of higher taxation would have to suffer the personal consequences of this selfish action, not the population as a whole.

'It is necessary to provide individuals, as individuals, not collectively, with much more opportunity to judge political matters by results, and to be able to reject, individually and non-collectively, policies they do not like,' Douglas said. The best solution was to abolish all political parties, which were nothing but a 'criminal absurdity' under the control of Jewish finance anyway, and replace their candidates with independent, non-affiliated persons, whose only duty would be to sit in some kind of assembly called a 'union of electors' and push through laws that performed the popular will, not vote according to the narrow considerations of Party. The gap between the people and their rulers was steadily growing, but, under Douglasite methods, no such gap would be possible. Douglas recommended that, as MPs were generally not knowledgeable in most of the issues they actually legislated upon, many areas of national life should be wholly administered by unelected but qualified experts – if Michael Gove is reading, he may at this point begin vomiting blood, but actually Douglas wanted experts to be the *servants* of the people, not their self-appointed masters. Douglas argued that most MPs were a bit thick, and their only true function was to listen to what a majority of their constituents wanted on any given issue, and then instruct more qualified persons to go away and implement this desire via whatever means the technocratic elite deemed best. For instance, the public might say 'we want better national defences', but it would be up to experts commissioned by MPs to decide whether this meant investing in more nuclear weapons or commissioning new battleships, not Joe Public. Or voters may say, 'we want lower immigration', and the technocrats would have to develop a scheme for making it so, not call them dim racists and then do precisely the opposite. Once people had elected their MP, it would be their responsibility to keep hounding him upon issues of individual interest. By assessing which topics his local constituents really cared about, the MP could then consult with other MPs, and together determine what the will of the people was. Contrary to popular belief, Great Britain had *never* been a democracy, Douglas said, and would not be so until his own programme for constitutional and economic reform was implemented.[93]

Oh, Canada!

The big question about Social Credit was whether or not Major Douglas' actual basic economic assertions themselves, once stripped of their lunatic racial and mystical content, were viable? If ever enacted in a concrete way, rather than remaining forever in mere theoretical form within his many books and pamphlets, would they actually have worked? The experience of the world's most successful Douglasite organisation, the Alberta Social Credit Party, which governed the Canadian province in question for some thirty-six uninterrupted years from 1935 until 1971, suggests not. The Canadian Crediteers ushered in a huge and decades-long economic boom, hence their long period in power – but only did so by failing completely to implement any kind of meaningful Social Credit policies whatsoever. The man who led the Douglasites into power in Alberta was one William 'Bible Bill' Aberhart (1878–1943), a popular radio preacher who from 1932 onwards had latched onto the Major's ideas in spite of the fact he didn't understand any of them, something he happily admitted. Bible Bill didn't *need* to understand the financial dogma he was preaching, however, because as Douglas himself had argued, it was results, not theory, that truly mattered. Aberhart knew how to flick a switch and turn on a lightbulb, he explained, but had no inkling of the precise technical process through which such a result occurred. Electricity was a total mystery to him, but he could still turn the lights on. Social Credit was a complete conundrum too, but if he flicked the legislative switch and all of Alberta's financial problems were then inexplicably solved immediately, then what did it matter? If someone wanted to know in academic detail precisely how the miracle had been wrought, they should just buy one of C. H. Douglas' books and see if they could make out what the hell the mad Scotsman was going on about, because Aberhart certainly couldn't. It appears that many of his colleagues within the Party had a similarly limited understanding of Douglas' theories too, because when they won the 1935 provincial elections by a landslide, gaining an almost monopolistic fifty-six seats out of sixty-three in the Alberta legislature, they basically wet themselves.

Not really expecting to win, Aberhart had promised every Albertan citizen $25 in National Dividend money per month, then a sizeable sum, in return for the simple fact of their own existence, something which understandably won his Party great popularity – Jeremy Corbyn take note, it's the Labour Party's next logical step. Alberta in the 1930s was a poor, mostly rural place (many Social Credit MPs were farmers), a large number of whose inhabitants had been reduced to near starvation by the Great Depression, and who as a result were willing to believe Bible Bill's wild promises. A real populist, during his campaign Aberhart had delivered numerous rousing speeches about the evil bankers and 'super-dictators' whose 'slimy octopus' of finance was 'wrapping his clammy blood-sucking tentacles around every man, woman and child in this Canada of ours' and making them starve. While he never specifically claimed that this octopus was a Jew, Bible Bill blamed the bankers and 'eastern capitalists' of the big cities like Toronto and Montreal for creating this giant man-eating beast, cities which his audience were well aware included fairly large Jewish populations (although Alberta itself had very few, less than 0.5 per cent of the provincial population). Like Douglas, William Aberhart claimed not to be anti-Semitic himself, even going so far as to address the Canadian Jewish Congress in 1939, and once giving an interview to the *Jewish Post* calling for more Jewish refugees to be allowed to enter into the country from Nazi-occupied Europe. Then, however, he would go away and ruin such good work by making weird and paranoid comments implying that, as soon as the Anti-Christ arrived on Earth, if indeed he were not present here on it already, most of the world's Jews would be stupid enough to accept him as their Master, happily aiding him in his project to destroy Christianity and thus the entire world. Possibly Aberhart wasn't actually anti-Semitic himself, but understood that many of his fellow Albertans were so prejudiced and was cynical enough to exploit this for cheap and easy electoral gain. Or, then again, maybe he was just an idiot. Whichever it was, in 1943 Bible Bill died of old age, and a whole new chapter was opened in the history of the Alberta Social Credit Party.

During his time in office, William Aberhart had been frustrated by his total inability to introduce Social Credit policies into Alberta, on the simple grounds that he had no legal power to do so. Overarching macroeconomic policy and the control and issuing of currency were the sole legal responsibility of the Canadian national government, not regional legislatures, something the Social Crediteers had blithely ignored when running for office. It turned out that Aberhart and his men, once in power, could no more turn Alberta into a Social Credit paradise than a local council today could promise to bring back hanging. This was rather embarrassing for Bible Bill, who was almost totally unable to keep his campaign promises and, his former loquaciousness notwithstanding, he failed to give even a single speech in Alberta's Parliament for a full four years following his election. Aberhart did his best to annoy the Canadian government by aiming to default on payment of various taxes and bonds, trying illegally to cancel farmers' debts, and attempting to censor the freedom of the Press so newspapers couldn't tell everyone what a mess he was making, but each time he tried to pull such sly tricks, the government in Ottawa overruled him and said he couldn't. Bible Bill's successor as Party leader, Ernest Manning (1908–96), knew that continuing in this vein was going to lead to complete electoral disaster, so began the arduous task of

A 'Prosperity Certificate' issued by the Alberta Social Credit Party during 1936. A somewhat incompatible combination of C. H. Douglas' ideas and Silvio Gesell's rival notion of stamp-scrip, it came from the organisation's early years, before their new leader Ernest Manning began actively arguing against his Party's own programme. Seeing as the stamps kept on falling off the damned thing, maybe he was right! (Courtesy of A. W. McPhee)

reinventing the Social Credit Party as an organisation that was directly opposed to actually implementing its own stated policies in any way, shape or form. Naturally, many members objected to this radical realignment, and a number of splits occurred, particularly when Aberhart began chucking out the Jew-haters. Given the general anti-Semitic climate within Social Credit circles, the fact that their programme of radical Douglasite reform had utterly failed was blamed by some hardliners on the influence of the Jews, who had proved that they really did run the world by refusing to let Aberhart do what he had been elected to do by the ordinary farm folk. The simple truth was that a substantial part of the edifice of Social Credit was based upon the idea that an evil Jewish octopus ran the world, and so to expel the Douglasite True Believers from the Party was also, happily, to expel the most hardened anti-Semites at the same time.[94]

Hard to Credit

The Canadian scholar Janine Stingel has performed in-depth research into the extent to which the Social Credit movement in her homeland was connected to anti-Semitic causes, making many disturbing findings. In 1946, for example, *Vers Demain*, the French-language Social Credit newspaper of Quebec, ran a complete serialisation of the *Protocols of the Elders of Zion* over a full eight months' worth of issues so its readers could discover just exactly what the Rothschilds were up to. Other Social Credit publications made claims that the Jew-controlled Bank of England was directly and deliberately responsible for a mass wave of some 2.5 million poverty-linked suicides across the British Empire. In particular, Canadian Social Crediteers, like Douglas himself, hated the London School of Economics, which they claimed had been created by Jew-funded socialists with the sole purpose to 'train the bureaucracy of the future world Socialist State', something they 'proved' by pointing out that the father of the modern welfare state in Britain, Sir William Beveridge (1879–1963), had once been the LSE's Head.

Furthermore, the victorious Allies' economic plans for post-war reconstruction were really Jewish plans for post-war enslavement of the white race, it transpired. Henry Morgenthau (1891–1967), President Roosevelt's Jewish Treasury Secretary, came under particular fire for his proposal to turn Germany into a largely agricultural economy, so the Huns would never be able to use heavy industry to reconstruct their armies ever again. Although Morgenthau's plan *was never actually put into action*, the editors of the *Canadian Social Crediter* apparently considered this fact to be a mere trifle, writing in 1946 of how the immoral scheme had somehow still caused the starvation of 'more German babies than there ever were Jews in Germany' and led to the mass Reich-wide rape of 'hundreds of thousands of German, Austrian and Hungarian girls and women from eight to eighty'. Apparently, Morgenthau's plan was responsible for the deaths of 'five times as many Germans in one year of peace as died during the five years of war', which makes you wonder how bad things would have got had it ever actually been implemented. As a result of such loony oddness, the *Canadian Social Crediter* received various letters of complaint from concerned non-mad citizens. Their response to one particular letter was especially revealing. In it, the organ's editors politely explained that, actually, they were not anti-Semitic at all, and the fact that the letter-writer thought they were simply demonstrated that he was part of a worldwide Jewish conspiracy.

The new transnational institutions of the post-war world, from the UN to the IMF, were condemned as simply yet more squirming limbs of the Jewish octopus. Social Credit MP Norman Jacques (1880–1949), for instance, suspected such institutions were designed to force upon the free Anglo-Saxon peoples of the world 'the surrender of [their] national sovereignty so as to render all peoples and all nations powerless and helpless to resist this accursed slavery of gold – the crown of Midas, Judas and Shylock.' In July 1943 Jacques openly quoted from the *Protocols of the Elders of Zion* in the Canadian House of Commons. Jacques' basic belief was that, having failed to enslave the world via the medium of Hitler Rothschild and his Jewish Nazis, the Zionists would endeavour to do so via 'the union of Shylock and Marx' instead. He even tried to deny that such a thing as anti-Semitism even existed; because, to Jacques, most Jews were Communists, whenever a true patriot like him tried to criticise their Leninist ways, to confuse the issue they just shouted 'racist!' at him, when in fact he was not racist at all, he simply disliked Jews for being Red. This insight then allowed Jacques to further perceive that all Jewish 'refugees' from Nazi Europe were really Communist agents. After all, if Hitler was really trying to kill them all off, like the fake Jews' fake news media said, then why did the Nazis let them flee instead of just shooting them all? If Jews were free to leave Germany, as during Hitler's early years they were, then this meant they were free in other all other senses, too, with the whole myth of Nazi anti-Semitism being merely a 'Communist smokescreen'. Instead of giving them asylum in Canada, why not let such Marxists settle safely within the 'Communist Paradise' of Soviet Russia? Worse, one Social Credit journal claimed that a one-world currency would soon be introduced, named the 'shekel' after the ancient coinage of the Jews, while another publication warned that the proposed UN Atomic Energy Agency was not going to be an impartial global watchdog, as claimed, but a means by which Shylock could get his hands on atom bombs with which to blackmail us all into financial submission.

Elements within the Canadian Social Credit movement also had direct links to an organisation called the Basic Book Club, which sold copies of the *Protocols* via mail-order, as well as various distasteful titles such as *Father of Lies*, which made the bizarre claim that Judaism itself was nothing but an quasi-occultist 'phallic cult' of perverted penis-worshippers, and came complete with a charming picture of a snake covered all over in obscure Jewish symbols on its front cover; according to one Social Credit publication, the very term 'usury' was derived from the Hebrew word for 'viper', *nesek* (actually it meant 'bite', whether from a snake or otherwise[95]). This is the precisely the kind of crazy thinking that Ernest Manning came to think had no place in his Party. While he himself did believe in the existence of an international financial conspiracy aimed at destroying Christianity, he never specifically said in public that it was a Jewish one, and could see that such claims, which were growing increasingly mad in nature, were doing the Party damage in terms of media coverage and relations with the government in Ottawa. Once he had successfully kicked out the noisiest Jew-bashers by the end of 1948, Manning embarked upon a rather more mainstream economic programme based mainly upon the fact that Alberta had large reserves of oil which could be sold for huge profit upon the international market, a highly sensible policy which made Alberta one of the richest provinces in Canada. Conservative in outlook on most social matters, but far more pro-business and pro-capitalism than Major Douglas would have liked, Ernest Manning's new, rebranded Social Credit Party was way more conventional in nature than that of Bible Bill's, and far more economically successful to boot. Anti-Semitism, it seemed, just wasn't that profitable an industry in Canada anymore.[96]

The Incredible Shrinking Man

As this whole regrettable episode shows, Social Credit may not have been truly workable, but there was yet another early economic influence upon Ezra Pound, too. Though it may have sounded incredibly original and new, Mr Potato-Head's bright idea of vegetable-money was in fact derived directly from the notion of 'stamp-scrip' or *Schwundgeld* ('shrinking money') proposed by a German-born economist of Belgian descent named Silvio Gesell (1862–1930). Gesell was an interesting man, especially for a Belgian, and a talented writer to boot, of the kind almost designed specifically to appeal towards Pound's *outré* tastes. For one thing, he had no official economic training, and so had a mind utterly unpolluted by the false professors who preached the wicked word of the Jewish gombeen-men at their so-called 'universities'; as such, he still had the capacity for independent thought and original ideas. In 1887 Gesell had moved to Argentina, hoping to pursue a career in commerce, but while there a particularly bad global recession hit the country, badly affecting his business. Disturbed, Gesell began to think about what might have caused the financial crash in question, drawing the conclusion that massive monetary reform was needed across the whole planet. Giving away his business to his brother, Gesell moved back to Europe, settling down in Switzerland and establishing a magazine named *Monetary and Land Reform* in 1900, a publication which, rather embarrassingly, was forced to fold during 1903 due to unforeseen financial reasons.

Seeking further answers about why his businesses kept on failing, Gesell was open to all kinds of fringe economic, social and even spiritual ideas in the hope of stumbling across the path to a better tomorrow. He joined a radical fruit-growing and jam-making vegetarian commune just north of Berlin, the *Vegetarische Obstbau-Kolonie Eden*, became a proponent of popular land-reform ideas, and ended up becoming a sort of wandering anarchist or libertarian socialist, who believed in wild dreams such as radical feminism, pacifism, free money, the abolition of all borders and the creation of a whole new social order. In April 1919 Gesell suddenly popped up in Munich, where a city-wide socialist revolution had just taken place, and found himself appointed Finance Minister of the short-lived Bavarian Soviet Republic, a kind of Communist-Anarchist workers' city-state. Delighted, Gesell immediately began making preparations for implementing a policy of *Schwundgeld*, but the Soviet Republic only lasted for six days, which was unsurprising given that most members of the amusingly amateurish government were unworldly mystics, poets, playwrights, actors, cabaret artists, film stars and the mentally ill.

One of them, the playwright Ernst Toller (1893–1939), described the farcical takeover as 'The Bavarian Revolution of Love', but a rather more accurate contemporary *New York Times* report described 'a saturnalia of political madmen', some of whom couldn't even speak German, who were 'conducting [a] campaign of confusion' in the Bavarian capital, and being treated with open contempt and mockery by the actual citizens in whose name they professed to rule. Most notorious was the conduct of the city-state's new Deputy Foreign Minister, Dr Franz Lipp (1855–1937), who had more than once been forcibly incarcerated in a mental asylum, which perhaps explained why after talking office he immediately declared war on Switzerland and sent an urgent telegram to Lenin, complaining that when the Minister of Bavaria had fled the scene during the uprising he had taken the only key to the ministerial toilets with him, causing much inconvenience for the revolutionaries. Then, claiming to be a 'good friend' of Benedict XV, Lipp is said to have contacted the Vatican, seeking the blessing of 'Comrade Pope' for the future success of the new Republic. As Munich descended into Trotskyite chaos, a gang of proper, hardened Communist thugs saw their chance to take charge, overthrowing their dilettante rivals and declaring yet another new Workers' Paradise. Sadly, as one of the Communists' main policies was that of openly welcoming the death of babies due to a city-wide milk shortage as an excellent way of eliminating the useless parasitic offspring of the bourgeoisie ('We are not interested in keeping them alive. No harm if they die.'), they did not prove themselves particularly popular with the people either. Following the eventual restoration of order by the German army assisted by some 30,000 paramilitary *freikorps*, Gesell was thrown into prison for treason. At his trial, however, the autodidact economist proved so eloquent when speaking in his own defence that the authorities effectively just let him off.[97]

The Potato in Your Pocket

Gesell's main literary opus, *The Natural Economic Order*, appeared in two parts in 1906 and 1911, but was not published in English until 1929, with

Gesell's untimely death from pneumonia coming only a year later. However, the book did make a smallish splash in the English-speaking world, with several prominent experts prepared to give it a fair hearing, including the great J. M. Keynes (1883–1946), the twentieth century's most prominent economist, who called Gesell a 'strange and unduly neglected prophet ... whose work contains flashes of deep insight'. Bombarded with copies of Gesell's work by the Belgian's disciples, Keynes initially thought he was a mad veggie crank, but eventually began to realise his theories possessed a slight limited worth. Keynes defined Gesell's economic thought as being a kind of 'anti-Marxian socialism', and boldly declared, with regrettable inaccuracy, that 'the future will learn more from the spirit of Gesell than from that of Marx.'[98] Most mainstream economists did not agree with Gesell's proposals, but, as the Oxford economist and future Labour Party leader Hugh Gaitskell (1906–63) put it in his own 1933 profile of the man, his ideas were so odd, and his writings so energetic, that they were 'by no means without entertainment value'. His highly original notions, said Gaitskell, made Gesell worth reading whether you agreed with him or not, a bit like David Icke.

The basic problem with the current economic system, said Gesell, was that at present the bearer of capital had a perpetual advantage over the bearer of goods. When a farmer grew a crop of potatoes and tried to sell them on the free market, the man with money could easily try to increase his profit by offering the farmer something less than they were really worth. The farmer could refuse to sell them on, but only in the knowledge that, the longer he waited, the more rotten his potatoes would grow. The bearer of capital, however, could call the farmer's bluff and just leave his money in the bank, accumulating interest, until such time as his opponent was forced to give in. Selling potatoes for something less than they were truly worth was better than letting them rot and getting nothing for them whatsoever, after all. (Alternatively, perhaps the farmer required to borrow capital from a lender in order to get his potatoes properly distributed, but the lender would only give him credit at a profitably usurious interest rate.) The problem was that capital, to use the lingo of economists, possesses liquidity, meaning that it can be deployed at almost any time or place, being transformable into goods, housing stock, bonds or whatever you like, whereas things like potatoes have almost no liquidity value at all, unless you happen to know a shopkeeper or mortgage lender mentally disturbed or hungry enough to accept payment in them.[99] Gesell, writing in the days of the Gold Standard, summed up the difference between the permanence of the gold upon which the value of capital stood and perishable non-liquid goods like potatoes thus:

Rust, damp, decay, heat, cold, breakage, mice, moths, flies, spiders, dust, wind, lightning, hail and earthquakes, epidemics, accidents, floods and thieves wage war continuously and successfully upon the quantity and quality of wares ... Gold neither rusts nor decays, neither breaks nor dies. Neither frost, heat, sun, rain nor fire can harm it. The holder of money made of gold need fear no loss arising from the material of his possession. Nor does its quality change. Gold which has lain buried for a thousand years remains unconsumed.[100]

You almost wonder if Gesell might have based his rhetoric here upon the biblical advice of Matthew 6:19: 'Lay not up for yourselves treasures upon Earth, where moth and rust doth corrupt, and where thieves break through and steal.' The obvious solution was to try to somehow address this disgraceful imbalance between currency and perishable produce. It being impossible to turn potatoes into metal, or to replace physical potatoes with abstract accounting-based numerical representations of potatoes inside special potato banks, it was clear that instead capital itself had to be forced to become more spud-like – something Gesell said should happen via the medium of stamp-scrip or *Schwundgeld*.

Stamp Collecting

Gesell's stamp-scrip is an easy idea to grasp, and can be summed up by his useful phrase, 'rusting banknotes'. Basically, Gesell proposed that money should, just like potatoes, rot within its bearer's pocket in order to discourage hoarding of the stuff. Wishing to free money from the safes and piggy banks in which it had been imprisoned, Gesell also gave his proposed currency the name of *Freigeld*, or 'free money'. This latter term, of course, had the advertising advantage of making it sound as if people were getting something for nothing, as with a Citizens' Wage, whereas in fact they were being asked to accept a currency which turned to dust within their very hands. Gesell's proposal as to how this demurrage – the technical term for a monetary 'rot rate' – was to be achieved lay in the idea of making banknotes big enough to bear a hundred tiny stamps on their face, each of which signified a stage in the death of your assets.

Imagine you have a £100 note. Under Gesell's scheme, after a month you are required to attend a Post Office and get a scrip-stamp, which you affix to the back of the note, where there would be a series of little numbered squares just waiting to be filled up, like in a Panini sticker album. This officially reduces the value of the note by 1 per cent, meaning the £100 is now worth £99. Every month, by force of law, this trip to the Post Office has to be repeated, for all your banknotes; so ten months later, you will have ten stamps on your £100 note, reducing its value by 10 per cent, and leaving it worth only £90. This would go on, month after month, until your £100 note had 100 stamps, reducing its value by 100 per cent, and making it utterly

An example of a half-stamped 1 Schilling *Schwundgeld* 'rotting banknote' issued in the Austrian village of Wörgl during the depths of the Great Depression, and marked with a slogan relating to its quasi-magical ability to give men 'Work and Bread'. Allegedly, its adoption led to a localised economic miracle occurring – but could this wonder really have lasted forever? (Courtesy of the Austrian Government)

worthless for anything other than blowing your nose and wiping your bum on, preferably in that order. In short, what you would have on your hands, rather than a lovely crisp £100 note, would be one seriously rotten potato, wholly unfit for human consumption. Nobody would keep a bag of chips for 100 months and expect them still to be edible; why should a person be able to hoard money for decades and still be able to spend it? The specifics of this scheme kept on altering – maybe sometimes the proposed loss of interest would be 5 per cent per annum, or 0.10 per cent per week – but overall, the aim of Gesell's proposal remained constant. As a further added bonus, Gesell also claimed his system would reduce interest rates down to a perpetual 0 per cent, stabilising prices and wages forever, and slaying the dragon of hyperinflation.[101] Ezra Pound considered Gesell's idea to be a kind of wonderful 'counter-usury', a sort of inherently anti-Jewish money whose operation, unlike that of the Hell Banks' finances, was blissfully easy to understand; stamp-scrip, wrote Pound, was 'not beyond the mental capacity of a peasant' as 'anyone is capable of sticking a stamp on an envelope'.[102]

As Hugh Gaitskell pointed out, however, there were several problems with Gesell's theories. What if the greedy, capital-bearing plutocrats started paying for things by cheque instead? In fact, most large business transactions were already carried out by just such means, so the *Schwundgeld* idea wouldn't really help out farmers much at all when selling their goods wholesale. If the greedy capitalists' money is left safely in the bank until the point that the cheque clears, when it magically appears in the farmer's bank account, then it will not have rotted away by even a single penny (unless, of course, deposits from transactions were only to be stored within special rotting accounts with negative interest rates). Eventually, ordinary everyday consumers might start paying for everything in cheques too, causing queues and chaos in the world of commerce, especially if the cheques bounced. And what if prices of goods did not remain stable, and began to fall? If prices fell faster than the rate at which stamp-scrip notes declined in value, then it might be worth holding on to them after all, and the bearer of capital would still hold the whip-hand over the vendor of spuds. J. M. Keynes suggested another objection. Money might at present have the best liquidity value, but if all ordinary notes really were replaced, then might not some other long-lasting commodity which did not rot and rust come to be used as a rival alternative currency? People could start to trade in long-lasting jewels or blocks of granite instead, if they really wanted to.

However, while neither economist agreed with their amateur rival's financial ideas in a wider general sense, both Keynes and Gaitskell did see some limited potential for vegetable-money during certain specific desperate circumstances, just so long as the stamp-scrip was used as an alternative currency *alongside* that issued by a Central Bank, as opposed to as a total *replacement* for it. During a severe depression, said Gaitskell, if such rusting banknotes could be distributed within the affected locality, then it would act as a temporary spur towards spending as people rushed to get rid of the dying cash from their wallets, and the merchants who accepted it then rushed to spend it in their turn, buying in more supplies from wholesalers and industrialists, who would then pay their employees in it. These employees would soon rush to spend their shrinking *Schwundgeld* in the shops, and a virtuous circle of the kind Ezra Pound so admired in the sheep-based finances of Siena would temporarily be created prior to the money becoming worthless, hopefully stimulating the local economy and getting it back on its feet again through a kind of transitory artificial boom of consumption.[103] Could it therefore be that stamp-scrip was not *that* bad an idea after all?

Burning Good Money

When he owned his giant sawmill back in the 1800s, Ezra Pound's grandfather Thaddeus had paid his employees in a self-printed pseudo-currency dubbed *shink-shank*, so Ezra felt confident such an idea could really work, in actuality. Thaddeus' employees had accepted payment in such notes, so why shouldn't others?[104] There is actually a long history of alternative currencies gaining acceptance among the public, as you will know if you have ever used a book-token or a Bitcoin. During the decade following the First World War there was a widespread craze across the defeated and bankrupted nations of Germany and Austria for trade in something called *notgeld,* or 'emergency/

necessity money'. *Notgeld* had no validity as money in terms of being issued by a legitimate Central Bank; but in another sense it *was* money, just so long as people were willing to *pretend* that it was. Due to hyperinflation, there was a shortage of currency in the Teutonic lands, with printing presses struggling to keep up with demand for ever-higher new denominations; these were the days when Germans might have to pay millions of Reichsmarks for a loaf of bread. When it came to coins, the actual metal the coin was made from was often worth more than the sum stamped upon its face, leading to hoarding of such items as being valuable in themselves, rather than because of what they were meant to represent. With physical money running in short supply, a number of local authorities and companies began issuing their own *notgeld* notes for use by citizens instead, thus apparently proving Pound correct in his assertion that more monetary 'tickets' could always be printed to enable goods to be better distributed whenever the need arose. Other examples of *notgeld* were not even proper paper notes, being simply made up from whatever random materials lay conveniently to hand, such as playing cards, aluminium foil, postage stamps, leather, porcelain and even lumps of condensed coal-dust. Then, if the monetary value of the stamped denomination should ever fall below the inherent value of the coal, it would be more economically sensible to simply toss your coal-coins onto the fire than use them to buy a smaller amount of coal with; perishable money indeed![105]

Notgeld is not the same as *Freigeld*. However, during the early 1930s some actual *Schwundgeld* had in fact been put into direct usage, and it had worked quite well. Indeed, if you believe the reports put out at the time, Gesell's stamp-scrip had given birth to nothing less than a full-blown economic marvel – the so-called 'Miracle of Wörgl'. Wörgl was a small Austrian town with a population of 4,000, of whom 500 were unemployed, with another 1,500 persons in the immediate vicinity similarly suffering as the town's industries collapsed due to the Great Depression; the local cellulose plant went from employing 350–400 workers in 1930 to only four men in 1933, whose sole job was to guard the idle machinery. However, salvation was at hand, as the town's mayor, Michael Unterguggenberger (1884–1936), was familiar with events that had recently occurred in the Bavarian village of Schwanenkirchen where in 1931 the owner of the local coal-mine, Max Hebecker (1882–1948), had tried out a Gesellian experiment himself. Hebecker's mine had been closed for two years, but Hebecker was aware of the work of a close follower of Gesell called Hans Timm. Timm had gone so far as to print his own supply of *Freigeld* called the 'Wära', from the German words *ware* and *währung*, meaning 'goods' and 'currency'. These Wära were intended to decrease in value to the tune of 1 per cent per month, and this, combined with their dubious legal status, was meant to make people move them on from their wallets as soon as they had them.

Herr Hebecker bought up 40,000 Reichsmarks worth of Wära with the proceeds of a bank loan, and told his old employees he would be willing to get the mine going again if only they would accept payment in the invented pseudo-currency. They agreed, on the proviso that the local shopkeepers would accept payment in Wära too. The shopkeepers agreed in their turn, on the condition that wholesalers and suppliers from whom they bought their stock would also accept payment in Wära. The suppliers agreed to do so, if only the manufacturers and farmers who produced the goods they distributed would agree to accept payment in Wära as well. Just so long as they could pay part of their employees' wages or their energy-fees for coal from Hebecker's mine in Wära too, the manufacturers also agreed to participate. The workers in these factories were then able to pay for their goods at the local shops in Wära and, because everyone wanted to get rid of their cash as quickly as possible, the speed with which this money changed hands (its 'velocity', in technical economic terms) increased massively, in what seemed like a never-ending virtuous circle. While the Wära was undoubtedly a wholly fake currency, with no more legal validity than chocolate coins, the situation apparently worked perfectly. However, it was impossible to determine whether or not the cycle could succeed indefinitely, or at least until the stamp-scrip completely shed its value in 100 months' time, because Berlin, nervous that the authority of its Central Bank was being undermined, responded by passing an emergency law banning the Wära. Predictably, the mine closed down again, and the miners of Schwanenkirchen returned to a life on the dole.[106]

The Magic Money-Go-Round

Because Wörgl was over the border in Austria, where German law's writ did not (yet) run, Mayor Unterguggenberger saw a window of opportunity to try to get his own village back on its feet again before the Austrian authorities had the chance to pass their own anti-*Schwundgeld* laws. Wishing to score an immediate moral victory over his likely critics, when he had his stamp-scrip made up, Unterguggenberger had the following mini-manifesto printed on one side, as propaganda:

> TO ALL: Slowly circulating money has thrown the world into an unheard-of crisis, and millions of working people are in terrible need. From the economic viewpoint, the decline of the world has begun with horrible consequences for all. Only a clear recognition of these facts, and decisive action, can stop the breakdown of the economic machine, and save mankind from another war, confusion and dissolution. Men live from the exchange of what they can do. Through slow money-circulation this exchange has been crippled to a large extent, and thus millions of men who are willing to work have lost their rights to live in our economic system.

The exchange of what we can do must, therefore, be again improved and the right to live be reimagined for all those who have already been cast out. This purpose, the "Certified Compensation Bills of Wörgl" shall serve. THEY ALLEVIATE WANT, GIVE WORK AND BREAD.[107]

And how could you possibly disagree with any of that? When they heard of the initial apparent success of the scheme, representatives of some 170 other towns and villages across Austria poured into Wörgl to hear the Mayor give speeches outlining the theory behind his 'magic money'. Seeing the large number of unemployed lingering within his parish, Unterguggenberger naturally conceived of putting the jobless to work on large public infrastructure projects for the community's benefit. But how to pay for them, when the town had almost no cash? Unterguggenberger's solution was to deposit a sum of real money in a local bank (accounts differ as to how much – at most, 40,000 Austrian schillings) in Wörgl's name, as backing for the local authority's subsequent issuing of *Freigeld*. The first issue of 1,000 of these scrip-notes took place on 31 July 1932, with them being forced upon council employees as 50 per cent of their salaries (later, it was 75 per cent). More *Schwundgeld* was then printed and distributed to a body of newly employed public labourers in the form of 100 per cent of their wage-packets. As in Schwanenkirchen, this led to the creation of a temporary local economic boom as workers desperately raced to spend all their cash before it declined in value and died, a bit like a real-world *Brewster's Millions*.

It was the fact that the council workers' money circulated so quickly following its original distribution in their pay-packets which stimulated the boom. Had they been paid in ordinary Austrian schillings, they would have been likely to hoard it to get through tough times. Hoarding *Freigeld* has no benefits, however, and the velocity of the new pseudo-notes increased the flow of cash through the local economy massively; the equivalent of 100,000 schillings' worth of spending was done with only 8,000 schillings' worth of scrip-notes (i.e. each schilling was rapidly re-used an average of 12.5 times in different transactions). Just as good, when citizens came towards the end of the month and still had some stamp-scrip left, rather than paying a 1 per cent demurrage on it by buying a stamp to stick on the back, they preferred to pay off their debts and back-taxes owed to the municipality, making Wörgl's coffers bulge with an extra 78,000 schillings during the eighteen months or so that the experiment continued. Some people even used the stamp-scrip to pay off their anticipated future taxes for the next year or so, thus leaving them in credit. Furthermore, the village's real deposited legal tender schillings, which guaranteed and underwrote the whole scheme in the first place, were accruing a generous 6 per cent interest in the local bank. As more and more money poured in, Mayor Unterguggenberger's main problem became thinking of more schemes to set his labour force loose on;

he eventually commissioned the building of a nice, but wholly unnecessary, new ski-jump for the village. One of the municipalities that soon copied Wörgl built a gigantic municipal swimming pool. If things carried on at this rate, would every small settlement in Austria end up with similar expensive public novelties too? The nation was never to find out because, in 1933, the Austrian Central Bank followed the lead of its German counterpart and outlawed all such stamp-scrip schemes, in the name of maintaining its own monetary monopoly.

Ever Decreasing Circles

Had the experiment been allowed to continue, then what would have happened? Probably, a cycle of diminishing returns would have set in. While *Freigeld* can be an excellent way to stimulate local short-term growth in the face of an economic emergency, in the long term the effects fizzle out. For one thing, there is the fact that, by definition, shrinking money eventually shrinks down into nothing. You could just print more and more scrip, admittedly, but the positive effects of this decrease over time. This is because, in order to lend the pseudo-currency enough credibility that people will be willing to accept payment in it, the stamp-scrip is usually made convertible back into real-life pounds, dollars or schillings upon presentation at a local bank. In the usual model of scrip-schemes, actually doing so is penalised by a one-off transaction tax on the conversion (2 per cent in Wörgl's case, meaning every schilling you deposit would be worth only 98 groschen, or pennies), in order to discourage such behaviour. However, standard wisdom has it that, once people have run out of debts and back-taxes to pay off, this is precisely what they will begin to do. If you owe $100 in back-taxes and have $10 of *Schwundgeld* spare at the end of each month, it makes economic sense to dispose of that cash at the tax office immediately while it still bears its maximum worth.

Once you have paid the $100 off, though, you might reach the end of the month with no immediate necessities to spend that $10 upon. At first you may pay off your next year or two's taxes, but nobody is going to want to pay off much more; why settle your bill for the next ten years when you might drop dead in five? You could just use the spare monthly $10 to go on a shopping splurge, but eventually people would tire of doing this too. Rather than spend it right away on goods you don't need, you would be better advised to just deposit your spare $10 in the bank, at a low one-off conversion cost of 20 cents, rather than keeping it in your pocket at a continuing loss of 1 per cent per month, especially if the bank offers a decent savings rate, in which case your immediate 20 cent loss would be utterly cancelled out. At this point, hoarding of money within private accounts begins once more, and the bank accumulates large numbers of scrip-notes which it is then unable to get rid of, as their period of usefulness seems to be coming to an end. The bank will become reluctant to take in any more stamp-scrip deposits beyond the value of the sum of real cash initially deposited in there by the local council as a guarantee, leading to a run on the bank as locals, nervous their *Schwundgeld* will stop being accepted as quasi-legal tender, all descend upon the bank tellers, seeking to swap their scrip for real-life currencies guaranteed by the nation's Central Bank. A local bank crash then leads to another local economic recession – and everyone is back where they started, except the local bank, which is now dead. That's the theory, anyway; the intercession of the Austrian authorities prevented us from being shown beyond dispute if this was really so.[108]

Democratic politicians were not the only ones to try to stamp out stamp-scrip. Gesell gained thousands of followers throughout Germany and Austria during the inter-war years, who formed themselves into quasi-political pressure groups termed *Freiwirtschaftsbunds* (Free Economy Associations), before attempting to lobby more mainstream politicians into accepting their hero's ideas. In 1932, two years after his death, a Gesell-supporting Free Economy Party stood for election to the German Reichstag, but failed to make any real mark – unlike their ballot-box rivals the Nazis. While Gesell's disciples continued trying to influence Nazi politicians following Hitler's appointment as Chancellor in 1933, they did not have much success; in 1934, all such organisations and their publications were outlawed and forcibly disbanded. While Gesell was certainly against usury, he was not an anti-Semite like Ezra Pound, so his teachings found little favour among the Nazi high-command – although they did confiscate the vegetarian commune Gesell had once inhabited and turn it to their own uses under the policy of *Gleichschaltung*.[109] As a result of this persecution, if you really wanted to see Gesell's ideas being tested out under real-life conditions during the 1930s, then you had to abandon Europe and sail across the Atlantic to the Great Depression-hit USA.

Financial Suicide

The key figure in the spread of *Freigeld* in America was Irving Fisher (1867–1947), a professor at Yale University and probably the world's first ever 'celebrity economist'. Admittedly, one of the reasons he was so well known was because of his mistaken pronouncement, immediately prior to the Wall Street Crash, that the stock market had reached 'a permanently high plateau' of value and would never again fall, but, this minor error aside, Fisher had made many valuable contributions to the world of finance. The idea of 'index numbers' – the values given to the FTSE 100 and Dow Jones that you see being read out on the news every night – were Fisher's invention, for example. One other idea of his, which caught on for a while during the early 1930s, was that of combating the malign effects of the Great Depression by copying the demurrage schemes of Silvio Gesell.

Like Keynes and Gaitskell, Fisher dismissed Gesell's general theories, but saw in stamp-scrip a brilliant means of what he called 'priming the pump', or getting the money supply within a depressed local economy going again. The key event came in October 1932 when a businessman named Charles J. Zylstra, living in the town of Hawarden, Iowa, proposed that the local council should issue $300 worth of $1 stamp-scrip notes to the ranks of the town's unemployed, and set them to work repairing roads. Labourers got a dollar a day, and had to pay 3 cents to buy a stamp from the council as soon as they spent the note. Every subsequent transaction carried out with the Hawarden Dollar also entailed a 3 cent stamp-surcharge, until its face was filled up with thirty-six stamps, equalling $1.08 of stamp-tax, the extra 8 cents covering the council's overheads in running the scheme. The demurrage rate of the *Freigeld* here wasn't actually time-linked, as it ideally should have been to increase its velocity, but the initial experiment still worked really well. Eager to see what Silvio Gesell's ideas looked like for real, Irving Fisher quickly turned up on the scene, and was mightily impressed. 'Stamp-scrip,' he said, 'offers the most promising method of a quick way of snapping us out of the Depression.' As the Hawarden Dollar ran out of value as soon as it accumulated enough stamps, Fisher declared it to be a new kind of 'self-liquidating' currency, meaning that the Federal Reserve had nothing to fear from it, as all such scrip-notes would soon become utterly useless once their initial short-term work in priming the economic pump had been done; the Hawarden Dollar was nothing less than money which willingly committed suicide in the name of a greater cause, like Kamikaze pilots or jihadists.

Promoting the Hawarden experiment in his syndicated newspaper columns, Fisher helped lend Zylstra's system mainstream credibility, leading hundreds of small towns across the USA to try to copy it. To aid them in their task, in 1933 Fisher helped produce a small, quickly made 'how-to-guide', called simply *Stamp Scrip*. The panacea proved an easy sell to starving small-town America, which had been hit hard by the 1929 Crash, and between 1932 and 1934 new and ambitious scrip-schemes sprouted up from state to state in their hundreds. Demonstrating typical American entrepreneurship, Charles Zylstra himself swiftly copyrighted the specifics of his own Hawarden Dollar, and franchised it out to other towns for a fee. Results were mixed. While some places did well for a time, elsewhere the plan failed miserably, and Fisher himself discontinued his promotion of vegetable-money within less than a year of his guide being published. Problems with the programme varied. In some towns, shopkeepers proved reluctant to take the scrip, making it useless; in others, workers refused *en masse* to be paid in it, thinking the funny money fraudulent. Some towns saw a massive burden placed on their merchants, as scrip-notes dominated their takings to an excessive degree, making it hard for them to continue to trade, especially as most of their customers wanted their change given in real US Treasury coins and notes, not suicidal ones. In Chicago, scrip-notes were massively over-issued in stupidly large numbers, so much so that an army of so-called 'scrippers' had to be hired to pound the sidewalks trying desperately to convince their fellow citizens to make use of the pointless pseudo-money. As the scrippers themselves were paid purely in scrip, they were effectively begging passers-by to enable them to spend their own wages! Eventually, President Franklin D. Roosevelt laid down the foundations for the modern welfare state in America, issuing the poor and unemployed with benefits payments to help them through hard times, thus making the whole idea of stamp-scrip redundant; if you're getting free actual dollars from Uncle Sam anyway, why bother breaking your back digging roads for dud ones? By 1934, Fisher's nationwide cult of dying money had itself croaked its last.[110]

Why did an acknowledged economic expert like Irving Fisher so like Gesell's strange scheme? Partially it was because he knew of the alleged 'miracles' of Wörgl and Schwanenkirchen. In addition, it was because he knew that the effects of the Great Depression across America had been so devastating that in some areas people had resorted to a system of primitive Stone Age barter economies. The process began, Fisher said, with farmers swapping their crops for goods with local merchants, as neither had any spare money to facilitate trade. The farmers also began paying crop pickers in a portion of the crops they picked, and the idea of trading labour, goods and services for other labour, goods and services before long spread to such an extent that, by Fisher's estimation, there were a million people across the US who had simply stopped using money. Next, printed swap-bulletins began to appear, in which people offered to exchange spare vehicles for stores of gasoline, food for furniture, or even entire houses and farms for other houses and farms in different locations. Some swap-notices collected by Professor Fisher sound like pleas from a particularly depressing and weird episode of Noel Edmonds' *Multi-Coloured Swap-Shop*: 'Will swap man's overcoat, in good condition, for slide-trombone, piccolo or French horn.' Eventually, groups called Exchange Associations sprang up, accumulating large warehouses full of goods, to which they gave a notional dollar value, before issuing voucher receipts to the goods' donators, who would then search through the warehouse, spending their new vouchers on other similarly priced items donated by their poverty-stricken peers. In such Exchange Association schemes, Fisher saw an American version of *Notgeld* markets at work – 'By agreement, a dollar receipt does whatever a [real] dollar would do if you had a dollar to use', he wrote – so it would be only a short step to actual *Freigeld* markets then being introduced, in his view. As the Professor wrote, 'It becomes more and more evident that, if there was no money, 1933 could invent it all over again.'[111]

More Speed, Less Waste

Fisher thought that, in times of crisis, all kinds of daring experiments were worth giving a go, several of which he cited approvingly in his *Stamp Scrip* book. Consider events at Tenino, Washington State, where, after the collapse of a local bank, the town's Chamber of Commerce had bought up part of the bank customers' deposits, hoping to save innocent citizens and avoid their accounts being wiped out. This was a noble venture, but the problem was that the Chamber of Commerce didn't actually have enough real money to go through with the scheme. Therefore, they came up with the unique solution of making a cache of fake wooden coins of no actual value at all, and offering these to the failing bank in return for partial control of the depositors' assets instead. Because the bank was on the point of death anyway, they said yes. The curious thing was that these wooden coins soon became collectors' items due to their unusual nature, meaning that, while intrinsically worth next to nothing, the Chamber of Commerce was able to sell on large amounts of spare ones to members of the public for $2.50 each as novelty souvenirs. In this way they made a 150 per cent, $6,500 profit, bought back the bank's building and persuaded another banking service to move in, which agreed to administer the local citizens' accounts in real money once more.[112] Problem solved!

Another benign insanity cited by Fisher was that of the German 'Speed Money' movement of the 1930s. Speed Money was an ingenious means of cancelling out multiple persons' debts in one fell swoop, and was invented by a certain Dr Nordwall of the town of Norden, who placed an advert in his local paper one day saying that he would give away, for free, a 10 Reichsmark bill to the first person who owed someone else such a sum who turned up at his office the next morning. The first man who did turn up was shown the 10 RM and told that he must settle his debt immediately. To ensure that this took place, the 10 RM note was actually handed over to a waiting messenger-boy on a bicycle. The debtor simply told the boy the address of the person to whom the money was owed, and it was taken off to him post-haste. Because virtually everyone in 1930s Germany was in debt to someone, however, the messenger-boy did not actually physically hand over the 10 RM to the next man. Instead, he told him his debt was now fully paid, with the 10 RM note he waved before his eyes, and asked him who *he* might owe 10 RM to in his turn. Being told this, the messenger-boy raced off to this next person in the debt chain and repeated the process. This went on all day long, with debt after debt being eliminated by means of the same single banknote, until it was time for the lad to finish work. At this point, he let the last debtor in the chain keep the 10 RM until the next morning, in return for a temporary receipt, and went back home, having cancelled out an average of 120 RM of debt in a single day. For providing this service, the messenger-boy was given a tip of a few pennies per debtor, thus improving his own economic situation too – customers were unlikely to refuse the opportunity of wiping out 10 RM of debt for only a handful of pfennigs, after all. If only the messenger-boy could pedal fast enough, maybe eventually he would help the whole German nation get back on its financial feet again, and all for the price of a tenner?[113]

If such apparently loopy schemes could succeed – which, according to Irving Fisher, they did – then why not stamp-scrip, too? Desperate times call for desperate measures, and on 17 February 1933, a pair of US politicians, Senator John H. Bankhead (1872–1946) and Congressman Samuel B. Pettengill (1886–1974), attempted to get a Bill through Congress, authorising the Federal Government to issue a series of massive nationwide caches of rusting banknotes for as long as proved necessary, to prime the country's financial pump again. Professor Fisher greatly approved, but those who held the actual levers of power did not; the Bankhead-Pettengill Bill was never passed.[114] So, from all this we can clearly see that the idea of vegetable-money had been long established both prior to and during Ezra Pound's enthusiastic promotion of this very same thing through his poems and prose. Pound's only true economic innovation was to propose some kind of merger of Major Douglas' Social Credit ideas with Silvio Gesell's dream of a stamp-scrip economy. This synthesis of the two models Pound christened 'Volitionist Economics', and he devoted a good part of the 1920s and '30s to uniting Douglasites and Gesellites beneath a single banner. Sadly, the majority of Social Crediteers and *Schwundgeld* fans could not be made to see that their plans were in any way compatible – Major Douglas himself sarcastically dismissed Gesell's notion of shrinking money with the phrase 'as if money did not disappear fast enough already' in a 1936 speech.[115] It was this total failure to unite the two camps which ultimately led Pound into the arms of Mussolini. Pound spied an opportunity to get his ideas enacted through *Il Duce*'s patronage, and tried his best to get Benito on-side. As we have seen, that he ultimately failed to obtain the fascist dictator's stamp of approval was certainly not through want of trying.

2

Pennies from Heaven

Buddhist Economics, the Economy of Eden and Talking High Finance with the Ghost of Mrs Thatcher

No man can serve two masters ... Ye cannot serve both God and Mammon.
Matthew 6:12

A compendium of alternative-minded schemes for spiritualising our economy, from encouraging Indians to embrace poverty by imitating the divine wisdom of birds, to directing a bemused proletariat to eat the World-Soul by sucking it out of magic paintings.

In 1955 one of the nation's most highly regarded economists, sent out to the former colony of Burma by the British State, presented the government in Rangoon with a much-anticipated report about how best to develop their economy along Western lines. Its advice could be summed up in one simple word: DON'T. According to the report's peculiar conclusions, Burma would be well advised not to bother developing any kind of advanced economy at all, with its people being much better served by continuing to live in poverty and embracing Buddha's message that worldly goods alone did not bring human happiness. The Burmese government, unhappy with this counsel, gave the man who had presented it with some guidance of their own – think again, chum.

This bearer of such strange economic tidings was E. F. Schumacher (1911–77), a high-ranking employee of Britain's National Coal Board (NCB), and later to become one of the most celebrated – if controversial – economists in the world. Schumacher was born into a distinguished family, at least in terms of its intellectual credentials. His father Hermann had been a Professor of Economics who, during the Weimar Republic years of hyperinflation, had acted as an advisor to the German government, helping develop options to alleviate the crisis. His younger sister Elisabeth, meanwhile, had married the quantum physicist Werner Heisenberg (1901–76), developer of the famous 'uncertainty principle'. In 1930, Schumacher attended economics lectures given by the great analyst of capitalism Joseph Schumpeter (1883–1950) at Bonn University, helping spark his interest in the field. Soon Schumacher was in England, where he met no less a figure than J. M. Keynes, who was most impressed by the young man. The rise of Nazism not being to his taste, Schumacher continued his studies in New York and Oxford, eventually accepting a short-lived job as an investment advisor in London. Come the outbreak of the Second World War, Schumacher was interned in a Welsh border POW camp as an enemy alien, but his well-placed university pal David Astor (1912–2001), the aristocratic future newspaper magnate, used his connections to get Schumacher released to join the staff on his uncle's country estate of Eydon, where he could live in a small cottage and help out with the farm work – a task Schumacher found he greatly enjoyed.

While interned in the POW camp, Schumacher used his spare time to write an academic paper, *Multilateral Clearing*, aiming to lay out rules for a better post-war system of trade. This paper came to the attention of Keynes, with whom he struck up a new correspondence. According to Schumacher, the global post-war economic settlement Keynes helped establish during the legendary 1944 Bretton Woods fiscal conference over in New Hampshire held certain suspicious similarities to his own ideas – ideas which Keynes had apparently discouraged him from publishing. In 1946, Schumacher became a British citizen and, Left-leaning as he then was, accepted an offer from the post-war Labour government of a position on the British Control Commission, whose responsibility was to help administer and rebuild the shattered West German economy following Hitler's defeat. By 1950 he was back in London, where Labour, fresh from nationalising the British coal industry, gave him a job as Chief Economic Advisor to the National Coal Board, a gigantic new organisation with more than 500,000 employees.[1] Proud of his sharp intellect to the point of arrogance, Schumacher had for most of his life been a staunch materialist with little time for flaky nonsense like religion or spirituality, who considered qualities like rationality, logic and clearness of thought above all else, an outlook which had served him well so far – but all this was about to change …

The Constant Gardener

The key event of Schumacher's time at the NCB was his 1950 purchase of a large house in the Surrey green-belt town of Caterham. Named Holcombe, the house came with a four-acre garden attached. Given this, Schumacher thought he had better take up gardening, and found he loved it. Not only did he beautify the grounds, he started up a large allotment, growing fruit and vegetables for his family to eat. He also joined the Soil Association, a body formed in 1946 to promote the idea of organic farming – between 1971 and 1977, Schumacher later served as the Association's head. Enamoured by the Soil Association's proto-Green message, Schumacher became obsessed with his new-found hobby, rising at 6 a.m. every morning to tend his soil before catching the train to work in London, and spending much of his annual holidays producing huge piles of compost (as it were). He also began conducting a series of small-scale agricultural experiments, one of which involved him getting hold of some grains of wheat found in the pyramid tombs of ancient Egypt, and planting them to see if they would grow. Remarkably, they did! While the garden's soil was originally far too chalky, Schumacher was determined to improve it using the organic methods promoted by the Soil Association, with the intention of making his family self-sufficient in terms of food as quickly as was possible. By settling down for good at Holcombe, the former international *wanderlust* of Schumacher was transformed into a desire for permanence in his life, of which his new regard for the idea of self-sustainability was only one aspect. Like the plants he grew, Schumacher was finally putting down roots.[2] This fascination with gardening lent him a whole new way of seeing the world, as he explained in a letter to his sister in 1951:

> In many ways, our house is an oasis in the desert of today's civilisation … This is my great aim – to prevent [my] children becoming mere consumers without having a creative attitude to their lives. For that reason I have started all sorts of new things, for example baking bread for the family … The bread made from whole-wheat and stone-ground flour is infinitely more tasty and healthier than any bread from the baker. Home produce from the garden has the same purpose: only in this way can the children of the modern world get some idea of what life and work really is.[3]

In an era in which many children can't even tell you what animals simple products like bacon and milk come from, or think that eggs drop from cows and cheese grows on trees,[4] Schumacher may have had a point. His thinking here was derived greatly from the Soil Association, whose basic philosophy ran thus – look after the soil, and you will grow healthier crops and raise healthier animals; eat healthier crops and animals, and you will grow to be a healthier person, in body and mind. Rejecting the use of chemical fertilisers and pesticides, and decrying the increasing mechanisation of agriculture, the Soil Association advised mankind did things the old-fashioned way, in line with the perennial wisdom of our ancestors, a wisdom whose enduring relevance they saw as being permanent in nature, not old-fashioned or obsolete. The trouble was that some of the 'ancient wisdom' upon which the Soil Association's philosophy was based turned out to have been derived from some very unusual sources which were not particularly ancient or wise in nature at all …

Doctor Who?

Foremost among these unusual sources was Rudolf Steiner (1861–1925), an Austrian-born sage who towards the end of his life developed some very odd ideas about agriculture, doubtless after having read up on the topic in the Akashic Records, a kind of disembodied psychic Wikipedia, inherent within the universe around us, to which he claimed to have clairvoyant access. Steiner, whose adolescence and childhood were filled with alleged supernatural encounters with the dead, was something of a prodigy who started out his New Age career as a member of the Theosophy cult which was all the rage in turn-of-the-century Europe. In 1913, he broke away from the Theosophists and started his own spiritual movement, Anthroposophy, or 'Man-Wisdom'. Possessing much Man-Wisdom himself, Steiner applied his vast brain to numerous areas, from architecture to literature, from medicine to education; his chain of Steiner Schools is still going today, offering pupils an alternative form of pedagogy based upon topics like reincarnation, in which Steiner steadfastly believed. Another specialist field of Steiner's was that of the interface existing between economics and politics, upon which he often delivered lectures – some 6,000 in total, over twenty-five years. Known to admirers as 'The Doctor', and habitually donning a series of flamboyant and archaic bow-ties, Steiner could have stepped straight out of the William Hartnell-era TARDIS. As his lectures often contained psychically derived details about life in ancient Atlantis and his conversations with ghosts, his initiation into esoteric mysteries by an unknown individual called 'The Master', and his previous incarnations in other bodies (he really was a Time-Lord!), Steiner's speeches were rather more entertaining than those of most public figures today.[5]

Following the First World War, Steiner published a book, *The Threefold Commonwealth*, which sold 80,000 copies in its first edition alone and proved popular among followers of Silvio Gesell and C. H. Douglas, with whose theories Steiner's were sometimes thought compatible; Douglas occasionally gave speeches at meetings of London Anthroposophists, and quoted Steiner (albeit not that enthusiastically) in his own work.[6] Like Douglas, Steiner wanted a tripartite structure to civilisation, believing there were three spheres in any successful society, the economic, the legal/political and the cultural (this latter consisting of a mini-trinity of arts, sciences and religion), none of which should be allowed to dominate the others, and each of which ought to support one another just as Douglas said the Father, Son and Holy Ghost did in the Holy Trinity. For example, Britain does not currently have entrance fees in public museums and art galleries, thereby indicating that culture is a sphere apart from economics; and yet it was politicians who decreed that tax money raked in from the economy should pay for this free entry, thus allowing the three spheres to interact usefully while still remaining separate from one another, as neither politicians, taxpayers nor businessmen are supposed to get to decide what goes on display or what opinions are expressed in such places. However, where this Trinitarian balance has broken down, as with the National Trust's bizarre 2017 campaign to spread gay propaganda during its guided tours of stately homes, one sphere (here, that of political correctness) can come to dominate over all others. The French Revolution's slogan of *liberté, egalité, fraternité* was, apparently, an early unheeded call for just such a Threefold Commonwealth to be created. Steiner's theories also included a lot of weird stuff about successful businessmen, or 'spiritual workers who direct production', being given control over various industries based upon their personal level of 'spiritual enlightenment', and a complex argument that all workers' wages are really fictional, and based upon a form of cash-disguised barter.[7]

Unholy Trinity

Steiner further proposed another form of vegetable-money. Thinking human civilisation was really a disembodied living psychic organism, he said the trick to a truly balanced society was to stop the tripartite elements fully separating out from one another like invisible amoebas. This was because, once one sphere had loosed itself entirely from the others, it would cannibalise them; for example, if the economic sphere, which Steiner characterised as a huge sentient stomach, guzzled the other two smaller amoebas in the trinity, it would swallow their souls and we would end up living in a kind of hyper-capitalist dystopia. In his 1922 lecture-series and book *World Economy*, Steiner laid out a plan to prevent such hyper-capitalist psychic amoebas from devouring us all lock, stock and barrel. The basic proposal was that because all wealth was derived ultimately from the land via agriculture, all money, like fruit, really did grow on trees after all, and should eventually be turned back into compost in order to create fresh, juicy new capital to replace the rotten, tired old money currently in circulation, which gradually became literally 'spent out' over time. Wealth creation was thus but another branch of farming cash-crops, or 'the substitution of a Nature-currency for a gold-currency', like Ezra Pound wanted. Ideally, we should 'let the sign [banknote] mimic the object [vegetable], let the money die'. In this model, excessive accumulations of capital in bank accounts or massive family inheritances were like blockages in the natural cycle of life which had to be removed, just like a blockage in your bowels – cash should be being spent, not gathering dust and interest in a banker's colon.

Steiner proposed a range of measures to remove the economic bum-blockage from the natural business cycle, thereby preventing the hyper-capitalist amoeba from growing too large and all-consuming, such as placing upper limits upon family inheritances, and stamping all cash with a strict use-by date. Money whose Gesellian death was impending Steiner termed 'gift-money', presuming that because it would soon be useless and so was worth much less than it originally had been, its owners would use it to fund altruistic gifts such as free university education, which would help fertilise society's future economic and cultural growth – a possible solution to the current tuition fees impasse, maybe? Alternatively, you could give it away to starving artists, bequeath it to museums, or use it to fund scientific research as so-called 'seed-money'. As one recent student of Steiner's ideas put it: 'The youth of money is the beginning of agriculture, its maturity is [investment in] industrial expansion, and its death is spiritual emancipation [through] growth of the arts and sciences.' Naturally, the tripartite, Holy Trinity-aping nature of this life-cycle was no accident.[8]

Silvio Gesell, too, considered society to be a kind of 'social organism'. When Gesell wrote *The Natural Economic Order*, it was the way that the current system of finance and usury contradicted the basic laws of Nature which annoyed him the most, just as with Steiner. The sin of speculators hoarding money rather than spending it or lending it out and thereby gumming up the normal cycle of trade during a recession was compared by him to the blocking up of the blood-supply in a human body, leading to death, a comparison Steiner himself also made. Gesell's idea of shrinking money, if applied properly, was supposed to allow such an ailing social organism to imitate the natural process of self-healing following an illness, and thus encourage the body-politic to return towards the state of equilibrium exemplified by the natural world around us. Nothing in Nature was eternal, so why should money be? By leading cash into the eternal cycle of life and death, Gesell was trying to make our economy less artificial, less separated from the land, in imitation of his own experiences within a vegetarian commune.[9] The difference between the two men is that, unlike the non-psychic Silvio Gesell, The Doctor ended up taking his regard for the spiritual and economic virtues of the blessed agricultural landscape into a whole new dimension of time and space...

Franken-Steiner Farms

In 1924 Steiner delivered the world's first organic farming course at Koberwitz in Silesia, where one of his followers ran a large agricultural estate. Here, Steiner railed against modern chemical-based farming methods, particularly the Haber-Bosch process, an industrial procedure invented in 1909 allowing for the mass production of cheap, synthetic, nitrogen-based fertilisers, which he blamed for degrading Europe's soil. Steiner had much better ideas about how to make the crops grow, telling attendees of his theory that every farm in existence was a 'living organism' with its own soul, a sort of *genius loci* or 'spirit of place'. According to Steiner, there was an inherent correspondence between the growth of plants and the movements of the stars and planets, meaning that, if a farmer wanted to gain the highest and healthiest yields of crops possible, he had to take astrological factors into account when doing his planting. Without the influence of the stars, said Steiner, our cereals would 'look very queer indeed' as all plants 'would have more or less pyramidal forms', or else 'the form of the cactus, which strikes us as abnormal'. If we didn't want such vegetable horrors to occur, we had better start taking more account of astrology when sowing our seeds.

Steiner felt that old rural proverbs about crops growing best when planted during certain phases of the moon were not outdated superstitions, but expressions of ancient folk wisdom. Sadly, however, a more mechanical image of Nature had increasingly displaced this traditional idea of the farm being connected to the cosmos, leading to a sad decline in the quality of vegetables. 'Why ... is it impossible today to eat such potatoes as I ate in my youth?' Steiner asked plaintively during one of his lectures. It was because agriculture was now thought of as a purely economic activity, rather than as a form of benign stewardship of the land enabling the farmer to draw closer to God. Soil contained a holy 'astral principle' within itself, and if this was not heeded, then the decline in potatoes would be joined by a wider decline in Western civilisation itself. For example, if we derived our firewood from trees which had been 'planted in the earth without understanding of the cosmic rhythms', purely for profit, then when burned in a fireplace, this wood would 'not provide the same health-giving warmth as firewood from trees that were planted intelligently'. If the natural world was manipulated purely for financial gain, then the foodstuffs and consumer objects derived from it, from turnips to tables, would be evil and unhealthy, and pass on their baleful influence to mankind at large as they entered into the economic supply chain.

Economists, Steiner said, were constantly lecturing farmers on how to best maximise their profits, but their words were 'manifest nonsense' and 'mere empty talk'. How could such people, sat away in their city offices and universities, possibly know better than actual experienced farmers how to manage the land? When it came to country matters, the problem with economists was that they continually 'look at a beetroot as a beetroot' rather than as a divine localised expression of the Godhead. Anybody who considered a beetroot to be merely a beetroot, Steiner explained, was 'still far from understanding the beetroot'. In order to *truly* comprehend a beetroot, a person had also to understand 'the living-together of the beetroot with the field, the season of the year in which it ripens and so forth', because the growth of the beetroot 'depends on countless conditions, not only of the Earth as a whole, but of the cosmic environment'. Therefore, when economists blithely encouraged farmers to use large amounts of industrial

Haber-Bosch fertiliser to increase crop yields, they were to be ignored, as such methods broke the eternal link between the universe and the beetroot, so would degrade and ruin the soil. It would be far better if farmers were to return to working the land 'by instinct and not by scientific theory' by throwing away their chemical sprays and instead burying a variety of bizarre random items beneath their fields. Everything from cow horns filled with dung, the bladders of red deer, and the skulls of domesticated animals stuffed with pieces of bark could be placed under your soil and left to rot into a form of highly effective natural compost, said Steiner, in a revival of old folk magic. In this way, a 'biodynamic farm', as he called his desired joint astrological-agricultural enterprises, could become self-sufficient, without having to rely upon the importation of harmful chemical substances from outside, thus pleasing the farm's guiding spirit and drawing down celestial forces from the heavens, causing the soil (and the people who ate its star-infused products) to rejuvenate. The soil, Steiner said, had a psychic 'inner life', with the Earth itself being a gigantic living organism, whose belly was the mud and dirt. Could it be that the dyspeptic convulsions of the modern world were really nothing more than a bout of economist-inspired global indigestion?[10]

Eco-Fascists

Such ideas may seem amusing, but they had a dark side too, as Steiner was something of a pan-German nationalist. Dying in 1925, Steiner wasn't a Nazi himself, but many of his obsessions later struck a chord with those who were. He staunchly denied that Germany had been responsible for the outbreak of the First World War, blaming instead a conspiracy perpetrated by money-worshipping British Freemasons, and claimed to be in direct contact with the ghost of General Helmuth von Moltke (1848–1916), German Chief of Staff during the early phase of the conflict. Steiner also had an immense portfolio of loopy racial ideas, thinking that the yellow-skinned Japanese were descended from ancient Atlantean stock, and that, because black skin was a clear sign of demonic influence, white women should not read any 'negro books' during pregnancy, otherwise they might give birth to black devil-babies. Steiner promulgated what has been called a kind of 'cosmic eugenics', which taught that 'in the grand cycle of spiritual evolution, the Germanic race had advanced the furthest.' Intermarriage between pure Aryans and blacks and Jews, therefore, was a form of reckless biological vandalism. Such fantasies also fed into Steiner's idea of a *Volksgeist*, a kind of governing archangel underpinning a nation or ethnic race's sense of self, and presiding over their ancestral lands rather like one of his *genius loci* presided over a biodynamic farm.

This final strand of Steiner's thought was in line with that of several so-called 'Green Nazis' such as Hitler's Agriculture Minister Walther Darré

(1895–1953), who themselves believed in a doctrine of 'blood and soil' which, hymning the mystical relationship between the German people and their land, made direct links between the apparently unconnected ideas of racial and environmental purity. The popularity of the widespread German *Lebensreform* ('life-reform') movement, in which proto-Greens set up clean-living vegetarian and organic communes like the one Silvio Gesell had inhabited, was also significant in helping spread Steiner's ideas; because so many Germans had already been exposed to eco-friendly, Nature-worshipping ideas through such channels, Steiner's teachings didn't sound as nutty as they might otherwise have done. Despite the Anthroposophic Society being dissolved throughout the Reich in 1935 on the direct orders of SS chief Heinrich Himmler (1900–45), the activities of its individual members remained uncurtailed for much longer, with several prominent Nazis being sympathetic to Steiner's aims; according to Deputy Führer Rudolf Hess (1894–1987), those sceptics who criticised biodynamic methods on scientific grounds were just 'carrying out a kind of witch-trial' against Steiner's followers. Hans Merkel, a Nazi bureaucrat in the Reich Food Estate organisation, sought to use his position to promote biodynamic agriculture as the best means for creating a 'new peasantry', back in touch with the soil of their ancestors. Merkel despised the 'soulless ways of thinking' of modern Western capitalism, feeling it had made the German people lose touch with the old ways, their 'Ür-wisdom', as he had it. Bemoaning how the modern farm 'had become a factory', Merkel proposed using Steiner's methods to reacquaint country folk with their ancestral *Volksgeist*, which had been made a stranger to them by the agents of rootless modern capital – that is, the Jews.

If you listen to various Nazis' special pleading for biodynamic methods, they begin to sound like precursors to the modern-day eco-fascists of the Green Party – adopting Steiner's ways was desirable on environmental grounds, they argued, leading to less pollution of the soil, and desirable on anti-big business grounds, too, as it challenged the monopolistic dominance of giant chemical companies. Key to the movement's spread was one Erhard Bartsch (1895–1960), founder of the Reich League for Biodynamic Agriculture, who tirelessly propagandised Steiner's methods to various Nazi economists and well-placed SS men; he even tried to convert Hitler. The Nazis planned making the German economy into a self-sufficient autarky as far as was possible, and Bartsch argued that Steiner's methods might reduce the Reich's reliance upon foreign-manufactured fertilisers, while at the same time allowing current German manufacturers to divert their limited chemical reserves to other areas. The rather *völkisch* Heinrich Himmler also embraced the cause, asking the SS economist Oswald Pohl (1892–1951) to develop plans for restocking Eastern Europe with a series of farms 'along organic lines' following the conquest of Poland, hoping to create a Nazi 'agricultural empire' there; seeding a generation of 'soldier-farmers' to defend the sacred soil of the Third Reich from bands of sub-humans from the East was the general idea. Together with Walther Darré, Himmler dreamed of these warrior-farmers living in pseudo-medieval houses, healing one another with natural herbs, reviving the old pagan way of life and following the farming methods of Rudolf Steiner. There was even a network of biodynamic farms inside the Jewish death camps! While Steiner's cult may officially have been disbanded, its influence lingered throughout the Third Reich nonetheless, the idea being that, while following Steiner rather than Hitler was wrong, you could still make use of some of his more useful teachings, but in the name of National Socialism, not Anthroposophy. Walther Darré, who got only a short prison sentence following the collapse of Nazism in 1945, once went so far as to call Steiner's methods 'farming according to the laws of life', and maintained contact with Anthroposophists at home and abroad following his release.[11]

One of Darré's correspondents was Jorian Jenks (1899–1963), a member of the British Union of Fascists (BUF) and a founder member in 1946 of the Soil Association. A one-time farmer, Jenks was forced to abandon his calling due to a slump in pre-war agricultural prices, so adopted a dual role as a writer and farming advisor to the BUF. Embittered by the failure of his farm, Jenks pronounced himself unhappy with the contemporary way of organising the rural economy, and campaigned for Britain to become an entirely self-sufficient autarky in terms of food production. As suspicious as Steiner of modern science, following the end of the Second World War Jenks dreamed of creating a 'spiritual ecologism', which would enhance the sacred bond between man and the land – a watered-down variant of 'blood and soil'. Believing like Steiner (and indeed Jamie Oliver) that a decline in the standard of vegetables being consumed across Europe would eventually lead to the complete collapse of Western civilisation, he became a founder member of the Soil Association, editing its journal *Mother Earth* as a vehicle for his cranky views. While the Soil Association took a sharp turn to the Left in the years following Jenks' death in 1963, during its first two decades it was a haven for Far-Right thinkers and Steinerites – as well as the occasional normal person.[12] One of these normals was the exceedingly un-fascist figure of E. F. Schumacher, who joined up for gardening tips, not to play at being Sir Roderick Spode. Nonetheless, regular exposure to the ideas of men like Jenks evidently had its effect; after his death, Schumacher was found to have several texts by Rudolf Steiner contained within his own personal library.

Fertile Soil

Schumacher's love for the unconventional organic approach promoted by the Soil Society was later credited by him with opening his mind to the alternative mode of thinking which came to dominate his life and work. As his daughter and biographer Barbara Wood put it, Schumacher's acceptance of the organic approach was really 'in a sense an act of faith', because there was 'little scientific evidence ... to convince the doubter of the "muck and mystery" way of thinking' that had been adopted by the group in defiance of prevailing preferences for chemical-based agriculture.[13] As a young man, in thrall to materialism, atheism and a rigidly logical and rationalistic outlook on the world, there is no way Schumacher would have been open to the teachings of such a group, but his new-found love of Nature opened the way for a whole different worldview as he entered middle age. During his daily train journey to work, Schumacher started reading books about the history of non-Western civilisations, noticing how their thinkers and philosophers based their systems of thought upon different cultural assumptions to those of contemporary Westerners, privileging qualities such as enlightenment and inspiration over pure intellect and logic. Gradually, he decided such minds had a point; after all, less developed nations like India and China hadn't been responsible for such recent disasters as the Holocaust, had they? Schumacher's dawning conclusions seem couched in metaphors relating to the organic, whole-world outlook of the Soil Association:

> The present condition in human affairs is due to a profound crisis in human consciousness, a lapse from the organic wholeness of life. There is a tendency to overlook the spiritual and exalt the intellectual ... Everything is stripped of soul, of inner life.[14]

At the age of forty-one, Schumacher's whole mindset was turned upside down, becoming so holistic in nature that, for a brief period, he was open to accepting almost anything of a fringe nature into his ever-expanding worldview. He joined the Society for Psychical Research, and developed a sudden enthusiasm for flying saucers. No matter how little sense some of the things he was looking into made, this did not in itself mean they were necessarily untrue; perhaps such topics could not be understood by the rational Western intellect, and had to be taken on faith or intuition, as with the teachings of the Soil Association. Bizarrely, his path down this road was greatly aided by the unexpected fact that the National Coal Board was at this point in time a real hotbed of occultism – or one of its associated bodies, the British Coal Utilisation Research Association (BICURA), was. BICURA's head was John G. Bennett (1897–1974), who was not only an acknowledged expert on coal, but also upon the teachings of the prominent mystic G. I. Gurdjieff (c.1865–1949), of whom Bennett was a true disciple. Every weekend, Bennett put away the Bunsen burners and transformed BICURA's premises into a retreat for seekers after hidden truth. In 1946, Bennett bought outright the Sussex estate of Coombe Springs, where BICURA's labs were located, and transformed it into a permanent centre for divine development. Here, Bennett gave classes in ancient wisdom, and developed a new system of 'five-dimensional geometry', which included eternity as a hitherto neglected element of Creation. Mankind in the present day was suffering from 'eternity-blindness', he said, which was just as limiting as only being able to see a 3-D shape in two dimensions, and led us to pursue short-sighted goals in direct conflict with the teachings of our past and the interests of our future. Disturbed by the short-termism of contemporary politics, Bennett proposed building a new Noah's Ark, in which 'everything worth preserving' was to be stored and conserved in order to protect it from whatever imminent catastrophe foolish modern man was about to unleash upon himself. In 1948 Bennett travelled to South Africa, looking for a suitable spot to locate this second Ark, but was unable to find one (or perhaps he was just refused planning permission).[15]

The Soul of Coal

The turning point in Bennett's life had come in 1918 when, out in France with the Royal Engineers, he was blown off his motorbike by a German shell. He remained in a coma for six days, during which time he underwent an out-of-body experience. Fluent in Turkish, following his recovery Bennett was posted to Constantinople as a liaison officer. One of his tasks was to monitor the wave of refugees passing through Turkey *en route* to safety in the West, one of whom was G. I. Gurdjieff. Introduced to Gurdjieff by a Turkish prince with an interest in Anthroposophy, Bennett learned all he could from the great man prior to his departure for mainland Europe, and pursued further research into esoteric matters throughout the 1920s, during which time he also used his contacts to become involved in the Turkish coal-mining industry, which accounted for his appointment as the first chairman of BICURA in 1938.[16] Naturally, such an unusual figure, whose areas of expertise ranged from the design of fuel-efficient fireplaces to the hidden depths of the human soul, had much appeal to Schumacher – but what had even more appeal was what Bennett had to teach him about Gurdjieff.

Born in Armenia around 1865, and raised in the Caucasus, Gurdjieff grew up to be a great spiritual teacher. A student of ancient traditions who had spent time wandering across India and the Middle East hunting hidden knowledge, his basic teaching was that man spends most of his life asleep, operating on a kind of automatic pilot, but that, through following his patented programme of sacred instruction and exercise, termed 'work', it was possible for a person to 'wake up' into a higher state of consciousness. In 1922, Gurdjieff established the Institute for the Harmonious Development of Man, a spiritual camp near Paris, where, to the untrained eye, he exploited his disciples – including A. R. Orage, the magazine editor who did so much to promote the financial theories of Ezra Pound and C. H. Douglas – by getting them to maintain the grounds and do all his hard outdoors work without pay. To those in the know, however, Gurdjieff was up to something different. When he ordered new arrivals to get their hands dirty by performing repetitive and laborious tasks like chopping wood or digging ditches, he was actually hoping to develop their souls. The idea went that, by working yourself beyond the point of exhaustion, the chattering voice inside your head would become quiet, allowing you to develop a sense of inner stillness and calm akin to that gleaned from meditation. By abandoning the mental stresses and strains of modern civilisation, and engaging in the traditional labour patterns of rural peasants, Gurdjieff taught that mankind could regain his lost sense of inner balance, making him capable of great things. When he handed you a spade and told to you dig, therefore, Gurdjieff was not being cruel or exploitative. He was simply inviting you to engage in a form of 'practical yoga'.[17]

Economic Enlightenment

Schumacher became eager to test out Gurdjieff's concept of 'work' for himself, and embarked upon a daily programme of early-morning meditation and yoga exercises, aiming to clear his mind of all distractions and become less of a 'sleeper' – viewed in this light, his constant labours within the garden were another kind of practical yoga, modelled after Gurdjieff's wise example. Work of the right kind – that is to say, physical labour in the great outdoors – helped Schumacher to 'wake up', as Gurdjieff would have wanted. In his 1977 book *A Guide for the Perplexed*, a sort of spiritual self-help text, Schumacher spoke of how it was impossible for man to live 'without systematic work to keep in contact with, and develop toward, Higher Levels than those of ordinary life', words which could have come direct from the Armenian Master.[18] Schumacher fell under the influence of other gurus too, such as the Anglo-German scholar Edward Conze (1904–79), who claimed to be the reincarnation of a Tibetan Buddhist monk who had been reborn in the West to save it from modernity. Conze convinced Schumacher of the reality of astrology, having as he did the uncanny gift of recognising which star-signs people were upon first sight. Henceforth, Schumacher became a devotee of the hidden messages which allegedly lay written in the stars; I wonder if he took the heavens' influence upon his crops into account when planting them, as Steiner would have advised?[19] The end result of all this exposure to the wells of Eastern wisdom came one day in 1954 when, during his regular morning yoga session, E. F. Schumacher suddenly 'woke up' for good:

On Monday February 1st, during my daily quarter of an hour, I came into contact with 'X'. As one can read in all the books, this cannot be described in words. But suddenly all sorts of things that I had not understood became completely clear – and in the same simple manner. Not that anything dramatic happened – no light, sound, vision or experience; but merely an indescribable detachment from all that which usually tries to distract one ... and then, with that, a new understanding.[20]

In the autumn of 1954 Schumacher received a second sudden illumination, not about God or *nirvana*, but the rather more prosaic matter of rates of global coal-consumption. During the 1950s, as the shattered economies of bombed-out Europe rapidly rebuilt themselves, the main problem faced by the coal industry was that sky-high rates of demand far exceeded rates of supply. One aspect of Schumacher's job at the NCB was to work out how best to increase rates of coal production to meet this demand. His second abrupt enlightenment, however, revealed to him a rather disturbing answer – that industry's demands for ever-more coal could *not* be met, at least not indefinitely. Governments appeared not to realise there was only a finite supply of coal (and natural oil and gas) stored away beneath the world's surface and once it had all been extracted, that was it, the advanced Western economies would be doomed to eternal collapse; as John G. Bennett had warned, contemporary man was indeed suffering from a bad case of eternity-blindness. Schumacher compared this to a person living on a large one-off amount of capital such as an inheritance, which would one day run out, leaving them in poverty, as opposed to a person living off a small but steady income, which would not. In this analogy, the industrialised nations were rapidly burning through their finite capital of coal, whereas the undeveloped countries of the Third World were more sensibly relying upon the steady income of burning renewable things like wood to satisfy their energy needs. Such nations were pursuing a way of life which was not only self-sufficient, but also sustainable – like biodynamic farms on a larger scale.[21]

Naturally, such an insight was not one his superiors at the NCB wished to hear, and the inconvenient truth was ignored. In 1951, Schumacher had been asked to contribute to discussions about ways of aiding Third World nations to industrialise which had been arranged by Britain's future Labour Prime Minister, Harold Wilson (1916–95). This invitation coming prior to his spiritual and economic enlightenment, Schumacher had made some relatively standard and therefore well-received suggestions to the MPs and other officials who had attended Wilson's conferences, something which in 1955 led to an offer from Whitehall for him to travel abroad to Burma to fill a temporary UN-sponsored role as economic advisor to the Burmese government. The question Burma's leaders wanted Schumacher to answer was 'How can you make us rich?' The question Schumacher himself wished to address, however, was rather different: 'Can one really help the Burmese [economically] without harming them?' Once he had landed safely in Rangoon, the enlightened economist was quickly to conclude the answer was 'no'.[22]

Indian Summary

Schumacher had been spending some of his valuable time on the train to work busily absorbing the financial thoughts of history's best-loved seditious Middle Temple lawyer, Mahatma Gandhi (1869–1948), hero of the Indian independence movement. The basic economic theories of Gandhi are easily glimpsed by taking a quick look at the flag of India, towards the design of which Gandhi contributed. Gandhi envisaged India becoming a quasi-autarky, an alliance of thousands upon thousands of separate villages whose individual mini-economies would centre upon the production of textiles. As such, he proposed the Indian flag feature a big spinning wheel, and be made of a variety of home-spun silk called *khadi* (from which all Indian flags still have to be manufactured, by law). However, immediately prior to Indian independence in 1947, Gandhi's spinning wheel was combined with the *Ashoka Chakra*, a holy Hindu and Buddhist 'wheel of fortune' representing the flow of karma. Karma is the destiny created for each person's soul by the merit (or lack of) in their actions, which leads them to be reincarnated in either a higher or a lower state come their next life; whether you return as an ant or a princess represents a turn one way or the other upon the karmic wheel. Gandhi's idea was that, via the adoption of small-scale, traditional village economies, the karmic spinning wheel would propel India onwards from colonial domination into a better, more meritorious and sustainable way of life. The three coloured stripes on the flag, meanwhile, stood for disinterestedness and the renunciation of material wealth (orange, like the *hare krishnas* wear), divine wisdom (white, like the pure light of the Godhead) and harmony with Nature and the soil (green, like the forests and fields). By blending these three things together in a tricolour, it was hoped Midnight's Children would come to inhabit a better, saner economic world – a Threefold Commonwealth, you might say.[23]

In spite of his appalling dress sense, Gandhi was obsessed by the textile industry, deploring the way that, in his view, Britain had colonised India largely to provide a vast captive market for Midlands mill owners to sell their tatty mass-produced wares to on the cheap, thereby destroying the traditional Indian economic way of life, which he saw as being based around happy villagers spinning and weaving. As such, Gandhi wished to make India largely self-sufficient in food, clothing and other such necessities, and to reject Western consumer goods. Viewing the free market as stoking the artificial 'multiplication of wants' – persuading people to buy things they don't really need – he wanted the Indian economy to be based upon the 'fulfilment of needs' instead. Rather than assessing an industry's value in

Fashion-conscious Mahatma Gandhi.
(Public domain)

monetary terms, economists should assess the effect it had on a person's soul; so working in a profitable and efficient textile factory was good for GDP but bad for the soul, whereas working as an independent small-scale craftsman weaving rugs on your own was inefficient and bad for GDP, but good for the soul. Almost always, the latter option was to be preferred, with spiritual dividends, not shareholder dividends, being most honoured. Things like GDP were false measures, and you should prefer to experience rises on the karmic wheel, not on the stock market. Desiring 'an ordered anarchy', Gandhi saw no point in India continuing as it had done under British rule, only with brown-faced bureaucrats instead of pink-faced ones.

Pursuing a capitalist mode of life would show the Indian people's minds remained colonised, so he proposed that every village become an *ashram*, a sort of self-supporting agricultural and cloth-producing commune whose contact with the outer world would be limited, and where spiritual development would be privileged over material wealth – a bit like the vegetarian commune Silvio Gesell had once inhabited. The government's main job would be to provide a supportive national framework within which such *ashrams* could flourish, and then leave everyone alone, as well as guaranteeing a perpetual market for village-spun cloth by forcing all public employees to wear hand-produced clothes to work (they would also ensure that spinning yarn was one of the major subjects on the school curriculum). To copy the European-style economic structure imposed by the

British Raj would be to transform India into 'Englishtan', Gandhi mocked. Maybe Indians could make use of small-scale Western technologies which made their lives easier on an individual scale, like Singer sewing machines, but not giant inhuman factory production lines. If this policy meant fewer consumer goods in the shops, then all the better. Indians should renounce all possessions, as Gandhi had done, and get their hands dirty working the soil so as to maintain contact with the eternal truths of Nature. Everybody, he said, should perform some 'bread labour' like Schumacher did in his garden at Holcombe. India's first post-independence Prime Minister Jawaharlal Nehru (1889–1964) did not like the idea of getting his hands dirty in this way, however, and chose the more mainstream economic option of turning India into a low-rent economic Englishtan after all.[24]

Kumarappa the Crapper

One of Gandhi's main allies was his friend J. C. Kumarappa (1892–1960), a philosopher and Professor of Economics who was imprisoned four times by colonial authorities for his prominent role in the independence movement. A committed Christian and former chartered accountant, Kumarappa considered Gandhi's economic programme was just what Christ would have wanted for India Himself, had He been in Gandhi's sandals. Kumarappa used a 1945 spell in prison to write a strange tract, *The Economy of Permanence: A Quest for a Social Order Based on Non-Violence*. Much of it repeats Gandhi's ideas outlined above, but some of Kumarappa's own additional notions were a little odder. Known as 'The Green Gandhian', Kumarappa promoted conservation and the use of clean, renewable energy, and possessed outspoken opinions upon chemical fertilisers strikingly similar to those of Rudolf Steiner; he proposed a whole natural industry be created in stirring together piles of human waste with the bones of dead animals, to make horrible compost. Bones and human excrement should not then be made available for export, he said (who would *want* them?), but kept close to where they had been dropped and transformed into manure cakes, so villagers and their cattle could fuel the local circle of life, not rely on any foreign muck. As a side benefit, said Kumarappa, this would also keep the toilet-less village streets clean of their residents' vast piles of rotting poo. He should have been called 'The Brown Gandhian', not the Green one.[25]

Kumarappa also made a close study of the alleged economic systems he thought had been adopted by various members of the animal kingdom, closely observing the birds and the bees to see what humans could learn from them. According to Kumarappa, there was an entire economic cycle at work in Nature, in which most animals, acting out of their own self-interest and self-preservation, accidentally contributed to the well-being of the whole of Creation. For example, in burrowing through the soil in search of food and water, worms churned up that very same soil, allowing plants and trees to take root as a by-product of their wriggling. Or a bird may eat a fruit, swallowing its seed, then plop it back out elsewhere, allowing another fruit-tree to sprout, from which its avian descendents will later be able to gain more food. The worm and the bird are unlikely to be particularly well-versed in the concept of sustainable forestry, but they inadvertently do their bit to promote it nonetheless, with their selfishness becoming generosity by mistake.[26] Strangely, this directly mirrors one of Adam Smith's most famous passages in *The Wealth of Nations*, where he argues that, in the free market:

> It is not through the benevolence of the butcher, the brewer or the baker that we expect our dinner, but their regard to their own self-interest. We address ourselves not to their humanity but to their self-love, and never talk to them of our necessities, but of their advantages.[27]

Apparently, therefore, animals and plants are free-market capitalists, but Kumarappa appears not to realise this, although he does claim that, when a bird has a distant poo, it is performing actual work, and when it later eats another fruit or berry, it is being paid Nature's wages for the prior labours of its anus. Kumarappa then creates a complex moral hierarchy for the 'economic' activities of animals and vegetables, ranging from financial parasites like fleas, fungi and blood-drinking tigers at one end of the scale to members of the 'Economy of Service' at the other end, such as mother-birds who, being spiritually advanced, feed their young meals of fresh insects through pure love, gaining nothing tangible from such labour themselves. Newly-independent Indians, argued Kumarappa, should aim to imitate the divine wisdom of mother-birds and transform their free nation into a gigantic Gandhian Economy of Service.[28]

Dead Rubbers

To act for short-term economic benefit at the expense of the future of mankind is only to kill mankind in the long-run, he says, citing the example of condom factory owners, who privilege short-term lust over long-term repopulation of the planet. As if to reinforce the insanity of such things, Kumarappa claims condoms make you go mad, leading to 'nervous disorders and derangement of mind' – but on the other hand, so does having children.[29] Therefore, what we needed was not pursuit of quasi-sexual immediate economic gratification, but the deferred gratification of *total economic sustainability*. Kumarappa even imitated Gesell by labelling money as unnatural because, unlike crops, it did not rot, cash's comparative immortality compared to their vegetable wares encouraging senseless short-term thinking by greedy farmers.[30] Unfortunately, the restrictive legal measures Kumarappa proposed to try and create his ideal Gandhian society – making farmers apply to the State for permission to grow the precise crops they wanted to grow, permission which would be automatically denied if the State thought they might be able to make a profit from them, because all crops should be intended almost exclusively for local village use, and valuable export-products like tobacco banned – would be calculated only to produce mass poverty and probable starvation. Surplus milk and honey could be traded locally for the different surpluses of nearby villages, such as wheat, but that was basically it. Agricultural exporters were nothing but 'traitors to the land' who had to be stopped at all costs, because the soil was 'a social asset', not something for private individuals to make money from.[31] Stalin and Mao would have said something similar. Maybe it's a good job Gandhi got shot after all.

Reading Kumarappa's book, it seems obvious Schumacher's coal-related moment of enlightenment sitting behind his desk at the NCB was inspired by it. Consider the following passage:

> There are certain things found in Nature which apparently have no life and do not grow or increase, and so get exhausted or consumed by being used. The world possesses a certain stock or reservoir of such materials as coal, petroleum, ores or minerals like iron, copper, gold, etc. These being available in fixed quantities, may be said to be 'transient', while the current of overflowing water in a river or the constantly growing timber of a forest may be considered 'permanent' as their stock is inexhaustible in the service of man when only the flow or increase [in economic terms, the 'surplus'] is taken advantage of ... The secret of Nature's permanency lies in the cycle of life.[32]

Appropriately enough, Schumacher was recycling other people's ideas and repackaging them anew for the West. As if to repay his imaginative debt, Schumacher made a trip to India in 1961. Finding horrific poverty everywhere he looked, he concluded India was a dying civilisation, whose culture and economy had been fatally polluted by the long incursion of the British Empire, and then through the well-meaning but catastrophic influence of transnational institutions like the IMF. According to Schumacher, the vast amounts of international aid pouring into India at such bodies' behest only served to create tiny oases of high-tech industrialisation amidst a morass of abject destitution, putting traditional small-scale workers out of business on a vast scale and making poverty worse. If aid-funded factories destroyed entire cottage-industries in their wake, then who was going to buy their mass-produced goods? And if there was nobody left able to buy such goods, then how were the factories meant to stay open? The question of how to provide India with what Gandhi had once called 'production *by* the masses rather than mass-production' had not been solved.[33] The situation seemed hopeless, and the general impression Schumacher got from India was much less positive in nature than that he had gained while visiting Burma. There, the perennial ideas of economic and spiritual wisdom still prevailed – for now. It was Schumacher's quest to ensure that they continued to do so for as long as possible.

Burmese Days

When Schumacher arrived in the Burmese capital of Rangoon in January 1955, he was absolutely delighted by the poverty he found lurking all around him. This may sound callous, but it was not, because the Burmese people, in their complete ignorance of Western standards of living, appeared much happier with their lot than the average Westerner did. The ordinary folk he met were all smiles, with Schumacher praising their 'innocence', 'dignified and composed manners' and 'loveable' nature. The Burmese, he thought, were simply *better* than most whites were, and the best advice he could give them would be to ignore any 'nonsense from the West' and go on 'following their own better natures' instead. Measures of GDP made the nation sound dirt-poor but because they had so few artificial wants in terms of consumer goods, the Burmese came across as being genuinely content. Instead of measuring poverty purely in crude financial terms, perhaps poverty should be measured in cultural terms too, or by the rate of happiness of the people – in which case, Burma was far richer than Great Britain.[34] Schumacher later admitted the real purpose of his visit to Burma had actually been to learn the advanced Buddhist mediation technique of *Sattipatthana* – he spent his weekends locked away in a Buddhist monastery, not a hotel room[35] – and this latest revelation about the true values to be sought within an economy stood as yet another great enlightenment in his life. As he concluded: 'In Burma the people are so happy because they have no wants; they have so much time because they have no labour-saving machinery and methods; their heads and hearts are kept free for inner matters because they are not obsessed with outer things.'[36]

Tragically, however, Burma's leaders had surrounded themselves with American economists whose outlook was wholly materialist in nature. Pushing the idea of imitating the economic schemes that had successfully revived West Germany, the Washington advisors did not seem to realise – or care – that Germany was a Western country, filled with Western traditions, while Burma was an Eastern land, with Eastern ways of doing things. For the Americans, there was only one kind of economy because there was only one kind of man – *Homo Americanus*, as embodied by themselves. Needless to say, Schumacher disagreed. 'The science of economics,' he perceived, 'does not stand on its own two feet; it is derived from a view of the meaning and purpose of life.' Economic models from the West were based upon a materialistic outlook on life, and the pursuit of profit, whereas the native economic models traditionally pursued within nations like Burma were based upon other precepts and assumptions about human nature. As such, by encouraging non-Western lands to implement Western models, which were utterly alien to them, we were doing them more harm than good. 'All peoples,' Schumacher once wrote, 'have always discovered a pattern of living which fitted their peculiar natural surroundings.'[37]

Schumacher placed these views within a paper entitled *Economics in a Buddhist Country*, later presented to the Economic and Social Council of Burma. They were not best pleased to be told that the US-influenced path of economic modernisation they were embarking upon was not only unlikely to work, but also 'evil, destructive [and] uneconomic'. The government should reverse its policies, Schumacher advised, and dismiss its blind Western advisers. Rather than trying to build up Burma's cities, resources should be diverted towards the countryside, to develop a culture of economic self-sufficiency. Why pay to import rice when your own people could grow it? Why import clothes when rural cottage-industries could, as Gandhi had dreamed, be nurtured to provide for the nation's needs? The notion of economic 'progress' (the inverted commas are Schumacher's own) only held true up to the point that national self-sufficiency in terms of life's basic necessities was achieved. Starving masses or homeless people wandering about in rags were obviously bad things, but once such problems had been solved, any further levels of economic development only led to a Western-style consumer culture, which would be bad for the Burmese soul. Furthermore, as the world's coal, steel and oil supplies would one day run out, by trying to build an economy reliant upon such materials Burma would condemn itself to future death. By avoiding reliance upon such things, however, Burmese society would ensure its own permanence, and outlive the forthcoming demise of the West, whose civilisation 'bears the sign of death' upon it, being a mere 'abnormality in the history of mankind'. The choice before the Burmese nation was between economic 'misery, sufficiency and surfeit' and, as Buddha himself had recommended, it was always wise to take the Middle Path. Burmese officials disagreed, however, and the only path Schumacher himself would be taking any time soon was one leading straight back to London.[38]

Traditional Thinking

Back in England, Schumacher systematically delved into holy texts from every major religion, including his formerly hated Christianity, concluding all creeds were but different ways of expressing the same basic truths about the world. He also began to read authors belonging to a philosophical movement called 'Traditionalism', in particular René Guénon (1886–1951), a French student of hermetic knowledge who spent much of his life in Egypt. In books such as *The Crisis of the Modern World*, Guénon enunciated his fears that the modern West was due for a major collapse. Western global supremacy, he argued, was based upon nothing more substantial than industrial and technological superiority. Beneath this, there was nothing; no spiritual foundations whatsoever. Like Schumacher, Guénon felt the contemporary West was 'a veritable anomaly', as it was the only civilisation throughout all of history that had been inspired by a false and misguided doctrine of materialism and reason and an all-pervading cult of 'progress', qualities Guénon deemed illusory. The post-medieval age was nothing but an age of 'inversion', in which all true virtues had been turned upside-down, with their evil and opposing twins reigning in their stead; logic triumphed over mysticism, for instance, and the urban dominated over the rural.

Borrowing a concept from Hinduism, Guénon deemed his own day to lie within the temporal bounds of the *kali yuga*, a period of precipitate and apocalyptic decline in all things – even consumer goods. One of the central signs of the *kali yuga* was the privileging of quantity over quality, as with the cheap mass-produced goods which, ever since the economic upheaval of the Industrial Revolution, had been rolling out of Europe's mechanised factories at an unstoppable rate. (Rudolf Steiner, too, had once linked the sad decline in potatoes and other mass-produced crops back to the *kali yuga*.[39]) In order for our civilisation to survive, Guénon argued, we had to imitate the examples of the East, and of Islamic societies, where there were still worthwhile things left for people to believe in. His argument was not that incompatible foreign spiritual practices like Islam had to be imported here wholesale, but that we must 'restore to the West an appropriate traditional civilisation' of its own.

The specific traditional wisdom Guénon thought the West should re-found its civilisation upon anew was the *philosophia perennis*, or 'Perennial Philosophy', a term coined by the Renaissance priest and Platonist Marsilio Ficino (1433–99). Ficino was intrigued by the way that certain arguments made by the ancient Greek philosopher Plato (427BC–347BC) could be used to support the teachings of Christianity, even though Plato had lived about 350–400 years prior to Christ's birth. His solution to this puzzle was that even before Christianity had been revealed to mankind, God had seeded the world with various messages, which could be used to support its truth. He had done this by creating a kind of primordial root-religion at the beginning of time, the Perennial Philosophy, whose tenets, lying implicit within the universe itself, were in accordance with those of Christianity, and from which all other subsequent 'true' religions and spiritual philosophies had later grown. Thus, to study Platonism was simply a way to access the truths of Christianity by another means. By the nineteenth century, the corpus of the Perennial Philosophy had been added to as knowledge of the religions of the East, namely Buddhism, Hinduism and Islam, came increasingly to be spread by scholars and travellers with links to Europe's growing colonies in Asia. However, while the width of the Perennial Philosophy's textual corpus might have expanded in recent centuries, its mainstream influence had not, with newer modes of rationalistic and scientific Enlightenment thought pushing all meaningful knowledge of such things to the margins of society, to be pored over only by obscure occultists. Both Guénon and Schumacher alike felt the time was now ripe for such ancient wisdom to be rediscovered by wider Western society.[40]

For those in the know, it is easy to see the influence of Traditionalist thinkers upon Schumacher's own writing. The following passage of his, for example, clearly derives from Guénon's negative ideas about quantity replacing quality:

> The reign of quantity celebrates its greatest triumphs in 'The Market'. Everything is equated with everything else. To equate things means to give them a price and thus to make them exchangeable. To the extent that economic thinking is based on the market, it takes the sacredness out of life, because there can be nothing sacred in something that has a price.[41]

Progressive Decline

The Reign of Quantity was the title of a 1945 book by Guénon, whose argument is rather interesting. Firstly, Guénon argues that, if 'the domain of manifestation that constitutes our world' is considered *in toto*, it represents a kind of overwhelming unity, akin to that of God. However, as 'the existences contained therein … gradually move away from the principal unity, [they] become progressively less qualitative and more quantitative'. Creation as a whole, like God, might be considered perfect; but once things start to separate themselves out from this wider whole, they become progressively less so. Imagine you look out to sea, and view the magnificence of the ocean, perfect, blue and beautiful. Then you pick up a beaker-full of water from this apparently flawless source, and find it is full of floating crumbs of faeces from a nearby coastal waste-pipe. The sea as a whole is qualitative, or perfect in nature; the beaker full of excrement is quantitative. If you could bottle up all the sea-water from the coast, and were left with millions of tiny beakers full of brown-tinged filth, you'd soon see that, once separated from the mother-sea, the individual beakers do not share the ocean's beauty, because the glorious sea is greater than the sum of its shitty parts.

The Western industrialised world, argued Guénon, was busily engaged in just such a unity-destroying project. By pushing the pernicious myth of 'equality', the West was pointlessly educating its young citizens on the fundamentally flawed belief that all of them were equally educable, even though this was obviously not true, and giving everyone a standardised education. The further the uniformity of this educational straitjacket was imposed, the less likely any genuinely remarkable children would be able to develop and express their genius properly. To level out opportunity thus meant only to level-down those minds that would otherwise rise above the masses. Modern education was, therefore, yet another shift from the qualitative towards the quantitative, one that Western man was determined to impose upon other races too, via colonialism, 'so as to make the whole world uniform', but in a negative way, a 'sort of caricature of unity' most unlike the primal unity of the Godhead. For Guénon the mass-production of low-quality identikit minds was simply another aspect of the mass-production of low-quality identikit objects, designed to make men into robots. Bestselling objects were lent genuine mass appeal despite their often low quality only on account of the fact that people's desires had all been homogenised through the brainwashing effects of education, advertising and the media. After all, mass-production of consumer objects will only work if the consumers' souls and wants become mass-produced, too; yet another victory of inversion for the evil forces of the *kali yuga*.[42]

Such alleged 'progress', wrote Guénon, was only 'dragging humanity towards the pit where pure quantity reigns', with the kind of pseudo-education that aimed to make school leavers equally fit to become bricklayers, factory hands, delivery drivers, office workers or housepainters in the name of the great god Economy robbing every man of the right to a true sense of vocation. Once, many men had been lucky enough to have possessed crafts, which were qualitative in nature; now, almost all men merely had jobs, which were quantitative. For a medieval stonemason, who required personal skill and a capacity for invention to do his job, be that carving a gargoyle or lettering a gravestone, there was a continuum between his craft and the world of art. Now, however, a small minority of fortunate fops went around claiming to be sculptors, a calling which was generally regarded as an elite pastime, totally divorced from the world of normal employment, 'a sort of closed domain having no connection with the rest of human activity'. So, there were still a few artists left, but hardly any artisans. However, during the medieval period, when people had allegedly worked not only for their own economic benefit but also for the larger benefit of God and Christendom, Guénon viewed craftsmen of the old guild systems as seeing themselves as part of a greater tradition, links in a chain between craftsmen of the past and future, and thus living parts of a greater qualitative whole. Furthermore, while for the average modern Westerner the religious realm began and ended at the church-door (if they attended at all), for more qualitative cultures such as medieval Christendom or the Islamic world, 'religion is not something restricted, narrowly bounded and occupying a place apart, without effective influence on anything else ... on the contrary ... it embraces within its domain everything which constitutes that existence and particularly social life', including the world of work, sentiments Gandhi and Kumarappa would have agreed with.[43]

That was why so many guilds once had ritual initiation ceremonies for new members, as with the Freemasons, because in such a qualitative culture 'every profession is a priesthood'. Once, 'the most ordinary actions of life [had] something "religious" in them', said Guénon, with everything sharing an aspect of the sacred, and every sincerely-produced product being infused in some small way with the personality of the individual artisan and the tiny yet discernible share of the Godhead which dwelled within him. Now, though, economic gurus preach the virtues of mobility of labour and transferrable skills, meaning each worker is encouraged to view his (increasingly temporary) profession as being 'something wholly outside himself, having no real connection with what he really is, that by virtue of which he is himself, and not anyone else.' The modern labour-market forces workers to become quantitative in nature rather than qualitative: 'individuals are regarded as no more than interchangeable and purely numerical units', a radical and inverted break with tradition which would rupture the divinely-ordained cosmic order, causing the West to implode. After all, by forcing square human pegs into round job-based holes in this way, occidental man was going against the divine Hindu principle of *svadharma*, which taught that everything had its right and proper place within the cosmic dance. Abandoning vocation for mere convenience of employment was thus a sin against God and Nature – so burn down your local JobCentre![44]

The Pound in Your Pocket

You should burn your banknotes too, because in a chapter of his book entitled 'The Degeneration of Coinage', Guénon decries our current monetary system as yet another manifestation of the quantity-obsessed *kali yuga*. Money, Guénon says, was once qualitative in nature, having had sacred import and been covered all over in traditional religious symbols, with mystic cults such as the Druids supposedly having a hand in its design. If no part of ancient society had been wholly separate from the religious realm, as Guénon thought, then this fact must have applied to coinage, too. Also, due to the fact they used to contain actual portions of gold, coins were once based upon genuine physical stores of God's wealth, unlike the Treasury-printed fiat currency banknotes of today. In this age when everyone knows the price of everything and the value of nothing, however, the old qualitative aspect of money has disappeared to be replaced entirely with the quantitative; indeed, says Guénon, nowadays 'nobody is able any longer to conceive that money can represent anything other than a simple quantity'.

A pound coin today is what a loaf of bread costs, not a holy manifestation of the temporal and spiritual power of the God-chosen Queen whose head it currently bears. Coins still have value, but the word 'value' used to have a higher meaning beyond 'price'.

However, the more quantitative our concept of money became, for Guénon the less real it became too, with the probable end result that it would eventually end up disappearing altogether. Consider the value of the pound coin, just mentioned; today it (might) buy you a full loaf, but fifty years ago you could have bought several loaves and still have had enough change for the bus-fare home and a fish-and-chip supper afterwards, at least according to our grandparents' recollection of the matter. Did this mean that the pound coin was slowly dying, that all money was now nothing but Gesellian *Schwundgeld* whether we liked it or not? Maybe so. We no longer have halfpenny pieces, even though you could buy a whole newspaper for one within living memory, and there have been repeated calls from retailers for the Royal Mint to stop producing pennies these days too, as they have shrunk to almost nil value in terms of purchasing power, and represent only an irritating burden to shopkeepers. Inflation and the excessive printing of money – nowadays also called *quantitative* easing, remember – have indeed helped destroy the value of our coinage, both in terms of monetary value and aesthetic worth, with now-obsolete coins like threepenny bits being far more attractive and collectible than their modern equivalents. For Guénon, the slow disappearance of value from our coinage was a symbolic foretaste of the forthcoming vanishing of Western civilisation itself, which was currently (quantitatively) easing itself out of existence:

> Since money lost all guarantee of a superior [religious] order, it has seen its own actual quantitative value, or what is called in the jargon of the economists its 'purchasing power', becoming ceaselessly less and less, so that it can be imagined that, when it arrives at a limit that is getting ever nearer, it will have lost every justification for its existence, even all merely 'practical' or 'material' justification, and will disappear of itself ... from human existence ... for since pure quantity is by its nature beneath all existence, when the trend toward it is pressed to its extreme limit, as in the case of money ... the end can only be a real dissolution ... the real goal of the tendency that is dragging men and things toward pure quantity can only be the final dissolution of the present world.[45]

Science Fictions

Some of Guénon's ideas may seem odd, at least to mass-produced modern minds, but E. F. Schumacher had some sympathy with them, concluding that taking steps to actively reduce rates of industrial productivity might be the best way to overcome the current *kali yuga* reign of cheap and nasty consumer goods, and make them once again more qualitative in nature. Lowering productivity to one sixth of present-day standards, Schumacher wrote, would give us 'six times as much time for any piece of work we choose to undertake – enough to make a really good job of it, to enjoy oneself, to produce real quality, even to make things beautiful' as with Guénon's ancient craftsmen.[46] Another of Schumacher's ideas Guénon would have applauded was the idea that Western philosophy had taken a terrible wrong-turn during the Renaissance and Enlightenment, with early materialist philosophers of science like Francis Bacon (1561–1626) and René Descartes (1596–1650) representing no increase in human understanding but a 'withdrawal from wisdom'. This opinion chimed with Guénon's notion of inversion because the very word 'philosophy' was supposed to mean love ('philo') of wisdom ('sophia'), whereas modern-day scientific materialist conceptions of the world privileged, in a Traditionalist view, the very reverse of sagacity.[47] Schumacher made an important distinction between the old occult sciences of Perennial Wisdom, which he termed 'science for understanding', and the degraded materialistic science of Bacon and Descartes, or 'science for manipulation':

> The purpose of the former was the enlightenment of the person and his liberation; the purpose of the latter is power. 'Knowledge itself is power,' said Francis Bacon, and Descartes promised men they would become 'masters and possessors of Nature' ... Science for understanding has often been called 'wisdom', while the name 'science' remained reserved for what I call 'science for manipulation' ... This has been the history of Western thought since Descartes ... The old science looked upon Nature as God's handiwork and man's mother; the new science tends to look upon Nature as an adversary to be conquered or a resource to be quarried and exploited.[48]

Similar views were held by Rudolf Steiner, who towards the end of his (most recent known) life came to believe that a malign spiritual entity or 'super-sensible Being' of the Anti-Christ type named Ahriman was due to incarnate himself upon Earth, and was busily beaming out 'Ahrimanic forces' across the planet which aimed to lead mankind astray by making him worship the kind of 'science of manipulation' Schumacher later associated with Bacon and Descartes. According to Steiner, these Ahrimanic forces had been doing their evil work ever since the Renaissance (or 'the Fifth Post-Atlantean epoch', as Steiner preferred – basically an alternative *kali yuga*), causing Western man to see Creation in a way which was 'robbed of spirit, robbed of soul, even of life', with the universe remodelled as 'a great mechanism' rather than a living organism or emanation of the Godhead. Ahriman was 'the power that makes man dry, prosaic, philistine – that ossifies him and brings him to the superstition of materialism', an outlook which would make man easy meat to 'fall a prey to Ahriman when he appears in human form' in future years. Ahriman had 'the greatest possible interest in bringing men chemistry, physics, biology and so on ... and in making man believe that these are absolute truths', but as Steiner had shown by rebelling against the tyranny of nitrogen-based fertilisers, running your society upon scientific methods alone was a sure-fire path towards unleashing moral and environmental downfall. Even worse, Ahrimanic forces had now managed to convince Western man to create the nonsensical field of 'social science' as yet another means through which the 'scientific superstition' of the future Anti-Christ could spread. The chief agent behind the promotion of such evil Positivist claptrap as sociology, Steiner said, was the figure of the economist, a fairly recent arrival upon the world scene:

> For, you see, Ahriman skilfully prepares his goal beforehand; ever since the Reformation and the Renaissance, the economist has been emerging in modern civilisation as the modern governing type. That is an actual historical fact ... Rulers are in fact merely the handymen, the understrappers of the economists. And all that has resulted by way of 'law' and 'justice' ... is simply a consequence of what economically-oriented men have thought.[49]

Obviously, Schumacher himself did not literally believe in the coming incarnation of Ahriman, but Steiner's ideas about the sinister figure's influence over modern man may have been enjoyed by him in a metaphorical way, as a personification of the inverted economic processes Guénon had been talking about in less outré terms. While Schumacher was not a full-blown Traditionalist *per se*, it can clearly be seen that he absorbed elements of their message, and in 1971 the former arch-atheist embraced the traditional ancestral religion of his race and became a Catholic. At last, he had escaped from the 'anti-Christian trauma' of his youth, with its hard-line atheism and materialism; he even began to read the Rome-tinged economic tracts of the Distributionists.[50] Soon, it would be time for him to write his own Good Book trying to reintroduce this same Perennial Wisdom rediscovered by Ficino during the Renaissance back into the minds of a much wider audience than René Guénon's brilliant but complex works had managed to attract.

It's a Small World

In 1970, Schumacher took semi-retirement from the NCB, and settled down to spend time writing the book which would make him a household name, 1973's *Small Is Beautiful: Economics As If People Mattered*. This widely-read text – some of whose royalty-cheques made their way to the Soil

Association – sold millions of copies, opened numerous doors for its author, and is often cited as one of the major launch-pads for the then-nascent Green movement which has become so popular today. In its wake, Schumacher became something of a celebrity, asked to give lectures all across the globe, meeting Presidents and Prime Ministers, hoping to get his message across. The central core of Schumacher's unexpected best-seller was derived not only from his own experience of a life spent mixing with many of the greatest economic theorists of his day, but also from his reading of less mainstream figures like Guénon, Gandhi and Gurdjieff. If Schumacher's moral were to be summed up in a single phrase, it would simply be that the modern West represents a short-sighted retreat from Perennial Wisdom. As he put it:

> Ever-bigger machines, entailing ever-bigger concentrations of economic power and exerting ever-greater violence against the environment, do not represent progress: they are a denial of wisdom. Wisdom demands a new orientation of science and technology towards the organic, the gentle, the nonviolent, the elegant and the beautiful.[51]

It would be easy to read Schumacher's book as a long economic diatribe against nothing less than the increasing incursion of the *kali yuga*. The most interesting chapter was entitled 'Buddhist Economics', and drew upon Schumacher's experiences in the East. Here, he referenced the concept of 'Right Livelihood' as espoused by Buddha as an element of the Noble Eightfold Path towards enlightenment. The key concepts of Right Livelihood were considered practical expressions of wisdom within the world of work, and involved ideas such as balanced living, lack of greed, and the importance of honest toil for the soul.[52]

All Work and No Play

Having introduced this concept, Schumacher went on to lay out many of the notions he had presented to the Burmese government twenty years beforehand. Western economic ideas, he argued, were inapplicable in the East, and often a great social evil in the West itself. In particular, he laid into the idea of division of labour lauded by Adam Smith in *The Wealth of Nations*, where the example of a pin factory was used to demonstrate how breaking down the manufacturing process into as many small stages of unskilled, repetitive labour as possible allowed pins to be made in a more economically efficient manner than by getting skilled craftsmen to make each one in its entirety from start to finish. From the point of view of Right Livelihood, however, such an approach was totally misguided, as it gave the worker no chance to develop his natural creativity, and thus his soul – toiling in a factory was not exactly the kind of beneficial 'work' Gurdjieff would have recommended to wake his disciples up. To a Buddhist, argued Schumacher, such unskilled mass-production demonstrated 'a greater concern with goods than with people, an evil lack of compassion and a soul-destroying degree of attachment to the most primitive side of this worldly existence.' Because the central aim of Buddhism was 'the purification of human character', following Adam Smith's prescriptions would have a negative effect upon mankind, as a man's work helps form his character – 'you are what you do repeatedly' as Aristotle once said. However, work when 'properly conducted in conditions of human dignity and freedom blesses those who do it and equally their products.'[53] By adhering to Smith's wrongheaded teachings, said Schumacher, Western economists and industrialists were:

> ... standing the truth on its head by considering goods as more important than people and consumption as more important than creative activity. It means shifting the emphasis from the worker to the product of work, that is, from the human to the subhuman, a surrender to the forces of evil ... While the materialist [Western consumer] is mainly interested in goods, the Buddhist is mainly interested in liberation [from them] ... For the modern economist this is very difficult to understand. He's used to measuring the 'standard of living' by the amount of annual consumption, assuming all the time that a man who consumes more is 'better off' than a man who consumes less. A Buddhist economist would consider this approach exceedingly irrational: since consumption is merely a means to human well-being, the aim should be to obtain the maximum of well-being with the minimum of consumption ... and the smallest possible input of toil. The less toil there is, the more time and strength is left for artistic creativity.[54]

You might hope that the increasing amount of automation beginning to be seen in the West would free up more spare time for workers to spend in useful leisure, but this was not so, said Schumacher. Instead, with increasing mass-production came a corresponding increase in the artificial wants of the public, thus meaning that many workers had less free time than ever before. Just as bad were the mental strains placed upon Western professionals and office workers, whose labour, while still often meaningless and unsatisfying, had a tendency to take over their lives:

> The widespread substitution of mental strain for physical strain is no advantage from our point of view. Proper physical work, even if strenuous, does not absorb a great deal of the power of attention, but mental work does ... I say, therefore, that it is a great evil – perhaps the greatest evil – of modern industrial society that, through its immensely involved nature, it imposes an undue nervous strain and absorbs an undue proportion of man's attention.[55]

Buddha had taught what was needed was a Middle Way, and Schumacher aimed to provide one with his concept of 'intermediate technology'.[56] Examples of such intermediate technology might include more efficient and hard-wearing hand-ploughs, potters' wheels powered by foot-pedals, steel-rimmed wheels for ox-carts, and other such instances of traditional tools given a modern twist which may, Schumacher hoped, allow individual craftsmen and small-scale businesses to compete with soulless factories by increasing their efficiency while still allowing their labour to retain an element of creative dignity to it – 'Technology with a Human Face', as Schumacher had it, imitating Gandhi's approval of Singer sewing machines. Schumacher talked of the pressing need to 'make things simple again' in the world of work, on account of the fact that 'modern technology has deprived man of the kind of work that he enjoys most, creative, useful work with hands and brains, and given him plenty of work of a fragmented kind, most of which he does not enjoy at all.' While Schumacher admitted this state of affairs was now so advanced it would be rather difficult for mankind to reverse, 'we jolly well have to have the courage to dream.'[57]

Green Vegetables

Much of Schumacher's book argued the need for a sustainable economy, an idea which derived ultimately not only from Buddhism and his work at the NCB, but also secretly from Rudolf Steiner and his eco-friendly biodynamic farming.[58] Echoing J. C. Kumarappa, he spoke of the need for 'an economics of permanence', saying this was the only way for economics to be considered wise. Schumacher recommended people should be encouraged to return to the land, as he had done in his farm-cum-garden at Holcombe, so workers could 'regain the dignity of man'. By his own assessment, 'we should be searching for policies to reconstruct rural culture, to open the land for the gainful occupation of larger numbers of people, whether it be on a full-time or a part-time basis, and to orientate all our actions on the land towards the threefold ideal of health, beauty and permanence'; echoes of Steiner's 'Threefold Commonwealth' and the dreams of cow-loving G. K. Chesterton.[59] One way we could do this was by rethinking our attitude towards trees. By endlessly chopping down forests for industry and fuel without replanting new ones, mankind was despoiling the environment and ignoring the ancient injunction of Buddha to respect trees, Schumacher said. 'Much of the economic decay of southeast Asia', he wailed, 'is undoubtedly due to a heedless and shameful neglect of trees.'[60]

Schumacher himself was indirectly responsible for the death of numerous trees, however, as his book sold so well. Sadly, while Schumacher became widely lauded as some kind of guru, the message gleaned from his text by the vast majority of its readers was simply one of Green environmentalism, with all the coded references to Guénon and the Perennial Philosophy falling upon deaf ears. The book's success roughly coincided with the formation of eco-campaign groups like Greenpeace and Friends of the Earth, and it was interpreted at the time very much in light of such organisations' newly articulated concerns – Schumacher's plea of 'Save the Trees!' found an eager contemporary audience, for example, but one which wholly ignored the Buddhist teachings underpinning it. Schumacher suffered a sudden death in 1977, probably caused by the stresses of travelling the world to meet uncomprehending politicians. He may have attracted a large quantity of readers but, as Guénon could have warned him, that is no substitute for *quality* of readers. Nonetheless, while Green movements may have largely ignored the esoteric aspects of Schumacher's thought, some of his economic ideas have occasionally been adopted and adapted, most notoriously in the case of the 2015 General Election Manifesto of the British Green Party, which memorably included a promise to make us all poorer for our own good, whether we liked it or not. Among the many rather unpopular pledges in this unintentionally amusing document were promises to lower the level of international trade and creep back towards a system of barter, to encourage subsistence-level agriculture, and to set a target of 'zero or negative economic growth to slow consumption and help the planet'. Asked whether she really wished to push the nation into recession, the Green Party's then leader, Natalie Bennett, replied:

> It depends if you want to measure success by GDP. Even the people who invented GDP said it's a lousy tool for [measuring] progress. The age of significant growth is over. We need to look at human measures now, not profits but a better quality of life. We have been driven by this neo-liberal Thatcherite idea that what motivates people is money. We want to focus on the fact that people don't just want to work to earn more and more money, they want to do other things.[61]

Bennett went on to urge voters to spoil their ballot papers by scribbling a 'rude word' ('growth', maybe?) on them if no local candidates' opinions were in accordance with their own. Perhaps E. F. Schumacher would have lent the Greens his vote had he still been alive, even if only from pity, but precious few other people did. Possibly voters did not particularly like the sound of Bennett's policy of reducing international trade and opposing globalisation in favour of 'local community import substitution, rather than export promotion' and 'local food growing in place of cash-crops for the international market'. This sounds rather like Gandhi and Kumarappa's ideas about encouraging local cottage-industries to flourish, but this is Great Britain, not the subcontinent, and Schumacher never advocated massive deindustrialisation on the scale imagined by the Greens, merely a more sensitive approach towards issues of sustainability and labour. He advised us to lower production in certain industries, yes, to reduce pollution and reliance upon fossil-fuels, and encouraged people to get back in touch with the land, but he didn't want us to close down all our factories!

If every town and village made its own products, in a form of ultra-local autarky, then not only would you be unable to purchase various useful devices from televisions to telephones (do you know anyone in your street who can source all the necessary raw materials and then make them from scratch?), all products, including genuine essentials like food and clothing, would be vastly more expensive due to the abandonment of economies of scale – at a time when people would, simultaneously, be becoming poorer by design. Also, small-scale subsistence farming of the kind imagined by the Greens provides so little food that, quite apart from people going hungry, you would need to use more soil to produce crops on, thus leading to less land being left free as a habitat for wildlife. And if every town had its own blast-furnace for local production of steel, say, as was tried in Communist China during the disastrous 1950s and '60s economic experiments of Chairman Mao (1893–1976), there would end up being more pollution, everywhere, rather than just some, somewhere. Or, to put it another way, the Greens' plans were dangerous and adolescent in equal measure. Similar criticisms have sometimes been laid by economists at E. F. Schumacher's door down the years too – one literary riposte to his most famous work was memorably titled *Small Is Stupid* – but you have to remember that Schumacher in fact recommended a Buddhist Middle Path as regards such things, not an extremist one like the stupid Greens.[62]

From Marx to Madonna

Another person who anticipated some of Schumacher's thinking was the Russian philosopher, priest and economic theoriser Sergei Nikolaevich Bulgakov (1871–1944), who developed the notion of a so-called 'Sophic Economy' which centred not upon the creation or distribution of wealth, but worship of the divine goddess Sophia, the spirit of holy wisdom or 'rightness', and an aspect of the Lord God Himself. Given this, some might dispute whether Bulgakov was really an economist at all, but he certainly *thought* he was, and his writings make copious reference to the likes of Karl Marx (1818–83) and Adam Smith, figures towards whom he was implacably opposed. Perhaps Bulgakov could be better thought of as a kind of 'anti-economist', who sought to transform the 'Dismal Science', as economics is sometimes called, into a branch of theology. Bulgakov was born in 1871, the son of an Orthodox priest, whose forefathers had also been Orthodox priests, stretching back some five generations. However, priest or not, his father Nikolai still succumbed to the age-old Russian weakness of vodka (or perhaps it was Communion wine?), and died an alcohol-related death during Bulgakov's childhood. Two of Sergei's elder brothers followed their father into a drink-induced grave, a litany of woe that led his mother to descend into mental disturbance. Such unpleasantness was not calculated to induce a strong belief in the existence of a loving, benevolent God, and so it was that, around the age of fourteen, while studying in an Orthodox seminary and reading sceptical German philosophers on the side, Bulgakov lost his faith and, as he put it, 'accepted nihilism without a struggle'. Losing one religion in Christianity, Bulgakov soon found another in Marxism. Quitting his path to the priesthood, at age seventeen Bulgakov went off to study Law and Political Economy at Moscow University, where he became known for translating some of Marx's works into Russian, and for penning intellectually brilliant Marxist analyses of capitalist modes of production. However, ultimately Bulgakov was to lose this second faith too, and return to the religion of his childhood. Whereas Schumacher rebelled against capitalism, Bulgakov rebelled against Marxism – although in truth neither of the unrealisable economic models either man proposed were entirely of the Left or Right, but expressions of immaterial spiritual desire, kingdoms which, like that of Christ, were not truly of this Earth.

The reasons behind Bulgakov's sudden about-turn were many. For one thing, he travelled westwards into Europe in search of data for a planned magnum opus about the applicability of Marxism towards agriculture ... and found, to his dismay, that Marxism had no positive applicability towards agriculture whatsoever, as later proven by Josef Stalin's (1879–1953)

A 1907 caricature of Sergei Bulgakov, made during his early political period, prior to adopting the mystical idea of creating a Sophic Economy. (Public domain)

catastrophic famine-inducing experiments with collectivised farms. Secondly, there were his meetings and conversations with the novelist Leo Tolstoy (1828–1910), of *War and Peace* and *Anna Karenina* fame, during which the elder man managed to reorient his young friend's mind back towards religion, implanting the idea within his head that Marxism was really some kind of pseudo-religious millenarian myth, not an objective or practical political programme. Thirdly, there was a visit Bulgakov paid to Raphael's (1483–1520) famous painting of the *Sistine Madonna* in Dresden's Zwinger Palace Gallery during his stay in Europe. Here, he underwent a profound mystical experience of the 'Stendhal Syndrome' kind, in which being in the presence of a great work of art produces an overwhelming emotional reaction in the viewer, causing faintness, rapid heartbeat, feelings of uncontrollable elation and a sort of temporary nervous breakdown. Seeing it, Bulgakov stood enraptured before the masterpiece for several solid hours, weeping tears of joy at the presence of God in the world which he felt it revealed to him. This was the same painting before which another great Russian writer, Fyodor Dostoyevsky (1821–81), had stood enraptured himself some years beforehand, and which had caused him to formulate the maxim later expressed by the character of Prince Myshkin in his novel *The Idiot* that 'Beauty will save the world!' Raphael's image engendered a similar thought within Bulgakov too, who set out to develop a theory of economics which, unlike those of Karl Marx or Adam Smith, would contain within it ample provision for the world to become neither more rich nor more equitable, but more suffused with beauty – the divine beauty of the goddess Sophia.

By 1903, back in Russia, Bulgakov was publishing a book detailing his re-conversion to the Holy Russian Church, *From Marxism to Idealism*, which was hardly designed to endear him to the godless Commissars following the officially atheistic Soviet revolution of 1917. His 1912 title *Philosophy of Economy*, in which he laid out his non-Marxist ideas about developing a Sophic Economy, was a further black mark against his name in the eyes of Lenin & Co. As a result, in 1922 Bulgakov was placed upon one of the infamous 'Philosophers' Ships', vessels which took a select group of prominent anti-Communist intellectuals away from Russia to a life of enforced exile abroad. Eventually, Bulgakov – by now an ordained Orthodox priest – settled in Paris, serving as Dean and Professor of Dogmatic Theology at the Orthodox Saint Sergius Theological Institute from 1925 until his death from throat cancer in 1944. Here, he continued to write upon the topic of 'Sophiology', drawing official condemnation from one wing of the Orthodox Church back in Russia, who accused him of attempting to add a fourth, female, entity to the otherwise masculine Holy Trinity in the shape of Sophia. Rather than uniting the two fields of theology and economics, as he had desired, Bulgakov had succeeded only in uniting Russia's Orthodox theologians and Marxist economists in unlikely alliance against him.[63]

Perhaps by now the *kali yuga* was simply too advanced to have the quality of beauty reintroduced back into its unfolding?

Sophia, So Good

Bulgakov was introduced to Sophia-worship through his reading of another mystically inclined Russian philosopher named Vladimir Solovyov (1853–1900). Solovyov had great first-hand knowledge of the wisdom of Sophia – because he had actually met the goddess in person, in the depths of the Egyptian desert. Solovyov is often described as Russia's greatest philosopher, whose main aim was to try to unite the disparate religious and spiritual traditions of the *philosophia perennis*, such as Orthodox and Catholic Christianity, Buddhism and Judaism, into one united 'Universal Church' which would then, in itself, reconcile all other opposites, like East and West, male and female, and Heaven and Earth, into one larger, more coherent whole, allowing the fallen physical world to better share in the true nature of the transcendent Godhead – to become more qualitative, and less quantitative. Like Bulgakov, Solovyov temporarily lost his Orthodox faith in his early teens then rediscovered it in young adulthood. Repudiating the materialist views of his teenage years, Solovyov published a highly critical work repudiating scientific materialism with the rather Guénon-like title *The Crisis in Western Philosophy: Against the Positivists*, and began an intensive programme of investigating such arcane fields as Neoplatonism and Gnosticism. In 1875, apparently at the advice of Dostoyevsky, Solovyov decamped to London, then one of the main European centres of learned occultism, to advance his studies further. Here, he spent his nights attending séances and his days in the Reading Room of the British Museum, the very same place where Karl Marx had once studied while writing *Das Kapital*. Solovyov's researches did not centre upon economics, however, but upon the occult, with the brilliant young scholar working his way through as many tomes upon esoteric subjects like alchemy and Rosicrucianism as he could lay his hands on. [64]

A particular interest of Solovyov's was the *Kabbalah*, a contemplative practice in which Jewish adepts would meditate upon the divine names of God contained within the Hebrew Scripture. One of the key books in the tradition is a thirteenth-century work known as the *Zohar*, which Solovyov encountered in the British Museum. The *Zohar* focuses upon the ten *Sephiroth*, God's holy names, each of which symbolises an aspect of the transcendent Godhead, or *Ain Sof*, an emanation of the Infinite Lord within the finite world of material and worldly imperfection. The most significant *Sephirah* for Solovyov was that of *Chokmah*, meaning 'Wisdom'. Solovyov identified this particular aspect of God with Sophia, a name the Bible also uses to describe the wisdom of the Almighty.[65] There is scant direct mainstream biblical authority for treating Sophia as if she is an actual goddess, but for

Solovyov the situation was different. This is because Solovyov was sat in the British Museum Reading Room one day, endlessly staring at the same page in some Kabbalistic book or other (possibly the *Zohar* itself?) and meditating upon the mysterious nature of the Divine Sophia when, suddenly, she appeared there before him, amid the stacks of learned journals.

Solovyov recognised her instantly, for he had encountered the goddess once before, while in church on Ascension Sunday 1862. During the service, the nine-year-old Solovyov, brooding upon some childhood crush, got caught up within the beauty of a particular hymn, so much so that the priest and congregation seemed to disappear from his sight, to be replaced with a golden-blue glow of supernatural light. As he explained in his 1898 poem *Three Meetings*, Solovyov was then greeted by a vision of a young and beautiful girl his own age, more appealing than his original sweetheart by far, who was smiling 'a radiant smile' and holding out 'a strange flower from a strange land' towards him. Before he could reach out to grasp it, however, the girl 'inclined [her] head, then faded into mist'. This mysterious maiden, Solovyov later realised, was the goddess Sophia, and he spent much of his time in London longing to re-encounter her. By his own account, the signs were propitious that he would soon do so; while in the British Museum, he wrote in *Three Meetings*, 'Mysterious forces chose my/Every book; and I read only of her.'[66] While studying these tomes, and considering the *Sephiroth*, inside his head he was constantly wishing Sophia to reappear to him – which, suddenly, she did. The same golden-blue glow known from his childhood filled the Reading Room, from which numinous radiance emerged Sophia's beautiful disembodied face.

Desert Rose

Solovyov had seen Sophia's face, and now he was a believer; his 'soul went blind to mundane matters', he said in his poem, and all remaining vestiges of scepticism vanished from his mind. Sophia spoke to him, but her words 'were incomprehensible' in his ecstasy. He only managed to make out one particular phrase – Sophia's instruction to travel out to Egypt immediately, if he wished to enjoy a further meeting with her. By October, Solovyov was in Cairo, when he heard Sophia's voice in his room. 'In the desert I am – seek me there,' she said. Obediently, Solovyov set out into the Sahara, alone and on foot, dressed in town-coat and top-hat because he could not afford any proper explorers' gear, and was promptly captured by a group of Bedouins who were so perturbed by his odd attire that they held a tribal council to determine whether or not to kill him. Eventually, they led him out into the middle of the sands, loosed the ropes from his wrists, and left him there to find his way back home or perish as Allah so desired. Falling asleep between the dunes, Solovyov was later awoken by the smell of roses. Opening his eyes, he saw Sophia once more, standing there surrounded by 'a heavenly purple glow' and with her irises the colour of 'azure fire'. It seemed as if Sophia's eyes contained the sun-suffused blueness of the sky itself within them, and Solovyov suddenly perceived that Sophia was something akin to the 'World-Soul' spoken of by the Neoplatonists of old, containing as she did the whole of Creation within her. As Solovyov poetised:

Your gaze was the first blaze
Of world-filling, life-giving day.
What is, what was, what shall forever be ;
All, all was held here in one steady gaze ...
The seas and rivers blue beneath me,
Distant woods, snow-capped peaks.
I saw all, and all was one;
A single image of womanly beauty ...
Pregnant with vastnesses!
Before me, in me ... only You!

This third and final encounter with Sophia undoubtedly had a particularly significant impact upon Solovyov, to the extent that he later picked up the unwanted attentions of a philosophical groupie named Anna Schmidt who did her best to attract his attention by claiming to be the physical incarnation of Sophia herself, and explaining that he was a new embodiment of Christ – if so, they would have made quite the power-couple.[67]

The Whole Is Greater than the Sum of Its Parts

One of Vladimir Solovyov's key ideas was that, because Sophia the World-Soul contained all of Creation within her and infused it with God's life-force somehow, all humans should strive to allow her animating power to shine through them, thus linking the material world with God, and uniting all seemingly irreconcilable opposites within the human frame. In the Russian Orthodox tradition, there is a concept called *sobornost*, or 'multiplicity in unity', as exemplified by the idea of the Holy Trinity, which Solovyov felt was compatible with the *Kabbalah*. As Solovyov understood it, Kabbalistic tradition teaches that all things in existence are in some sense one, with the material world being the extension of the Godhead into matter, and matter being the extension of the material world into the Godhead, with the *Sephiroth* being the medium through which this process occurs – especially, for Solovyov, the *Sephirah* of *Chokmah*, or Wisdom/ Sophia. This was also one of the key teachings of the Perennial Philosophy elsewhere hymned by the likes of René Guénon. Through contemplation of such Kabbalistic mysteries, mankind – the highest form which matter can attain – can become suffused with Sophia, thus coming to act as a bridge between God and the world; Christ, as the fleshly incarnation of God, was the ideal example. Given that humanity connects the worlds of Earth and Heaven, it thereby followed that, through our actions, we could help these two realms become one, as in Eden. *Kabbalah* posits the idea that the true cause of mankind's expulsion from Paradise lay in Eve's sin causing the *Sephiroth* to separate from one another. By performing righteous acts, therefore, in which the love of God shines through them, human beings can gradually cancel out the effects of Original Sin and reconnect the *Sephiroth* again, causing humanity to 'fall back upwards' into a restored Eden. Thus, while *Kabbalah* was a mystical tradition, it was one whose adherents were encouraged not simply to sit alone in some high lonely tower at midnight hour and ponder over the *Zohar*, but instead to be active participants within their communities, to go out into the real world and help change it back into Paradise through good deeds like charity, prayer, public generosity and civic-mindedness.[68]

Such notions are reflected in Solovyov's key statement that 'Mankind is obligated not to contemplate divinity, but to make itself divine.' He felt that, through a long programme of spiritual exercises, it was mankind's ultimate destiny to evolve into immortal Christ-like beings, with this being what the Bible really meant when it talked about the eventual resurrection of the dead. Victory over death, Solovyov said, was 'a natural consequence of internal spiritual perfection'. Jesus' reappearance on Earth following his own crucifixion made him simply the first example of a newly evolved superior species, akin to the first human to appear among orang-utans (which Solovyov felt we had evolved from). This evolutionary process may take a long time, Solovyov admitted, perhaps 10,000 years, but if the correct spiritual disciplines were adopted, mankind's evolution into a race of Jesus-men would be as inevitable as orang-utans' evolution into humans. In fact, our current state was something like a 'de-evolution' from what humanity had once been before in the days of Adam Kadmon, or 'Adam the First Man', who had lived in perfect immortal harmony with Sophia in the Garden of Eden. The process of becoming immortal would happen miraculously, as the end-point of intense meditation and prayer, whereupon the corporeal frames of advanced holy men would suddenly become indestructible spiritual bodies which could not rot. This represented a rejection of growing Marxist ideas about humanity conquering Nature and establishing a future Paradise via scientific means. Instead, mankind must conquer the material world he had been cursed by Eve's sin to live in by infusing it with spirit and merging his soul with Nature itself, creating something greater than both – rather like the manifestation of Sophia that Solovyov had encountered in the Sahara, who held the sun and skies within her very eyes, with the *Sephiroth* of the *Kabbalah* thereby being rejoined once more into the all-encompassing Godhead of *Ain Sof*.

Sexual Union

Solovyov's key term here was 'syzygy', or the unification of paired opposites, in particular the unification of male and female through love and sex. Some Kabbalistic thought is known to insist that sexual intercourse is an inherently divine activity, with some of the *Sephiroth* considered male, and some female; the *Sephirah* called *Yesod*, or 'Foundation', for example, is often imagined as being God's great penis. In some sense, the different *Sephiroth* are said to impregnate one another, thus allowing God to impregnate the world with meaning and life through the *Sephiroth*'s own manifestation within it. Influenced by such teachings, in his book *The Meaning of Love*, Solovyov spoke of how the future immortal Christ-people would not simply be men or women, but some 'higher unity of the two', an LGBTQ-friendly evolutionary end-point which present-day men and women unconsciously expressed their desire for by temporarily joining their two bodies via shagging. In this view, idealising your chosen lover should not be an end in itself, but a means for enabling the contemplation of a higher, spiritual reality which lies *behind* that specific lover; much as Solovyov's brooding over his childhood crush during Mass that fateful day back in 1862 had ultimately enabled him to gain a glance of Sophia, the divine World-Soul behind all earthly beauty.

By transforming current notions of physical love into more spiritualised versions of the same, we could, wrote Solovyov, literally alter the physical nature of the world around us into something better, in imitation of Dostoyevsky's maxim that 'Beauty will save the world'. For Solovyov, the material world itself was not inherently evil, as it was for the Gnostic sages he had once studied, but temporarily Fallen and awaiting rescue; once fully re-infused with the life-force of Sophia, it would become Eden once more and the transfigured transgender dead arise, in a final 'resurrection of love' lasting for all time. For this to truly happen, however, mankind first had to fall in love with the actual physical environment around him too, as Nature-mystics and Romantic poets did, seeing a tree or mountain not merely as physical objects, but as manifestations of God in the world at large, much like the *Sephiroth* in the Kabbalistic tradition. Rather than exploiting Nature with gigantic collectivised farms like the Marxists wanted, man should strive to be in 'loving interaction' with the natural world around us, taught Russia's greatest philosopher.[69] All of which is very interesting, but sounds as if it has very little to do with economics – which it doesn't. Until, that is, Sergei Bulgakov got his hands on such theories …

I Am Not a Number

Bulgakov was aware the twin fields of economics and theology were generally considered to be completely unconnected. However, he claimed that the very idea of economics had grown directly from religion itself. His 1909 essay *The National Economy and the Religious Personality* is an interesting exercise in attempting to claim that the very basis of the modern-day economies of Europe lay ultimately in ancient Christian notions about the dignity of labour and the early economic actions of monks and nuns. Already in this essay, several of Bulgakov's major ideas can be found in embryo. For a start, there is his profound dislike of the idea of *Homo economicus*, or 'economic man', which had been pushed in their books by Adam Smith and Karl Marx alike. To Bulgakov, *Homo economicus* was an essentially statistical and fictional creation, a wholly rational and therefore wholly unrealistic creature motivated purely by notions of profit and loss, money and wages, production and consumption, someone who 'does not eat and sleep but always calculates interests, seeking the greatest benefit at lowest costs; a slide-rule that reacts with mathematical accuracy to the outer mechanisms of [economic] redistribution and production.' Bulgakov saw this model of man was a complete abstraction, which took no account whatsoever of the fact that most people are not motivated by money alone. The whole 'science' of economics was thus misguided even on its own, mathematical terms, dealing with only a 'fractional value' of man, not the unmeasurable 'whole unit' of any individual. When such partial depictions of *Homo economicus* were then scaled up to gain a bigger picture of any national economy, they led to crude, vastly over-simplified depictions of a purely money-based society which simply did not exist, with human beings and the complex world they inhabited converted into a mere 'sack of atoms' – a process that sadly continues today. With books like Marx's *Das Kapital* being based upon such irrationally over-rational thinking every bit as much as Smith's *Wealth of Nations*, Bulgakov viewed an over-reliance upon statistics as a cardinal sin committed just as much by socialists as by capitalists.[70]

However, the Original Economic Sin was definitely committed by Adam Smith, when he drew a distinction between so-called 'productive labour' and 'unproductive labour'. Productive labour, in Smith's terms, led to the creation of items or services of direct economic benefit to the producer, whereas unproductive labour did not. Bulgakov thought this a most unfortunate distinction, as it meant that the efficient manufacturing of some pins within a factory in a few seconds was an inherently more valuable activity than, say, spending hours tending a garden and making it beautiful for zero financial gain. Only in crudely economic terms is a pin more valuable than a rose; Bulgakov preferred to argue it was the nature of *labour itself* which carried true value, not the monetary worth of that labour as later expressed in wages or cost of items produced.[71] To argue otherwise, it might be said, would be to claim that Christ would have made a much greater contribution to His local community if He had stayed working as a carpenter instead of wandering around raising the dead all day long, free of charge, or putting local bakers

Adam Smith and Karl
Marx, twin creators of
Homo economicus and
chief economic demons of
Sergei Bulgakov's worldview.
(Courtesy of the Library of
Congress/John Mayall)

out of business by multiplying loaves *gratis*. Upon these narrow terms, Jesus was 'economically inactive', as they say, having made no significant contribution towards Judea's GDP since He stopped nailing together chairs and tables, and so was utterly unworthy of the esteem in which He has since been held.

Would You Adam and Eve It?

By separating labour into productive and unproductive modes, Smith had helped formalise the idea of Adam's Curse, the punishment placed upon Adam and Eve by God when ejecting them from Paradise that they would henceforth have to earn their living by the sweat of their brow rather than, as in Eden, simply by existing in harmony with the natural world, effortlessly. The irony was that, according to Bulgakov's analysis, it was religion which had caused Adam Kadmon to be transformed into his evil inverted anti-self Adam Smith in the first place. There was once a time when much human labour had been a kind of intrinsic worship of God, said Bulgakov, but this had since been lost. He cites numerous pre-modern religious authorities on the inherent Christian dignity of labour, such as St Augustine's (354–430) statement that 'labour in some respect equals prayer'. The true value of such spiritually worthwhile toil, says Bulgakov 'lies beyond the labour process' itself, as could be seen in the work-ethic of the monks of medieval European monasteries, who spent years busily creating beautiful illuminated manuscripts purely for the greater glory of Christendom, not for cash. However, while doing so, the monks had inadvertently helped lay the foundations for the wider, lay economy. In clearing woods and converting wetlands into fertile fields fit for agriculture, in establishing retreats in remote environments and taming the previously hostile land, the medieval monks may well have been transforming wild Nature into something slightly more Edenic in God's honour as Solovyov (or indeed Rudolf Steiner and E. F. Schumacher) might have liked, but they also provided the foundations for other people to come along and settle in such reclaimed locations, building up towns, villages, trading-posts and other such settlements in their wake.[72]

During this early stage of Europe's economic development, much labour, being rural in nature, was in Bulgakov's opinion still fairly close to God. The word 'economy', we will recall, was not used in the sense that we currently understand it, as relating to the financial, industrial and monetary affairs of a specific country or trade-bloc, until the late nineteenth or early twentieth century. As we saw earlier when discussing Distributism, the term originates from the combination of two Greek words which, when put together, equate to 'household management', and the first known instance of the word in that sense is found in a manuscript thought to have been produced in a European monastery around 1440. Managing the economics of a monastery or farmland did not simply equate to a crude notion of profit and loss (although obviously such things had to be taken account of), but also involved taking good care of the land, vineyards, crops and livestock, taming the natural world and making it more productive, but in a sustainable, non-destructive and sensitive way, thereby maintaining respectful contact with the *genius loci* ... rather like on a biodynamic farm. In the view of Bulgakov, rural labourers and monks were stewards of the land as much as economic actors in the modern sense, who acted to infuse elements of Sophia back into Nature through the dignity of their labours. According to Psalm 24, 'The Earth is the LORD's, and the fullness thereof', so us humans were merely minding it for Him and making sure it looked nice.[73]

Paradise Lost

Of course, this does all ignore the fact that much rural labour was back-breaking, dirty and unpleasant and that many monasteries did make rather a lot of money from their activities – think of the financial importance of the monk-dominated wool-trade to medieval England – but this is what Bulgakov thought. He might sound naïve, but other economic historians would have agreed with his assertion that, during medieval times, the economy was managed with reference to many things other than the naked pursuit of gold. In his classic 1926 book *Religion and the Rise of Capitalism*, for example, the historian R. H. Tawney (1880–1962) spoke of how, within the medieval Catholic outlook:

> Material riches ... have a secondary importance ... [and purely] economic motives are suspect ... There is no place in medieval theory for economic activity which is not related to a moral end, and to found the science of a society upon the assumption that the appetite for economic gain is a constant and measurable force, to be accepted, like other natural forces, as an inevitable and self-evident *datum* would have appeared to the medieval thinker as ... irrational or ... immoral ... At every turn, therefore, there are limits, restrictions, warnings, against allowing economic interests to interfere with [more] serious affairs ... It is right for a man to seek such wealth as is necessary for a livelihood in his station. To seek more is not enterprise, but avarice, and avarice is a deadly sin. Trade is legitimate ... but it is a dangerous business. A man must be sure that he carries it on for the public benefit, and that the profits he takes are no more than the wages of his labour.[74]

The problem was that into this rustic old-world idyll had come the heresy of Protestantism. Bulgakov had read the famous 1905 text of the German social historian Max Weber (1864–1920), *The Protestant Ethic and the*

Spirit of Capitalism, and absorbed its theories wholesale. Weber noted that the most economically successful nations tended to be Protestant, seeing certain offshoots of this schismatic religion, particularly Calvinism and Puritanism, as the accidental seedbeds of modernity. The central doctrine of Calvinism was 'predestination', the idea that God had already chosen a select group of people for Heaven, and condemned all others to an eternity in Hell, before they were even born. However, nobody knew precisely who among the wider mass of Calvinists God's actual chosen ones were, so the only way for an individual to ascertain whether they were destined for Paradise or the Pit was to monitor their day-to-day behaviour and moral character. Those who worked hard, had great self-discipline and possessed a thrifty, ascetic nature were more likely to be destined for Heaven, it was thought – and, as a natural by-product, to do well in business too. Therefore, the better you *did* do in business, the more you appeared to be favoured by God, hence the old saying 'God blesseth trade'.

From now on you did not *pass* your time, you *spent* it, a most instructive metaphor. Old biblical injunctions about it being easier for a camel to pass through the eye of a needle than for a rich man to enter Heaven began to be disregarded. In the new Calvinist outlook, a rich man desiring poverty was as foolish as a healthy man desiring sickness – such bouts of pointless virtue-signalling were condemned. While other sects did not share this precise doctrine, the general idea of trade being blessed nonetheless spread across Protestantism as a whole, especially among England's Puritans, who considered themselves God's chosen people not individually, like the Calvinists, but as a whole. Thus, developing the mercantile life of England became a kind of holy task on the Puritans' behalf, laying the foundations for Napoleon's later jibe that the English were nothing but 'a nation of shopkeepers'. Ironically, however, the Puritans' ostensible asceticism actually led to the earliest manifestations of the consumer culture of today, because the continued accumulation of goods and capital, just so long as they were not enjoyed too conspicuously or frivolously, became another clear sign of God's love for the successful Protestant capitalist.[75] As Bulgakov wrote:

> The more the property, the heavier the sense of responsibility to perpetuate it for the glory of God and to multiply it through ceaseless labour. Thus, little by little, the capitalist fetishism [of consumer objects and capital] so well known to us now has been elaborated ... [Puritanism] liberates accumulation from traditional ethical barriers and develops ascetic ways of accumulation for the sake of asceticism itself, not only legalising the drive to enrich, but directly interpreting it as a deed that pleases God ... Puritan asceticism is at the cradle of contemporary economic man, operating on the stock exchange and the market ... The strength of this religious asceticism has ... [created] the current-day bourgeois entrepreneur – sober,

conscientious, unusually hard-working, attached to their labour as to a divine life-objective.[76]

As this attitude spread across the Protestant nations of northern Europe – which even today are among the richest on Earth – so it became increasingly impossible for their inhabitants to live within the world of the old and ever-more obsolete rural monastery-centred economies. As Weber had it, 'The Puritan *wanted* to be a professional; we are *forced* to be one.'[77] For Bulgakov this was an appalling outcome, which he set out to try to reverse – by using the power of Holy Sophia.

You Are What You Eat

Sergei Bulgakov's bizarre spiritual plan to save the world from mutated Protestant economics centred largely upon encouraging people to eat it. His chief 1912 masterwork *Philosophy of Economy* had the telling subtitle *The World as Household*, with the book laying out a complex Solovyov-inspired plea for mankind to throw off his current false role as *Homo economicus* and return to being a steward of the land, thus making Earth fall back upwards into the Garden of Eden. When he spoke of the global economy as being analogous to that of a household, Bulgakov meant that people should imitate the medieval monks of old by carving out a place to live from the materials of raw Nature in a way intended to glorify God through the sincerity and sacrifice of their creative labour, not to turn them a quick profit – imagine a priest playing *Minecraft*, and you're halfway there.[78]

The term economists use to express the way that people and societies gobble up goods and materials is 'consumption', a word also used to refer to the act of eating. In his 1912 book, Bulgakov chose to take this fact literally, arguing that 'economic life can ultimately be reduced to a metabolic process', like those of digestion and excretion. However, in a universe in which everything was connected, with every last atom of physical matter being an emanation of the Godhead, as the Perennial Philosophy of the *Kabbalah* taught, it was possible to conceive of all acts of economic consumption as really being one big cannibalistic exercise in eating God. Human bodies, Bulgakov pointed out, were constructed from all kinds of inert and non-living physical substances, such as iron, water and potassium, and yet when combined together in the right way these materials amounted to something much greater than the sum of their parts, a kind of *sobornost*, or multiplicity in unity, of the kind Solovyov had once glimpsed within the sky-filled eyes of Sophia.

A human or animal body, said Bulgakov, was a 'totality of organs by means of which life overcomes dead matter', something he described as 'the physical communism of being', with 'communism' here meaning something like 'inseparable union' as opposed to anything Marxist. If dead matter could indeed be transmuted into life in this way, then it meant that the entire cosmos was nothing but 'the potential body of a living being, an organism *in potentia*'. When considered *in toto*, the universe was basically God, the sum of all things, the Alpha and Omega, something like the Kabbalistic *Ain Sof*. If so, then we needed to be careful how precisely we consumed God, when we took Him inside our bodies. 'Our bodily organs,' wrote Bulgakov, 'are like doors and windows into the universe', with whatever we consume through our eyes, ears, mouths and mind becoming part of our bodily selves.[79] Look at a grand old oak in an economically utilitarian way, as a source of valuable timber, and the visual 'food' you take in will not be truly nourishing. Feast your eyes upon the oak as a visible expression of God's presence in the world, however, and the spiritual food you thereby consume will provide vital sustenance to your soul; recall Rudolf Steiner's lesson about the difference between wood derived from trees planted 'intelligently', or merely for profit. Even if you do make some use of the oak for your own economic benefit – lopping a few limbs off to whittle down and sell as walking-staffs, maybe – so long as you don't simply exploit and kill the thing purely for your own selfish immediate financial greed, you are still acting as a steward of God's world. Cutting off a few branches can be a spur to new growth, after all.

Bread with Nowt Taken Out

Proclaiming that 'we eat the world' via our interaction with it, Bulgakov goes on to provide a complex meditation upon the true metaphysical nature of our daily bread. 'What, then, is food?' he asks, before providing an answer based upon the Christian mystery of the Holy Communion, in which the crumb of wafer-bread held aloft by the priest during Mass is miraculously transubstantiated into the Body and Flesh of Christ. Food, writes Bulgakov:

> ... is the most vivid expression of cosmic communism ... The boundary between living and nonliving is actually removed in food. Food is *natural communion* – partaking of the flesh of the world. When I take in food, I am eating world-matter in general, and in so doing, I truly and in reality find the world within me, and myself in the world, I become a part of it ... For the history of this bread, as of every particle of matter, contains the history of the entire universe.[80]

More unadulterated than the bittiest slice of Warburton's Wholemeal, Bulgakov's special Sophia-infused bread contains within it a history of the entire universe of which it is only a transient localised manifestation, and thus tastes of God Himself. This is because, in order for any loaf 'to grow and receive its current form' it had not only to be baked, but 'the collective action of the entire world-mechanism in its past and present' had to have occurred, too. To Bulgakov, bread should taste not only of bread, but of the stars, suns, planets, soil, seeds, rain and all other things which had first to come into being before a loaf could materialise in our physical realm, an idea with echoes of biodynamic farming to it. By eating food – or, in a wider sense, consuming consumer goods – with such beliefs in mind, it should be possible for mankind to make the planet holy again, as in Eden.[81] The paradigmatic model for such consumption was found in Bulgakov's rapture before Raphael's *Sistine Madonna* as a young man, an ecstatic experience which first allowed him to fully perceive the precise feelings Solovyov was talking about when he wrote of encountering Sophia. According to the American academic George M. Young, Bulgakov:

> … first attained his [direct] knowledge of Sophia not by reading or debating or conducting a survey, but by standing before Raphael's *Madonna*, not trying to analyse the painting, but absorbing it, opening himself to a great artist's intuition of higher reality. He came to understand Solovyov through Raphael. To use his terms, he consumed the *Madonna*; she became part of Bulgakov, and Bulgakov became part of her. Raphael's great vision became an extension of his body and life, and he became an extension of Raphael's vision.[82]

The spirit of Sophia haunted Raphael's painting, and, like Dostoyevsky before him, Sergei Bulgakov ate it with his eyes and was transformed, in the same way the devout Catholic is transformed by swallowing Christ's body within the Communion wafer. Potentially, could all economic consumption of objects imitate this model one day, too? Only, concluded Bulgakov, if such items were crafted with the same sense of love, sincerity and glorification of God which Raphael had employed while labouring upon his *Madonna* – only, in short, if the profit-motive was abolished and human labour became once again wholly animated by the Edenic force of Divine Sophia.

Workers' Paradise

Naturally, eating haunted paintings with your soul is not an experience most ordinary workers can reasonably expect to undergo during their own lifetimes. However, Bulgakov's book was probably not intended for easy consumption by the masses, nigh-on incomprehensible as it was to anyone who did not possess a highly academic education in the humanities. Take the following passage:

> The real coming out of our I into the non-I and, conversely, this non-I's pressure on the I, the entire practice of mutual interaction of I and non-I,

establish the reality of the external world and fill the empty and cold realm of the non-I with strength, warmth [and] bodies, turning the mirage of the non-I into Nature and, at the same time, placing the I in Nature, organically fusing them in a single universe. This active, economic relation to the world constitutes the living basis for that "naïve realism" which comprises humanity's universal natural epistemology before any philosophical reflection and that is retained in practice despite any destructive, sceptical conclusions of philosophical solipsism.[83]

Are you listening, factory workers? They better had be, because Bulgakov had plans to alter their working lives forever. The above paragraph might sound like a laughable chin-stroking obscurity, but it is really just an overly complex re-statement of Solovyov's plea to infuse the material world (the non-I) with some aspect of the self (the I) to help reanimate the dying World-Soul of our planet. The difference is that Bulgakov felt the best way to do so was not through spiritual exercise alone, as Solovyov taught, but by transforming the whole field of human industry. Bulgakov's central question here was 'How is production possible?' How was it that mankind was able to produce consumer goods or yields of crops through agriculture? The obvious answer was by imposing his will on the world, by taking an idea for a product which lay within his mind, such as a table or a field of corn, and then manipulating and altering physical Nature in order to make such an idea manifest. Defining man as 'the subject' and raw materials as 'the object', Bulgakov declared that any product manufactured from such substances by man is in fact a third thing, a new entity called a 'subject-object', something 'in which the distinction between subject and object is extinguished.'[84]

It therefore followed that the central 'bridge' between the two worlds of subject and object was labour, which fused all three elements together in a state of *sobornost*, symbolic of 'the mystery of the Holy Trinity'. The problem with employment in the modern age, however, as E. F. Schumacher also later taught, was that it was almost always evaluated in light of Adam Smith's exceedingly reductive notion of 'productive labour' in which the manufacture of a warehouse full of pins might be valued more highly than the production of a great poem, because the latter usually has far less monetary value to it.[85] This kind of limited perspective had to be overcome if the planet was to be redeemed. Viewed correctly, said Bulgakov, economic activity should be seen as nothing less than the quest to defeat both death and Satan by infusing Sophia into the world by humanising Nature, thereby facilitating 'the transformation of the entire cosmic mechanism into a potential or actual organism' which, like Solovyov's Christ-men, would live forever, thereby conquering death.[86] But such a thing could never occur within the dark satanic mills and dingy, mechanised production-lines of modernity. For Bulgakov the entire Industrial Revolution had been nothing more than a 'sly magic trick perpetrated on feeble humanity by the Anti-Christ', in which ever-greater ability to change the world was granted mankind, but without the necessary dose of Sophia which would allow him to remake the world in honour of God, not Mammon, to reshape the environment sustainably, not degrade and destroy it – compare Steiner's ideas about *Homo economicus* being duped by a black alliance between scientists and economists into entering the inverted *kali yuga* age of Ahriman.[87]

In the Gnostic tradition there is a figure named the 'demiurge', a kind of lesser god whose station is below that of the actual Godhead, and whose task it was to create the material world by the manipulation of physical matter. Gnostics usually viewed this figure in negative terms, but Bulgakov disagreed, saying that mankind had to imitate the demiurge in his creative labours, thereby making 'the economic system into a work of art' filled with Sophia. The purpose of the economy was not to enrich people, as the evil Adam Smith had implied, nor to reduce them all down to the same level, as the wicked Marx wanted, but to transform the world into 'a cosmos – a chaos that has been conquered, tamed and illuminated from within'. The true success of any economic system, Bulgakov argued, should not be measured through artificial concepts like GDP, but by how much its products allowed for 'the cosmic victory of beauty' over meaningless chaos. 'The goal of economic activity,' he wrote, was to 'restore the primordial unity of living Nature' which had once existed in Eden.[88] Man was supposed to mirror the world, and the world to mirror man, as taught in the old hermetic concept of microcosm reflecting macrocosm, but in the present climate, where man had been redefined as *Homo economicus* and encouraged to think of his own narrow financial interests first within a competitive capitalist economy, the mirror had been 'broken into many shards, each of which reflects the world in its [own] peculiar way'.[89] Through rediscovery of the concept of holy monkish labour, we had to abandon such hyper-individualistic notions and reclaim instead that animating spark of Adam Kadmon which still lurked somewhere within us all, a common human heritage connecting mankind as a species back to the lost economic Paradise of Eden.[90]

Feast of Eden

The idea of striving to express the Adam hidden within us through our labour is all very well, but how can such aims actually be achieved? Bulgakov suggested the development of an entire Sophic Economy, in which the manufacture of objects was based upon the concept of 'Platonic Forms'. Back in ancient Greece, Plato had proposed that underlying all physical things in the world was a perfect, immaterial template of that very same thing in the spiritual world. These templates Plato termed 'Forms'. All things of any particular type in existence were simply imperfect expressions of their original Form; the Form-template of man, for instance, stood as a perfect man, like Adam, in whose nature all men to some degree shared, with men usually having a head, torso, two arms and legs and so forth. The more like this original Form a person was, the more perfect they were, although it was never possible to share in such perfection completely, even if your only blemish was a single freckle. These Forms emanated from the mind of the Godhead, and every single thing in existence had to have been preceded by the existence of its immaterial Form in the spiritual world, as God, being perfect, had thought of all possible things which could ever conceivably exist beforehand. Thus, said Bulgakov, any consumer products mankind *thought* he had invented had actually been invented by God the Creator, countless aeons ago. 'Knowledge is really remembrance', said Bulgakov, again echoing Plato, a recollection of that for which God had already drawn up the designs. When mankind invented everything from the wheel to the Twix bar, he was therefore simply implementing God's pre-existing blueprints for such products within the physical realm for the first time, not truly making anything new; technically, God could sue us all for infringement of copyright.

However, God had given mankind the gift of free will, as reflected in the economic choices he was free to make – namely, in terms of which of God's Platonic Form blueprints he decided to manufacture. If he chose to expend his effort making beautiful artworks, like Raphael, then that particular man had chosen well, in accordance with the will of Sophia. If he chose to spend all his time manufacturing mundane items like pins, however, then he was doing the work of the Devil, 'shaping a shadowy, Satanic world' for us to inhabit, instead of a bright, shining, Sophic one. In practice, mankind today dwelled within a Fallen realm wherein a truly Sophic economy was not yet attainable – people still *needed* pins, after all – but our task was to use our free will to choose to make objects of which God and Sophia, as opposed to Satan the pin-manufacturing fan, would approve as much as was humanly possible. Once we were immortal and Paradise had been regained, of course, we wouldn't need pins at all – not even to secure fig-leaves over our genitalia.[91] As Bulgakov concluded, 'economic activity is a Sophic process that gradually raises the world to a higher level until, ultimately, that Sophia which now shines in the beauty of a flower or of the starry sky becomes fully realised' within the world as a whole, something which would finally allow us to overcome the materialistic 'kingdom of objects' within which we had been cursed to live by Satan and the Serpent.[92] Ultimately, then, the modern-day Western economy, and the dull and degraded forms of drudgery which financial circumstance forced most workers to perform within it, were nothing less than the dismal, real-world results of Eve having bitten that apple:

The current economy was preceded by a different one, [with] a different type of labour – free, selfless, loving, in which economic activity merges with artistic creativity. Art has preserved the prototype of this primordial type of economic labour. Originally, economic activity was the harmonious interaction of man with Nature; this was the Edenic Economy, preceding the historical process that began with the Fall ... But after the Fall of Man ... the meaning and motivations of economic activity changed dramatically. The heavy shroud of economic need descended on economic activity and hid its Sophic character; the struggle for survival became the goal of economy, and economic materialism became its natural ideology. The economic process became the realisation of God's judgement on sinful humanity: 'in the sweat of thy face shalt thou eat bread, till thou return unto the ground; for out of it wast thou taken'. (Genesis 3:19)[93]

So, if you hate your job, then rest assured – everybody else hates theirs too, for this is the Will of the Lord. If capitalism and Marxism alike had helped create a world in which the human soul was so alienated from the world around it that objects had become more valued than the people who produced them, then the only solution was to reunite the I and the non-I by infusing your labour with a constant sense of the immanent presence of God and Christ, thus booking yourself a one-way ticket to Paradise – which, of course, is all well and good if you are a mystically inclined holy man, philosopher, poet or theologian like Bulgakov and Solovyov were. Persons whose job it is to pick up dog-turds from public streets with a grab-stick all day long for the minimum wage may well find Sophia rather harder to perceive shining transcendent from within their own 'creative' economic labours, however.

A Shared Wisdom

It should be obvious that there were several similarities between the thought and lives of Sergei Bulgakov and E. F. Schumacher – although, as far as I know, there is no evidence that the latter man had ever read so much as a single word of his predecessor, who in turn could clearly not have read any of Schumacher's books, unless from beyond the grave. There was the bout of materialism and atheism during early life, for example, followed by sudden enlightenment which led to a new, more spiritual outlook, with both Bulgakov and Schumacher returning to the religion of their ancestors. There was also their twin adoration of Sophia and Perennial Wisdom, and their borderline Nature-worship. Their hatred of mass-production and the consequent degradation of Earth's environment were also shared, as was their opinion that factories turned people into robots. Likewise, both believed strongly in the redemptive potential of creative work. In her biography of Schumacher, his daughter Barbara Wood speaks of how his exposure to Buddhism and Gurdjieff taught her father that the true purpose of work 'was more than fulfilling material needs, that its function was also the development of human potential and man's relationship ... towards God.'[94] Schumacher put such principles into practice in his huge garden at Holcombe, a real labour of love based around the monk-like reshaping of the soil from chaos. For Bulgakov, Schumacher's well-tended lands would surely have had unmistakable intimations of Eden.

Another resemblance lay in their mutual contempt for Adam Smith's idea of man as *Homo economicus*. Like Bulgakov, Schumacher talked with disdain about 'the religion of economics', a religion which, paradoxically, made the fake claim it was a science. Contemporary economic doctrine, Schumacher said, was a subjective idea misperceived in objective terms and then inappropriately universalised, forcing everyone to live as if the current norms of American-style capitalism were eternal and rational in nature. This was dangerous, because 'to the extent that he becomes *Homo economicus* ... man ceases to be man.'[95] 'The great majority of economists,' Schumacher wrote, 'are still pursuing the absurd ideal of making their "science" as scientific and precise as physics, as if there were no qualitative difference between mindless atoms and men made in the image of God', a statement mirroring Bulgakov's own complaint that economic statisticians were reducing mankind to 'a sack of atoms'.[96] Finally, Schumacher also conceived of the world as a kind of household, with the following Bulgakov-like words printed at the end of *Small Is Beautiful*:

> Everywhere people ask: 'What can I actually do?' The answer is as simple as it is disconcerting: we can, each of us, work to put our own inner house in order. The guidance we need for this work cannot be found in science or technology, which utterly depends on the ends they serve; but it can still be found in the traditional wisdom of mankind.[97]

These are, appropriately enough, wise words – but I wonder how many of Schumacher's millions of readers would have recognised the layers and layers of esoteric thought which lay buried carefully beneath them? Students of Vladimir Solovyov might have done; when Schumacher's library was catalogued after his death, it was found to contain several works either by or about Russia's greatest philosopher.[98] Solovyov's notion of Sophia was a Perennial Philosophy indeed; as we shall now discover, even a recent British Prime Minister ended up becoming an accidental disciple at her altar.

You Can Keep Your Silver, You Can Keep Your Gold ...

'Wisdom is better than rubies' – so says the Bible (Proverbs 8:11). A more recent variation of this message was made at Bombay International Airport one day in 1979 by the 4th Dragon King of Bhutan, Jigme Singye Wangchuck, who was returning to his mountain kingdom from an international summit in Cuba. Accosted by Indian journalists who wanted to know more about the obscure Himalayan country, His Majesty was asked a number of questions, one of which was 'What is Bhutan's Gross National Product?' (GNP being a variant of GDP) 'We do not believe in Gross National Product,' the Dragon King replied. 'Why not?' the hacks enquired. 'Because Gross National Happiness is more important!' came the reply, appealing words which were then splashed across the world's media. Perhaps the King had been reading *Small Is Beautiful*, wherein E. F. Schumacher had similarly claimed that 'The substance of man cannot be measured by Gross National Product.' As Schumacher subsequently explained, it was 'The quality of life – not the quantity – yes, that's what matters. GNP, being purely a quantitative concept, bypasses the real question: how to enhance the quality of life.'[99] It was a problem which had also once been posed by René Guénon.

Bhutan would have been the ideal place for Schumacher to have visited back in 1955, not Burma. Unlike Burma, Bhutan had not flooded itself with American economic advisors in the aftermath of the Second World War, and remained an essentially closed country to the West until as late as 1961. By the time the 4th Dragon King came to the throne in 1972, aged only sixteen, his new kingdom was still in a state of extremely low development. Bhutan's economy was almost entirely agrarian, there was little modern infrastructure, and levels of literacy were so low that the education of most of the country's civil service had ended in junior school. Nonetheless, Bhutan was coming under outside pressure to adopt US-friendly economic ways. This fact disturbed the Dragon King, who was eager not to allow his land to change too much, too quickly, thus destroying its traditional culture. To get to know his subjects better, the King travelled the realm on horseback, talking to peasants around campfires at night. Like Schumacher in Burma, the King realised that the people seemed largely happy in their poverty and concluded that, while raising levels of prosperity was a desirable goal overall, it was not worth destroying political stability, environmental well-being and the age-old ways of Bhutanese culture for. Instead, the Dragon King wisely determined to set his land upon a Middle Path, and today the concept of Gross National Happiness, or GNH, is enshrined in the country's constitution, which states that 'if the Government cannot create happiness for its people, there is no purpose for the Government to exist.'

The annual state of the nation address made by Bhutan's Prime Minister is always made in relation to the concept of GNH, all policy-proposals are examined in light of various GNH indicators, and in 2008 the government devised some complex statistical formulae which they (rather implausibly) claim can mathematically measure the nation's overall levels of happiness. Unusual policies have been implemented in the country, such as a monthly 'pedestrian day', in which no privately owned vehicles are allowed on the roads, and there is also an official pledge to ensure that 60 per cent of Bhutan's territory is left covered by forest in perpetuity, in the name of sustainability – or permanence, as Schumacher and J. C. Kumarappa might have had it. At school, children are taught basic agricultural techniques, and have daily sessions of meditation. In recent years, Bhutanese officials have tried to spread their ideas abroad, through bodies like the UN. Whether Western electorates would be happy to see their rulers implementing such ideas in their own societies is another matter, of course. While Bhutan has doubled its people's life-expectancy and vastly increased access to education in recent decades, figures from 2012 showed that around 25 per cent of its inhabitants were living on less than $1.25 a day, and 70 per cent had no access to electricity. It's not easy being Green.[100]

Evil Tory Cults

One Western leader who decided to imitate Bhutan and give the Good Life a go was former Tory PM David Cameron who, not long after entering 10 Downing Street in 2010, announced his intention to force the Office of National Statistics (ONS) to begin measuring something termed 'General Well-Being', an idea clearly modelled upon the Dragon King's GNH. In 2006, Cameron changed the Conservative Party logo to a scribbly green oak tree as part of his ongoing campaign to 'detoxify' the Tory brand by associating it with positive-sounding Green issues. Dubbed 'the muesli offensive' by some, Cameron's attempts to turn the blues Green could just have been an attempt to steal votes from the more authentically muesli-eating Lib Dems. However, the now-defunct 'Green Tories' campaign could also be viewed as an effort to earn the vote of the ghost of E. F. Schumacher, especially with Cameron's repeated comments that 'There's more to life than GDP.' The first speech in which Cameron expressed such sentiments was made before none other than the Soil Association, during their 60th anniversary conference in January 2006. In his speech, Cameron hymned the Schumacher-like qualities of 'sustainable agriculture and a good environment', although he was accused of peddling empty rhetoric by the Green Party, which condemned Cameron's plan to 'make Britain a better place to live without constraining economic growth', on the grounds that economic growth was in itself inherently evil.

In spite of such smug criticisms, it later transpired that Cameron's campaign really had been directly based upon an appreciation of *Small Is Beautiful*. In 2011, one of Cameron's chief policy-advisors, Rohan Silva, confirmed that much of Cameron's environmental agenda came straight from Schumacher, with the much-hyped, though ultimately failed, 'Big Society' programme of that era being inspired by the same source. It was Number 10's intention, said Silva, to introduce the concept of 'enoughness' into national discourse, and transform Britain into 'a contributor society rather than a consumer economy', something which was allegedly part of a wider global trend which, I must confess, I appear to have missed. Cameron's plans to measure Gross National Happiness were actually implemented during his time in power, with the ONS producing a few reports on the issue, but they elicited little public interest, beyond the predictable moan that they were a waste of time and tax money.[101] Ironically, by trying to gauge the nation's happiness levels, poor old Dave had only succeeded in making citizens feel a tiny bit more miserable with their lot under his wishy-washy rule – something he later rectified by spreading unconfined joy throughout the land by accidentally facilitating Brexit and then resigning in June 2016.

Happy Chappies

Maybe Cameron approached the idea of GNH from entirely the wrong angle. In attempting to draw Perennial Buddhist-style Wisdom from Schumacher and the Dragon King, he was stupidly getting his information second-hand, rather than direct from the Buddha's mouth. If only he had known about the existence of a unique Japanese political organisation called the Happiness Realisation Party (HRP), then he could have made a long-distance phone-call seeking true enlightenment. This is because the 'Happies', as they are known, are headed up by a man who is not only a qualified economist and former city trader, but also the reincarnation of Buddha himself – and, in this particular economic guru's opinion, the best way to ensure the spread of happiness and Right Livelihood is to embrace not poverty, but Thatcherism.

The HRP's leader is one 'Master' Ryuho Okawa, who founded the HRP as a political offshoot of his Happy Science religious movement in 2009. Happy Science itself was founded by Okawa in 1986, following an ecstatic experience he terms 'The Great Enlightenment'. He is certainly a most enlightened character himself. According to a detailed hagiography on Happy Science's website, Okawa started out as the employee of an unnamed 'major trading company', working in the Foreign Exchange Section of their Tokyo HQ before being transferred to their New York office, inside one of the now-fallen Twin Towers, where he was considered a likely future executive. On 23 March 1981, relaxing during a rare break from work, the young Okawa suddenly sensed an 'invisible presence' somewhere in the room with him. Realising it wished to communicate, Okawa grabbed a pencil. Then, he said, 'my hand holding the pencil began to move as if it had a life of its own. On card after card it wrote the words "Good News, Good News, Good News …"'. The Good News was that he was the reincarnation of Buddha. Surprisingly, rather than renouncing all worldly goods, Buddha continued to grease the wheels of global commodity-exchange until, on 17 June 1986, numerous 'high spirits came down one after another from the heavenly world' to tell him to resign and pursue a nobler path in life.

A month later, after turning thirty, Okawa handed in his notice and (it says here) 'stood up alone for the salvation of all humanity'. By October, the Happy Science movement had been founded, officially being certified as a religious organisation in Japan in 1991.

Okawa is a highly erudite man, who has written over 2,000 books – that number is not a misprint. Some of his titles have become best-sellers, with his early work *The Laws of the Sun* shifting in excess of a million copies. Admittedly, Okawa has had a little help in penning these works, as they have mostly been channelled down from discarnate spirits via a process of automatic writing. The original entity from which Okawa drew literary inspiration was called El Cantare, described as being 'God of the Earth' and 'The Tree of Life', and known as 'Elohim' in the Bible – that is to say, God Himself, the ultimate source of all religions. Occasionally, El Cantare allows His 'core consciousness' to descend to Earth and inhabit a human body in the form of an avatar, or living god; previous incarnations have included Hermes in ancient Greece and, 2,500 years ago, Gautama Buddha in India and Nepal. Gautama was El Cantare's last incarnation prior to 1956, when Master Okawa was born, thus making him both God on Earth and the latest version of Buddha. But what is Buddha doing promoting 1980s-style free-market capitalism?[102]

Angel Investors

It is telling that Okawa bills himself not only as a spiritual Master, but also as 'CEO of the Happy Science Group'. Photographs show a well-groomed, presentable *salaryman*-type in smart suit and tie, not a semi-naked, grey-bearded guru. He has built up Happy Science into a professionally run international organisation with a claimed 12 million members worldwide, who gather at temples called 'Happy Science Shojas' – 'town squares of the soul' and 'lighthouses shining heaven's light to the surrounding areas' – to recite sutras from one of Okawa's books and arrange charity work. Here, a practice known as 'Happiness Planting' takes place – i.e. the soliciting of financial donations. Contributions are voluntary, but promoted in such a way as to have echoes not only of traditional religious teaching, but also of Okawa's career in finance. There is such a thing as 'seed-capital', in which investors give money to start-up businesses in the hope of seeing them grow, thus contributing to the growth of the wider economy and the investor's own bank balance. Happiness Planting seems similar. By giving money to them, Happy Science say, 'not only do you contribute to creating more prosperity in this world, you store spiritual wealth and virtue for when you return back to Heaven. Let us all aim to become angels of wealth.' As an acknowledged Master of the Universe in both a financial and a religious sense, your investments will be safe with Okawa.[103]

But if Okawa can work such wonders for a Japanese person's soul, then why not also for the failing Japanese economy which, after runaway success during the 1980s, has been on the slide ever since? Could Okawa magically multiply yen just like Jesus did with loaves and fishes? Via astute financial management, Okawa thinks he can, and tried to put his theories into practice by founding a political wing of Happy Science, the aforementioned HRP, just in time for 2009's general election. Run initially by his wife Kyoko, whom Okawa said was the earthly incarnation of the goddess Aphrodite – all husbands think that at first – the HRP put forward 345 candidates, but failed to gain a single seat (although they did get a million votes!). Their strange and alarming manifesto was well-explained in an interview Okawa gave to the *Japan Times* prior to polling day. Avowedly Right-wing liberal in outlook, Okawa explained that the HRP aimed to make Japan great again by lowering taxes to encourage growth, and reverse the nation's terrible demographic decline by throwing open Japan's borders to hordes of economic migrants to roughly double the dwindling population to 300 million. If such measures are not taken then, according to the HRP, in thirty years Japan's rapidly aging population will lead it towards economic collapse, as there will be way too many pensioners for the younger, working-age population to support with taxes. In other words, the HRP wishes to recreate Japan's 1980s boom-years by imitating the policies of Thatcherite-Reaganite economic liberalism, which their leader saw working at close-hand during his years trading in New York.

The Iron Lady-Boy

Master Okawa's other main claim to fame is that he can speak to the dead, the vast majority of whom also love the economic, social and military policies of the HRP (Okawa is big on increasing Japan's martial prowess, urging it to build nuclear weapons in case North Korea attacks). These are not just any old ghosts Okawa spends his time chatting with, however, but prominent dead economists, businessmen, politicians and other major figures from world history. The Prophet Muhammad, Nelson Mandela, John Stuart Mill, Kublai Khan, Jesus Christ – all agree with or embody different aspects of the Happies' basic platform. Indeed, it was upon the advice of such spooks that Master Okawa entered politics in the first place. So frequent are his channelled chats that eventually Japan's publishing industry could no longer keep pace, so Happy Science felt compelled to create its own online newspaper in 2010. Called *The Liberty Web*, it seeks to provide 'not only spiritual, but also political, economic and educational advice on a global scale', pointing 'the direction in which this confused and drifting planet should go'. What this amounts to in practice is rather like a surprisingly pro-immigrant Japanese *Daily Mail*, as written by Spiritualists.

As a proud *Mail* reader myself, I agree with editor Jiro Ayaori's desire to prove that 'Marxist income-distribution and a controlled economy produce nothing but poverty' – but I would not choose to try to prove this by running interviews with like-minded ghosts.[104]

The website includes a wealth of bizarre material. Because Okawa reckons that even living people have spirits resident within their minds, in the form of their immortal souls, he has been able to speak to the brain-ghosts of various current world leaders such as Donald Trump, the Kims of Korea and even Vladimir Putin, who is secretly the reincarnation of the Roman Emperor Augustus, hence the Russian strong-man's growing imperial tendencies. Most spiritual interviews on the website, however, take place with the actual discarnate dead. On *The Liberty Web*, not only do Happy journalists provide sympathetic write-ups of talks their leader has had with deceased Japanese war-criminals such as Generals Hideki Tojo (1884–1948) and Iwane Matsui (1878–1948) – in 2013 the group also gained a world-exclusive first interview with the newly deceased Margaret Thatcher (1925–2013) while her corpse was still so fresh she hadn't yet realised she had snuffed it. It was definitely her, as her spirit, which was 'puzzled by the sudden summoning', said things like 'Yes, [I am] the Iron Lady, I'm not very kind, and I have a short temper.' As Okawa said, this was 'a big scoop', and he used it to ask her about the lessons Japan could draw from her successful free-market reforms of the 1980s.

On 23 November 1990, the day following Maggie's tearful announcement she would resign as PM, Master Okawa had already given a speech declaring that the great woman was really an 'angel of light' who originated from the seventh dimension, as well as a man who had chosen to be born into a woman's body in order to advance the feminist cause by swinging her handbag at all and sundry – so Mrs T was really Mr T! During a 1986 interview with the 1,000-year-old ghost of the early female 'novelist' Murasaki Shikibu (*c*.973–*c*.1014), Okawa had discovered that, this time around, the gods had given permission for Thatcher to be born with a vagina instead of the penis he/she normally had. In fact, it transpired that Thatcher's previous Earthly incarnation had been as the demonstrably male Otto von Bismarck (1815–98) – Germany's 'Iron Chancellor' transforming with surprising logic into Britain's 'Iron Lady'! While the Happies run a legal disclaimer before certain interviews with the dead along the lines of 'please note that spiritual messages are opinions of the original spirits and may contradict the ideas or teachings of the Happy Science Group', in Thatcher's case her ideology fitted in perfectly. As well as revealing her deep scepticism about the increasingly out-of-control EU and their blasted Euro, both of which she condemned as dire impositions upon the sovereignty of formerly free nations, she was asked to answer the question 'Why is socialism bad?' Her answer? 'Laziness! They love being lazy ... Labour unions love to indulge in playing, and they don't make efforts to achieve success, money or honour ... [The Left] is ruining the foundations of the UK. It'll lead to the death of the country in the end.' But what was the honourable *Thatcher-san*'s solution to this growing socialistic malaise? 'A small government is preferable, I think ... assist the privatisation of industries. There are too many laws, which prohibit the growth of private companies, so set them free and educate them to fight for themselves in order to obtain prosperity.'[105]

Herald of Free Enterprise

The fact that Mrs T had been stabbed in the back and forced to resign in the year 1990 held great symbolic significance to Master Okawa, as the new decade marked the end not only of the Cold War, but also of Tokyo's long 1980s financial boom. Sadly, with the twin guiding lights of free-market capitalism Margaret Thatcher and Ronald Reagan (1911–2004) – who had shared the same guardian angel in St Michael – now gone, and the world free forever from the threat of Soviet Communism, there was scope for a watering down of the two great Western leaders' proud legacy of prosperity and freedom. Had electorates had enough of free-market policies, and were they about to take an unfortunate turn Leftwards? An interview with the spirit of Victorian philosopher and economist J. S. Mill (1806–73), who warned Okawa about the dangers of 'the tyranny of the majority', suggested so.[106] In a 1997 speech, Okawa explained how, during the late 1980s, it began to appear as if Japan might overtake America as the world's richest country. However since 1990 Japan's GDP has remained stuck around the 500 trillion yen mark, while the US' GDP has tripled. Okawa theorised this was because the Japanese people, conditioned to be subservient to Washington since defeat in the Second World War, had subconsciously made the self-destructive decision to view themselves as a wicked nation who deserved all they got, and to wilfully rein in their runaway growth rates, so as not to antagonise their rightful conqueror, Uncle Sam. In The Master's view, 'the Japanese people have a group psychology ... that overtaking is a fearful thing'. Since 1990, this fear of impolitely overtaking the US's GDP had become firmly embedded within the Japanese psyche, with a prevailing view that 'economic growth [is] evil' holding them back. Whenever the economy showed signs of growth, people complained about inequality, demanding the rich be taxed and their wealth redistributed to the poor, something which harmed business and therefore made everyone worse off. 'Thus, the dark shadow of socialism now looms over Japan,' Okawa concluded, with *1984*-like plans afoot for every citizen to be given a special number which unified all of their financial affairs with their bank accounts, thus allowing the State to steal yen directly from their savings whenever they wished, in order to fund the ever-growing and ever-wasteful welfare state leviathan.[107]

The twin 1980s saviours of the Western economic world, who were both guided in their quest to deregulate free-enterprise by the Archangel Michael – at least according to the leading Japanese politician, necromancer and economic reformer 'Master' Ryuho Okawa. (Courtesy of the White House)

Today, under the *supposedly* Right-wing and free-market-friendly PM Shinzo Abe, who it turns out is really a big soft Lefty, Japan is headed only for financial disaster, says Okawa, at risk of becoming a unilaterally 'pacifist economy'. In 1989, in an act of unconscious economic sabotage, Japan had stupidly introduced a consumption-tax on goods and services, a Japanese VAT. It was no coincidence, said Okawa, that the Japanese economy had begun its slump soon afterwards, as this measure was bound to make consumers less likely to spend. Instead of seeking to abolish this insane tax, as was HRP policy, Abe and his government of clowns had raised it, with plans afoot to hike it even further. Predictably, Japanese consumer spending and commercial profits had since slowed yet more. To counteract this, in 2016 the Bank of Japan introduced a suicidal policy of negative interest rates upon certain deposits made inside commercial banks, the idea being to force banks to lend more cash to businesses, rather than seeing it rot away inside their vaults. Normal high-street depositors were not meant to be affected by this measure themselves, but some at the time warned that the banks in question would eventually end up passing on the cost of this measure to their ordinary customers through negative interest rates on standard current and savings accounts.

Possibly, this is what the Bank of Japan really wanted, but would prefer this to be done by proxy, so as to shift the inevitable anger of the electorate

151

onto someone else. If so, then this was a modern-day resurrection of the ideas of Silvio Gesell; with negative interest rates, if the Japanese people leave their hard-earned yen in the bank in the form of savings, with every passing month its value will decrease. Should such measures be universalised by the banks to claw back profits, the alleged government hope was that, once they saw their money disappearing before their eyes, consumers would draw as much out as possible and embark upon a massive, nationwide spending-spree, creating an economic boom. As Okawa correctly perceived, however, any such 'boom' would really be nothing but a temporary financial bubble, which would very soon burst. Following an initial short-lived splurge as they bought any desired items they had been putting off purchasing in favour of saving, Japanese consumers would work out they could easily avoid the effects of negative interest rates simply by withdrawing their money and keeping it at home under their beds.

Panasonic Boom

Furthermore, Master Okawa knew that such policies of so-called 'Abenomics' went against the teachings of the highly esteemed nineteenth-century Japanese philosopher, economist and agricultural reformer Ninomiya Sontoku (1787–1856), who had first promoted concepts such as compound interest to Japan. Sontoku's basic idea that 'the accumulation of small efforts brings great success' was hard-wired into generations of Japanese brains as being the very 'spirit of capitalism', but now negative interest rates were in severe danger of destroying the underlying intellectual basis of Nippon's prosperity forever. This was because, as Sontoku and Okawa had both warned, 'if people are unable to accumulate capital [due to negative interest], no one will be able to expand a business to make greater profit, and therefore the economy will never grow.' In distinctly Thatcherite tones, Okawa could only conclude that 'The Abe administration thinks that governmental economic policies can control economic conditions, but this approach will only make the Japanese economy plunge headfirst into darkness.'[108]

Hoping to avert this grim fate, The Master resorted once more to necromancy, and summoned down the spirit of Konosuke Matsushita (1894–1989) from the Land of the Dead. As the founder of the Japanese electronics giant Panasonic, and a man dubbed 'The God of Management' in his homeland, surely Matsushita would know what to do. Matsushita agreed to provide the Happies with a free business seminar from beyond the grave, advising them to ignore all these airy-fairy economic theorists who were busy running Japan into the ground and rely upon their own instincts instead. The average economist had never done a proper day's work in his life, said Matsushita, explaining 'in detail why intellectuals were unfit for business management'. Common sense policies like those of the HRP were needed, with a return to the gloriously successful free-market ways of the 1980s being long overdue. Excessive governmental interference in the economy at the instigation of the defeatist Left-wing media had only served to help ruin it, he said, leading to twenty years of damaging malaise, and a general weakening of the spirit of Japanese business.[109]

In order to restore this spirit to its fullest strength, Okawa recommended something predictably strange. The First World Japanese economy had become a victim of its own 1980s success, Okawa declared, with its consumers no longer particularly having any pressing needs, and so not wanting to buy as much as they had done in the past. Who needs the latest TV when you already have three perfectly good ones lying around your house anyway? In his 2015 lecture *The Mind That Calls Forth Miracles*, rather than just manufacturing more and more of such mundane products, Master Okawa recommended that Japanese *salarymen* instead open their minds to such an extent that they were 'able to connect and draw inspiration from other dimensions', thereby designing and producing fantastic new consumer products which 'touch people's hearts' and are infused with 'holy wisdom' – the kinds of things even René Guénon might be happy to buy. What will these products be, though? How about amazing vehicles which will instigate 'a transportation revolution that will save time and add more substance to life and work', 'space-development and ocean-development [tools] that will break through the frontiers of man', or simply 'things that will solve issues'? 'From now on,' says Okawa, 'businessmen will take on the role of creating enterprises that will move and impress people, through using the power of the subconscious to the full.' These legions of psychic businessmen, Okawa proposes, will reinvigorate domestic enterprise to such an extent that Japan's economy will quickly display qualities of 'infinite progress', with its GDP tripling to around 1.5 quadrillion yen.[110] Somewhere in the Heaven of the seventh dimension, the ghost of Mrs Thatcher must be looking down upon the good work of her enlightened Japanese protégé with immense angelic pride. Where there is currently economic discord, may he one day bring harmony.

What Would Jesus Do?

Surprisingly, Mrs T's own economic ideas while she was still alive were partly inspired by religious motives. A traditionalist, ideally she wanted her political programme to restore the ties that bind, and take Britain back into the cosy, cohesive world of the 1950s, not spin it ever onwards into the chaos of hyper-globalised modernity. 'Economics is the method,' she once said, 'the object is to change the soul.' The daughter (or secret transgender son) of a Methodist lay-preacher named Alf Roberts who also ran a grocer's shop, Maggie linked capitalism and Christianity together from an early age, and was inspired by daddy's sermons to try to restore the bond previously identified by Max Weber between the Protestant work-ethic and economic success. Alf constantly hymned the virtues of thrift, industry, saving, self-reliance and individual liberty. Indeed, during her youth, Thatcher dabbled in lay-preaching herself, later doing her best to link the Invisible Hand of the Market to the Invisible Hand of God by illustrating her economic values with reference to the Bible. A particular obsession was the parable of the Good Samaritan. In order to help out the injured man lying on the road in Jesus' famous story, Maggie carefully explained that 'no one would remember the Good Samaritan if he'd only had good intentions; he had [to have] money as well.' 'I wonder whether [welfare] state services would have done as much for the man?' she asked, in unconscious self-parody. The Lefty wets in the Church of England, beginning their long transformation into *Guardian*-reading mitred social workers, may have disagreed with Maggie, but she could easily have quoted St Paul's Second Letter to the Thessalonians (3:10) back to them, namely 'If a man will not work, he shall not eat.' So, cut the scroungers' benefits, Jesus would have done.[111]

Thatcher's creed came not only from her twin Holy Fathers of Alf and the Bible, but also from a Slovak-American Catholic theologian and economist named Michael Novak (1933–2017), who basically argued that, had Jesus been alive today, he would have been a CEO. Novak spent much of his youth in a seminary, but eventually concluded the priesthood was not for him. Seeking to spread social justice in the world by other means, he flirted with Left-wing nonsense in his youth, as so many of us poor sinners do, before going on to reject this adolescent folly also, becoming an adviser to Popes and Presidents upon the godly virtues of the free market. Mrs Thatcher invited Novak to Downing Street and showed him her personal copy of his key 1982 book *The Spirit of Democratic Capitalism*; it was full of annotations and underlinings. Novak's main idea was that capitalist corporations were doing God's work by spreading wealth around the world, thereby alleviating poverty, and setting men free from the tyranny of the Satanic Servile State. He advised young people considering career options that they would 'save their souls and serve the cause of the Kingdom of God ... by restoring the liberty and power of the private sector'. By facilitating the increase of ever-more pointless public sector jobs, the tax-and-spend Devil was making work for idle hands to do, thereby accounting for the existence of most bureaucratic busybodies and their hellish red tape. Business, Novak said, was a calling from The Lord, which unleashed the innate, God-given creative faculties of captains of industry. Jesus taught us never to hide your light under a bushel or bury your talents under the ground, and if your talents happened to include selling Coca-Cola to Mexicans, then this was nothing less than missionary work in disguise. Both echoing and inverting Sergei Bulgakov, Novak argued that, just as God was the Creator, so was the man who created a new brand of breakfast cereal, as the corporation's creativity 'mirrors God's' – this must be why Richard Branson thinks he is Christ, and trims his facial hair accordingly. Novak's teachings about capitalism producing 'morally better people than socialism does' provided for Mrs T 'the intellectual basis for my approach' towards the economy, she once wrote, praising the way Novak 'put into new and striking language what I had always believed.'

The Slovak Novak thought corporations were *Kabbalah*-like extensions of the Godhead down onto Earth, and that as such it was America and Britain's sacred duty to spread the word of *laissez faire* capitalism to every corner of the planet, like Victorians colonising Africa for the natives' own good. God disliked excessive taxation and burdensome overregulation, and made some countries poor on purpose so they would have a motivation to trade with rich ones, thus helping bring mankind together. Throughout the 1980s and '90s books with titles such as *Toward a Theology of the Corporation* poured from Novak's well-meaning pen, in which he explained that the Central American isthmus which joins North and South America together was a sign from God telling Ronald Reagan to bridge the ideological gap between the two continents by selling the Lefty Latinos lots of cheap stuff to help engineer a turn to the Right. Adoption of the free market, said Novak, inevitably produced a nation 'free in its polity, free in its economy, and free in the realm of conscience and inquiry'. Rebellious workers in 1980s Communist Poland agreed; copies of Novak's books circulated as *samizdat* underground literature there, inspiring those who wanted the Eastern Bloc to be free.[112]

Christ on a Bus!

But if Jesus were alive today, would He really vote Tory? Someday soon, it may be possible to ask Him. By an amazing cosmic coincidence, while Guatama Buddha is currently seeking high office over in Japan, his Western counterpart Jesus Christ has also been reincarnated and is employed as an NHS night porter in an unnamed London hospital, awaiting the perfect time to unveil his own economic doctrines to the world. That was the opinion of Benjamin Creme (1922–2016), a Scottish-born painter who made headlines in the 1980s by claiming to have discovered that Jesus had regenerated Himself as a Pakistani and emerged from a cave somewhere in the Himalayas during 1977, from whence He had flown to London and begun living undercover among His fellow subcontinental folk in the wonderfully vibrant and diverse Brick Lane area. Unaccountably, Tony Blair did not make any use of this fact when unilaterally throwing open the UK's borders to all-comers following his catastrophic election in 1997, seeing as here was a prime example of an immigrant from another culture successfully finding gainful employment, paying His taxes, and helping contribute to the upkeep of our precious public services. Apparently, from 1978 onwards, Brick Lane Jesus achieved the status of 'community spokesman' for the local Pakistani community, thus becoming the real-life equivalent of TV's *Citizen Khan*. You may think it surprising that London's Muslims accepted Jesus Christ as their self-appointed representative, but it transpires that Christ is simultaneously an entity called 'Maitreya', who is also somehow a reincarnation of Krishna, Buddha and the Imam Mahdi, a mystical Islamic figure fated to prepare the ground for the return of the Prophet Muhammad.

Jesus was now also an economist, and Creme claimed to have the ability to channel Christ's fiscal thoughts direct through his own mouth, tape-recordings of which he played before a small crowd on a monthly basis in a building opposite Euston Station. Occasionally Maitreya would also engage in a spot of light teleportation to spread His word directly, as in 1988 when He allegedly appeared before astonished onlookers at a Kenyan prayer-meeting, causing one onlooker to literally wet his pants. Having delivered an impromptu lecture and healed some cripples, Jesus (who often pretends to be a hitch hiker, in order to inform passing motorists about his theories before vanishing) accepted a lift home from a local man named Mr Gurnam Singh, and asked to be let out at the nearest terminus, so He could catch the number 56 bus. However, once Jesus exited Mr Singh's car and approached the bus terminus, He 'simply vanished into thin air' and returned to Brick Lane, hopefully in time for the start of His next hospital-shift. This was reported as 'fact' in the Kenyan Press of the time, complete with actual photographs! The British media proved more sceptical, though. In 1982, Creme spent £100,000 advertising the Second Coming of the Lord in newspapers across the world, and in 1984 arranged a meeting with Jesus and some journalists in an Asian restaurant, but Christ never turned up, being prevented from doing so by 'materialistic forces'. Creme assured the media that Jesus had definitely been spotted working part-time as a waiter in various Brick Lane eateries before, but when Christ later attempted to set up another interview on the BBC during 1986, which would involve Him being filmed in silence and broadcasting His thoughts out to global TV viewers telepathically in their own native languages, He was repeatedly thwarted by The Establishment, who objected to the nature of His stridently anti-Thatcherite message.[113]

To prepare the world for the implications of Christ's Second Coming, once the pathetic BBC would finally deign to announce it properly, Creme set up and edited a more-or-less monthly magazine, *Share International*, whose articles aimed to contain a peculiar synthesis of 'the political and the spiritual' by covering the economic priorities of Maitreya, defined as being 'an adequate [global] supply of the right food; appropriate housing for all; healthcare and education as universal rights; and the maintenance of ecological balance'. *Share International* is still going today and is available not only in English but also Dutch, French, German, Spanish, Polish, Slovenian and Japanese – I wonder if Master Okawa subscribes to it, and if so what he thinks about having a rival claimant to the title of Buddha? Having the motto 'Share and Save the World', the journal first appeared in 1982 and during all that time has never published a single advert, thereby remaining unsullied by the propagandist filth of global capital. In 1993, *Share International* carried an in-depth interview with Creme, in which the editor laid out Maitreya's economic philosophy in full. Interestingly, in his dialogue and its preamble, Creme appeared to predict the 2007/08 crash, stating that Western stock markets were due to 'plunge' on account of the way that many financial transactions had become purely ethereal and electronic in nature, being 'unrelated to any exchange of real goods and services'. Echoing a view of J. M. Keynes, he compared the post-Cold War free market to a 'global casino'. The idea of perpetual growth was an illusion, and the excessive consumption of natural resources in pursuit of this mirage was destroying our planet. Maitreya/Jesus was offering a different vision for world trade, one based upon sustainability and self-sufficiency, the fair and equitable redistribution of resources, strict population control and 'a crash programme of aid on a world scale to alleviate … suffering'.

Creme Crashes

The most interesting aspect of Maitreya's plan was to replace international trade based upon money with 'a sophisticated form of barter, on a global scale'. Apparently, specific technical plans for this return to bartering had already been drawn up by a crack-team of Spiritual Masters of Wisdom and 'economists, financiers and industrialists of great achievement', acting upon Jesus' basic vision, plans which were 'awaiting only the demand of humanity for their implementation'. Following the 2007/08 crash, some of Creme's followers thought this plan's time had finally come, on the basis that, due to a short-term food production problem in South-East Asia, the Malaysian government had announced it would be willing to swap its national store of palm-oil that year for a supply of rice-crop, 'with any rice-producing nation willing to make the trade'. However, this offer turned out to be a one-off blip due to special circumstances, and money is still king in international trade … for now. Free-market mechanisms 'have their place', said Jesus/Creme, but 'when they are followed blindly, they lead inevitably to destruction'. Denying that 'market forces are the saviour of mankind', as Michael Novak had argued, Creme warned the standing down of Cold War armies was only the prelude to something far worse:

> The energy which sent the planes into the sky and the tanks and troops onto the battlefield does not just disappear. It is a destructive force which

[Maitreya] says has been going around the world looking for a new home. He says it has found a 'new womb'. That new womb is commercialisation based on market forces, which, he says, are based on human greed. Maitreya calls market forces the forces of evil because they have inequality built into their very structure ... We are finding a situation where the rise in [economic] tension is so great it has within it the seeds of a Third World War, and that war would destroy all life.

The imbalance between the First and Third Worlds was ultimately 'created by disharmonic thought-patterns', argued Jesus, and, because He had predicted the pricking of Japan's 1980s economic bubble a year or two before it actually burst, Creme thought Jesus should be listened to. Scarily, the Tokyo bubble had been full of pure spiritual evil that was now floating across Western economies, leading to gross situations in which the EU held on to butter mountains and wine lakes to ensure high prices for French farmers, while poor Africans starved. On the other hand, the bursting of the Japanese bubble had the potential to be like the lancing of a nasty boil, in which all badness was expelled from the Western body-politic. While Japanese investors would alas soon 'start jumping out of high windows', Japan's malaise could also provide the wake-up call for mankind to realise it shared a single soul, thereby prompting the miserly EU to start donating its surplus butter and wine to Africa to feed the starving millions, or at least get them drunk and greased up. This would be the initial basis of the coming UN-run system of global barter, which would solve the world's problems forever, ushering in an era of universal peace, harmony and brotherhood of man; once each country on Earth had drawn up 'an inventory of its assets and needs', they could start swapping resources just as Malaysia tried to do with its palm-oil surplus. The eulogising of free-market competition had led to division within the World-Soul, but if we could learn to share and share alike, such rifts could be healed forever. 'We either share or we die, it is as simple as that,' concluded Creme.[114]

Identity Crisis

In 2010, Creme sensationally announced that he had seen 'The World Teacher' and 'Master of all the Masters' appear on a 'well-known television programme on a major network in the United States' under a false name. Creme refused to specify the show in question, but his followers checked through US TV schedules and discovered a recent appearance by a Left-leaning economist and former British citizen of Indian ancestry called Dr Raj Patel on a daytime chat-show. A critic of capitalism, Patel was the author of such books as *Stuffed and Starved: Markets, Power and the Hidden Battle for the World Food System* and *The Value of Nothing: How to*

Reclaim Market Society and Redefine Democracy, so certainly sounded as if he shared some of NHS Jesus's Corbynista-style political views. Furthermore, he had indeed entered Britain in 1977, the same year as Maitreya was meant to have done, but as Patel was thirty-seven at the time his 'true' identity was revealed in 2010, he must have been a toddler at the time, which does not fit in with Christ's previous biography. Also, the British-born Patel's 'entry into the country' was simply a return from a family holiday abroad, and so did not represent his emergence from a secret Himalayan cave at all, but from within a hotel room. Comparison of photos of Patel with photos taken of Jesus waiting for a bus in Kenya back in 1988 conclusively demonstrate that they are not the same man (although Creme thought Maitreya could shape-shift, potentially explaining this discrepancy).

Nonetheless, several of Creme's disciples eagerly e-mailed Patel, politely asking if he really was the Second Coming and, if so, would He mind them worshipping Him? Disappointingly, Patel said he had never even heard of Maitreya, and jokily modified the famous line from *Monty Python's Life of Brian* to read 'Sadly, I'm not the Messiah, I'm just a very naughty boy.' Some of Creme's followers interpreted this denial as further proof that Patel *really was* Christ, however, on the grounds that on one of Creme's channelled audio-tapes, Maitreya had stated that He didn't particularly want people to worship Him, something which chimed perfectly with Mr Patel's embarrassed words.[115] So, if you really do want to know what Jesus would do when faced with the ills of modern-day economic inequality, just buy one of Patel's books – it could well become your economic Bible.

3

Taxing Credulity

Gabriel Green and the Interplanetary Campaign to Abolish Income-Tax

Live long and prosper!
Mr Spock, well-known alien being

The neglected tale of how an obscure Californian politician hatched a revolutionary plan to abolish all taxation from our economically oppressed planet forever – upon the direct advice of friendly alien accountants from another world.

They say there are only two things that are certain in life – death and taxes. But what if someone came along promising you freedom from both? The kind person who was once to be found offering mankind just such a promise was Gabriel Green (1924–2001), a California-based economic theorist, alien Contactee and founder of the Amalgamated Flying Saucer Clubs of America, or AFSCA. 'Honest Gabe' ('Abe in 1860 – Gabe in 1960', ran the optimistic Lincoln-referencing slogan on one of his campaign pin-badges) was a two-time US presidential candidate whose political high-point came during the 1962 race for a seat in California's Senate, when, by his own account, he placed second in the State's Democratic Primary with some 171,631 votes, or 8.45 per cent of those cast. That's not too bad a showing for a UFO-nut, but nonetheless stood as something of a disappointment for Green himself; as a result of his many years of psychic contact with benign humanoid aliens, he genuinely believed that 'I have been selected [to become] President by folks from outer-space.' 'With the help of space-men I believe I can carry millions of votes,' Green once said, as 'hundreds of Space People' were 'walking the streets' in disguise, building support for his ticket – but not quite enough support, evidently. Maybe, as non-native citizens, they were ineligible to vote?

Billing himself as 'The Space People's Choice', Green's first failed bid for public office came when he announced himself as a candidate for Congress in 1958, under the auspices of the short-lived Economic Security Party, or 'ESP' for short (the letters 'ESP' also stand for 'Extra-Sensory Perception', a fancy name for 'psychic powers'). Two years later Green was back, running as a candidate during the 1960 presidential election, but that October he withdrew his candidacy, endorsing the eventual winner John F. Kennedy (1917–63) for the role instead. However, as both JFK and his brother Robert (1925–68) were clearly 'card-carrying members of AFSCA', and because Green himself was in regular telepathic contact with the Kennedy clan, it seems that Gabe had a direct hot-line to America's youthful new leader in any case, and so could influence economic policy in that way instead – or so he said. Just like George Washington, Honest Gabe could never tell a lie ... could he?

California Dreamers

If Gabriel Green was lying to anyone, then it was surely to himself. Obviously a sincere (if deeply deluded) individual, Green was typical of the 1950s Contactees – as people who claimed to have had contact with friendly human-like space-persons were then known – in that he was as much a trance-medium as an interlocutor with extra-terrestrials, engaging in a number of nascent New Age fads from past-life regression to channelling. While Green claimed a number of actual, physical encounters with solid-bodied Space Brothers, as the affable aliens of the period were dubbed, he would more often simply allow them to speak through his own body, like a Spiritualist at a séance. A California native, Green was well-placed to take part in the Contactee-craze which swept through the Golden State following the first well-publicised saucer-sighting of the era, made by commercial pilot Kenneth Arnold (1915–85) over Washington State's Cascade Mountains on the afternoon of 24 June 1947. A local Polish-American Contactee and mystic named George Adamski's (1891–1965) alleged meeting with a Scandinavian-looking Venusian space-hippie named Orthon out in the Mojave Desert in 1952 helped make California the early epicentre of America's saucer-scene, a fortuitous development which Green happily exploited. Drafted into the US Navy in 1942, Green returned to civilian life following the end of the Second World War, setting up his own photography studio and working for the Los Angeles school-system at their Visual Education Centre. In 1956 he made his first public foray into the world of the saucers, setting up his own amateur UFO-club called the Los Angeles Interplanetary Study Group. As well as making repeated visits to fellow Contactee George Van Tassel's (1910–78) annual 'Interplanetary Spacecraft Convention' held each summer out in the Mojave at a place called Giant Rock (charming *Life* magazine photos of Green wearing a pith-helmet made up to look like a stereotypical 1950s saucer exist), Green's most notable early activities involved publicising the comical claims of a man named Dick Miller, who affected to be in communication with a Martian named Mon-Ka, via his ham-radio set.[1]

Mon-Ka had first made himself known to a wider public in April 1956, live on-stage at that year's Giant Rock Convention, during which Miller had played a series of recordings upon which the entity's voice had supposedly appeared while the audio-tapes had been sitting in their sealed cans. Even though Mon-Ka – who claimed to be 'what you would call the head of my government' – spoke in the ridiculous cadences of a 1950s Ed Wood B-movie script, the credulous yet harmless crowd went wild, treating proclamations such as the following with a seriousness which they did not really deserve: 'On the evening of November 7, of this your year 1956, at 10.30 p.m. your local time, we request that one of your communications stations remove its carrier signal from the air for two minutes. At that time we will speak [over the radio] from our craft, which will be stationed at an altitude of 10,000 feet over your great city of Los Angeles.' This sounded like real first-contact was about to occur – until the local *Los Angeles Mirror-News* dug up a scoop that Miller had already been caught out faking a radio-communication from a flying saucer in his native Detroit some time earlier. Nonetheless, Mon-Ka's promise proved popular with thrill-seeking LA locals, who held two mass rallies in the imaginary Martian's honour in late October. When 7 November came around, two local radio-stations did indeed go off the air, hoping to gain some free PR, and a plane was sent out to look for Mon-Ka's spaceship hovering overhead. Sadly, the craft never made it to LA that night, and the airwaves remained entirely free of messages from Mars.[2]

Reflections in the Mirror

The *Mirror-News* was to play a major role in publicising Green's many odd claims throughout the late 1950s and early '60s, helping him gain the status of local celebrity which allowed him to enter the realm of politics. On 11 July 1959, for instance, under the headline 'Flying Saucer Clubs Still Hold to Gravity', the newspaper ran a long report on the newly rechristened Amalgamated Flying Saucer Clubs of America's first-ever annual meeting in LA. A new name AFSCA may have had, but some of Gabriel Green's old friends still turned up for the occasion nonetheless, including Dick Miller who was now in contact with an alien called Kla-La from the star-system of Aldeberan, a wise being who had suggested holding the conference in the first place. Considering that Green's dad Seth was listed as AFSCA's Treasurer, the outfit can't exactly have been big-time, but Green kept it up and running, even if only in name, right until his death in 2001. AFSCA was never a home for the more serious-minded UFO researchers of the day, but it proved very popular among those at the more unconventional end of the spectrum. As such, Press reports about Green were largely light-hearted, something he seemed willing to endure just so long as they helped get his message across.

Typical was a May 1966 interview with *The Houston Post*, in which Green tried his best to spread his personal economic message, while the *Post*'s reporter equally did his own best to ask silly questions about where precisely the aliens parked their saucers while they were visiting him. Because Green took such queries seriously, talking about spaceships being parked in the sky using special force-fields, he came across as something of a nut, a notion not dispelled when he was persuaded to start talking about how it was possible that Jesus Christ had been an alien, who had used 'a Martian levitation-belt' to walk across Lake Galilee. When he also boasted about receiving regular phone-calls from outer-space, and described meeting a 'casually dressed' Martian 'by appointment at a friend's home', the reporter's willingness to file some copy about boring old economic matters must have been slight – and so it proved. Although Green told the journalist he had selflessly resigned his secure photography job with the LA School Board in 1959 to 'help the space-men save civilisation' via financial means, only a single (and very vague) sentence about monetary matters was allowed to creep into the article itself.

The *Mirror-News* was much the same, it being obvious the newspaper viewed Green and his chums as a bunch of loveable loonies. You would never have guessed from the tone of their reporting that here was the man whose destiny was to end the problem of poverty forever. On 10 August 1960, under the headline 'Flying Saucer Man Runs for President', the publication ran a comical-looking photo of Green dressed in an old-fashioned bow-tie and checked-suit, which lent him the look of a stand-up comedian, while filling readers in on his latest tilt at leadership of the Free World. However, instead of focusing on his innovative economic policies, reporter Jack Smith focused upon the much more pressing issue of the 'spectacular' red socks the candidate was wearing. 'Did you get those from outer-space?' he was asked. 'No,' Green replied. What was wrong with these hacks? Didn't they want to ask about any of the really important issues? No. What interviewers really wanted to know was what the women were like in outer-space. 'Beautiful' was the answer; one of Green's friends had eyed one up recently, concluding she was 'really out of this world'. That was just great, but why had no aliens come with him to his Press conference that day? Didn't this prove he was lying? 'It doesn't prove you don't exist if you don't show up for work in the morning, does it?' pointed out Gabe. 'If we receive sufficient publicity … we will be in the White House this year.' Predictably, though, the lying fake news media proved little use to Green when it came to disseminating any meaningful details about his manifesto for office; if you wanted those, then you would just have to subscribe to his semi-regular newsletter-cum-fanzine *Thy Kingdom Come*, the world's number one source of UFO-related financial theorising.[3]

Blowing His Own Horn

Thy Kingdom Come was not what most people might have expected from a UFO magazine. For one thing, the front-page motto of its first issue dated January 1957 was not something like 'THE TRUTH IS OUT THERE' but advertised instead that the publication was 'DEDICATED TO THE PHYSICAL, SPIRITUAL AND ECONOMIC EMANCIPATION OF MAN', followed up by a declaration that the main aim of the periodical was 'To help initiate, through political and economic action, the procedures for providing abundance for all.' Doing so would 'help establish ... The Kingdom of Heaven on Earth', thus accounting for the title chosen by Green for his journal. Another regular cover-feature was a crude stick-man drawing of someone blowing a horn. This was a reference to a prophecy once made by the famed sixteenth-century English witch Old Mother Shipton (*c.*1488–1561) to the effect that: 'Storms will rage and oceans roar, when GABRIEL stands on sea and shore; and as he blows his wondrous horn, OLD WORLDS SHALL DIE AND NEW BE BORN.' To Green, this was nothing less than a genuine, centuries-old prediction of the key role he was destined to play in history as the man who ushered in a new utopian era of economic abundance upon Earth. In the Bible, the Angel Gabriel had announced the birth of Christ to the world; in the pages of *Thy Kingdom Come*, Gabriel Green announced the birth of something far more significant – Prior Choice Economics!

As editions passed by, the political and socio-economic content of the amateur fanzine grew ever-larger. In issue four, Green announced that in 1958's elections he would be standing for the position of US Congressman in the 24th District of California, under the banner of the ESP Party. By issue five, even greater news was announced; George Van Tassel, of Giant Rock fame, was throwing his hat into the ring to become President of the United States in the 1960 election, 'at the unexpected request of the Space People'. In his editorial, Green praised Van Tassel's decision, on the grounds that 'God helps those who help themselves'. 'The political actions now being undertaken by the disciples of today are for the purpose of setting up Christ's Kingdom on Earth,' Green explained, and Van Tassel's announcement was definitely 'a step in the right direction'. If you were a New Ager, then sitting around and waiting to receive enlightenment was no longer enough in this precarious Cold War era, the Space Brothers had declared. Instead, 'By their actions and words shall the children of God be known.' If readers didn't want their children to 'come into life with deformed, diseased and demented bodies' because of nuclear warfare, then they had to join the ESP Party and tell the hawkish goons and wannabe-Dr Strangeloves in Washington that all H-bomb testing had to cease immediately, and an era of global peace begin instead. But how could this nonviolent new world come about? Why, by adoption of Prior Choice Economics, of course! Billed as 'a unique economic system', which would allow people to 'easily' put their religious principles into practice like never before, Green said that Prior Choice doctrine would enable mankind to 'fulfil the glorious non-destructive prophecies and promises of the religions of the Earth', bringing about Nirvana, Valhalla and the New Jerusalem, all in one. The precise details, promised Green, would be printed in next month's issue – 'Be sure not to miss it!'

Emancipation Proclamation

Next month's version of *Thy Kingdom Come*, number six, dated December 1957, may have featured a huge image of a flying saucer on the front, as per usual, but its contents bore scant relation to UFOs at all, reading more like a special edition of *The Economist* gone horribly wrong. The publication's new slogan had become 'WHAT EVERY CITIZEN, TAXPAYER AND BUSINESSMAN IS LOOKING FOR', followed by the following seven-point summation of the magazine's contents:

1. How to reduce taxes or end taxation altogether.
2. How to increase sales and make more profit.
3. How to make a profit on everything you produce.
4. How to accomplish 100 per cent distribution of what you are capable of producing.
5. How to solve the employee and employer problems of automation, eliminate the present vested interest in inefficiency to unshackle the chains of industry, and usher in the automatonic age with its benefits to all people.
6. How to guarantee a free enterprise, individual-initiative form of society, and prevent Communism and Socialism.
7. How it may now be possible to bring 'World Peace Through World Trade'.

It sounds like the false prospectus of some shameless political scam-artist like Jeremy Corbyn, but Gabriel Green was absolutely sincere in thinking his system could follow through on each and every one of those impossible-sounding promises. On the back page of the same issue was a short biography of the man himself, in which he proudly announced that, with his Prior Choice theory, he had solved 'the problems of people', and compared himself to Abraham Lincoln (1809–65), 'The Great Emancipator' of America's black slaves. 'Some of those who know him,' he wrote of himself, grandly using the third-person like Julius Caesar, 'compare his ideals [to those of Lincoln] and draw a correlation between the emancipation of man from physical slavery in the beginning, and the emancipation of man from economic slavery in the end, as both parts of an overall goal to obtain true freedom under God, as was envisaged by the Founding Fathers of this great nation.'

Above and Opposite: 1960s US presidential candidate Gabriel Green's uncanny prediction of Internet shopping procedures, made as part of his promotion of his beloved 'Prior Choice Economics' system. Green's idea of accessing a 'Tele-Dial Automatic Vending-Machine Dept' on your TV before ordering goods to be delivered to your home was not too far from what Amazon.com does today in reality, using PCs, smartphones and tablets. (*Thy Kingdom Come* issue 6)

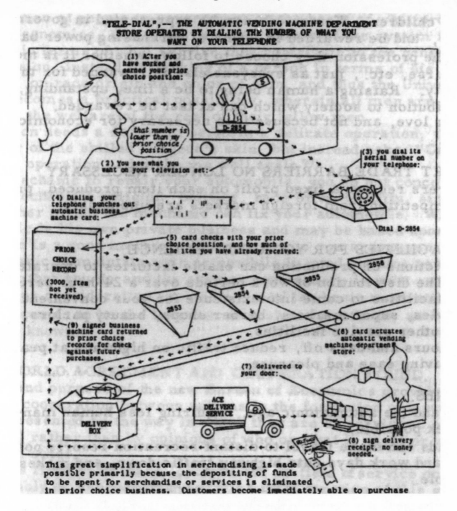

"TELE-DIAL", — THE AUTOMATIC VENDING MACHINE DEPARTMENT STORE OPERATED BY DIALING THE NUMBER OF WHAT YOU WANT ON YOUR TELEPHONE

This great simplification in merchandising is made possible primarily because the depositing of funds to be spent for merchandise or services is eliminated in prior choice business. Customers become immediately able to purchase

Make Prior Choice Your First Choice

The actual concept of Prior Choice Economics, as described by this latter-day Lincoln, rests upon one core principle, namely that 'Everything is ... the sum total of all that has taken place before', in economics as in history and Nature. Applied to the world of finance, this means that a person doesn't actually have any less money in their bank account once they have spent it. Under this wonderful system, explains Green, 'one's purchasing power is determined by the total amount [you] have done in your life', that is to say, the sum total of your paid labours over a lifetime, not by how much cash you have left in the bank since receiving your last paycheque. Say you start your first-ever job after leaving education, and earn $1,500 at the end of your first month. Under the current system, you would end up spending most of that, and adding what little remains to your next paycheque of $1,500. Under a

Prior Choice System, however, that original $1,500 never runs out. Instead, the sum total of the worth of your work is added up by government clerks after each and every monthly payday on a special credit-card, so that after one month you are worth $1,500, after two $3,000, after three $4,500 and so on forever, so that eventually everyone ends up rich. These 'dollars' are not really dollars at all, though, being better thought of as 'Credit Points', because under Green's scheme, money does not actually exist. Scanning your Prior Choice Card into a cash-register does not lead to any money or money-like tokens being exchanged, as you keep your total number of Credit Points so far accumulated. Nothing is ever 'spent'; instead, your Prior Choice Card simply indicates the maximum value of any given item in stock you are entitled to, as your lifetime human right, on account of your accumulated service to mankind. As Green put it, Prior Choice is 'A NON-MONEY, NON-SPENDING SYSTEM OF ECONOMICS; NOTHING IS EXCHANGED AT THE TIME OF PURCHASE.' One of its main principles was 'Do not destroy or get rid of, only create or increase', a law most hard-pressed workers would doubtless find agreeable.

The sole point of working, from a selfish personal point of view, thus becomes to get to the front of the queue when it comes to the distribution of new or rare goods. The reason for calling the system 'Prior Choice' is that those who have banked the most Credit Points get prior choice of the most scarce, and therefore most expensive, luxury items. The value of all products for sale, says Green, 'is determined by the amount of work done by the last person to which it can be distributed before its supply is exhausted', a value which is constantly declining as more and more of each product is manufactured. Imagine a new model of automobile is produced, and only 100 roll off the production-line in the first month. Only the 100 richest people in the country would be able to afford one, in the sense of being given first choice of purchase. In this case, the manufacturer looks up who that 100th richest person is, and how many Credit Points they have on their Prior Choice Card. Let's say they have 10 million. The price, therefore, would be set at 10 million Credit Points, or 'dollars', for tradition's sake. The next month, another 1,000 autos roll off the assembly line; now, they should be available to the richest 1,100 people in the land as there are 1,100 of the things in total, and nobody is allowed to be greedy and purchase two. The manufacturer looks up who this 1,100th person is, and sets the price accordingly. Maybe by the second month of production, the price of the car will have dropped down to a cool million. By the end of the year, perhaps 10,000 cars have been made, and the price plummeted to $50,000 per car. If the car becomes so popular that nearly every person in the country starts driving one, then the price will freefall to something like $500, meaning almost any adult with a work-record can have one upon request. By this point, however, the manufacturer will have designed an even better new model, which will initially be scarce, and begin to be sold at a high price of $10 million again ... and so on, forever.

Appliances which penetrate 99.9 per cent of homes, therefore, like vacuum-cleaners or TVs, will ultimately become dirt-cheap, and truly universal products everyone must have – such as clothes, food, medicine, utilities and basic housing – will cost literally nothing, meaning that anyone ascetically minded enough to live a truly frugal, non-materialistic life will be able to do so *gratis* until the day they die. A young university student, therefore, who has never done a day's paid toil in his life, would still be able to get as much food as he required even though his Prior Choice Card had a rating of $0, and would even have a simple home of his own, without having to pay for it. Maybe if he wanted a few extra things, such as books, to make his life more bearable, he could do a short stint in a factory until he had, say, $1,000 stored on his Card, enabling him to buy such things easily. If he was happy driving an old-fashioned, low-range $500 car, he need never leave higher-education and get a proper job at all, if he didn't want to. This is because, as no money is ever actually changing hands during any transaction, manufacturers, builders and retailers will, under Green's system, be forced by law to produce their products and services to satisfy demand from the population as a whole, not to make a profit. If everyone wants a private jet, for example, then it is the legal obligation of aerospace companies to keep on building them until everyone has one; not, as now, their task to gain profit by building only as many as they can sell to a few lucky billionaires. 'THE PURCHASE PRICE OF A PRODUCT FOR SALE IS ENTIRELY INDEPENDENT OF ITS ACTUAL VALUE', wrote Green, in excited capitals, allowing everyone to have one, eventually.

From the Cradle to the Grave

Rates of pay would be determined by a special government council, composed of representatives from every profession, who would determine the true social worth of each job, thus meaning that persons who truly served their community, like nurses and hangmen, would be given higher salaries than the bloated bureaucrats who currently oversee them – a nice idea, if woefully unlikely. Green's hope was that a person's Prior Choice Credit-Score would act as a numerical evaluation of their moral worth, an easily understood symbol of the state of a person's soul and true ethical character. Under such a system, the good would be like the rich of today and the wicked like the poor of today – at least relatively speaking, as in practice everybody would be well-off. The scheme had other advantages, too; there would be no drop in living-standards during retirement, people could work shorter hours due to their increased purchasing power, leading to full employment, and there was never any prospect of a person going bankrupt or losing their home. Great Depressions would be banished forever, and because products were made according to the needs of the public, not for the short-term profit of manufacturers, they could be produced at higher quality and made to last, rather than being built to break a few years down the line, so the manufacturer could sell you another one. Best of all, said Green, there would be no more need for taxation; hospitals and new roads would be built by construction firms simply because there was a public demand for them, and teachers, doctors, soldiers and policemen would not need to be paid, simply given Credit updates on their Prior Choice Cards each month, and all public transport would be free. In short, there would be 'CRADLE-TO-THE-GRAVE SECURITY WITHOUT HAVING TO PAY FOR IT', just like Labour voters want.

Furthermore, factory owners and service providers would be automatically given a Credit update on their own personal Prior Choice Cards for every item distributed or service rendered, and the economy would roll along happily in this way forever, like clockwork. Green promised that crime would then virtually disappear, along with most mental illnesses (other than his own). 'Adults being freed of [financial stress] ... can no longer work themselves into candidates for mental institutions, and these buildings can be put to more profitable use', Green explains. With less time devoted to work, people would have longer leisure hours and begin devoting themselves to cultural and spiritual pursuits. As families spent more time with one another, divorce rates would plummet and juvenile delinquency be eliminated. Housewives would not be forced out to work, but given appropriate recognition for their home-making and child-rearing skills on their Prior Choice Cards, thus making society even more coherent – maybe Green had been reading his Chesterbelloc. Once people realised that their high standard of living was utterly dependent upon every individual performing their individual jobs as well as they could, for the benefit of all, a sense of national community would flourish. As Green put it, 'The work that you do, and the service you render, is what you do for others, or how you show love or consideration for them, [so] the basic motivation of a society under Prior Choice comes to be the love that men show for others, as by their acts or their works they are known.'

In such a benign New Age climate, nations would declare universal peace, a One World Government appear, and the Brotherhood of Man be established globally. Communism would be smashed, and atom-bomb tests come to an abrupt end. In short, the Kingdom of God would be established upon Earth, and man live within Paradise forever more, amen. Furthermore, due to the coming advent of 'the automatonic age', machines would be able to perform all the most unpleasant and physically draining jobs which nobody wanted to do, as well as bringing wonderful new services and ideas into the world; remarkably, Green's magazine-essay actually includes a substantially accurate prediction of Internet home-shopping services such as Amazon.

com (albeit performed via a TV-set). Prior Choice Economics, Green says, is 'the greatest story ever told', and urges readers to spread the word. They should write letters to newspapers, badger their local Congressmen, demand propaganda-funds from rich industrialists or, best of all, club together and go to Hollywood to create 'A SUPER-MUSICAL EXTRAVAGANZA' to place before the American public's dazzled eyes. Once his readers have scraped together enough cash, Green suggests they should use it to 'obtain the best performers from the world of entertainment to publicise and dramatise Prior Choice, through beautiful and inspirational music, song, dance, colour, and food for thought!' 'YOU CAN TAKE THE ACTION TODAY TO MAKE A BETTER WORLD TOMORROW. START NOW!' he ended his encomium, and Green himself, at least, proved willing to do so.

Take Me to Your Leader

Thy Kingdom Come didn't make a single appearance during 1958. Presumably, Green was busy making plans to storm the White House. There is nothing in his belated next issue, for January 1959, about his planned 1958 run for Congress, but evidently it was not successful; perhaps Green did not go through with his candidacy after all. His ET-spotting friend George Van Tassel also seems to have had cold feet about running for President in 1960, given that by issue eight, for March-April 1959, Green is advertising for like-minded people to come to his house in California and engage in a heated public debate, which was intended to end with 'the drafting of a platform of principles for a new political party with New Age leadership' behind it, to succeed his old ESP Party. In this same issue, Green also takes time to explain the bizarre reasons that had convinced him to arrange this unparalleled political congress. First of all, Mon-Ka the Martian had got back in contact with Green's old pal Dick Miller via radio-wave again, warning that the entire US economy was about to collapse and its population become 'completely enslaved in a web of its own making'. Another, better system quickly had to be put in place, said Mon-Ka – and surely that system was Prior Choice Economics? Secondly, on 6 April 1959 Green had received a letter from a fellow Californian saucer-obsessive named Harvey Weeks, pleading with him to 'STAND UP AND BE COUNTED'. Deploring the unsatisfactory political situation of the day, Weeks proposed that all major California Contactees gather in Los Angeles on 4 July 1959, during US Independence Day – or, as Weeks had it, 'upon the anniversary of [the signing of] that Great New Age manifesto, the Declaration of Independence' back in 1776. Here, said Weeks, the ghosts of America's Founding Fathers would 'look down with approval' and help them write a New Constitution, fit for a New Age. The comprehensive programme for government drawn up could then be presented to rapturous delegates at the forthcoming AFSCA convention of 11–12 July, and a 'New Age Party' be founded to bring about Paradise on Earth. Apparently, Green was the only notable Contactee to respond positively to Weeks' suggestion, thus making him first in line to be America's next President, and the leader of what was termed 'God's New Political Party'.

Issue nine of *Thy Kingdom Come* was a souvenir-programme of AFSCA's convention, and contained much repetitive material about Prior Choice Economics. The only real development came in a more detailed account of how it was Green had become such an ardent proponent of Prior Choice in the first place. He had already made brief admissions in previous issues that he had not actually invented the theory himself, but now Green provided more details about the true father of the notion, a wandering mystic by the name of Addison Brown (1922–2000). Hailing from Portland, Oregon, Brown had developed his radical idea in 1947, the very same year in which Kenneth Arnold had enjoyed the UFO-sighting which set off the whole California saucer-craze in the first place. Brown had once been a student of nuclear physics at an unspecified US university, where he had undergone some kind of mystical epiphany/mental breakdown which led him to abandon his studies and adopt the name of 'John Believer', travelling from State to State preaching about spirituality, Eastern Wisdom and Prior Choice Economics. His subsequent books and pamphlets included such essential-sounding but nigh-on unfindable publications as *The Quest*, *Talking with Clouds*, *Conquering Death*, *All Problems Solved*, *The Portland Rainbow* and *A Prophet from the West*.

The way Green tells the story makes it sound as if Brown was, literally, the reincarnation of Jesus Christ. Apparently, Brown 'wore a beard and had long, wavy hair down to his shoulders', and was the re-embodiment of some great sage of times gone by, who 'had been called by many different names as he walked the Earth in the past', and had only adopted the pseudonym of John Believer 'lest his [true] identity become known before the proper time.' 'Could it be,' asked Green, that 'the Avatar of the New Age now walks the Earth as a "thief in the night", describing the solutions to mankind's problems and personally supervising the creation of a new heavenly world out of an old one of chaos and destruction?' To Green, the answer was clearly 'yes!' Jesus certainly had great timing. The 1960s saw the 100th anniversary of Abraham Lincoln becoming President in 1860 and freeing America's slaves in 1862/3, and Green was sure the centenary of black emancipation would be marked by the blossoming of a parallel programme of pan-racial economic emancipation too. Green never actually makes the claim in so many words, but you get the distinct impression that just as he believed Addison Brown was the Second Coming of Jesus, so he himself was the reincarnation of Abraham Lincoln. As he later admitted in his *AFSCA Information Sheet #3*, a thin newsletter-like successor to his magazines issued by Green during the

1980s, a number of his 'Light-Worker' friends on the Californian UFO-scene were really reborn versions of America's Founding Fathers, who were, he said, continually reincarnating 'over and over again to raise the quality of life and bring a greater measure of freedom to all mankind.' If so, then why should Green not have been the Great Emancipator 2.0, freshly emancipated himself from the prison of the grave?

Green Party Politics

In the run-up to the 1960 election, Green polished his rhetoric by giving talks to local universities, colleges and women's institutes, spreading Jesus' word through his oft-repeated lecture 'Heaven on Earth with Non-Money Economics'. The next meaningful development in the saga came with issue sixteen of Green's newly renamed *AFSCA World Report* magazine, which acted as a full manifesto for what was now being called the 'SPACE-AGE PLATFORM OF GABRIEL GREEN: CANDIDATE FOR THE OFFICE OF PRESIDENT OF THE UNITED STATES'. This time, Green had genuinely entered himself as an independent candidate for the role of POTUS, as promised, but under what are called 'write-in terms'; that is to say, his name was not actually printed on the ballot, as with the more mainstream candidates, but you had to write it in yourself in a blank space provided. Such votes would, however, then be officially counted, so he really was a genuine, *bona-fide* contender for the Oval Office.

Naturally, the first thing mentioned in Green's manifesto was a promise to implement his beloved Prior Choice Economics nationwide as quickly as possible, a pledge which came together with a short, bullet-point list of the scheme's many undeniable advantages, such as 'No more taxes' and 'Free medical and dental care for everyone'. Second came an unambiguous assertion of the reality of UFOs: 'We affirm that flying saucers are real, that in reality they are true spacecraft manned by people from other planets ... We deplore the actions of our government in withholding information on this subject which is so vital to the welfare of our nation and its people.' Third on the list was a pledge to launch a radical new space-programme: 'We advocate that the United States stop shooting tin-cans into outer-space and concentrate on building a true free energy-powered, man-carrying spaceship.' After this has been accomplished, 'We advocate that a message of friendship be broadcast to the Space People, offering to exchange diplomats with them.'

All this out of the way, Green then concentrates upon laying out the implications of Prior Choice Economics for the usual hot-topic electoral fields of Education (better-funded schools and better-paid teachers), Employment (a guaranteed job building new public infrastructure for anyone who wants one), Agriculture (no more EU-style butter-mountains and wine-lakes – all surplus products to be given away free to starving foreigners) and Crime (to be abolished immediately, thanks to nobody needing to steal anything anymore). Green even claims that Prior Choice will improve TV, with 'the blight of annoying commercials' being 'forever banished from the screen'. He also proposed setting up a new Department of Peace to help settle any remaining global conflicts, an idea so unrealistic it was recently floated by Jeremy Corbyn. Regular readers annoyed by all this ceaseless prattle about politics rather than planets, meanwhile, could simply turn the page to peruse a list of mail-order books about the periodical's more usual subject matter, with titles such as *The Inexplicable Sky*, *Secret Places of the Lion*, *Venusian Health Magic* and *The Rainbow People*.

Manifesto of Madness

Green also paid for a full-page ad in the *LA Mirror-News* of 22 July 1960, setting out his manifesto under the heading 'AMERICA NEEDS A SPACE-AGE PRESIDENT', albeit without specifically mentioning alien beings or UFOs anywhere in the main text. Although attentive readers would have noticed a cartoon saucer on the ad's mast-head, they may not have realised how seriously Green took such matters unless they read the small-print at the bottom of the page, where it was admitted the advert was sponsored by AFSCA. Instead of playing up the whole ET-angle, the ad painted Green as the champion of the common man. 'HIS HEART IS WITH THE PEOPLE', the breathless spiel gushed. 'If you want the World of Tomorrow today and UTOPIA now', then you had to vote for Honest Gabe, whose list of absurd and often meaningless promises had now expanded to include, *inter alia*:

- Progress instead of prattle
- Principles instead of personalities
- Ideas instead of double-talk and ballyhoo
- Solutions instead of stalemates
- Survival instead of annihilation
- Peace instead of pieces
- Morality instead of moral degeneration
- Issues instead of smears, sneers and jeers
- A better tomorrow instead of no tomorrow
- New ideas instead of bombs and bullets
- Everyman a Richman tomorrow
- A passport to Paradise on Earth
- The true Stairway to the Stars instead of missile-fizzles and launching-pad blues

'ACT NOW!' the advert screamed. 'TOMORROW MAY BE TOO LATE!' And then, after all that effort, in October Green abruptly dropped his candidature, on the grounds that the Space People had made contact with him and let him know that John F. Kennedy would do a better job after all – something subsequently confirmed during JFK and Green's many in-depth telepathic conversations with one another. Nonetheless, the campaign had not been in vain. As revealed in *AFSCA Information Sheet #3*, by mentioning space-missions and Lefty notions about world peace and increased welfare provision, Green's crusade had helped lay the grounds for Kennedy's subsequent victory, and kept his more trigger-happy Republican opponent Richard Nixon (1913–94) out of office for the duration of the Cuban Missile Crisis of 1962, thus saving the world from obliteration. When Green had withdrawn from the race and endorsed Kennedy, that was the final straw which tipped the electoral balance against Tricky Dicky, according to a political scientist from Alpha Centauri named Renton, a four-foot dwarf who greatly resembled Captain Kirk from *Star Trek*. 'If it weren't for that Gabriel Green, I'd be President today!' Nixon was allegedly heard to curse, in the manner of a defeated villain from *Scooby Doo*. As both Nixon and Green originally hailed from the same small California town of Whittier, there is a minor possibility that the crooked future President might actually have heard of his obscure rival, although I sincerely doubt he thought Green had cost him the White House.[4]

Korendor Calling

Following his failure to become President in 1960 you would have forgiven Green for giving up, but this was not to be. After all, how could he have thrown in the towel when, in 1961, one of his close colleagues made direct radio-contact with a race of super-intelligent aliens from the planet Korendor – a planet where Prior Choice Economics was already up and running, and working miracles for the grateful population! The story began one night in July 1961, when a young Massachusetts radio-ham named Bob Renaud was surfing through the airwaves when he came across a curious high-pitched beeping sound. Was it another *Sputnik*? No, it was a beautiful female alien from the hitherto-unknown realm of Korendor named Lin-Erri, who spent the next few months spinning out an elaborate history of her home-world, interspersed with useful advice for Earth-politicians of the day. Eventually, in the middle of the night on 22 December 1962, a gang of humanoids drove up to Bob's house and told him to get in their car. They drove him to a field, where they demonstrated their ability to make boulders float, took him on a tour of their secret underground base, and gave him a quick fly-around in their saucer. They also gifted Renaud detailed instructions for how to build a special circular-screened television which could pick up broadcasts from outer-space. One of the alien TV channels was like an early version of Skype, allowing Bob to make video-contact with Lin-Erri, who turned out to be blonde and youthful, looking only around eighteen years of age – although she was in fact seventy-four, this being the long-lived Korendians' equivalent of human adolescence. Bob wrote off to Green, telling him of his adventures, and so began an interminably long series of articles given the collective title of *The Bob Renaud Story*, a new instalment of which was printed in just about every issue of Green's magazine from 1963 to 1969.

Renaud's account was full of enthusiastically childish nonsense, with information about everything from sports on Korendor (no football or baseball, but a form of basketball where players were armed with anti-gravity guns to make the ball float into the net), to painless alien methods of giving birth (by teleporting babies straight from the womb), to the vital-statistics and large breast-size of Lin-Erri herself ('37-22-36!!! Yes, 37-22-36! ... Talk about stacked!'). It was a good job she lived in zero-gravity conditions, otherwise she would have toppled over. Issue twenty-one of Green's magazine – now called *UFO International*, having changed its name yet again – featured an exclusive interview with Korendor's Business Minister, Damon Rel, in which Rel revealed that Prior Choice Economics was used on his home-world, under the alternative name of 'Universal Economics', or 'UnEc' for short. This name had been adopted, he said, because Korendor was part of a wider Universal Alliance of Planets, like the Federation in *Star Trek*, all of which made use of the same financial methods – hence, it was a truly universal way of doing things. Indeed, adoption of the UnEc scheme was a legal prerequisite for full membership of the Alliance, much like adopting the Euro is for those countries stupid enough to want to join the EU today. A gigantic central computing-centre full of 'huge Memory Consoles' had been built on the distant planet Andamian-III to store the Prior Choice Credit-Score of every ET in the galaxy, explained the Business Minister, thus demonstrating how the extremely complex record-keeping operation was managed. Damon Rel also spoke of how, on Korendor, the average worker had three days in, followed by two days off, together with a further fifty days of guaranteed vacation-time per annum, meaning that everyone went through life happy and relaxed. 'Sounds like a very pleasant work-situation,' commented Bob Renaud, by way of ending the exclusive interview. 'I hope that we can approximate it here [on Earth] in the near future.'

A Universal Panacea

Renaud was quite the fantasist; in issue twenty-seven of *UFO International*, he explained how he was really the first man to walk in outer-space, not the Soviet Cosmonaut Alexey Leonov, as well as engaging in a weird daydream about how all Earth-women should be obliged to undergo a session of 'artificial defloration' from their gynaecologists prior to marriage, as allegedly happens to the pristine bodies of lovely space-teens like Lin-Erri on Korendor. However, his tales of Prior Choice Economics being adopted by the denizens of other worlds proved surprisingly influential among a small number of dedicated UFO-buffs with a hankering for a different way of running our own terrestrial affairs. Consider the bizarre 1969 Dutch book *Extraterrestrial Civilisation*, later translated into English as *Operation Survival Earth* in 1977, before being expanded in 1982 under the final title of *UFO Contact from Planet Iarga*. This book was a smash-hit in Holland, partly because its pseudonymous author, 'Stefan Denaerde', or 'Steve of Earth', was apparently revealed as being a prominent Dutch businessman who ran a company importing lorries made by the Swedish company Scania into the Netherlands. The book, which purports to be factual in some editions and fictional in others, tells the story of how Denaerde's family sailing-holiday off the Dutch coast is interrupted by a close encounter with an alien submarine-cum-spacecraft, aboard which he is invited by a race of squat, horse-faced brown ET mammals with square pupils in their eyes, named the Iargans. Here, Denaerde is given a video-lecture about the Iargan system of economics, which allows every citizen to live the life of a rich man/mammal:

> Nothing is paid for on Iarga, only registered. What a consumer uses is registered in the computer-centre ... and this may not exceed that to which he has a right ... You cannot *buy* anything ... [although] the right of use remains for life ... all the articles are made to such a high standard that repair is never necessary ... [manufacturers] work on a cost-price basis, whereby the term 'profit' is replaced by 'the cost of continuation [of manufacture]' ... [Iarga's] economy was as stable as a rock .... [Any item's] cost-price was computed on the standard work-hour, the 'ura' ... What is conveniently called 'price' is in fact purely a method of expressing the production-time demanded by a certain article.

Or, in other words, the Iargans made use of the very same system of Prior Choice Economics which had been independently developed down here on terra firma by Gabriel Green and Addison Brown – an important point, as it meant the system must have been based upon truly universal laws of financial logic, rather than an arbitrary invention of deluded New Age Earth-men. Green sold mail-order copies of Denaerde's book through his magazine, and English editions of it were co-written by the American UFO-investigator Wendelle Stevens (1923–2010), who had also made a close and approving first-hand examination of Bob Renaud and his claims, so it does seem as if there were links of some kind between all these people, allowing them to help maintain one another's fantasies by continually adding new chapters and episodes to them. Indeed, a book co-authored by Green, Stevens and Renaud, *UFO Contact from Planet Korendor*, is now available online.[5]

ET Economics

The in-depth study of extraterrestrial economics continues today, in the shape of the Dutch fringe-researcher Gerard Aartsen, who has made a long-term investigation into the nature and extent of socio-economic development upon other worlds, and published some of his findings in a 2015 book, *Priorities for a Planet in Transition: The Space Brothers' Case for Justice and Freedom*, as well as penning the occasional article in Benjamin Creme's *Share International* magazine. A proud 'student of the Ageless Wisdom teaching for over thirty years', Aartsen has chosen to search for *Sophia Perennis* not within the works of Ficino or Guénon, but within the key texts of the Contactee movement. According to Aartsen, the benevolent Space Brothers feel that mankind's way of life 'makes no sense on any level beyond a profit-motive', something he has tried to prove by mining the Contactees' numerous books for quotes. ETs 'have repeatedly voiced their concerns about the way we have chosen to organise society around the need to earn money for daily living', it seems, with Aartsen finding one group of aliens, no doubt fully signed-up Social Crediteers, who condemned usury, or 'making money from money', as being 'absolutely unacceptable'.[6]

However, scholarly research has since concluded that there would be problems with using credit cards in space, which would seem to rule out the intergalactic adoption of any kind of UnEc/Prior Choice cards, as described by Gabriel Green. Quite apart from the fact that space-radiation would prevent the magnetic strips on such cards from functioning properly as soon as an astronaut took one from his shielded space-wallet, planets are so far away from one another that transmission of electronic data from a Korendian supermarket checkout to a space-bank's databases located on Andamian-III would take an unacceptable amount of time for each transaction to be processed. Physical currencies, too, pose a problem, as traditional 50p-like coins with pointy edges would float around and poke aliens in the eye. To counter these issues, an actual variety of usable space-coin has now been developed by scientists at Britain's National Space Centre. Termed the QUID (Quasi Universal Intergalactic Denomination), they are not like Earth-coins, as they are spherical polymer-based bubbles with no sharp edges, so you won't accidentally blind any Zeta Reticuleans should you drop your change in a zero-gravity off-licence. Further research into these issues is planned by an unholy-sounding alliance of PayPal, SETI (the Search for Extraterrestrial Intelligence – a body which scans the skies for messages from Mars) and Richard Branson's Virgin Galactic commercial spaceflight service.[7] However, as Korendor's Business Minister Damon Rel made no mention of such phenomena as spherical bubble-coins with the face of Richard Branson stamped on them during his interview with Bob Renaud, we can only conclude that there must be some flaw in these innovative and wholly plausible plans which has as yet not become fully apparent.

Kirby's Dream Land

Because Bob Renaud had provided Gabriel Green with indisputable evidence that Prior Choice Economics was already in use across most of the galaxy, he knew he couldn't give up on his quest for high office just yet. Green's finest political hour came when, by focusing upon anti-nuclear pacifist issues rather than flying saucers, he managed to gain more than 171,000 votes in the 1962 Democratic Senate Primary, coming second to the eventual winner Richard Richards (1916–88) with nearly 8.5 per cent of votes cast; an excellent result for a figure like Green. However, the next stage of his political career took a most unexpected turn, when he teamed up with Kirby J. Hensley (1911–99), a California-based pseudo-religious con-man who also took it upon himself to try and reform the US tax-system.

Hensley was the founder in 1962 of the notorious Universal Life Church (ULC), which has been condemned as an 'ordination mill' whose only apparent purpose (while under the control of Hensley, at any rate) was to ordain as many people as ULC Ministers as it possibly could, at a low, low cost of $5.00 per certificate – while also selling them books, pamphlets and training courses to turn a profit. The Church had little actual doctrine beyond 'We only believe in that which is right.' So vague was this creed that the ULC under Hensley felt free to accept not only Christians into its ranks, but also Buddhists, Wiccans, Satanists, humanists, atheists, pagans, Jedi mind-warriors from *Star Wars*, and even people's pet cats and dogs, if their owners were prepared to pay for their diplomas. By 2008, the ULC had allegedly ordained some 18 million persons (or animals) worldwide. Perhaps Hensley was so welcoming to all people of other faiths and none because he himself had no belief in any particular God either. Indeed, because he was allegedly illiterate, he had not actually read the Bible, although he had listened to the best bits on tape. He evidently didn't believe much of what he heard through his earphones, controversially stating that 'Jesus was a good actor', 'The Bible is full of lies from one end to the other', and 'I always stand for freedom, food and sex; that's all there is.'

Hensley intensely disliked the fact that churches and church leaders in America were to some degree tax-exempt, thinking this was a bigger con-trick than any he was involved in, so made it his mission to ordain as many ULC Ministers as possible, to starve the US Treasury of tax-income. Adverts were bought in American newspapers, informing readers of the financial benefits supposedly to be derived from signing up to the ULC. According to one such ad from 1981, 'Recently a whole town in Hardenburg, New York, became Universal Life Ministers and turned their homes into religious retreats and monasteries thereby relieving themselves of property taxes, at least until the State tries to figure out what to do.' If he could only persuade enough people to be ordained, then Hensley reckoned the government would have to change their rules and start taxing churches, synagogues and mosques, and those who preached in them, or else go bust. 'I just want to raise all the hell I can, and get all the kooks and what-have-you [classified] as churches,' Hensley admitted. 'Then they will have to tax them all!'

One of the most amenable such kooks, naturally, was Gabriel Green, with whom Hensley joined forces in 1963 to found the Universal Party, which I presume was named after the Korendians' brand of Universal Economics. Hensley's religious movement had originally just been called the 'Life Church', but once he and Green got together, it too adopted the 'Universal' prefix. Soon, Hensley was, like Green, expressing belief in reincarnation and alien life, and proposing that Earth appoint official ambassadors to liaise with the Space Brothers. Hensley ran for President in 1964 and 1968, but fared appallingly upon his programme of guaranteeing 'civil treatment to visitors from other worlds'. In 1964, he gained only nineteen votes, rising to sixty-four in 1968, so in 1970 left to set up a rival People's Peace and Prosperity Party. The Universal Party still continued, however, and in 1972 Gabriel Green campaigned under its auspices to be President yet again, standing against his old enemy Richard Nixon, and with another prominent Contactee, Daniel Fry (1908–92), as his Vice-Presidential running-mate. This time, Green actually paid to appear as a printed option on the ballot ... but only in Iowa. The percentage of votes he gained nationally was so low that it failed to register statistically; look up his final standings and you will find he officially gained 0.00 per cent of that year's support, with a mere 199 crosses next to his name. After this disappointing debacle, Green seems to have split from Kirby J. Hensley completely, whose most notable subsequent scam was declaring himself King of the non-existent country of Aqualandia in 1986, selling 'citizenship' to the place to innocent fools at $35 a pop. Even his promise of tax-relief for ULC converts transpired to be based on false premises; only churches as institutions are fully tax-exempt in US law, not those who preach in them. Indeed, ever since its inception, the ULC has come under investigation from American tax-authorities, with bean-counters sometimes judging it to be a real religion, worthy of tax-relief, and sometimes deciding the exact opposite, decreeing it a mere business, devoted to the enrichment of Pope Hensley himself. The ULC still continues today, under the leadership of Hensley's son, André – whose belief in God seems more sincere – and is apparently doing rather well.[8]

World Weird Web

Following the demoralising failure of his 1972 campaign, Green is often said to have withdrawn from the political scene into a reclusive retirement in California's Yucca Valley, but this is not quite true. While he didn't stand for public office again, Green continued promoting Prior Choice Economics right until his death, funding his efforts by providing past-life regression sessions, utilising techniques he had supposedly learned direct from the Space Brothers. He also offered to put you into psychic contact with your dead relatives, Ascended Masters, aliens, your Higher Self or even King Arthur and the Knights of the Round Table. Or perhaps you would prefer to be trained how to have psychic visions of the sunken kingdom of Atlantis, or the amazing world which lies hidden within our hollow Earth, or secret alien bases concealed upon the moon? If so, all you had to do was cross Green's palm with enough silver to help him keep a roof over his head. Alternatively, you could buy obscure paperbacks with titles such as *UFO Contact from Reticulum*, *Flying Saucerama*, *Space Aliens Took Me to Their Planet* or *Golden Moments with the Ascended Masters* from him via mail-order, for reasonable sums. Disciples were also encouraged to post Green donations of $25 per year, to help him fund candidates to run for election on the platform of his new United World Party which, as well as promoting Prior Choice, also called for the creation of a Global Parliament that would be run according to the rules of a new electoral system called 'Multi-Aspected Proportional Representation' which Green had invented. Such a Parliament would, said Green, be 'a theocratic democracy' – one run according to the principles of God Himself. It certainly sounds better than the useless self-righteous talking-shop that the UN has become in recent decades.[9]

Prior Choice Economics did not quite die with Gabriel Green, however, with the commercial advent of the Internet around the turn of the millennium facilitating a certain minor revival in the notion. There were two main reasons for this. Firstly, there was the fact that such a huge advance in IT appeared at last to provide an opportunity for us to imitate ET and put the once-impossible plan into practice, with massive, globally connected databases recording each and every citizen's lifetime history of purchasing and earning and then transmitting all this onto special electronic Prior Choice Cards for use at cash registers being now feasible to create, at least in theory – supermarket reward cards seem like an early step towards such a scheme. If some of Green's formerly far-out predictions such as online home shopping had quite genuinely come to pass, then why shouldn't some of his other equally outlandish ideas do so, too? Secondly, of course, the advent of blogs and do-it-yourself websites provided a far more efficient and less costly way for enthusiasts to spread their message to a far wider potential public than small-circulation magazines such as *Thy Kingdom Come* could ever hope to reach. One of the first surviving Contactees to try his hand at this new-media way of doing things was Green himself who, in the years immediately before his death in 2001, set up an official AFSCA webpage devoted to spreading news of what he too was now calling Universal Economics, 'because it had been used for aeons of time universally throughout the galaxy.'

Most of Green's website was made up of short reprinted items from his old magazines and breathless slogans along the lines of 'LIGHT-WORKERS UNITE!', 'WERE YOU THERE WHEN THEY CRUCIFIED THE LORD?' and 'FLYING SAUCERS ARE REAL, AND THEY'RE COMING OPENLY SOON!', although there were a few new titbits to absorb. For example, Green speculated that King Arthur and his knightly friends had written an early precursor of the US Constitution while sitting at the Round Table in Camelot one day. Furthermore, it seems that 'the phenomenon of the worldwide outpouring of Universal Love and Compassion' (or sickening, senseless hysteria) unleashed by the death of Princess Diana in 1997 meant that planet Earth was about to 'enter into the Photon Belt', thereby giving mankind access to 'new energies from our Galactic centre, The Great Central Sun', which would quickly unleash the optimum conditions for Prior Choice Economics to be implemented across the globe. This, explained Green, 'WOULD ALMOST IMMEDIATELY RESOLVE MOST OF THE PROBLEMS THAT MANKIND IS COMPLAINING ABOUT', from poverty to pollution to marital discord to traffic-jams. According to Green, 'when the Universal Economics system is adopted it will make it possible to finance the work of building world-transforming autos that hover over present-day freeways' which will consequently be 'turned into beautiful flower-beds'. 'Wouldn't it be wonderful not to have to pay taxes, or to have to fill out complicated tax reports?' Green asked, in August 2000. Almost exactly a year later, on 8 September 2001, Green at last achieved such freedom from the oppressive American taxation-system – by dying. I wonder if, had he just lived on a few days more to see the horrific, world-shattering events of 11 September 2001, Green would still have thought a wonderful New Age of peace and love was about to dawn upon the Earth? The old temples of American high finance were indeed due to crash and burn, but not, perhaps, in quite the way Gabriel Green and his peacenik pals from outer space had once anticipated.[10]

Oh, Mr Wu – What Did You Do?

Another strange website appeared at around the same time as Green's, maintained in the name of none other than 'John Believer' himself, the self-described 'Prophet-Writer-Inventor' Addison Brown, the original Earthly father of Prior Choice Economics. Apparently maintained by a disciple of Brown's named Alan K. Wu, a Canadian computer-programmer who 'used to work with and under the supervision of Mr Brown', seemingly as his sole remaining follower, the site stood as something of a shrine to the wandering preacher and his words. Prior to suffering a debilitating stroke in 1996, followed by his death in 2000, it turns out that Brown had hoped to set up a Foundation to continue his work, which had recently moved on from pure economic theory to a further, and even more advanced stage of knowledge – raising the dead.

According to Wu's account, Brown's ambitiously named 'Human Reincarnation and Resurrecting the Dead Project' grew directly from his work on economics, and was brought to a successful conclusion during the late 1990s, when the two men had developed a very special piece of software named 'Miracle.zip'. This amazing programme – available for free download direct from Brown's website until March 2017, when the pages were tragically taken offline – would reputedly allow PC users to raise from the dead any person they so desired. I couldn't get it to work myself, but it sounds as if Miracle.zip was some kind of astrology programme which allowed you to work out 'how best to time the birth of a child using computerised horoscope-timing so as to … duplicate the soul-shape and consciousness of a person previously alive but now "deceased"'. Naturally, said the website, 'if you are not interested in overcoming death', then there were other files available for use, but I'm sure most people would have put Miracle.zip at the top of their download list. Initially, it seems hard to see what necromancy has to do with economics, and the strange and impenetrable way in which the website was written did little to help. According to Wu, finding the text perplexing was 'an almost universal response' from readers, with 'about twenty people in three years' e-mailing in to tell him so – that's how many people their idea must have reached.

An Idea Which Resonates

Some of the website was written by Addison Brown himself, and in a FAQ section Brown addresses those intrepid web surfers who grumble that they have not understood what the hell he is talking about – the main such complainant being Alan K. Wu! The central thing for Mr Wu to appreciate was that for Brown the entire physical basis of the universe was reliant upon something called 'resonation physics'. Consider how a bell, when struck, continues to vibrate, echoing out a repeat of the original sound, until eventually it fades away. We say that the sound resonates, or repeats itself in a declining fashion, like ripples from a pebble thrown into a still pond. Brown claimed that Creation itself was modelled upon such a pattern of wave-like resonance, the universe being nothing more than 'a system of interacting resonations or repeating events'. If this was so, then repetition was an inherent quality of the cosmos. While the nature of many of the cosmic waves rippling throughout the universe were as-yet unknown to mankind, their fleeting manner of combination at the time of a baby's birth determined the exact shape of its soul by virtue of their combined pressure upon it. Therefore, if you could work out the precise state of such cosmic waves at the time of Einstein's birth, you could wait until such an arrangement of waves reoccurred (which it inevitably would, these waves being perpetually resonant and repetitive in nature) and then 'put Einstein back in a new body on purpose to let him continue his work'. Sometimes, dead souls had been reborn again in babies' bodies quite by chance, which explained all those cases of apparent reincarnation, but Miracle.zip allowed parents to do such a thing intentionally with, Brown said, a tempting one-in-three success rate – psychic IVF.

In a resonant universe, every human being was to all intents and purposes 'a radio-like broadcasting and receiving device', with our physical bodies tuning in to the particular cosmic-wave frequency broadcast by the cosmos at the time of our birth, a frequency which, if it could be mapped out properly by astrology, would trace out the shape of our soul. In this way, human bodies could be thought of as walking biological TV sets, which could easily be replaced when broken down beyond repair. When your TV set was knocked over, Brown pointed out, you did not mourn but went and bought a new one that you then tuned in to 'the same wave-shape of repeating events phenomena [i.e. channel frequency] as the TV that fell off a table and died', to begin watching exactly the same programmes you did before; the absence of a receiver does not imply the absence of a broadcasting wave. In much the same way, when a person's body died, the interactive TV show of their soul was still being broadcast somewhere in the universe. All that needed to be done to resurrect the dead was to tune back in to the correct resonant frequency of a dead person's soul-shape by conceiving a new infant at the precise astrologically determined time for the incipient foetus to be influenced by the relevant cosmic waves in question. Then, the baby would automatically become the deceased figure of your choice as soon as it exited the womb and began receiving resonant, soul-shaping space-waves through its internal biological antennae – that is to say, your baby would be a reincarnated human being. 'Turn on, tune in, drop out', as they say.

The connection to Brown's economic ideas came in the way that Miracle. zip exposed the gross fallacies of mankind's present approach to problem-solving. Currently, scientists viewed death as a physical problem to be cracked by building artificial hearts to replace malfunctioning ones and so on, until eventually a human body, given the correct medical attention, could last forever. For Brown, this aim was impossible, because bodies, as aspects of a resonating universe, were as doomed as everything else to echo away into nothing one day, like a ringing bell fading into silence. Therefore, instead of approaching the issue of death – or 'death', as Brown preferred to call it, in inverted commas – as a problem to be solved by eliminating the individual causes of bodily decay, like the clogging up of arteries, you should approach it as a problem the universe has already solved by itself. Rather than destroying the immediate causes of problems – replacing a non-beating heart inside a patient's chest – what we really had to do was rearrange the repeating resonant aspects of the universe. Because mortal human bodies repeated and replaced themselves in the form of babies, it was far simpler to rearrange the time of a child's birth so that a dead person's soul-shape could be reborn anew in the maternity-ward than it would be to spend billions on creating entire artificial bodies. The universe could perhaps be thought of as a gigantic Rubik's Cube; if you have a face of the Cube which is mostly blue, but with a single red square left on it, you don't paint the red square blue and call it solved. Instead, you rearrange the squares some more, until the red ones are in their correct place, and the Cube's original colour co-ordinated harmony reigns again. This, said Brown, was how the global economy should be organised and arranged, within our new networked age.

Homo Economics

To Brown, the advent of the Internet meant mankind had literally evolved into a new species; from *Homo sapiens*, we had become *Homo net*. Brown produced pamphlets with the phrase 'HOMO NET' written across them in capital letters, urging the open-minded to log onto his site and make personal contact with him, although I fear some young males who read them may have got the wrong idea. Nonetheless, Brown's utopian aim of using humanity's newly networked existence to create 'TEAM HUMANS ON THE EARTH' was couched by him largely in economic terms. Describing the problem of growing computer-piracy, in which files and programmes were illegally copied and then shared for free across the web, Brown accurately anticipated such practices would have a disruptive economic impact for intellectual copyright holders. However, using the same logic that had allowed him to solve the problem of death, Brown declared that web-piracy was no problem at all, but an opportunity. By trying to eliminate the cause of piracy by prosecuting the pirates, corporate lawyers were inadvertently imitating the idiot doctors who tried to eliminate death by removing diseased hearts. What was really needed was a complete re-ordering of society – by introducing Prior Choice Economics into it. Apart from much mention of using the new-fangled World Wide Web to administer the whole programme, Brown's basic scheme had not altered in any significant way since Gabriel Green's tilt at the presidency back in 1960; it was just that the underlying rationale underpinning it had become more overtly mystical, rather than related to UFOs and ETs, subjects Brown nowhere mentioned.

Prior Choice Economics was now billed as part of a wider cosmology, 'a way to fit ALL the pieces of a jigsaw puzzle … together … not a solution only to business problems.' Brown asks us to consider the way that the ultimate sum total of mass in existence in the universe always remains as a constant. Nothing is ever truly destroyed, only transformed – its existence resonates forever throughout the cosmos. Burn some wood, and the wood still exists, but in another form; as ash and smoke, as separated rather than bonded atoms of carbon, and so forth. If this simple physical law is applied economically, said Brown, then the value of any labour an individual worker has ever performed must still exist, too. Say you work for a single hour, at a rate of $5 per hour. A packet of cigarettes cost $5, so your hour's worth of labour will allow you to buy one packet, and then no more – forever. But where has that $5 gone? It still exists, in the shopkeeper's till. You earned it, so why not keep it? Under Prior Choice, you *can* and *do* keep it, forever! That hour's worth of expended labour, and the $5 you accumulated, resonates outwards from your bank account eternally, keeping you in $5 packets of cigarettes for life. Just as a Miracle.zip baby tunes into a dead person's soul, still resonating outwards across the universe, so a special Prior Choice credit-card, which links to the Internet with every till purchase, will tune in to the resonance of your accumulated 'financial soul', as it were. Once again, the way ahead is not to *destroy* the worker's hard-won $5, but to *rearrange* the wider financial system so that it, just like the soul which earned it, becomes immortal.

Doing the Work of God

Brown's economic and cosmological theories could also be combined to prove the literal truth of the Bible. As Wu put it, Brown's plans would 'help to fulfil, along with the resurrection of the dead, the major CREATIVE prophecies of Christianity'. Prior Choice, he said, 'serves as a Mirror that reflects and echoes prophecies of the Christian religion, how "in the Last Days the dead shall be resurrected" and how "by thy WORK thy shall be judged" … for the whole world to see' (seemingly an alternative version of Romans 2:6, which explains that God shall 'render to every man according to his deeds'). The ultimate unspoken conclusion to be drawn is that one's Prior Choice Credit-Score could be maintained after death, when passing between material bodies, like permanent financial karma. When you turn a TV off one day and switch it back on tomorrow, that day's episode of your favourite show follows on from the last one, rather than starting all over again at the beginning, and when a person's soul-shape is reincarnated via tuning a baby into the correct resonance-waves, the child retains some of the memories of its previous life within its brain too. You could read this as implying that, come the Day of Judgement, God will assess your Credit-Score accumulated over several lifetimes, and assign you a place within Heaven or Hell based upon it; 'by thy WORK thy shall be judged' at the End of Time. Because for Brown God was just another term for the universe as a whole – which itself was really little more than a giant 'difference-arranging machine' within which phenomena of varying resonance could organise themselves properly – in his outlook, a man's soul could be subjected to a moral bookkeeping process. So, the higher your cumulative Prior Choice Credit-Score, the cleaner your soul. When Addison Brown is finally reincarnated himself by someone with access to both a surviving copy of Miracle.zip and a willing, astrologically attuned female with spare room in her womb, he surely deserves infinite credit for the originality of such thoughts.[11]

A small group of people devoted to promoting Addison Brown's idea under its alternative, Korendian-derived title of Universal Economics, still exists online today. As far as can be told, the main mover is a journalist named William Patrick Bourne, who describes himself as 'an independent researcher/generalist with published papers on fortean phenomena, cosmology/particle physics and the new catastrophism in geology'. It seems Bourne had some direct contact with Addison Brown prior to his death, which led him to become interested in UnEc and later 'write the definitive essay on the system', which I have been unable to source; however, he has also helped produce an animated documentary for YouTube, laying out the details of UnEc for anyone who is interested. The actual UnEc website is very small and undeveloped as of yet, although it does feature a basic online shop where you can purchase various branded goods, the best being a T-shirt with an Andy Warhol-style print of Addison Brown's face on it. However, it says everything about UnEc's chances of ever catching on that the prices charged upon the site are listed in US dollars, not Prior Choice Credits.[12] Linn-Erri, Damon Rel and the good folk of Korendor may do things that way but not those down here on Earth – at least not yet. Maybe in another lifetime …

4

Going Caracas

Hugo Chávez and the Economic Murder
of Venezuela

*The curious task of economics is to demonstrate to men how little they
really know about what they imagine they can design.*
Friedrich von Hayek, economist

*The tragic tale of how an oil-rich country was utterly destroyed by the
unworkable policies of a Yankee-hating Marxist, and a warning about how
his deluded international cheerleaders would happily have their own lands
follow him blindly along the road to serfdom.*

It says everything about the current state of Venezuela's withered economy
that should you have won the recently cancelled domestic version of *Who
Wants To Be A Millionaire?* you would have taken home with you a jackpot
worth approximately £50, at current exchange rates. Considering that due to
rampant inflation an average trip to McDonalds would, as of 2016, set you
back the equivalent of £110, the show should really have been renamed *Who
Wants To Win Half a Happy Meal?*, and yet it still had no trouble attracting
contestants – presumably because a large section of Venezuela's 31 million
people, forced into a state of extreme poverty by the government's insane Far
Left policies, are suffering from severe malnutrition and reduced to queuing
up and scavenging scraps from bins like stray dogs. As an estimated 82 per
cent of the population now lives in poverty, such trash-can food-lines are
doubtless very long.[1]

In some ways it is pointless detailing figures here, as the situation worsens
daily, but here are some anyway. Because the government suspended the
release of national economic data some years back, we have to rely on
outside estimates, which can vary, but Ricardo Hausmann, the Harvard-
based Venezuelan economist, has calculated that the nation's collapse

'dwarfs any in the history of the US, Western Europe, or the rest of Latin America'. During the Great Depression, US GDP fell by 28 per cent; in Venezuela, since 2013 alone, GDP may have fallen by between 30 and 35 per cent, depending on which alleged lying Yankee stooge you listen to. By August 2017, the value of the minimum wage was reported as having shrunk by 88 per cent in five years, to the equivalent of £27 per month. Come September 2017, officials raised the minimum wage by 40 per cent but, considering that food prices rose 51 per cent between August and September 2017 due to hyperinflation, this 'pay rise' was truly a pay cut. The government had to hike the minimum salary no fewer than five times in the nine months between January and September 2017. Instead of acknowledging that this was as a result of their total mismanagement of the economy, the government in the capital, Caracas, actually *boasted* that this 'record' showed they cared for the poor, not that banknotes were now virtually worthless, having lost 99.81 per cent of their value against the US dollar. The IMF predicts that, come 2018, annual inflation will hit 2,000 per cent. Some say it will hit 10,000 per cent.

So worthless is the national currency, the bolivar, that for a long time the Venezuelan Treasury couldn't even afford to have any new banknotes printed. The traditional top denomination note, worth 100 bolivares, was due to be replaced with a much higher denomination years ago, but this proved impossible until January 2017, when a new 20,000 bolivar note, worth an amazing £5, was issued nationally. The problem was that, like almost everything else in Venezuela, the notes were not manufactured domestically but imported, and the government was running out of money to buy new money with, as ridiculous as that sounds. They wanted some 10 billion bank notes, but as they owed one foreign banknote-printer alone $71 million in unpaid fees, the new notes proved difficult to source. To try to avoid the possibility of physical cash supplies running out, in September 2017 a law was implemented, limiting daily withdrawals to 10,000 bolivares per person – a sum which, thanks to continuing hyperinflation, was by now worth only 31p. So, the highest 20,000 note in the country – which, to ensure that it wouldn't run out, you couldn't even withdraw from a bank anymore, less than a year after its much-hyped introduction – was actually worth 62p. Remember a single Happy Meal costs £110, so it is no wonder 93 per cent of the population now say they can't afford enough food to live on. The only practical solution would be for the Treasury to arbitrarily decree that all 20,000 bolivar notes are now actually 200,000 bolivar ones, and get citizens to draw the extra zeros on with a biro, should they by some miracle be able to afford to buy one. In some areas, primitive modes of barter are now in operation, with IOUs more valuable than cash.[2] Venezuela was once the richest country in Latin America, and has, so it claims, the world's largest proven oil reserves, so things should not be this way. What has gone wrong?

Capitalist Cancer

Partially it is down to bad fortune. Following record highs, global oil prices have since collapsed to record lows. From 1999 to 2008, prices climbed upwards inexorably, hitting a dizzying peak of $147 per barrel in 2008, before then plummeting back down to a modern nadir of $26 per barrel in 2016. Prices have since recovered somewhat to hover at around $50 per barrel, but that's still about two thirds less than the 2008 high. This has inevitably negatively affected the economies of all oil-producing nations – and yet the masses aren't starving in lands like Qatar, Saudi Arabia, Nigeria, Norway or Scotland. Such countries, however, never had the mixed fortune to be ruled by the supposed economic genius that was Hugo Chávez (1954–2013), Venezuela's initially very popular President between 1999 and 2013. Chávez died of cancer at the young age of fifty-eight, an illness he liked to blame on the intervention of Yankee imperialists from the superpower up north. 'Would it be so strange that they have invented the technology to spread cancer and we won't know about it for fifty years?' he once asked. Chávez's main ally in the region, the Communist Cuban dictator Fidel Castro (1926–2016) – also now dead, scarily enough – encouraged him in such notions. According to Hugo, 'Fidel always told me, "Chávez, take care. These people have developed technology. You are very careless. Take care what you eat, what they give you to eat ... [All it takes is] a little needle and they inject you with I don't know what."' Come Chávez's death in March 2013, the official tone had hardened further; according to Hugo's anointed successor, moustachioed former bus driver Nicolás Maduro, his mentor had most definitely been 'attacked' by Venezuela's 'historical enemies', the US. 'We have the intuition that our commander Chávez was poisoned by dark forces,' Maduro told his mourning countrymen, while also announcing an official inquiry into Chávez's 'murder' and dismissing a number of US diplomats from Caracas in protest.[3]

As this conspiracy-narrative implies, Chávez thought most things Western and American were inherently evil, in particular capitalism, which was apparently the single most destructive force in the universe; you might almost call it a cancer, and '*El Comandante*', as Chávez liked to be known because of his well-known army background, was prepared to fight it by any means necessary. On World Water Day 2011, for example, he suggested that capitalism, by driving global warming, might be causing all kinds of environmental disasters. 'Careful!' he warned. 'Here on planet Earth where hundreds of years ago or less there were great forests, now there are deserts.' It wasn't just our own sphere which was being affected by such evils, either. 'Maybe,' Chávez opined, Mars was currently a dry and lifeless desert-world because 'capitalism arrived there, imperialism arrived and finished off the planet.' When low rainfall led to Venezuela's hydro-electric dams beginning to fail in 2009/10, Chávez mirrored this theme, trying to avoid any responsibility for the consequent blackouts by blaming such 'horrific phenomena' on 'the destructive system of capitalism'. This all showed that private companies, which allegedly used the most electricity (because they were the most productive!), were destroying the country, with the power-grid probably being sabotaged by US agents in any case. To solve the problem, Chávez said he had borrowed special equipment from Fidel Castro, and was personally going to fly a modified military aeroplane into the sky and shoot the clouds to make them rain: 'Any cloud that comes in my way, I'll hurl a lightning bolt at it; tonight I'm going out to bombard.' To save water, he also suggested people should stop singing in the shower. 'What kind of Communism is that?' he asked, angrily.[4]

The real problem may have been that electricity prices were so heavily subsidised under Chávez's regime that Venezuelans had become South America's largest per capita energy consumers. Cheap power made Hugo popular, though, so he didn't dare try and reduce consumption by addressing this. Instead he targeted industry, ordering the factories of the remote and expensively equipped industrial heartland Ciudad Guyana region be powered down. Ciudad Guyana was supposed to wean the nation off its profound economic overreliance upon oil, but was sacrificed by Chávez in the name of short-term electoral gain. Smelters and furnaces can't just be unplugged like a TV set without destroying them, but government officials did so anyway, because the area was relatively underpopulated compared to other voter-rich regions and cities. Nonetheless, even though the factories were ruined, their employees were still kept on the public payroll, using

Cuban dictator Fidel Castro, who once lent Chávez some 'special equipment' so he could shoot at capitalist-allied clouds from an aeroplane. (Courtesy of the Library of Congress)

reserves of national oil-money; 6,000 workers at one aluminium factory alone. Worse, State-controlled firms were ordered to cease exporting their goods to the United States in favour of seeking out 'ideologically friendlier' (yet far less profitable) trading partners elsewhere – such as the hard-line, but certainly non-Yankee-aligned, dictatorship of Belarus. Because such markets were basically fictional, goods were stockpiled, thus accumulating no profit at all. Anyhow, due to the furnaces being sabotaged, many products were now simply of too low a quality to be sold abroad. It was only due to endless and massive injections of cash from the State that industry could keep going at all, something which ate up ever more petro-dollars. To compensate, Marxist theorists were dispatched to set up Workers' Councils in Ciudad Guyana's factories and mines but, predictably, the workers just wanted to do their work and go home, not spend hours discussing dialectical materialism with bearded academics, and a system of 'co-management' was introduced there instead; that is, normal top-down management from above, given a euphemistically Leftish name. Whenever actual trade unionists objected to all this madness, naturally, all talk of 'solidarity' with the people suddenly disappeared and bolshie strike leaders were imprisoned for years at a time.[5]

Oil's Not Well That Begins Well

It was only in 2004 that Chávez had declared Venezuela's transition towards full-blown socialism, or *chávismo* as it is often called domestically. Chávez initially maintained sane economic policies that diverted money to the needy in an affordable fashion, while using the undoubted force of his personality to persuade his fellow members of OPEC – the cartel of oil-producing countries which runs the world oil-market – to cut production and raise prices, leading to a boost in Venezuela's finances. Sure, he enjoyed accusing the wealthy private sector 'oligarchs' who supposedly controlled the country of being vampires, pigs, perverts, bags of crap and suchlike, but this just seemed as if he was playing to his natural audience within the *barrios*, or slums, in whose name he professed to rule. Doubtless, the gap between rich and poor in Venezuela was disgraceful at the time (it still is) and if Chávez was going to do something about it in a reasonable manner, then great. His first December 1998 election victory was a genuine landslide and, while he played up his military background, he was not actually a full-blown dictator, so deserved his initial chance at the helm. In many ways he seemed benign, if wildly eccentric and hubristic, with genuine concern for the poor. He paid off national debts and improved tax collection, and his professed radicalism seemed largely rhetorical. Some disappointed socialists accused him of not being Left-wing enough. He even intended to privatise the telecoms industry, like Mrs Thatcher. Actually, he was just biding his time, removing moderates from positions of civil authority and replacing them with loyalists, while simultaneously turning the middle and working classes against one another, for future electoral advantage. Conflating the rich plutocrats who had traditionally sucked up much of the oil wealth with the ordinary middle classes, Chávez successfully sowed division. Gradually, the perverts, pigs and vampires came to hate him and took part in street protests against his rule – thereby allowing Chávez to portray them to his main constituency, the poor, as being opposed to the People's Champion, and only interested in their own selfish wellbeing. It was classic divide and rule.[6]

Carried by the votes of the slums, Chávez sailed on, winning vote after vote until in 2004 an upcoming referendum concerning his rule hung on a knife-edge. The economy had become flat, and the alienated middle-class 'shit-bags' (Chávez's words) were in open revolt. Turning to his friend Fidel for advice, he was told to open the floodgates in terms of public spending. And so began the profligate spree for which Chávez became a hero to the international Left – a ruinous spree motivated not primarily by compassion but by electoral need. *El Comandante*'s main idea was to establish an extensive programme of social services throughout the *barrios*, named *misiones*. Most famously, free health clinics were established for the poor, staffed with 20,000 Cuban doctors and nurses sent over by Castro in return for 95,000 barrels of Venezuelan oil per day. Undoubtedly these doctors initially did much good, winning Chávez even more support among the slum voters. Programmes of free education slashed illiteracy rates, while soup kitchens and subsidised food fed the hungry. Thanks to such largesse, Chávez won the 2004 referendum easily, and Venezuela's future course was fixed – long-term bankruptcy for the sake of short-term benefit.[7]

Even the jewel in Venezuela's economic crown, the State-owned oil company PDVSA, which accounted for half of all foreign revenue in 1999, ended up being partially ruined, which was unfortunate as it now accounts for 95 per cent of such revenue. It was already nationalised and corrupt before Chávez came to power, but, after shrewd initial reforms, he began overloading it with irrelevant social tasks that had nothing to do with refining and selling crude, and foreign drilling firms became reluctant to invest in proper infrastructure due to fear the Marxists might one day expropriate it all. Production and profits dwindled, even as oil was being expected to subsidise more and more of the economy. You could fill your entire engine with subsidised petrol for less than $1, which cost the State $21 billion a year, double the annual pensions budget; as this only benefited car owners, it wasn't even doing any good for the slum-dwelling poor. Chávez admitted this was 'immoral', but continued anyway, to avoid electoral reprisals. PDVSA's profits also subsidised artificially low prices for food, clothes, mobile phones, electricity and more besides, thus buying voters' allegiance while simultaneously undercutting and thereby destroying yet more private enterprises along with the general tax-base.[8]

Hugo Chávez, looking presidential as always. He was the one man on Earth who knew that capitalism had destroyed life on Mars. (Courtesy of Karel Fuentes)

PDVSA is now in such poor financial straits that, in May 2017, the *chávistas* swallowed their pride and sold government bonds in the company with a face-value of $2.8 billion to the hated Wall Street capitalist investment bank Goldman Sachs, giving the government an immediate emergency windfall of $865 million to piss up against a wall. Goldman Sachs negotiated a heavy discount, paying 32 cents in the dollar for each 'hunger bond', which was decried by some as exploiting the situation for their own profit – which is true, they were, but whose fault was it that Caracas was by now desperate enough to go through with such a terrible deal? Quite how the government's pact with Wall Street fitted in with their simultaneous claim that there was an American boycott against the country aiming to pummel it into economic submission was never explained, by the way. In fact, as of August 2017 the US bought half of Venezuela's oil exports, so, considering that almost all Venezuela actually now exports is oil, there was no meaningful Yankee imperialist embargo in place whatsoever, the government in Caracas had destroyed their international trade all by themselves. There are specific US financial sanctions in operation against certain members of the ruling regime, but America has thus far largely refrained from boycotting actual normal commercial trade with the country, recognising that this will only make the ordinary bin-scavenging public suffer further.[9]

The Price Is Wrong

The economic collapse that followed the tumble in oil prices was utterly predictable. Chávez knew perfectly well that over-reliance upon crude

194

was dangerous, as a previous economic crisis caused by this very same problem had led to a wave of riots during 1989, provoking the non-socialist then-government to send out troops who shot hundreds of restless slum-dwellers to put down the revolt. This set the stage for Chávez himself, then a lieutenant-colonel, to stage the abortive 1992 coup which gained him national prominence in the first place. When he won his first election in 1998, one of the promises which led to his victory was to reduce Venezuela's over-reliance upon oil, the so-called 'Dutch Disease', named after a 1960s financial slump in the Netherlands. At that stage Holland thought it had struck gold during a 1960s gas boom, but gas revenues strengthened their exchange rate so much that it became cheaper to import products rather than develop native industries, leading to ultimate disaster.[10] The historical examples were all there but, post-2004, Chávez chose to ignore them in favour of bribing the public. Chávez used petro-dollars to foster an unsustainable boom by artificially increasing wages and boosting production in State-owned industries, which then led to more consumer spending as better-paid workers bought these same products back again. Meanwhile, inflation was kept under control by an artificial system of price-fixing; Chávez's government had armies of officials whose job it was to decide how much thousands of goods, from butter to bread, from coffee to coffins, should cost in shops. Then, an *actual* army was used to enforce this system, with soldiers sent into supermarkets to make sure items had the correct price-tags on them. Those retailers who did not comply were labelled 'enemies of the people' and prosecuted.

Sadly, artificially low prices mean that neither shopkeepers nor producers can make any profit, with the result that many close down. Using reserves of petro-dollars, a foolish government just shrugs and imports what they need instead, which is fine until the petro-dollars start to run low. Then, shortages appear, with products disappearing off shelves, seemingly at random. Consumers end up queuing for hours hoping to buy a loaf of bread, only to come away with a tin of sardines, because that's all the shops have in stock, like it or lump it. The reasons why one product ends up available and another doesn't become simply incomprehensible; milk is apparently almost impossible to buy in Caracas these days, but there is an inexplicable glut of yoghurt, and nobody seems to know why. Strangely, those goods with government price controls slapped on them tend to be scarce, whereas goods sold on the free market are plentiful; so if you want liquor or *foie gras* rather than bread and milk for breakfast, you're fine, so long as you can afford those goods, which you can't, because you are limited to withdrawing 31p per day.

Eventually, queues for State-subsidised mystery items become so long that wives quit their jobs and stand in them as a form of surrogate full-time employment, so their husbands and children can have something excitingly unknown to eat of an evening. Naturally, general economic activity therefore declines, and tax-revenues dip further. The black market booms and the government devalues the currency and tries to limit imports to stimulate domestic industries which have already gone out of business anyway, leading to ever-more inflation and ever-greater shortages. Seizing foreign assets – a General Motors plant was one recent victim – seems like a good wheeze, until it leads to a freeze in outside investment from selfish international enterprises who unaccountably don't want their factories and equipment being stolen in the name of Marx. Wages thus need to be raised by the State to compensate, leading to ever further inflation, until eventually a 100 bolivar note is worth 2p, GDP freefalls and the population starves and dies, although not the politicians, naturally. As long as oil prices stayed high, this fate could be staved off temporarily, but not fully and not forever. Chávez may have spent an estimated £500 billion in alleviating poverty in the short-term, but only increased it in the long-term.[11]

Criminal Enterprise

Another result of this madness has been the effective criminalisation of large sectors of the population. From 2015 onwards, citizens have had to be fingerprinted when buying price-controlled items in shops, to prevent them making multiple purchases of staple foodstuffs. This 'anti-fraud device' was billed as a way of preventing evil-doers from stockpiling goods at the expense of others, or engaging in smuggling activity. To be fair, smuggling is indeed now rife in Venezuela – people are forced into it, as this is one of the few ways to make any actual money. Because petrol is so heavily subsidised, people fill up their cars, drive them across the border to Colombia, and sell the contents of their tanks to foreigners for real money at a large mark-up. Those who don't have any cars just take it across in bottles or cans, or else try their luck illegally exporting different State-subsidised goods, from toothpaste to underpants; allegedly, during 2014, 40 per cent of all price-fixed items were sold on in this way. Soldiers have been ordered to try to stop this trade, with 17,000 being posted to the Colombian border in 2014 alone. Troops are also under orders to patrol warehouses, inspecting the prices of one of the 15,000 different categories of item that have had their values 'scientifically' determined down the years. To avoid being arrested, some shopkeepers deliberately keep their shelves bare, rather than buy in products and sell them at a loss.[12] Actual crime, too, has risen exponentially, with Caracas now being the murder capital of the world. Admittedly, national murder rates were high when Chávez came to power in 1999, at 4,550 per year. By 2013 when he died, however, almost 25,000 persons were being killed across the country, the vast majority of whom had probably not been secretly injected with cancer by the CIA.[13]

Because Chávez had imitated his fellow anti-imperialist idol Robert 'Comrade Bob' Mugabe in nationalising privately owned farms before handing them over to peasants who had no idea how to run them, with criminals given semi-official leeway to steal crops, livestock and vehicles from the capitalist scum who rightfully owned them, food supplies suffered even further. Hugo spent around $1 billion equipping 1 million hectares of seized co-operative peasant farms with subsidised tractors and suchlike, but 90 per cent collapsed. So, he ordered another million hectares be seized, and another billion dollars be wasted. Real farmers, naturally, sold up, took their cash and fled. So much food then ended up being imported to make up the shortfall that it couldn't be dealt with, so 300,000 tonnes rotted at the nation's ports. Chubby Chávez's solution was to appear on TV surrounded by mountains of food, telling his people they had never had it so good. 'Mmmmm, look at that, smells delicious,' he would say to camera. At this point, some viewers probably tried to eat the telly. To alleviate problems, he would arbitrarily announce the creation of things like a 'Socialist Rice' company on screen one day, then forget about it the next, leading to administrative chaos. Having announced it, that was it, his work here was done.[14]

Moral Bankruptcy

Chávez's chief economic henchman, Jorge Giordani, an ultra-thin ascetic nicknamed 'The Monk', was obsessed with creating abstract financial theories so complex nobody else could understand them. Giordani was sacked by Nicolás Maduro in 2014, and has since accused the government of engaging in a programme of 'fiscal nymphomania' – i.e. screwing the entire country – as well as having 'the Midas touch in reverse', thus transforming Venezuela into a 'laughing stock'. 'We need to acknowledge this crisis, comrades,' he now urges, a sentiment which would have been admirable had he not helped cause it all himself. Wishing to establish an entirely logical – and therefore entirely unrealisable – centralised command-economy, Giordani started by having officials wilfully underestimate the then-value of oil at $35 a barrel instead of $100. The difference would then be funnelled off into secret government accounts, for Chávez to spend without this sum appearing in official figures, thus rendering the ballooning national budget beyond scrutiny. As the hidden billions were supposed to be lavished on the poor, this was well-intentioned, but open to obvious criminal plunder.

Giordani – who was not personally corrupt himself, just an ideologue reluctant to face reality – then opened the floodgates to further sleaze by establishing a double exchange rate. Essentially, PDVSA was obliged to sell its petro-dollars to a body called CADIVI, which then allowed Venezuelans who needed foreign cash to use their bolivares to buy US dollars. As foreign banks wouldn't accept bolivares, if businessmen needed to import equipment from abroad they needed to swap bolivares for dollars, and then buy what they needed with these. The trouble was, CADIVI did not have enough US dollars to go around, so people well-in with the regime, or else able to pay bribes, got to the front of the queue. If you were first in the line, you got access to the privileged exchange rate of $40 to 100 bolivares. If you were at the back of the line, because you were poor and unknown or out of official favour with Hugo, there weren't enough dollars left to sustain this exchange rate, so you had to seek out the black-market, where you got only $16 per 100 bolivares. As the economy began to fail, the gap between these two exchange rates widened, then yawned. As of August 2017, the lucky few could swap ten bolivares for a dollar. The unlucky many could swap 19,000 bolivares for a dollar. Those upon whose loyalty the regime relied in order to function, primarily the politicians and bureaucrats themselves, together with the security forces, would be granted privileged access to the more valuable rate. As a result, the armed forces have thus far failed to institute a major rebellion against Chávez's successor, President Maduro, which makes sense when you consider that to keep them on side, Maduro recently promoted 195 officers to the rank of General in a single day, has twelve out of thirty-five government ministries staffed by military men, and allows the army to hold key stakes in hundreds of businesses, including a bank and a TV station. It doesn't matter whether these institutions are profitable in and of themselves. As prominent stakeholders in such important companies, Venezuela's 2,000 Generals get access to the privileged exchange rate in order to facilitate all of their 'legitimate business interests' abroad – drug-trafficking, for example.[15]

Naturally, if anyone disagreed with Chávez's ideas, then they were either agents of the dreaded gringos, or else clinically mad. One critic was accused of having had a CIA mind-control chip implanted in his brain by Bill Gates, causing him to 'act strangely' – that is, begin criticising the regime. Apparently, opposition groups have shown 'clear signs of insanity' when protesting against *chávista* rule; Microsoft must have been manufacturing an awful lot of those crafty brain-scrambling chips lately.[16] Alternatively, opponents could always be labelled as Jews, or being under their evil control. Long an uncritical friend of the Palestinians, like many blind men on the Left, Chávez eventually began wondering aloud if his opponents had been hypnotised by Israelis rather than Bill Gates. Following his success in the 2004 referendum, he warned those who had voted against him not to allow themselves to be 'poisoned by those Wandering Jews; don't let them lead you to the place they want you to be led.' In 2005, meanwhile, he complained that 'A minority has taken possession of all the wealth of the world.' Who could this minority have been? Why, they were 'the descendents of the same ones that crucified Christ, the descendents of the same ones that kicked Bolívar out of here and also crucified him in their own way.' By Bolívar, Chávez meant the revolutionary hero Simón Bolívar (1783–1830), who had helped eject Spanish colonialists from Latin America, and whose ultimate downfall he liked to blame on rich oligarchs; by conflating the powerful rich with the Jews, Chávez was blatantly playing to classic anti-Semitic stereotypes. Predictably, he then denied this, calling such accusations 'a lie', and blaming the very idea upon 'an offensive of the [American] Empire' and their (no doubt Jewish) media propagandists.

When Chávez came to power in 1999, there were 22,000 Jews in Venezuela. By 2015, there were 7,000. Considering how the government's main political opponent Henrique Capriles, who is of Jewish descent, was allegedly accused of being a stooge of 'Zionist capitalism' while on the campaign trail in 2013, who only acted on behalf of the shadowy imperialist 'Jewish Lobby', it is no wonder so many Jews have fled. Absurdly, however, in May 2017 Nicolás Maduro – playing upon the self-proclaimed fact his own grandparents were apparently Jewish – had the nerve to announce that, in his view, members of the Venezuelan government were 'the new Jews of the twenty-first century that Hitler pursued', with their vicious capitalist opponents at home and abroad being nothing but 'twenty-first century Nazis'. Opposition rallies were just the same as Nazi rallies, he said, while he and his fellow *chávistas* 'don't carry the yellow Star of David', as during the Holocaust, but 'red hearts that are filled with desire to fight for human dignity'.[17] With both Jews *and* Nazis after them, what chance did these poor persecuted socialist souls ever have? No wonder Chávez ended up being murdered.

A Little Bird Told Me

If the dreaded American imperialists really did assassinate *El Comandante*, then perhaps it was actually a mercy-killing, because he was thereby spared having to observe the effects the global oil price slump had upon his cherished dream of a socialist utopia; since 2012, Venezuela's non-oil-related tax-revenues have dwindled by 70 per cent, smashing his plans forever.[18] President Maduro, however, has had to deal with such consequences of *chávismo* misrule from his first day in office, and as a result has never been anything like as popular. Despite Chávez saying it was 'as clear as the full moon' that Maduro should be his successor[19], 'Tropical Stalin', as he is sometimes known, has nothing like Chávez's level of personal charisma. With annual inflation levels already hitting 50 per cent (those now seem like golden times …) and basic staples running low due to the malfunctioning command-economy, Maduro had neither his predecessor's almost messianic persona nor his fistful of petro-dollars to hide behind when he assumed power in 2013. With blame for Venezuela's woes increasingly being heaped upon Chávez and Maduro's PSUV Party, there seemed real danger that

Tropical Stalin would lose April 2013's elections to his more moderate capitalist opponent, the supposedly Zionist-controlled Henrique Capriles. And so, Maduro did something astonishing. Rather than admitting the regime's economic errors, he began claiming to be in touch with the ghost of his dead predecessor. According to Maduro, when he was praying in a chapel one day during the election campaign, he saw a small bird enter the room, turn around three times and land upon a wooden beam, where it began whistling. Maduro, inexplicably entranced, stared at the bird and whistled back at it. The bird then 'looked strangely' at the politician, as it was surely entitled to, flew around and left. According to Maduro, this was really no bird at all, but the spirit of the dear-departed *El Presidente*, tweeting his support the old-fashioned way. In 2014, Maduro then claimed that this bird had since returned and begun *talking* to him, saying things like '[because of your rule] *El Comandante* [is] happy, full of the love and loyalty of his people'.[20]

There is no way of knowing how much influence this story had upon the subsequent election results. Probably most voters had things other than Lefty ghost-birds on their minds, given the state of the national finances. The PSUV won; albeit by the narrowest of margins, gaining only 1.5 per cent more votes than the opposition. However, on 8 December 2013, municipal elections were due, and Henrique Capriles' MUD alliance were pushing hard to sweep up the protest vote, transforming dull local ballots into an unofficial referendum upon the PSUV's fiscal competence. Things did not look good for the socialists. This was an election in the month leading up to Christmas and Press reports implied that, due to foreign currency restrictions, there would be a shortage of toy imports to keep the nation's kids quiet that festive season. Not wanting to be known as the Commie who stole Christmas, Maduro sprang into action. As well as announcing the formation of the incredibly Orwellian-sounding 'Deputy Ministry for Supreme Happiness', he also attempted to bribe public-sector workers by bringing forward part-payment of their Christmas bonuses to mid-November. But, with no toys to fill the shelves, what would the huddled Venezuelan proletariat have to spend their dying currency on? With the nation's Catholic priests complaining that they were unable to buy any fresh Communion wine, people couldn't even turn to the Church for solace.[21]

Learning from this debacle, in 2014 Maduro launched his 'Operation Merry Christmas', in which Barbie dolls were suddenly reduced down to only £2 in price by force of law, triggering a rush on them; quite a reversal of attitude, as Chávez had once denounced 'the stupidity of Barbie' as a capitalist icon, and had dolls of himself manufactured and distributed instead, which spouted Marxist slogans when you pulled a little string on the back.[22] Back in 2013 it was adults who were thought to need bargain-priced Christmas presents the most, though, so Maduro claimed that innocent sellers of televisions, radios and other electrical goods were a secret capitalist 'enemy within', who, like typical Yankee counter-revolutionaries and imperialist running-dogs, were exploiting the poor by marking up prices. As such, he ordered the Venezuelan army to invade the 'Daka' chain of electronics stores and hand out flat-screen TVs and other such goodies to the public at a massive discount. However, the boost in popularity Maduro derived from this act was short-lived; due to chronic mismanagement of the country's power infrastructure there were, yet again, numerous blackouts nationwide, rendering even the most top-of-the-range gadgets temporarily useless.[23] After these embarrassing public displays of no power to the people, which Maduro blamed upon 'fascist' saboteurs, there had to be another way to get the workers back on-side ...

Dialectical Immaterialism

'Chávez is everywhere, we are all Chávez,' the increasingly desperate politician said at a Press conference held in late October 2013 to inform the world about a miracle that had been performed in *El Comandante*'s name. 'A look, it is a look of the homeland that is on all sides, including on phenomenons [sic] that do not have an explanation,' babbled Maduro incomprehensibly, as he stood on stage wearing a distinctly ill-fitting tracksuit emblazoned in the colours of the Venezuelan flag, and pointing excitedly at a blown-up photograph with a little stick. The photo showed a form of optical illusion known as a 'simulacrum', a spontaneously occurring natural image of what appears to be a face, as when people claim to see Jesus in the burn-marks on their toast. One of these images had just appeared in rocks beneath Caracas, while workers were digging out tunnels for an underground railway. Supposedly, the face was none other than that of Hugo Chávez himself, returned from beyond the grave – at least if you squinted at it a bit. Maduro presented this mundane event to his countrymen as a full-blown secular miracle. According to him, Chávez's face had appeared underground at 2 a.m. one morning and been snapped by a worker with his phone, before mysteriously vanishing into thin air. 'So, just as it appeared, it disappeared ...' said Maduro unconvincingly, before going on to imply that the face had talked to the construction workers somehow.[24] Did Maduro's ploy really influence the electorate, though? The outcome of the December elections (held, suspiciously, on the new annual 'Loyalty and Love to Hugo Chávez Day') suggested they did not. The vote was split, with about 49% going to the PSUV and about 43% to Capriles' MUD-men.[25] Venezuela remained a country divided.

There is no doubt, though, that a substantial number of Venezuelans really did – and still do – worship Chávez as a kind of god. His bizarre regular television show *Aló Presidente* (*Hello, Mr President!*), in which the avuncular demagogue would sit in a studio and cheerily rant for six hours at a time, often surprising his own ministers by announcing silly new schemes like the confiscation of the nation's golf-courses, or showing off his ability to ride a bike, was surprisingly popular viewing; you might almost say some people watched it religiously. It does sound entertaining. One day he would tell you in intimate detail about his diarrhoea, the next be seen on horseback or in a tank, or even perform a rap. He could sing, dance and tell jokes. Sometimes ordinary schedules would be interrupted without warning for footage to be broadcast demonstrating to the nation that Chávez knew how to drive a tractor, shoot a gun or operate a large industrial drill. Ministers would often learn about their sackings not face-to-face, but via TV. Unhappy with the management of the PDVSA oil-firm, he called its executives onto his show and fired them, one by one, by blowing a whistle like a football referee, shouting 'Offside!' and sending them off the field of financial play forever. Such programmes were largely improvised. People could phone in, asking their leader for a free house or holiday, and he would consider their request. Once, he announced the arbitrary mass expropriation of jewellers' shops in Caracas in the name of the people, leading to the jewellers themselves, who were watching, sneaking back into their premises after dark, boxing up all their wares and driving away with them, thus meaning the State got neither gold nor taxes.[26]

Say a Little Prayer

So, the Robber Prince certainly had a large and loyal audience, and the scenes of widespread mourning at his funeral made him look like a modern-day saint. In life Chávez had explicitly encouraged this very same assumption, making use of the slogan 'Christ is with the Revolution!' and claiming that Jesus was, like him, a tax-and-spend socialist.[27] *El Comandante* lives on still, with recordings of his speeches and videos of him dancing regularly being played at PSUV rallies. Samples of his handwriting have even been digitised by a group of young 'anti-imperialists' in the shape of the ChávezPro computer font, should you wish to make it appear he has written you a message (or a blank cheque) from Heaven.[28] Plans were also made to embalm Chávez's body and put it on public display like Lenin's, but, as his death was allegedly kept secret by the government for two months, this reputedly proved impossible as he had rotted away like *Schwundgeld*.[29] Perhaps most risibly, in 2014 the PSUV rewrote the Christian 'Lord's Prayer', rededicating it to Chávez instead of God Almighty and had it read out by a delegate at their conference:

> *Our Chávez, who art in Heaven, the Earth, the sea and we delegates,*
> *Hallowed be your name,*

May your legacy come to us so we can spread it to people here and
elsewhere,
Give us your light to lead us every day,
Lead us not into the temptation of capitalism,
And deliver us from the evil of the oligarchy (like the crime of
contraband),
Because ours is the homeland, the peace and life,
For ever and ever,
Amen. Viva Chávez![30]

It may have lost something in translation. Exploitation of widespread Catholic feeling in the country by the PSUV is widespread. Just prior to Easter 2017, Nicolás Maduro – a former altar-boy – claimed that members of the opposition, being capitalists, were 'the Anti-Christ'. 'I'm not exaggerating,' he added, alleging that, as economic agents of Beelzebub, they were trying to disrupt Easter and 'betray the sanctity' of the festival by organising Satanic anti-socialist street protests. To reassert the message of Christ in the face of such evil, Maduro announced all public sector workers could have an extra five days off immediately, something which was not at all yet another blatant bribe. Amusingly, some citizens took advantage of this extra free time to create straw effigies of Maduro and burn them on bonfires instead of the traditional Venezuelan Easter Judas dolls.[31] In reality, official Catholic 'support' for the regime is such that in August 2017 the Vatican issued a statement condemning Maduro's government, accusing it of 'encouraging a climate of tension and confrontation' which 'mortgages the future' of the entire country.[32]

Doctoring the Figures

I dwell upon Chávez's deification because, as the reader will surely know, *El Comandante* has his disciples here in the West too, particularly in Britain. Chávez's acolytes at the top of the Corbyn-captured Labour Party feel particularly motivated to worship at Hugo's feet on account of his professed love of free, NHS-style healthcare. In truth, however, even *El Comandante*'s much-lauded medical schemes have now descended into unmitigated disaster. The expansion in State payment for healthcare was partially a con, in which the *barrios* clinics were funded at the expense of the already-extant main hospitals which, having mostly been built by previous governments before Chávez came to power, Hugo couldn't claim credit for. So, he let them slide into disrepair, underfunding them to the extent that doctors, desperate to top up their pathetic pay (now £15 a month for some qualified surgeons), resorted to trying to flog their patients DVDs, while black-market touts proliferated outside entrance-lobbies, selling the sick supplies of bandages, tampons, toilet-roll, nappies and other such necessities, because the hospitals had none in stock.

Chávez didn't really care about this, however, as the Venezuelan Physicians' Association was seen as a bastion of bourgeois opposition, so sod them. Soon, the hospitals themselves were in dire need of some intensive care. The plentiful 'Out of Order' signs on lifts, medical equipment and broken lighting were replaced with the slogan 'Socialist Modernisation [Under Way]', though they really should have said 'Fix It Yourselves, Plebs'. Demoralised, it is estimated 14,000 doctors have now left the country to work elsewhere, doubtless for slightly more than £15 a month. Instead of public hospitals being flooded with cash, as is constantly hymned by *chávistas* abroad, in 2014 estimates put Venezuelan spending on healthcare at only 4.6 per cent of GDP, against a Latin American average of 7.6 per cent. This was not only down to freefalling tax-revenues after the initial mad splurge on Cuban clinics, but also due to some seriously twisted priorities. That very same year, the UN estimated that the government spent three times as much on subsidising virtually free petrol for voters as it did on healthcare. At least those in unbearable pain could easily afford to set themselves on fire to end it all, then. Another path out of a life spent in medical agony was simply to await your possible murder upon hospital premises. So crime-ridden have such institutions now become due to general social collapse that there have been cases of gangsters breaking into operating-theatres and shooting patients going under the knife; such victims would doubtless have been in the perfect place for their bullet wounds to be dealt with, had the surgeons only had access to the necessary equipment to save their lives. Of course, physicians could always try buying medical supplies from those very same gangsters on the black-market, but anyone who has ever seen *The Third Man* knows how that particular story would end.

Naturally, PSUV politicians can afford to go private, but when Cuba eventually began pulling its doctors out from the *barrios* clinics due to cost considerations and because many of them were fleeing northwards to the US in search of an escape from socialism, the poor had no choice but to go to the deliberately neglected normal hospitals again, where by now medicine was out of date, facilities were filthy, painkillers had run out, water had been cut off and cockroaches infested the operating rooms. One thing these institutions are absolutely overflowing with, however, is dying infants; according to Caritas, a Catholic aid organisation, around half the children it monitors in the country are suffering from starvation, with 11 per cent classified as severely malnourished. The best hospitals can offer these pathetic figures is sympathy; due to food shortages, nurses themselves end up buying babies milk out of their own pitiful wages, although God knows how. Despite this, Nicolás Maduro for a long time refused to allow aid supplies into the country, on the pretence that there was no humanitarian crisis at all, because the PSUV are socialists, and socialists always look after the poor, unlike wicked capitalists. Also, if they accepted aid from Westerners, this would rather undermine the PSUV's fake narrative that their Yankee-allied oligarch enemies were deliberately stealing and hiding all the medicine, to make the government fall or, even worse, *to make them privatise their NHS*! It was not until March 2017 that Tropical Stalin gave in and made a humiliating plea to the UN to help him out in sourcing new supplies of medication – I suggest they give him a large bottle of strychnine with strict instructions to drink the whole lot in one go.

All this is covered up, though unsuccessfully, like placing a tarpaulin over a dead racehorse. According to Maduro, 'I doubt that anywhere in the world, except in Cuba, there exists a better health system than this one', though you could be forgiven for thinking otherwise. Official figures on malnutrition are, strangely, no longer being published, and while there is no money for medicine, there is always enough spare cash to pay armed guards to stand outside Caracas' hospitals, keeping nosy foreign journalists (if not criminal gunmen) out. When in 2014 a cartoonist on a popular newspaper dared draw a cartoon criticising the dire state of Venezuela's NHS, she was sacked within hours of its publication. Clearly, she had committed sacrilege against the ultimate socialist sacred cow. Surprisingly, in May 2017 Venezuela's Health Minister, Antonieta Caporale, made the unaccountable blunder of allowing true national health statistics to be published on a government website. They revealed a 30 per cent rise in infant mortality, and a 65 per cent jump in maternal mortality, as well as massive upsurges in malaria and diphtheria, hardly surprising when there is no medicine available. These figures had been kept secret for two years because, announced the PSUV, they risked being subject to 'political interpretation' – namely, the political interpretation that the government was bloody useless. Naturally, Caporale was speedily sacked by President Maduro; whether for letting the figures slip out or for presiding over needless death and suffering, who can possibly say?[33] It all rather puts the alleged 'Evil Tory Cuts' to hospitals that the Chávez-loving British Left are always complaining about over here into some kind of perspective, doesn't it?

Labour under a Delusion

Like the Blessed St Hugo, Patron Saint of Lost Causes, Britain's own hallowed J. C., Jeremy Corbyn, is also worshipped as a Christ-figure by some of his more over-exuberant followers, and not only because of his beard and sandals. Here are just a few of Jeremy's (conflated) opinions on Venezuela, many of which, funnily enough, have now been erased from the websites where they once appeared. All these statements date from long after it had become apparent that Venezuela was sinking, but before Jezza became leader of the Labour Party in September 2015:

> It is a cause for celebration, the achievements of Venezuela, in jobs, in housing, in health, in education, but above all its role in the whole world as a completely different place ... Venezuela gives every child a future, a school, a doctor – a chance [N. B. recent research appears to show that children have access to schools and doctors in Britain, too] ... There is an alternative to austerity and cuts, and enriching the richest and impoverishing the poorest, and it is called socialism![34]

Or 'State-enforced poverty', to give it its technical name. As a seemingly hopeless long-term backbencher with no true responsibilities besides endless bouts of moral masturbation, Corbyn had previously acclaimed Chávez as 'an inspiration to all of us fighting back against austerity and neo-liberal economics in Europe' as well as praising his 'huge contribution ... to conquering poverty' and his ability to demonstrate that 'there is a different and a better way of doing things', fiscally speaking. Such comments would suggest that wanking does indeed make a man go blind. Upon being asked to condemn a violent State crackdown upon opponents in 2017, which cost around 100 lives and saw 5,000 people arbitrarily detained in prison, Corbyn simply replied that he condemned the violence performed by 'all sides, in all this'. According to the UN, however, the worst violence came from one side in particular, with policemen firing nuts and bolts from guns at anti-PSUV protestors, then giving out electric shocks and threatening to sexually abuse their families following arrest. Given how often he appears at anti-austerity rallies, I would have thought Corbyn would be in favour of people's right to engage in peaceful economic protests? Maybe not if the economic policies people are protesting about happen to be Left-wing in nature. Praising the 'effective and serious attempts' made to reduce poverty in Venezuela, the most Corbyn was willing to admit about the Chávez experiment's utter failure was that 'the issues ... are partly structural because not enough has been done to diversify the economy away from oil – that has to be a priority for the future'.[35] But recalling that when Chávez came to power petro-dollars from PDVSA accounted for about 50 per cent of export income, and now account for about 95 per cent, surely the regime actively did the precise opposite of this in order to gain immediate electoral support? Corbyn makes it sound like an oversight, not the inevitable result of their insane policy decisions. In July 2017, obscure Tory MP Marcus Fysh stood up in the Commons and criticised Corbyn's thinking about Venezuela. 'What a complete wanker,' Corbyn appeared to respond, although his office later denied this.[36] It takes one to know one, Jeremy – although, as Corbyn still cannot see that Chávez and Maduro alike were both colossal, world-class onanists, perhaps it doesn't.

Red in Untruth and Claw

In most countries, politicians who once backed *chávismo* are now backing away from this stance. José Mujica, Uruguay's extremely Left-wing former President, has branded Nicolás Maduro 'loco', while Spain's radical Far Left Podemos Party, whose leader once acted as an adviser to Chávez, have also begun to drop their former support through embarrassment and shame.[37] In Britain, the situation is rather different. Many sensible Labour figures have criticised the Venezuelan regime, but regrettably the non-sensible ones now hold the reins of power. Because their liking for Venezuela is basically religious in nature, not rational, it is literally impossible for such people to see the obvious truth about their fallen idols. In 2007 Corbyn's Shadow Chancellor and fellow Far Left hardliner John McDonnell addressed a conference of the 'Hands Off Venezuela' campaign group in London, arguing that the British government had to make a choice between supporting 'democracy or oligarchy' in Caracas, an issue that one day soon 'no MP would be allowed to dodge'. This meeting, by the way, saw a motion approved condemning 'economic sabotage' being pursued against the country before its economy or global oil prices had truly even begun to enter full meltdown – getting their excuses in early, I suppose.[38]

Meanwhile, Corbyn's extremely close ally Diane Abbott has claimed that Venezuela's voting system is 'less liable to fraud and impersonation' than the UK's, something which, as large numbers of students appear to have illegally voted for the Labour Party twice during the 2017 General Election, may well actually be true. Certainly, representatives from Jeremy Corbyn's good friends in Sinn Fein, invited over to Venezuela to monitor their last Constituent Assembly elections, thought the process 'fair and equitable', although Luis Almagro, head of the Organisation of American States, called it 'the biggest electoral fraud in the history of Latin America', while the chief executive of Smartmatic, the company that provided Venezuela's electronic voting machines, estimated that 'the difference between the actual [voter] participation and the one announced by authorities is at least one million votes'. For some unaccountable reason, Venezuela has not allowed the usual internationally recognised bodies of impartial observers into the country at election time since 2006, preferring to fly in its own hand-picked people instead ... such as Chávez cheerleader Diane Abbott, who acted in just such a role in 2012.[39] She never has been very good with figures, has she?

Domestic trade unions, too, seem to be in love with Venezuela. The Venezuela Solidarity Campaign (VSC), which applauds the 'progressive developments' allegedly underway in the country, claims to have links to eighteen British trade unions, including Unite, Unison and the GMB. According to *The Times*, its HQ is located in the same London building as the HQ of Unite and any donation cheques are to be made out 'c/o Unite' which, all things considered, would indeed appear to link them back somehow to Unite. Unite's website has boasted that 'record levels of investment in public services have seen four million Venezuelans lifted out of poverty', although it failed to mention that they were then plunged straight back into it again and now have to chew refuse from bins. Len McCluskey, the renowned Nelson Mandela-like figure who heads up the union, once backed a VSC motion applauding the 'advances in social progress and workers' rights' in Venezuela, and he is not alone in such magical thinking. Frances O'Grady, General Secretary of the TUC, signed her name to a 2015 petition opposing 'Right-wing, anti-democratic violence' in Venezuela too – but how did such people feel when Chávez had union leaders imprisoned when they stood up to him over his deliberate mismanagement of heavy industry in Ciudad Guyana? Mr Mandela once said it would be justified for British workers to break the apparently unfair strike laws of the Tories, so presumably he believes in the right for people to protest and withdraw their labour without being arbitrarily imprisoned by the State, especially as he once spent so many years locked away in Robben Island himself?[40]

Shameless Seamus

Most myopic of all may be Seamus Milne, an extremely scary former high-up journalist at *The Guardian*, now Jeremy Corbyn's chief spin-doctor, who simply cannot accept that *chávismo* could fail because it was inherently flawed, preferring to believe instead that its external and internal enemies have worked to destroy it. In 2014, during his time at the newspaper in question, Milne embarked upon a trip to Venezuela to interview Nicolás Maduro, giving him a platform to blame the US for fostering a 'slow motion' coup and 'revolt of the rich' against him, to 'get their hands on Venezuelan oil'. The Yankees were engaging in 'an economic war to cut the supplies of basic goods and boost an artificial inflation', Maduro implied, so they could justify sanctions and maybe even invasion. They would surely fail, however, as Venezuela was 'a country where the rich protest and the poor celebrate their social wellbeing', and 95 per cent of all deaths during protests were the responsibility of 'Right-wing extremist groups', he said, alleging that the US helped fund the opposition (this latter allegation being not actually that implausible, in limited terms). Less plausible was Maduro's claim that, being 'a little bit hippy, a little bohemian', if the street-marchers were correct about the State causing food shortages, he would have joined the protests himself. You get the impression Milne would not have done so, though, as he bought

Maduro's argument completely. 'What are portrayed as peaceful protests have all the hallmarks of an anti-democratic rebellion,' he wrote, 'shot through with class privilege and racism.' Venezuela was 'very far from being the basket case of its enemies' hopes', he proclaimed, thus demonstrating that 'there are multiple social and economic alternatives to the failed neoliberal [economic] system that still has the West and its allies in its grip.'[41]

By this, Blind-Man Milne meant socialism. After Chávez's death in 2013 Milne praised *El Comandante* as 'someone who was an outstanding champion of the poor and the oppressed' (other than those he happened currently to be oppressing), who oversaw 'the rebirth of socialism in our time'.[42] Milne would doubtless like to see socialism reborn, as he appears to be a fan of Josef Stalin and, so it has been said, believes that the wrong side won the Cold War. In his own words, we should always remember that 'Communism in the Soviet Union, Eastern Europe and elsewhere delivered industrialisation, mass education, job security and huge advances in social and gender equality.'[43] Indeed so. No matter what your class or gender, Stalin would happily have you shot or tortured in the name of equality of opportunity – and, as we all know, Stalin's slave labourers had jobs for life, in the sense that they were frequently worked to death in gulags.

Chris Williamson, Corbyn's former Shadow Fire and Emergency Services Spokesman, agrees with Milne that America, which has 'a very shady record', is the true villain behind Venezuelan suffering. In a now infamous August 2017 *Newsnight* interview, Williamson said he wished not to condemn Maduro's regime, but instead to 'facilitate talks and encourage the Right-wing opposition to stop these protests'. Thus, the victims were really the oppressors, and the oppressors were really the victims – Guénon was right, this is the age of inversion. Like his boss, Williamson admitted that the Marxists 'didn't do enough to diversify the economy', but speculated that the 'violent protests' were being 'aided and abetted by the United States of America'. Bare shelves were a result of 'manufactured shortages', not price-fixing and socialist incompetence. 'When a government is doing good things, as they certainly were under Hugo Chávez … that's surely a good thing we should celebrate,' he added. Writing – where else? – in Commie newspaper *The Morning Star*, Williamson further claimed reports of violence and decay in Venezuela were simply part of 'a proxy war against Jeremy Corbyn' rather than, for example, a major international news story about mass killings and enforced public starvation, blaming the 'hysterical media' for peddling such hyperbole.[44]

Deaf to the West

Former London Mayor Ken Livingstone also believes Venezuela is the victim of an economic conspiracy. In 2006 Chávez travelled to London for a two-day visit and was hosted by Ken, with *El Comandante* being greeted as the Messiah he so clearly was by hordes of cheering Lefties including Jeremy and his usual gang of useful idiots. He also spoke to the TUC, and praised the Labour Party (or one specific abnormal section of it, anyway), telling them that 'we must take power' because 'the only way forward for humanity is socialism'. It was not especially surprising, therefore, that in August 2017 Ken went on TalkRadio to claim: 'One of the things that Chávez did when he came to power, he didn't kill all the oligarchs; there was about 200 families who controlled about 80 per cent of the wealth in Venezuela, he allowed them to live, to carry on.' Livingstone emphasised that he was not suggesting Chávez *should* have killed them, merely that he would not be surprised if a lot of these businessmen whom *El Comandante* had generously refrained from shooting in the head were 'using their power and their control over imports and exports, medicines and foods, to make it difficult and to undermine Maduro.' If they had been executed, he said, these people 'wouldn't be able to undermine the present government'. While certainly 'not in favour of killing anyone' himself, some listeners mistakenly gained the reverse impression. Therefore, Ken released a statement clarifying his words further, saying the point he was trying to make was that 'contrary to some misrepresentations, Hugo Chávez didn't repress the former ruling elite in Venezuela', which was why they were still alive and ruining the country.

On the radio and in separate media comments, Ken argued that the true villains of the piece were the evil Americans, who had a 'long record' of 'screwing up' socialism in Latin America. So, did he support the PSUV government? 'Oh God, yes,' he told *The Times*. He even said that Britain should try following Venezuela's lead and start reforming its constitution, which is pretty disturbing as the main reason Venezuela has been reforming its constitution of late is to ensure permanent one-party rule and the *de facto* end of democracy. But as Ken was reported as thinking that stories of government crackdowns in Caracas were mere 'propaganda that's circulating around the world', and that the true nature of goings-on in Venezuela would not be known 'for decades' until secret US spy-files were released, he does not seem to wish to realise this. 'Armed people on the streets from the opposition [are] killing people', he said – quite a contrast to Hugo Chávez's vast reserves of mercy towards his own oligarch enemies.[45]

Economic Sabotage

So, is there any evidence that the Venezuelan economy has been deliberately sabotaged by gringo scum and capitalist wreckers? What Red Ken *et al* are referring to are the events of 1973, when the Leftist government of Chile's Salvador Allende (1908–73) was toppled with American backing, so the Right-wing dictator General Augusto Pinochet (1915–2006) could be installed in his stead. In a 2015 speech to the VSC, Corbyn himself asked 'Look at what is happening in Venezuela … is that different to what happened to the government of Allende in Chile in the 1970s?'[46] As Donald Trump has recently threatened Venezuela with military intervention, the Far Left fear the CIA might be preparing to depose Nicolás Maduro too. This rather ignores the fact, however, that Maduro himself is clearly on a fast-track to dictatorship himself, and that such intervention – which appears to be yet another typical empty threat from The Donald anyway – has only been made because of the violent government-led repression which is going on there, not because of any inherent desire for regime-change in Washington, which continues to enjoy buying Caracas' cheap oil.

In 2002/03, though, there genuinely was an attempt by Venezuelan businessmen and the middle classes to depose Chávez by wilful economic sabotage and the deliberate creation of shortages. Led by PDVSA executives, managers, union leaders, media moguls, businessmen and owners, a general strike ensured that banks, schools, warehouses and factories were temporarily closed down, with food shortages and queues appearing in supermarkets. The rebels hoped to pass blame for all this on to Chávez and get him deposed; an attempted April 2002 coup against him hadn't worked, so maybe this would. As Chávez and Maduro's supporters rightly say, this was a genuine and cruel disgrace, which caused hardship and cost the country billions … but it didn't work. People could see what was going on, and increasingly supported Chávez in the dispute. Within weeks, the general strike was broken. Soldiers commandeered supplies from warehouses and distributed them to shops. Chávez sacked 19,000 troublesome PDVSA workers, assumed full control of the oil industry and de-fanged the hostile media. And, naturally, private enterprise filled the gaps created by rebellious businessmen, as new businesses sprang up to sell and distribute the very goods which their striking peers were refusing to put on the market, thus stealing their custom and forcing them to give in.[47] With this event in mind, people like Livingstone claim that history is simply repeating itself. But if so, then how has it been able to go on for so long now? Are the oligarchs really so brutal that they are willing to let millions starve for years on end, and blockade all access to medicines? Do they hate Maduro so much they are willing to let their own businesses collapse and their capital and savings fall victim to a potential 10,000 per cent rate of hyperinflation? Why haven't the army simply been able to commandeer hoarded goods again and distribute them, like last time? And why have no rival enterprising businessmen stepped forward once more to fill the gap? Could it perhaps be that, whatever happened in 2002/03, this time the socialist government really is to blame?

As President Trump said to the UN in 2017, 'The problem in Venezuela is not that socialism has been poorly implemented, but that socialism has been faithfully implemented.'[48] Considering that so many on Britain's Far Left manifestly consider Mr Trump to be a vulgar, subhuman thicko, what does this make *them* if even he can see the obvious truth here and they can't? Nothing in this chapter is classified material – I've got it all from easily available newspapers, websites and Rory Carroll's excellent standard English-language biography of Chávez, *Comandante*, which perhaps Jeremy, John, Diane, Ken and Seamus should try reading some time instead of *The Morning Star*. As Carroll is a *Guardian* journalist, Milne in particular surely cannot claim this text is merely another product of the lying Right-wing mainstream media, participating in the Uncle Sam-inspired cover-up of Chávez's incredible economic achievements and profound care for his disadvantaged countrymen?

A Corbyn Copy?

So, if Labour gained power, would they try to copy the Venezuelan model? 'What an example to any future Labour government in this country', John McDonnell said of Chávez's socialist State in 2007.[49] This rather implies that they would ... except, of course, they couldn't because, dwindling supplies of North Sea oil apart, we have no petro-dollars to burn. Therefore, Labour would either have to print vast amounts of cash, thereby destroying the currency, or else have to borrow billions on the international lending markets to fund their proposed unaffordable spending sprees and mass nationalisation programmes, which would be even worse than what Chávez did – at least the money he blew actually existed, and was his Treasury's own. On the other hand, Labour have announced no plans to engage in the centralised price-fixing of goods, thankfully, nor is there any need for them to introduce a double exchange rate (yet). The Corbynistas do seem quite eager to imitate Chávez's highly successful policy of bribing voters with numerous impossible financial promises, however, and John McDonnell's talk of 'requisitioning' (a fancy word for 'stealing') local houses and apartments in the wake of the 2017 Grenfell Tower tragedy carries uncomfortable echoes of Chávez grandstanding on TV and ordering the immediate expropriation of Caracas' jeweller's shops.[50] Would the Modern Marxists like to try out such things here too? I hope not, and I also hope that, if you are reading this in years to come, such fears will seem inaccurate, outdated and maybe even rather quaint. Thinking that Labour would seek to transform us into a carbon copy of Venezuela is perhaps slightly hyperbolic. *Chávismo* may well be one of their main basic inspirations, but not a detailed blueprint. Here's Seamus Milne, writing in 2012:

> Venezuela's revolution doesn't offer a political model that can be directly transplanted elsewhere, not least because oil revenues allow it to target

resources on the poor without seriously attacking the interests of the wealthy. But its innovative social programmes, experiments in direct democracy and success in bringing resources under public control offer lessons to anyone interested in social justice and new forms of socialist policies in the rest of the world.[51]

In 2013, he had this to add:

Ever since the crash of 2008 exposed the rotten core of a failed economic model, we've been told there are no viable alternatives. As Europe sinks deeper into austerity, governing parties of whatever stripe are routinely rejected by disillusioned voters – only to be replaced by others delivering more welfare cuts, privatisation and inequality ... [Venezuela] makes a nonsense of the idea that ... nothing can be done but more of the same ... [Leaders like Chávez] have shown there are multiple alternatives to neoliberal masochism – which win elections, too.[52]

Don't Let Them Eat Cake!

Milne is correct to say that Venezuela offers the world lessons, but not the ones he would like to imagine. He may have a point about 'the rotten core' of certain forms of hyper-capitalism, but the rotten core of Venezuela's brand of hyper-socialism is even worse. In Venezuela, the economic insanities and obscenities keep flowing on a daily basis. In March 2017, Maduro had several bakers arrested due to their illegal baking of cakes, accusing them of engaging in a 'bread war' against the government. Decreeing that, due to the shortages he himself had caused, 90 per cent of all wheat now had to be used to bake bread with, not decadent capitalist luxuries like iced buns, Maduro sent troops into 700 Caracas bakeries, to make sure they were complying. When two men were caught making brownies, they were carted away by police. Of course, as 80 per cent of bakeries had no wheat at all, it proved easy for most bakers to comply with this sudden rule. The bakers' union protested anyway, explaining that their members' business models depended upon selling a certain number of high-priced cakes to turn a profit, but Maduro did not want to know. 'Those behind the bread war are going to pay,' he warned, threatening to take over bakeries in the name of the revolution if need be.[53]

In September 2017, meanwhile, Maduro's Urban Agriculture Minister, Freddy Bernal – the man who is charged with telling ordinary people to grow their own food on the roofs of their houses because Donald Trump has apparently blockaded all the crops – suggested that citizens should start breeding rabbits and eating them if they were hungry. 'A rabbit is not a pet,' he explained. 'It's two-and-a-half kilos of meat.'[54] But where were the people going to get all these rabbits from, and what would they feed them on if they had no food? Thin air? Possibly they could not even afford to do that, as in 2014 it was announced that, to raise funds, a tax would be placed on breathing. Thankfully this applied only at Caracas' international airport, where a £12 surcharge was placed on all tickets for the 'luxury' of experiencing ozone-infused air being pumped into the building.[55] This is the kind of lunatic economic and political regime that the people who run the modern-day Labour Party genuinely think is a good and noble thing. Disturbingly, increasing numbers of voters appear willing to trust them on this. Are they all going Caracas?

5

Loose Change
A Pocketful of Fool's Gold and Bad Pennies

There is always an easy solution to every human problem – neat, plausible and wrong.

H. L. Mencken, American journalist

A varied portfolio of other odd economists and financial ideas for you to invest your valuable interest in, from the woman who thought an unholy alliance between gravity and vampires controlled the stock exchange to the man with a wobbled brain who invented the incredible 50/50 Split.

There is such a thing as the 'rational markets hypothesis' which purports to formally 'prove' that the Invisible Hand of the Market works in an almost supernaturally logical and judicious fashion. Developed by the Nobel Prize-winning economists Gene Fama and Harry Markowitz, it was later developed into a supposedly foolproof method of making a killing on the stock market ... a method Markowitz himself refused to use because, irrationally, it just didn't feel right to him. Many scientific studies performed by figures like the Israeli psychologist Daniel Kahneman appear to demonstrate conclusively that human beings frequently make irrational choices; if economics claims to be a 'science', as it sometimes does, then how can it afford to simply go against the findings of other branches of scientific discipline? Disturbingly, a 2003 study of historical trading patterns on twenty-six separate major international stock exchanges found that, across the average year, share prices did 24.8 per cent better on sunny days than they did on cloudy days; i.e. nearly a quarter of historical market rises could apparently be attributed to the idea that traders feel more optimistic when the sun shines (although we must always remember that correlation does not necessarily imply causation). No wonder we talk about Black Monday and

Black Wednesday; those must have been the colour of the clouds hovering over New York and London at the time. How appropriate that early models of financial forecasting were specifically modelled upon the science of weather forecasting.[1] If you need final proof that those economic models predicated upon the idea that human beings are inherently rational in nature are wrong, then the stories that follow will surely provide it; I have saved the very loopiest economic theorists from throughout history until last. These people and their ideas are so mad they make Hugo Chávez look normal ... almost.

£BO Problem: Robert Eisler, Werewolves and Money Banco

One of the greatest problems of the Great Depression was the spectre of hyperinflation. To dispel this demon, extreme measures were needed – and one possible response was proposed by yet another fringe-theorist of the day, Dr Robert Eisler (1882–1949), who suggested that every affected nation should create two complementary currencies for people to use at the same time. An Austrian Jew and follower of the mystically inclined Swiss psychologist C. G. Jung (1875–1961), Eisler's true area of expertise lay in the fields of religious and cultural history, but in the 1930s he switched tack and began producing books with titles such as *Gold* and *This Money Maze*, which seemed far removed from his previous works, such as *Orpheus the Fisher: Comparative Studies in Orphic and Christian Cult Symbolism*. As his researches into financial matters progressed, Eisler became convinced he had the solution to the world's woes. Under Eisler's proposed scheme, there would be two pounds and two dollars, a pair of non-identical twins, one of which lived in the bank and one of which lived inside people's wallets. The first type was eternal, but the second faded away over time, like an old soldier. In books such as 1932's *Stable Money*, Eisler laid out his hope that all workers' wages could be fixed to a central Index so they would rise and fall in accordance with prices. However, the precise way in which Eisler proposed to implement this fairly simple idea was, in the accurate words of Hugh Gaitskell, 'extremely complicated and in places almost impossible to understand'. Essentially, Eisler wanted to create a perpetual distinction between the coins and banknotes people carried around and used in shops, which he called 'current money', and money held in banks, which he called 'money banco'. Current money (£cr or $cr) would be like the money we have now, which can rise or fall in value according to fluctuations of the market. Money banco (£bo or $bo), however, would remain eternally stable in terms of worth.

The point of this scheme would be to ensure that, no matter what happened to the value of the £cr, the purchasing power of individuals would be forever protected, in terms of the £bo. Imagine you have £10,000 of savings in the bank and then, like in 1929, the global market crashes, leading to a sudden freefall in the value of the pound. That £10,000 which you thought was safe in the bank might drop to being worth only £5,000 overnight; it would be as if half of your money had been stolen, even though, physically, it was still there. Even if there was no major crash, the constant small increase in inflation year by year gradually eats away at the value of your money like moths at cloths, so that £10,000 in 1917 might have lasted a man for decades, whereas £10,000 in 2017 would have been less than a year's wages. However, with the advent of £cr and £bo, such problems would be solved forever. When a person needed money to purchase goods and services, they would go to their bank and withdraw the correct sum for what they needed. In doing so, they would convert the £bo which they were withdrawing into £cr, in accordance with that day's exchange rate. Say in January £1.00 in £bo was worth £1.50 in £cr. If you withdrew £2.00 of your saved £bo, you would be handed over £3.00 in £cr. However, say the economy then suffered a wobble, prices rose, and by February £1.00 in £bo was worth £2.00 in £cr. If you withdrew £2.00 of your saved £bo under these circumstances you would receive £4.00 in £cr, not £3.00 as in January, thus meaning your purchasing power had remained unaffected. Just so long as you didn't keep hold of the physical £cr for long enough for it to gradually decrease in worth inside your pocket, you would be shielded from inflation forever. Because wages would be paid direct from employers' bank accounts into their employees' bank accounts in the shape of £bo, and all major financial transactions like debts, loans and contracts would also be conducted in terms of £bo, unfortunate situations like being in negative equity on your mortgage should theoretically never occur.

Eisler's scheme was certainly novel, but it never caught on. Quite apart from being fairly difficult to comprehend, it may also have had the probable side-effect of bankrupting shopkeepers. As far as can be told from Eisler's confusing writings, a shopkeeper would pay his employees' wages, as well as rent, etc, in £bo, by force of law, but he then puts his goods on sale to ordinary customers in £cr, having had to pay for them wholesale in £bo. What if the economy subsequently develops in such a way that the value of the £cr drops in the interim between him buying the goods wholesale and then putting them on sale to the public? He may have paid £1bo for an item from the warehouse, which equates to £1cr at the time. But what if the worth of £1cr then drops in relation to £1bo? He will in effect receive less for the item when he sells it to the customer than he paid out to the wholesaler when buying it. Even if he tries to raise his prices to compensate for this, the Treasury will just raise the number of £crs that £1.00 in £bo is worth to combat the consequent price-inflation, thus rendering this measure futile. End result? A lot of bankrupt shopkeepers. If Eisler's scheme ever had been implemented, the Great Depression might never have ended at all!

Following the end of the Second World War, Eisler returned back to his old topics of scholarship, abandoning all talk of implausible monetary reform for the altogether more sensible subject of werewolves. Eisler is best remembered today not for his authorship of *Stable Money*, but for his 1948 book *Man Into Wolf: An Anthropological Interpretation of Sadism, Masochism and Lycanthropy*. Partly based upon genuine archaeological and textual scholarship, and partly upon the Jungian analysis of mental patients' dreams, the book advanced the very unusual notion that, once upon a time, mankind had been a peaceful, herbivorous animal but that, somewhere along the line, humanity had split into two groups, one of which remained veggie, the other of which were a bunch of violent, carnivorous sex-fiends. His theory was that, during the Ice Age, this latter group had sought to imitate the successful predatory techniques of the wolf-packs they saw thriving all around them, overcoming snow-based food-shortages by becoming hunters who dressed in animal-skins. Transforming themselves imaginatively into bloodthirsty wolves as they did so, they thus gave birth to the widespread European myth of werewolves – if, indeed, it was truly a myth at all. Unfortunately, said Eisler, werewolves were psychologically real, and the genetic descendants of these wolf-men, being more ruthless and aggressive, now dominated the Cold War corridors of power, sending us hurtling towards nuclear oblivion. The solution was for us all to return to being plant eaters and to live in harmony with Nature, or else face annihilation. Just as £bo and £cr had the potential to shape-shift into one another, thus being a kind of werewolf-money, so the wolf-men in the Kremlin and the Pentagon had quickly to morph themselves into sheep, for the benefit of the entire quivering human race.[2] Not only did Eisler wish to transform our financial system, he now desired to change the whole world. Sadly, he ended up just howling at the moon.

Somewhere over the Brainbeau: Lt George E. Lemon and the Amazing 50/50 Split

One day in 1943, an ordinary US soldier fighting in the Second World War named Lt George E. Lemon (d.1992) was involved in a jeep accident in Tunisia, during which he received a severe bump on the head. The injury was so grave that it led not only to the brave GI's immediate discharge on medical grounds, but also 'wobbled' his brain so much that plain old Lt Lemon, American war-casualty, magically transformed into his fabled superhero-like alter ego J. C. Birdbrain Brainbeau, developer of a comprehensive '4-WAY PEACE-PLAN' which, he said, was 'the only way to end war, inflation, unemployment, trade-deficits and death'. 'All my brain needed was a tilt,' Brainbeau later explained, to make him engage in a ceaseless 'me-to-me talkathon', which would end up with him solving all of mankind's economic and social problems forever. However, to maintain plausible cover for his secret identity, Mr Lemon spent several decades living with his two unmarried sisters in their obscure Bat-Cave in Youngstown, Ohio, working quietly as a metalworker for the Youngstown Sheet and Tube Company until his retirement, aged seventy-two, when he suddenly began placing an endless series of very bizarre cryptic advertisements in American fringe-magazines of all kinds.

Everywhere from underground music fanzines to cheap sex-mags and mail-order guides to massage-parlours, weird little classified ads started to appear, telling readers of a coming change in the global financial world order which 'will prove who the real birdbrains are, and you could be among them unless you change your thinking'. If you were intrigued enough to do as Brainbeau suggested and send him off a Self-Addressed Stamped Envelope (SASE) to PO Box 2243, Youngstown, Ohio, then you may have expected to get a letter-box full of detailed explanatory pamphlets in return, laying out what precisely Birdbrain's great new idea was. However, all you would actually get would be a series of other equally enigmatic ads created by Lemon, as many photocopies as he could fit onto a few sheets of A4 paper. Brainbeau's economic philosophy was so complex he wanted it to be deciphered by kindred souls alone, those rare persons whose brains had also been 'wobbled' by the modern world in such a way that they would understand what the hell he was talking about. Some of these messages were, indeed, nigh-on incomprehensible:

$$\$$

WHAT IF THAT
Circus clown walking on stilts
tried it with just one stilt?
That's the trouble with each of
the world's defense forces. You
go into battle with a chance to
lose (get killed) but no chance
to win (go home). For a war-ending
strategy fire a SASE at:
LOSERS, WINNERS
(chance-selected) or simply WINNERS
BOX 2243
YOUNGSTOWN – OHIO, 44504

$$\$$

$$\$$

IT'S A NATURAL LAW THAT EACH
Fallen soldier (loser) should trigger a chance-
selected winner (civilian again). It's also

only natural that the PRINCE OF PEACE
should be the first BIRDBRAIN that concerns
him or her self with the adoption of
this non-suicidal, war-ending concept.
Drop a SASE on: BRAINBEAU'S Winners
BOX 2243
YOUNGSTOWN – OHIO, 44504
$$$$$$$$$$$$$$$$$$$$$$$$$$$$$$$$$$

Then again, considering how Lemon was not remotely embarrassed about advertising the fact his ideas were the result of profound mental illness caused by a bash on the brain, perhaps regular readers of his messages would not have been especially surprised that his words made little sense:

$$$$$$$$$$$$$$$$$$$$$$$$$$$$$$$$$$$$
IF BIRDBRAIN
BRAINBEAU'S CONCEPTS
Puzzle you it's because Nature
makes us adjust to the 100%
wrong way of doing things
which has been in effect since
the year one. Thanks to a W.W.II
jeep accident head injury incident
I got maladjusted in 1943.
Send SASE to:
4 WRONGS RIGHTED
BOX 2243
YOUNGSTOWN – OHIO, 44504
$$$$$$$$$$$$$$$$$$$$$$$$$$$$$$$$$$$$

Nonetheless, reading over Birdbrain's notices, it does become just about possible to discern the basic outlines of his theory. Lemon apparently believed that everything in existence could be split into pairs of opposing concepts such as wet/dry, day/night or hot/cold. The ones Brainbeau mentioned most frequently were men/women, winners/losers and odd/even. He believed that contemporary society was split down the middle into two contrasting groups, those who were fortunate and those who were unfortunate. Unfortunate people ('losers') might be unemployed, while fortunate people ('winners') had good jobs. Winners got given a cushy posting when called up to the Army; losers like him got sent off on dangerous missions where even the jeeps turned violent. Life was a giant lottery – so why not even things up a bit with something called the '50/50 Split'? Under such a regime, all companies would be forced to give 50 per cent of their profits to their employees, who would constitute 50 per cent of the national adult population, male and female, at any one time. In order to avoid the ills of mass unemployment, Brainbeau proposed that, in any given year, half the population should be forced to take a twelve-month holiday on full pay, while the other half filled all the nation's manual jobs. Then, come the end of the year, both sets of people simply swapped around, so that everyone worked in a one-year-on, one-year-off, shared shift pattern. In this way, 'everyone does ... his or her share of blue-collar work – no free-riders.' As for who would then do all the necessary white-collar work, I am unable to say; public-minded persons during their year off, maybe? Very possibly. Witness the following ad, in which Lemon gloats that half of the 'Mad Men' of Madison Avenue's world-famous advertising industry would soon be turfed out onto the streets performing some *real* labour for a change:

$$$$$$$$$$$$$$$$$$$$$$$$$$$$$$$$$$
IF MADISON AVENUE
Seems half-deserted maybe the deserters
are out on assignment wearing WORK
GLOVES. Send SASE to world-changing
(for the better)
EVEN AGE WORK FORCE PLAN
BOX 2243
YOUNGSTOWN – OHIO, 44504
$$$$$$$$$$$$$$$$$$$$$$$$$$$$$$$$$$

Madison Avenue is only *half*-deserted here, so it seems that the 50 per cent of the workforce who should have been enjoying a year off are instead happily spending their time coming up with new slogans to sell Coke and Pepsi; are they doing so voluntarily, so as not to get bored during their long holiday period? The unemployment-busting qualities of Lemon's plan were hymned again and again in ads like the following:

$$$$$$$$$$$$$$$$$$$$$$$$$$$$$$$$$$
A FIRST, SECOND OR THIRD
Rate mechanic shouldn't be out
of work and won't be when the
even age work force plan
IS ADOPTED.
Everyone works in tomorrow's
world ... and gets a year-long paid
vacation. End free-riding and
unemployment. Send SASE to
all-embracing inescapable

EVEN AGE
BOX 2243
YOUNGSTOWN – OHIO, 44504
$$$$$$$$$$$$$$$$$$$$$$$$$$$$$$$$$$$$$$$

Which cohort of the workforce you belonged to would depend purely on your age; those whose ages were evenly divisible by two would work one year, while those whose ages were odd and indivisible would not. A person would enter the workforce aged twenty and leave it aged sixty, and the fixed income of those pensioners, students and children who fell outside these age-brackets would be paid for by those who were not working that year, 'on a wheel-of-chance' basis, which would do away with all taxation in the usual sense, and see that year's non-workers split down the middle once more, into winners (who pay no cash to the government) and losers (who do). For reasons obscure, Brainbeau felt this system of 'UNFIXED WAGES' would lead to a perpetual 5 per cent rate of profit for companies, and a 5 per cent interest rate, rendering prices eternally stable. Everyone would be a winner in the sense of getting one out of every two years off, however, with a new problem of universal boredom due to excessive leisure-hours coming into play – but never fear, for Birdbrain Brainbeau had the answer ready to hand. He invented a new form of playing-card holder, dubbed 'THE CARD CADDY', and registered it with the US Patent Office. Billed as being a 'living room Vegas', Lemon hoped to sell such caddies for $10 apiece once his 50/50 Split had been adopted, thus earning millions while simultaneously bringing hours of joy to every household. Among Brainbeau's other patents (all registered under the name of George E. Lemon, curiously) were a magnetic dartboard, a quick-release arm-straightening device for golfers, an automatic ping-pong ball launcher, and some kind of 'target-game' which appeared to centre on model warplanes dropping bombs onto enemy shipping. Boredom, meet your final end!

Was there no socio-economic problem the 50/50 Split could not solve? The gender pay-gap would also be abolished in Lt Lemon's 'money-independent economy', and, because pay rates of 50 per cent of any company's profits would be standardised worldwide, the inexorable tide of mass migration from poorer countries towards richer ones would be stopped in its tracks. As Lemon put it, 'The daily invasion [of America] by two thousand illegal immigrants [from Mexico] could be stopped overnight'; under the 50/50 Split, with its guaranteed levels of full-employment and decent wages, 'those "greener pastures" [desired by immigrants] could be found right at home' in Mexico. Moreover, Brainbeau developed the further wheeze of abolishing all monetary pay in terms of dollars, pounds, yen and pesos, and instead issuing workers with Ezra Pound-like 'hours-worked certificates', redeemable only for goods manufactured in the country in

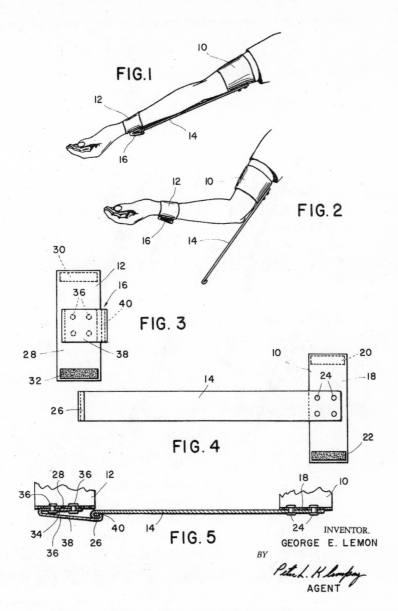

FIG.1

FIG. 2

FIG. 3

FIG. 4

FIG. 5

INVENTOR.

GEORGE E. LEMON

BY

AGENT

One of George E. Lemon/J.C. Birdbrain Brainbeau's many patents designed to help citizens fill in all their spare leisure hours once his amazing '50/50 Split' economic plan had given each member of the American workforce one out of every two years off. This is 'a device for preventing or restraining the bending of an elbow', designed to allow amateur golfers to improve their swing during all those extra free hours spent at the tee. To be honest, it looks painful. (Google Patents)

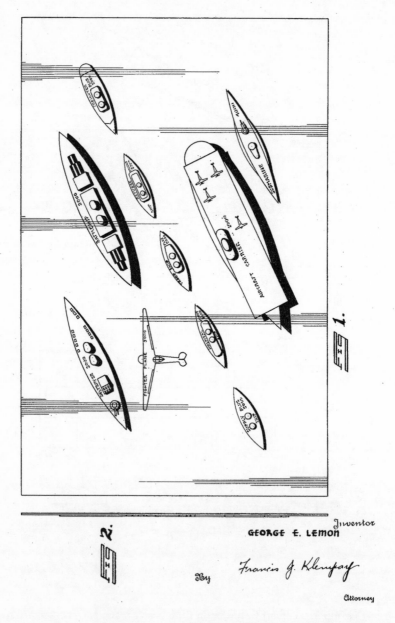

Sept. 2, 1941.

G. E. LEMON

Des. 129,262

TARGET GAME DEVICE

Filed Dec. 17, 1940

FIG 1.

FIG 2.

Inventor
GEORGE E. LEMON

By Francis J. Klempay

Attorney

More violent-minded members of the American public could always have a go at Lemon's 'Target Game Device', in which US warplanes dropped bombs on enemy shipping, if they so preferred. Interestingly, this patent was registered in late 1940, three years prior to Lemon's unfortunate 'brain-wobble', thus showing that he had always possessed a certain talent for invention. (Google Patents) which such certificates were earned, thus forcing all nations on Earth to become autarkies, and making it impossible to migrate into the US and still have anything it was possible to spend when you got there. Such fresh thinking, wrote Birdbrain, made it likely that he would become America's 'next President or maybe our next Jesus Christ or maybe both.' At the very least, as word of J.C.'s new gospel spread, the Free World's next leader would surely be 'some other guy, if one exists ... [who] thinks ... the way I do about ending war, inflation, unemployment, deficit-spending and death.'

But wait, what was all this stuff about ending death? To Lemon, there were four main human problems – war, atheism, unemployment and the Grim Reaper – and he reckoned his overall philosophy, the 4-WAY PEACE PLAN, held the answer to laming each of these Four Horsemen forever. Lemon's wider head-trauma-induced cosmology seems to have been conceptually compatible with his notion of the 50/50 Split, centring as it does upon the idea that two separate time-frames existed in the universe, termed 'herebefores' and 'hereafters' – or past/future, to you and me. Brainbeau believed in reincarnation, and reckoned that, in sum total, he had been alive for around a million lifetimes 'more or less' thus far, meaning he was approximately 70 million years old. Using this belief as the basis of a '20th century arithmetically and spiritually sound religion', Birdbrain appeared to think that spreading word of his plan would bring people back around to belief in God, and also solve the problem of death by demonstrating that we would all be reborn again one day in the hereafter, in a series of 'herenow reruns', or new bodies for our reborn souls. The particular herenow in which we were currently living was a kind of 'Hell on Earth', said Brainbeau, but things had been different a million years ago during a previous herebefore, when his 50/50 Split system had already been adopted – presumably we were all winners during this previous timeframe, but losers now, thus demonstrating yet again the law of 50/50 chance. Nonetheless, someday hereafter the cosmic factory-whistle would sound the changing of mankind's shift yet again, and the 50/50 Split way of doing things would be re-adopted; that was J. C. Birdbrain Brainbeau's one unshakeable faith, although he did admit it all sounded kind of hard to believe. 'I was as much an atheist as anyone until I wobbled my brain,' he once admitted – maybe the rest of us should start deliberately smashing our heads in too, in order to experience such a wonderful world-wobble.[3]

Silly Soddy: Frederick Soddy, Solar Economics and the Fight Against Perpetual Monetary Motion

Another somewhat wobble-brained economist was Professor Frederick Soddy, MA, FRS (1877–1956), an Oxford-educated scholar who won the

Nobel Prize in 1921 – for his fine work in the field of radiochemistry, not economics. A scientific genius, Soddy was jointly responsible for discovering what precisely radioactivity was in the first place, explaining it in terms of the decay of elements, perceiving that substances such as uranium would decay and transmute into radium, and radium into helium, producing alpha, beta and gamma rays. He also developed the theory of isotopes, and was among the first to perceive the future potential of atomic power and nuclear weapons. There is even a crater named after him on the moon, as well as the obscure radioactive mineral 'Soddyite', a variant form of uranium. In short, Soddy was no moron, and he knew it; a somewhat difficult man with immense confidence in the powers of his own mind, it was Soddy's scientific interests that ultimately led him towards the contemplation of economic matters. Essentially, Soddy perceived a certain similarity between coal and money, arguing that coal itself was an 'inherited accumulation of solar energy from the carboniferous period', a sort of lump-sum of capital that we spendthrift heirs of Nature's bounty were now working our way through at a frightening rate. Nonetheless, the sum of this carboniferous inheritance, which lay piled up within mankind's energetic bank account, was still enormous, at least for the time being, reasoned Soddy – so why were so many people still poor? His conclusion, not a million miles away from those of Ezra Pound (who read and admired Soddy) and C. H. Douglas (whom Soddy had his own qualified admiration for), was that it was the entirely fictional nature of bank loans that was to blame for this disaster. If human wealth within the industrialised world was based ultimately upon coal, then so should our money-supply be based upon something equally concrete – but it isn't, as by giving out their fictional loans the Hell Banks have caused it to be based upon airy nothing. This is unfair, because by doing so they have tricked governments into borrowing what they presume is real money from them, but really isn't, thereby leading to the destruction of the value of their national currencies.

To pay for the First World War, said Soddy, the British government could just have printed more and more banknotes, but refrained from doing so as they knew it would lead to inflation, reducing the value of the banknotes already held by British citizens, thus effectively robbing the pennies from their pockets. Instead, hoping to spare Britons this fate, the government had gone to the banks and borrowed money which they naïvely thought existed, but which was actually summoned from nowhere. The end result was precisely the same as printing excess money would have been; if the banks conjure up lashings of money on such a massive scale as to be able to fund a World War, then inflation still rages. Worse, in return for providing this 'service' to the State, the banks were now being unjustly rewarded with huge sums of taxpayers' real money in terms of the interest-payments politicians had agreed to pay on the original loans. This all went against the laws of Nature, said the chemist, as once a store of coal had been burnt – or 'spent', in economic terms – there was 'no way, thermodynamically, of extracting perennial interest from it'. If you have 100 lumps of coal, give them to someone else and he burns them, that's it, they're gone forever; their energy is used up and dispersed, via the process of entropy. But the banks were giving people and governments 100 lumps of coal and then expecting them to pay those 100 vaporised lumps back, plus an extra ten lumps in interest. It was simply unnatural and, in the end, unsustainable, pure usury.

Soddy claimed that by continuing to loan companies and governments their fake money, the banks were stoking up conditions for a future industrial recession, and affecting the stability of prices; he thought that a table that cost £1 in 1825 should still cost £1 in 1925, and that it *would* still do so if the currency hadn't been deliberately manipulated by the criminal con-banks. You never saw scientific measurements like the metre or the litre shifting about wildly from month to month, so why should the noble British pound? Soddy's solution was to ban the issuing of all these 'fictitious' loans from banks, and make the State regulate the value of the pound deliberately from Whitehall instead. This would be done by the Treasury printing more money and then distributing it to the people through the medium of higher public spending, and then performing a sudden about-turn and recouping large amounts of money back through ultra-high taxes, as and when the value of the pound seemed to be getting too high or too low, as determined by fluctuations in prices. Presumably, this might conceivably mean the nation running a massive surplus in one year, and then a massive deficit the next, which would prove exceedingly difficult for those poor souls in charge of trying to plan public spending, but for Soddy balancing the budget was nowhere near as important as balancing the value of the currency.[4]

Some of Soddy's other proposals for monetary reform were sensible, and have since come to pass. He argued for abandoning the Gold Standard, establishing floating fiat-currencies, creating consumer price-indexes, and for Central Banks and governments to be given macroeconomic tools to help manage the economy, as when the Bank of England fiddles with interest rates today. So, while once labelled a 'currency crank', Soddy could be viewed as being in many respects fairly sensible and ahead of his time from today's perspective.[5] The trouble is, if you actually read his original works, it is evident that something far, far weirder was going on in them, too. The basic problem stemmed from the fact that rather than simply promoting the field of science, Soddy also promoted the field of scien*tism*, that is to say, the arrogant presumption that all fields of human endeavour should be viewed through a purely scientific lens, and society subordinated to a kind of technocratic rule by men in white lab-coats – or by their theories and discoveries, at any rate. The modern world, Soddy said, had entered into a new Scientific Age which, as the disaster of the First World War with its tanks, zeppelins, flame-throwers, submarines and poison-gases had shown, the political methods of old were unfit to govern. If engineers invent the aeroplane, and statesmen wickedly co-opt it to drop bombs out of it, something has gone wrong. It was the same with modern economics, which claimed to be a science, but was truly a form of obscurantist religion, which failed to acknowledge that all wealth was ultimately based upon Earth's sun, whose concentrated energy was stored up in our fossil fuels, as coal was ultimately formed from the compressed remains of sunlight-eating plants and their herbivorous consumers. Even a carnivorous T-Rex was, ultimately, eating sunlight at third-hand, and when we burned a lump of prehistoric remains in the shape of coal, we were actually burning a condensed fragment of the sun's radioactive power. The world economy should thus be thought of as a sort of giant steam-engine whose powering fuel would one day run out, an argument which, so far, will have modern-day Greens nodding their heads in agreement. It is in the next part of Soddy's argument that things become increasingly bizarre.

Soddy's ideas, which went by several names, including 'Energetic Economics', 'Cartesian Economics' and 'Solar Economics', were expounded by him in a number of books and pamphlets from 1921 onwards, including *Money Versus Man*, *Money as Something for Nothing* and *The Wrecking of a Scientific Age*. His 1926 book *Wealth, Virtual Wealth and Debt* provided perhaps the clearest outline of his thought. Here, he saw dismal cosmic significance in the coincidence – or *was* it? – that both the modern steam-engine and the basic conceptual framework of modern capitalism had been created within a few years of one another by two sinister Scotsmen, namely James Watt (1736–1819) and Adam Smith. Watt's steam-engine had been perfected in 1775, while Smith's *Wealth of Nations* was published only a year later, in 1776. Smith, said Soddy, created 'the system of political economy under which the scientific era has developed', but the genuine science of Watt and the pseudoscience of Smith were 'mutually incompatible', so that, 'ever since, the world has been attempting to move in two opposite directions at one and the same time', causing financial distress for millions. Soddy held Smith and his followers responsible for the endless creation of debt and credit *ex nihilo* by the banking system, thereby fatally distancing it from the actual coal-wealth of nature. This was a profound mistake, because civilisation could not 'escape conforming to the laws of matter and energy' in the end, and the 'hopeless muddle' of the modern economic world was 'largely to be traced to [politicians and bankers] having no clear recognition of the physical principles underlying that subject'. Proclaiming that 'The Real Capitalist [is] a Plant', Soddy extolled the virtues of vegetation, which lived 'on the *revenue* of sunshine', as opposed to mankind which now lived on the large but ultimately limited *capital* of coal. Things had been different for cave-men, whose needs 'were met out of the solar energy of their own times' because 'the food they ate, the clothes they wore and the wood they burnt could be envisaged ... as stores of sunlight'. So, the plants were wise, living on the ever-flowing nuclear energy of the sun, whereas modern men were stupid, literally burning up the finite energy-wealth upon which their entire world depended; E. F. Schumacher and J. C. Kumarappa might have agreed (Schumacher did in fact read Soddy).[6]

This *should* all have been obvious, but people couldn't be made to see it. Why not? This was the Age of Science, was it not? It may well have been, but in such an age there was always the danger of science being abused by greedy con-men to dupe the ordinary people. It seemed to Soddy that pseudoscientists had now gained control of the levers of finance and, instead of admitting that they were operating a fiscal steam-engine, were busily tricking the masses into thinking they had invented a kind of economic perpetual-motion machine, one of those impossible devices that claim to be able to operate forever without fuel, like a car that never needs petrol. Money, said Soddy, was just a *symbol* of fossil fuels, upon which all our wealth was ultimately based; without coal, oil and gas, industry would collapse. So, really, every pound note was just a paper icon of coal reserves. Instead of a Gold Standard, it might be said, there should be a Coal Standard. When banks lent out money plucked from thin air, this was akin to the fake engine in a perpetual-motion machine plucking energy from thin air, too; a gigantic illusion, created by hucksters. Ever-expanding debts created through bank-loans were like giving people black-painted *papier mâché* nuggets to burn instead of real coal, meaning that money had become 'the nothing [empty symbol] you get for something [performing work or taking out a loan] before you can get anything [buy any consumer goods]'. The whole process contravened the First and Second Laws of Thermodynamics, hardly appropriate for a Scientific Age.[7] Nonetheless, many people were not scientifically educated, and, due to certain sad eternal defects in human nature, were prime candidates for being fleeced:

> Psychologically, the economic aim of the individual is, always has been, and probably always will be, to secure a permanent revenue independent of further effort, proof against the passage of time and the chance of circumstance, to support himself in old age and his family after him in perpetuity. He endeavours to do so by accumulating so much property [or capital] in the heyday of his youth that he and his heirs may live on the interest on it in perpetuity afterwards. Economic and social history is the conflict of this human aspiration with the laws of physics, which make such a *perpetuum mobile* impossible.[8]

Such simple-minded folk were easy prey for 'every conjuring trick' of the bankers who controlled the world, creating money from nowhere 'with a wave of the wand'.[9] You would think these references to wizardry were just metaphors, but apparently not. As a man of science, Frederick Soddy, MA, FRS, did not believe in magic; but he *did* seemingly believe in an international conspiracy of fraudulent sorcerers and fiscal hypnotists who were doing their best to enslave mankind with the black magic of money. In his 1934 book *The Role of Money: What It Should Be, Contrasted With What It Has Become*, Soddy argued that, in the Scientific Age, 'anything setting itself up against physical reality cannot be allowed to continue', in particular the abstract fictions of money, debt and credit, which were the basis of a new false religion to replace what he saw as being the old false one of the Bible.[10] All true human advances had come from science, said Soddy, and in pretending that wealth derived from banks, not from the sun as the physics of radiochemistry taught, the Hell Bankers were following an ancient and evil model of appropriating scientific discoveries in order to trick people into accepting false religions:

> It is a curious thought that the earliest description of the [primitive] steam-engine in antiquity describes its use for the 'magic' opening of the temple doors, when the priests lit the fires on the altars, to deceive the populace into ascribing to a deity what was [really] the work of the engineer. In much the same way today, the almost boundless fecundity of the creative scientific discoveries and inventions of the age are being appropriated for the purpose of the mysterious opening of doors into the Holy of Holies of the Temples of Mammon by a hierarchy of imposters and humbugs, whom it is the first task of a sane civilisation to expose and clear out.[11]

What was needed was a return to 'honest counting', of both money and coal. Sadly, this could never be, under the 'cabalistic abracadabra' of the modern financial system, which had to be overthrown – an obviously anti-Semitic phrase. In no way was such weird rhetoric at the time limited only to Frederick Soddy, though. Major C. H. Douglas, for example, once declared that 'Any serious endeavour to identify the origins of world unrest and war inevitably and invariably leads back to what is loosely called occultism.' Douglas seemed to believe that the mystical tradition of the *Kabbalah*, examined earlier, gave the hyper-Jews he so detested control over the ordinary everyday Jews-in-the-Street, bending them to their will somehow, arguing that the holy book of the Talmud 'so organised the Jews [by its influence] that the Masters of the Cabala were able to use them as one unit' in a kind of hypnotised economic army. Douglas even began subscribing to the genuinely loopy theories of the mad British conspiracy-queen Nesta Webster (1876–1960), a well-bred lady of (too much?) leisure who thought she was the reincarnation of a wronged aristocrat from the days of the French Revolution, an organised programme of Left-wing mass murder which she discovered had really been organised not by the rebellious French peasants but by, yet again, the Jews. Operating under the name of 'The Illuminati', Webster claimed that the Jews had since organised the Russian Revolution of 1917, as well as helping create the precursors of the IRA in Ireland and modern-day radical Islamists in Egypt, with the specific aim of destroying the British Empire via the twin viruses of Communism and terrorism, 'revelations' which she felt had put her in such potential danger from Jewish assassins that she never opened her front door to anybody without clutching a loaded pistol in her hand, something that must certainly have surprised the milkman. According to Webster, the Hidden Hand of the Jews was even behind the creation of the nudist movement and the American Civil Liberties Union – and, of course, behind the banking system, Theosophy and all alternative New Age religions and forms of esoteric thought (other than her own belief in reincarnation, presumably). In the interpretation of the occult historian James Webb, many of these monetary reformers of the day viewed themselves as being 'illuminated' in some way, having the power to 'see through money' as little more than a hallucination created by Jewish occultists, in much the same way that Gnostic initiates are able to 'see through' the illusion of matter created by the dismal demiurge.[12]

So, Soddy was not alone. But if wizards ruled the globe, then what was to be done? In a long and extraordinary passage, Soddy apparently calls for violent insurrection to take place against the black magicians, pseudoscientists and occultists who had engineered the Great Depression for their own selfish benefit, and who were apparently now preparing to instigate a Second World War via their perpetual-motion machines for the sole sake of turning a quick profit:

> Hampered by national frontiers, nothing can satisfy it [the Hell Bank system] till the whole world is made safe for banking ... Under the specious guise of a unification of humanity, it aims at absolute dictatorship under which none shall be allowed to live save by its favour and for the advancement of its transcendent whims ... Let us not, as other countries have done in the grip of these anti-social innovations, discard ... the freedom of the individual and personal life ... [It is] only now dawning on a duped world that, its loans being fictitious, its pawn-tickets can never afterwards be redeemed [i.e. national debts can never be fully paid off] ... Let us not enslave men that pretenders may rule, but take back our sovereign powers over money in order that men may be free. It is a road Britons have trod before ... Even as the heralds of a new Armageddon are taking wing, let the truth be tested – within or without the law ... Is it necessary to break the law to vindicate the law, or trust to democratic organisations, always officered in advance by the very interests they ostensibly oppose? ... [Modern finance] poisons the very air men breathe,

rots them for life or fattens them for death, and imputes its curse to science ... It serves the convenience of practising a worldly wisdom the exact opposite of that which is the foundation of the age. It prefers the dark in times when all men seek the light, and is sowing the seeds of hatred and war in a world weary to death of strife. It is poisoning the wells of Western civilisation, and science must turn from the conquest of Nature to deal with a more sinister antagonist, or lose all it has won.[13]

But who, precisely, were these Dark Forces of sinister antagonism? Today, Soddy might have fingered the unaccountable transnational tin-pot dictators of the EU or IMF. This being the 1930s, however, Soddy preferred to take after Nesta Webster and blame the Jews. This time, Shylock had got hold of a fake perpetual-motion machine that was inadvertently being powered by his own victims, who were kept endlessly running on the rat-race treadmill, until the point they simply keeled over and died to be replaced with another unwitting and utterly dispensable hamster-slave. In 1939, Soddy co-wrote a pamphlet printed by the Nationalist Press Association in New York, whose other output included such non-PC works as *Are All Jews Liars?*; I haven't read the text in question, but I'm guessing its authors would have concluded 'yes'. Soddy's own booklet was called *Abolish Private Money or Drown in Debt: Two Amended Addresses to Our Bosses*, and featured a number of blatantly anti-Semitic cartoons, such as a group of Tommies being marched off to war by a man waving a Star of David flag, and a front-cover image of an obese, big-nosed, oily-looking Jewish plutocrat examining yet another nice, fat gentile cheque that has just rolled in.[14] Worse, Soddy's already-mentioned 1926 book *Wealth, Virtual Wealth and Debt* featured an entire section, 'Is There a Financial Conspiracy?' in which the *Protocols of the Elders of Zion* is cited as evidence that Jews might indeed control the world's banks. According to Soddy, the whole plot was a kind of Oriental revenge upon Western science for having allegedly disproved the existence of the biblical God of Jews and Christians, and an Israelite attempt to enslave white men once more by substituting enforced worship of the Golden Calf, remoulded into the Gold Standard, for worship of Jehovah:

Hitherto in this field of high finance, the semi-Oriental, cradled in the battleground between East and West, has been supreme. Before the development of science, the flood of mystical half-truths that inundated the Western world from this quarter had effactually subjugated it intellectually. The Westerner, in trying to assimilate and digest this exotic spiritual diet, entirely lost ... any intellectual independence. He was fascinated and hypnotised by the iridescent bubble of [biblical] beliefs blown around the world by the Hebraic hierarchy, and even now, long after the lancet of science has pricked the bubble and let in the light, the alleged doings of the 'chosen people' thousands of years ago is still considered an essential part of everyone's education ... It would be unwise to underrate the influence of a dominant force of this magnitude over people's lives ... [In an Age of Science] We have given up the belief in physical miracles, only to be ensnared in metaphysical ones [of abstract finance]. Until the apparent miracle of Virtual Wealth is understood and mastered by those who would essay to influence the destinies of nations they will continue to be like clay in the hands of the astute financier ... Whether or not there is a conspiracy among the 'chosen people' to re-establish by Gold the dominance they were wont to derive from God ... it must be admitted that it would be a revenge on science for its iconoclastic tendencies, not without certain sardonic humour, if we wake up one day and find instead of the Ten Commandments a single Golden Rule.[15]

As evidence of this Jewish conspiracy, Soddy complained that his economics were often mocked in the Press, and that his ideas were constantly being suppressed by the publishing industry ... a complaint he made in print, within what can only be described as a book. Regrettably, therefore, it seems the Jewish grip upon the media wasn't quite strong enough, and Soddy somehow managed to get his scribblings out anyway. Perhaps it would have been better if he hadn't. Still, at least we can burn them as an expression of stored Solar Wealth, should all the coal indeed one day run out.

Defying Economic Gravity: Roger W. Babson and Newtonian Finance

Another man who tried to base his financial theories upon the supposedly solid ground of science was Roger W. Babson (1875–1967), a highly eccentric millionaire who stood for President on behalf of the Prohibition Party in 1940. Babson might have wanted to prevent people from getting wasted on drugs and alcohol, but he was quite happy for them to float Eight Miles High by another means – namely, through the development of anti-gravity devices. Gravity was Babson's life-long obsession, one which had begun when, while still a child, his older sister had drowned while swimming in Massachusetts' Annisquam River. In a 1948 essay, *Gravity: Our Enemy Number One*, Babson explained how this tragic event had first made him realise that gravity was a malign force, bent on humanity's destruction: 'Yes, they say she was "drowned", but the fact is ... she was unable to fight Gravity, which came up and seized her like a dragon and brought her to the bottom. There she was smothered, and died from lack of oxygen.' When in 1947 his seventeen-year-old grandson Michael was also drowned by 'Old Man Gravity', as he called this murderous force, Babson decided it was time to act, and in 1948 set up an organisation called the Gravity Research Foundation, devoted to clipping the dreadful dragon's wings.[16]

This makes it sound as if Babson unreservedly detested this dangerous Newtonian power. In fact, the situation was more ambiguous. Babson owed a lot to gravity, as the title of his autobiography, *Actions and Reactions*, implied. Born into a successful mercantile family in 1875, as a young man Babson was forced by his strict father Nathaniel to attend the Massachusetts Institute of Technology (MIT). Babson found the majority of his lectures boring, and his tutors utterly lacking in vision and imagination; while they were supposed to be world experts in the field of technology, they rubbished the idea of aeroplanes, and failed utterly to foresee the future impact of the automobile, radio set and cinema screen. The young Babson was rather more imaginative, trying to set up a business selling fish coated in chocolate, a venture which unsurprisingly failed because his products were disgusting. Nonetheless, such daring projects at least demonstrated a sense of invention and originality, qualities Babson also saw in Sir Isaac Newton, whose theories were virtually the only thing he enjoyed learning about at MIT. Upon graduation in 1898, Babson decided to follow in the former Master of the Mint's footsteps by seeking out a career in money. Landing a job in a Boston investment firm, he was quickly fired after repeatedly asking his greedy employers why they were selling their gullible customers bonds at crookedly high prices.

Roger W. Babson, pictured in 1918. Babson had a love-hate relationship with gravity, upon the one hand chastising it for killing several of his relatives and causing outbreaks of constipation, on the other hand celebrating it as the secret force which controlled the world's stock markets and made him a millionaire. (Courtesy of the Library of Congress)

In 1901, by now working for a less corrupt firm, Babson took a business trip to Buffalo, where he came down with tuberculosis. It seemed likely he would die before he even reached thirty. With the disease settling on his lungs, Babson ignored medical advice to move to a region with dry, warm air, remembered the teachings of his idol Newton, and theorised that, if he stayed in the hilly, mountainous area of Wellesely Hills in his home State of Massachusetts, the cold, high-altitude air would push the TB out of his lungs somehow, via the powers of gravity. (Babson felt, only half-correctly, that there was less water in higher air and thus more oxygen; when gravity made water-content drop down closer to the ground in valleys, seeding the air with moisture, people were being invisibly 'drowned' on dry land by Old Man Gravity, he said.) Lying in bed for two years while breathing in the frosty mountain air, Babson eventually recovered, using the free time afforded by his long convalescence to make plans for creating his own financial services company, Babson's Reports, Inc. Looking over the monthly financial reports of banks, railroads and other companies, Babson realised that, in every investment firm across the land, hundreds of statisticians were taking delivery of precisely the same reports he was, poring over the data, and compiling it for the use of their bosses. Would it not be cheaper if just one man, namely himself, did all this work and then posted out summaries to each investment bank that needed them for a small sum, instead of them having to keep all those expensive statisticians on the payroll? The idea was so simple it was amazing nobody had ever thought of it before, and, after a slow start, Babson's Reports began raking in millions; Babson is now regarded as one of the founding fathers of the entire American financial services industry.

The world of high finance was not the only thing on Roger W. Babson's mind during his illness. Brooding, Babson became increasingly possessed by his now uncontrollable interest in Sir Isaac Newton, who had also previously been subjected to an unprovoked assault by gravity one day while sitting quietly beneath an apple tree. If Newton's laws of gravity controlled everything in existence, from falling objects to the level of TB in people's lungs to the way that female relatives sank and died in large bodies of water, then might it not control the global economy too? Babson thought so and invented a novel method based on Newton's theories to help him beat the market. His idea boiled down to 'what goes up must come down'; when the market soars high, it will eventually plummet back down to earth again, and vice-versa. On 5 September 1929, as global stocks were riding high, Babson gave a seemingly contrarian speech predicting a 'terrific' crash was on its way; hours later, stocks declined by 3 per cent. By 24 October, the Wall Street Crash had struck, and so began the Great Depression – bad news for most men, but not for Babson. His reputation was made, and the newly christened 'Wizard of Babson Park' cashed it in wisely. He became a prolific writer, with some forty-seven books to his name, many of which were financial self-help titles, and got his own weekly columns in the *New York Times* and *Saturday Evening Post*. His already highly successful advice and analysis service went from strength to strength, as did his own personal investment portfolio; when he died in 1967, Babson was worth $50 million (about $367 million today).[17]

Babson's favourite Newtonian discovery was the English scientist's Third Law of Motion, which informs physicists that 'for every action there is an equal and opposite reaction'. Together with Professor of Engineering George F. Swain (1857–1931), the Wizard of Wall Street developed a new way of recording and predicting the vacillations of the stock market, in the shape of his once-renowned 'Babsonchart of Economic Indicators'. A Babsonchart resembles one of those temperature-tracking graphs you used to see pegged onto the bottom of patients' beds in hospitals, and sought to divide up the natural macroeconomic cycle into four simple stages – recovery, prosperity, decline and depression. By using the Babsonchart to work out what stage of the cycle the economy was in, investors could make informed decisions about whether to buy or sell stock. Babson thought that when it came to economics, history repeated itself, so he bought a full set of old copies of the *Commercial and Financial Chronicle* and, after working out what stage of the cycle the market was at on his Babsonchart, sought out an issue of the *Chronicle* in which similar conditions prevailed. Then, he looked in subsequent issues to see what had happened next, and issued his predictions and advice accordingly. He called this principle that of Action-Reaction, seeing financial falls as caused by financial rises in just the same way that, when a ball is

Sir Isaac Newton, scientific genius and former Master of the Royal Mint, to whom Roger W. Babson was so devoted that he ended up buying his antique bed. Seeing as each man shared a deep interest in both gravitational and monetary matters, they were clearly soul-mates across the centuries. (Courtesy of the Library of Congress)

tossed violently up into the air, it falls back down to earth again – before then bouncing up and falling once more. Imagining the ball bouncing up and down forever, in some idealised Newtonian paradise, Babson saw that this physical law must be what the financial world was based upon. Alternatively, the stock market could be envisaged as a pendulum, constantly swinging between boom and bust. If only governments and investors would heed Babson's advice, the pendulum's path could become subject to fewer violent swings, with stock market graphs being transformed into 'a straight but slowly rising line' as the economy gently expanded forever, guaranteed. If you don't want a ball to fall very far, then don't let it bounce too high in the first place; Babson recommended that, when times were good, governments should intervene to deliberately *cause* recessions, because, if the financial peaks were fairly low, then so would the troughs be.[18]

Babson's idea implied that the global economy was a kind of self-correcting mechanism like a gyroscope, which always returned back to equilibrium in the end. For Babson, business was like 'a cold spring; the more it is compressed, the greater becomes the potential snap-back' in terms of ultimate economic expansion. Therefore, the Great Depression would inevitably one day end: 'The page of history shows that the limit of [the spring's] elasticity has never yet been reached; never has business been so distorted as to be unable to come back.'[19] All economic phenomena could be explained along such lines. Prices would rise, until they got too high, and then they would fall – until they got too low, whereupon they would rise again, as the gyroscope corrected itself. It was the same for unemployment rates, interest rates, taxation levels, inflation and rates of government spending. Politics too was an inherently Newtonian field, whose pendulum swung incessantly between Left and Right, something that led the Wizard to propose a new law that would have all Congressmen starting their day by being forced to listen to someone reading stories from old newspapers out loud for half an hour. 'I am serious in this and speak with considerable authority,' Babson said, having built his own fortune upon similar methods. If the West's 'crazy' politicians were properly educated about the past, argued Babson, they would realise their limited scope to change the world, and so abandon all overambitious schemes for comprehensive, socialist-type change forever, seeking to put the world on a very gradual upwards curve instead, mirroring his ideal chart of the stock market. After all, 'it took a million years to teach men not to eat each other', and Rome wasn't weaned off cannibalism in a day. Alternatively, Babson proposed scientists should be put to work developing 'a tube', which 'would recover light-beams of bygone days'. Then, by comparing ancient footage of Nero fiddling while Rome burned with equally flame-filled images of the Great Fire of London, the time-tube would 'furnish dramatic proof that history is repeating itself' to its users, thereby enabling Congressmen to suss out for themselves that 'the only new thing about the present Depression is its date'.[20] Babson certainly identified a genuine problem about the historical ignorance of many politicians here; I'm just not sure about his solution ...

After predicting the Great Depression, Babson generously tried to alleviate its evils by paying the unemployed to begin carving and painting 'inspirational business insights' onto big boulders in the abandoned Massachusetts settlement of Dogtown, slogans like 'LOYALTY', 'KEEP OUT OF DEBT', 'HELP MOTHER' and, rather cruelly given the circumstances, 'GET A JOB'. The reasons behind Babson's choice of Dogtown as the home of this institutionalised graffiti-fest were characteristically peculiar. In his rather Pooterish autobiography, Babson devotes an entire chapter to his 'Hobbies and Recreations', where he admits his chief leisure pursuit is redecorating Dogtown, a place he had bought outright. Babson's relatives accused him of 'defacing the boulders and disgracing the family' with his antics, but he disagreed. Being a big fan of trite 'good cheer' books – self-help tomes, in today's parlance – Babson developed the severely deluded notion that reading such trash could cure mental illness. He even provided a list of the books he felt had the greatest curative properties for his more disturbed readers to make use of, including such essential-sounding titles as *Courage That Propels* by G. Ray Jordan, *I Dare You!* by William H. Danforth (don't give either of these to someone who's suicidal and standing on a window-ledge), *Tune in for Your Birthright* by Florence L. Clarke, *Thought Transmutation* by Henry Thomas Hamblin, *Blessed Be Drudgery* by William C. Gannett and *The Happiest Man in the World* by Harold F. Barber. Babson also airily advised that 'one having a nervous breakdown' could very easily be cured simply by reading a book about astronomy. Babson admitted he was trying to transform Dogtown into a gigantic 3-D self-help book, 'with words carved in stone instead of printed on paper'. This particular living book, however, would not be intended to cure people's mental illnesses but their financial ones, something facilitated not only by the slogans on the boulders, but also by Babson's incredible discovery that the flowers in Dogtown had for some reason been specially designed by God to illustrate the wonders of the beneficial nexus which currently existed within America between competitive and individualistic free-market capitalism and a conservative form of government, free from the wicked socialistic desire for endless and pointless change.[21] As he explained:

> I am always captivated by the native flowers [of Dogtown]. Wild roses, blue asters, bayberry and thistles bloom today identically as they did when this former village ... was at its height of activity. Why is it that through struggle and in spite of flood, drought, and even promiscuity, these native flowers hold their own and refuse to deteriorate? Yet our marvellous newly cultivated species will completely run out in a few years except with continued fertilisation and artificial breeding. The answer ... is

apparently as follows: through the centuries the native Dogtown flowers have developed some divine technique of invisible control from within, but which does not interfere with the freedom of the individual plants to propagate and grow as they wish. Scientists have not yet discovered how this has been accomplished; but they do know that it is a slow progress. In these days when we want government to quickly bring about a new social order, has not Dogtown a lesson for even political leaders? Dogtown teaches me clearly that progress comes only slowly and from developing within the individual self-control, high ideals and other fundamental immunities.[22]

Politicians and economists would therefore do well to talk to flowers like Prince Charles and take note of the blooming wisdom of Dogtown. Babson tried applying the laws of Newtonian physics to other areas as well. Having undergone a religious conversion experience aged fifteen, between 1936 and 1938 Babson held a high-up position in the General Council of Congregational-Christian Churches, and tried to prove that fluctuations in Church attendance figures followed a similar path to the ups and downs of the business cycle.[23] He went on to develop a strange theory that the path to God lay through gravity and undefined 'cosmic rays', deciding that Jesus' admirable message of 'do unto others as you would have others do unto you' was really just yet another restatement of Newton's Third Law of Motion. This teaching of Christ Babson called 'The Golden Rule':

> Young people should especially be interested in the fact that this Golden Rule is based on the same Law of Action and Reaction about which Sir Isaac Newton wrote in [his book] *Principia Mathematica* in 1687. In short, we should do right by others because what we do to them they ultimately will do to us. Kindness reacts as kindness, while meanness reacts as meanness. Only as this fundamental principle is universally recognised will the business cycle be flattened out and wars between nations become a thing of the past.

This sounds a generous enough creed, but in fact Babson thought Jesus was really an extreme social Darwinist, explaining that the only way to test Christ's teachings was to see whether they could defeat Communism, or indeed 'any other "ism"', for that matter. Decrying the 'wishy-washy doctrines' of those misguided fools who argued for expanding the welfare state or lighter sentences for criminals, Babson argued that such naïve Reds were destroying the nation and even Christianity itself. Lefties, wrote Babson, 'refer to Jesus' appeal for mercy and justice, but ... it is not merciful to let a race or a family become soft spiritually, physically, or intellectually; it is not justice to tax the thrifty to support the wasteful. Jesus appealed for a *stronger* race.' As if to back up Christ's unexpectedly eugenicist message, Babson also advised that missionaries to foreign lands should restrict their activities to 'teaching them birth-control' and, naturally, 'helping them harness gravity for power'. Desiring to prove once and for all that God and Christ were basically Newtonian, Babson penned the following short summation of his entire doctrine:

> THIS HOLY SPIRIT WHICH WE CALL GOD IS THE GENERATING FORCE OF EVOLUTION. THE POWER OF THE SPIRITUAL LIFE IS DUE TO THE SAME LAW OF ATTRACTION AS THAT WHICH HOLDS THE PLANETS IN THEIR COURSES. THE EFFECT OF PRAYER IS A LAW OF PSYCHOLOGY, PROVEN IN THE LABORATORY. THE GOLDEN RULE IS FOUNDED ON THE SAME LAW OF ACTION AND REACTION WHICH UNDERLIES PHYSICS, CHEMISTRY, MECHANICS AND OTHER SCIENCES. ETERNAL LIFE IS MERELY THE LAW OF THE CONSERVATION OF ENERGY APPLIED TO OUR SPIRITUAL EXISTENCE. THESE ARE THE GREAT MESSAGES WHICH JESUS TAUGHT. EVERY ONE IS AS DEMONSTRABLE AS A PROBLEM IN GEOMETRY.[24]

Such unique theological knowledge allowed Babson to draw a direct parallel between periods of boom and bust and periods of high and low religious sentiment; if the workings of the stock market and Christianity were alike based upon the Newtonian principles of Action-Reaction, then this conclusion made sense, at least to Babson. Therefore, recessions were truly caused by the lax moral standards engendered by periods of financial boom:

> Economic history plainly teaches that during past periods of prosperity there developed debt, waste, carelessness and crime. In fact, these agents were the real cause of the disaster which inevitably followed. When men are making money they are more likely to lose their faith, forget their God, and become, more or less, pagans … When, however, people are out of employment, when men are making losses, they find material things drifting away. Being unable to control the situation, they look to higher spiritual power. The first move is to stop waste; next, more employers and workers determine to do their very best; and finally, we begin to seek higher sources for aid and guidance … When 51 per cent of the people are actuated by the desire to be of real service [to God], conditions begin to improve and prosperity gradually returns.[25]

Babson also used his knowledge of Newton (and his immense wealth) to enter politics. His choice of allegiance was the Prohibition Party, the oldest existing third party in the US. Founded in 1869, the Prohibitionists helped ensure the passing of the 18th Amendment to the US Constitution in 1919, banning the sale and production of alcohol, but following this success their support sank rapidly. In the presidential election of 1904, their inappropriately named candidate Silas C. Swallow (1839–1940) had gained 258,596 votes, but by the time of Babson's candidacy in 1940, the Prohibitionists were in full-blown Newtonian freefall. Babson was unable to significantly halt the Prohibitionists' decline, coming fourth in the contest overall with 58,743 votes. Babson sought an explanation for this dismal failure and eventually found it in … gravity! His paper *Weather Conditions and Political Victories* analysed each presidential election between 1844 and 1948, 'proving' that gravity had been behind most winners. Apparently, gravity affects the weather, the weather affects crop-yields, crop-yields affect business, business affects employment, and employment affects elections. In 75 per cent of cases, said Babson, a Party kept its hold on the presidency when gravity had ensured good weather, and lost its grip when gravity made bad weather. FDR had thus beaten him in 1940 not because he was the better man, but because Old Man Gravity was on his side, rigging the vote.[26] Babson added another layer of meaning to the term 'Prohibitionist', however, wishing to prohibit not only the consumption of alcoholic beverages, but also the right of allegedly unfit persons to vote. The 'promiscuous voting' represented by universal suffrage only allowed the more sub-human element of the population to wave in welfare state measures designed to foster their ability to breed and live like parasites off decent taxpayers, a 'system of ignoring the fit and protecting the unfit' which was 'biologically unsound and will end in disaster'. According to Babson, votes for all had created a system of reverse-Darwinian de-evolution, in which huge sectors of the US populace had already degenerated into hideous humanoid semi-animals:

> [Just] because an early American document states that all men are 'created equal', does not make it a fact. Different families within the United States have reached different [levels] of domesticity. Speaking frankly, our nation is like one big farmyard. Roaming over our land are all kinds of human animals, from wildcats and foxes, skunks and pigs, to intelligent dogs and horses. The idea that the same freedom should be given to all is absolutely ridiculous. Wire fences and shotguns are as necessary for good government as for good farming.

At least 10 per cent of the population were too selfish and retarded to be allowed the vote, Babson argued. Politicians who sought to interfere with natural economic laws to satisfy the demands of morally mutated pig-people were sinning not only against God, but gravity. Criminals, welfare-recipients, public-sector workers, those 'with no family or useful responsibilities' and anyone unable to pass a simple written test, all should be denied the vote in the name of Newton. Furthermore, said Babson, 'democracy, to be saved, must be purged', with the welfare state being slashed and a race of superior beings like himself and his admirably named son-in-law Lewis W. Mustard Jr being left to take over as a new 'aristocracy of character, health and intelligence', a sort of 'Royal Family of America'. To this end, Babson recommended temporarily installing a fascist dictatorship, until such time as the people and politicians had got it drummed into their thick skulls that the government couldn't control gravity, and therefore could not control the economy in terms of abolishing the financial inequality which accompanied booms and busts. 'If such [a dictatorship] comes, I hope my descendants will co-operate therewith,' Babson concluded. Following the installation of a temporary *Duce*, Babson recommended that a 'Department of Character Training, headed by a Secretary of Character' should be set up in order to do for the sub-humans 'what the Secretary of Agriculture has done for cattle, sheep and hogs'. Men should be taught that the laws of economics paralleled the laws of Newton: 'stones will always sink and corks will always float'. Indeed, said Babson, 'laws cannot be made, they can only be discovered', as Newton had found when the apple fell on his head. Therefore, 'We cannot break economic laws, we can only break ourselves against them.'[27]

Flirtation with fascism apart, the teetotal Babson was undoubtedly a well-meaning man, but following his grandson's death in 1947 he simply lost all reason, blaming gravity for every problem. As he explained in 1948, gravity 'is not only directly responsible for millions of deaths each year', but also for 'millions of accidents' in which people fell over. Even constipation was gravity's fault; 'intestinal and other internal troubles are directly due to people's inability to counteract gravity at a critical moment,' he argued. Fortunately, Babson had the solution – Priscolene, a patented 'anti-gravity pill' he invented to improve circulation and digestion. In his paper *Gravity and Sitting*, Babson argued that ordinary chairs had negative gravitational effects, advising people to renounce them and squat around on low benches with their knees raised and balancing on their bum, as if playing crab-football. Furthermore, by sewing an uncomfortable rubber-ball into the back of your pyjamas, you could easily prevent the harmful Newtonian effects of sleeping on your back at night; Babson owned Sir Isaac Newton's own personal antique bed, so clearly had special insights into the matter. Babson also noticed that, as he got older, gravity made it more difficult to climb stairs; as such, he undertook research into whether or not it would be easier for him to go to bed during high-tide, when the stronger pull of the moon might help drag him upwards. He also speculated that nights when there was no moon might lead to more train-crashes occurring, or even to notable political events taking place, presumably due to people's brains being a bit weighed down by the lack of the moon's extra gravitational pull, causing unusual decisions to be made. Babson actually wrote to fifty-four separate railway companies, warning them to beware the absent moon. His paper *Gravity and Ventilation* featured a further original idea; if you were suffering from 'bad air' in your house, then why not make all the floors slope downwards so gravity will push the miasma out through a convenient hole in the wall? A model-home incorporating this design was actually built; hopefully its furniture wasn't on castors.

Such papers were issued under the auspices of Babson's Gravity Research Foundation, whose main function was to search for a special, hitherto-unknown alloy of metals with anti-gravity properties with which aeroplanes could be coated, thus making it impossible for them to crash (or indeed land). With the help of his unexpected colleague 'Captain' Clarence Birdseye (1886–1956), the man who launched a thousand fish fingers, Babson paid three permanent employees to sit in the US Patent Office at all times scanning through proposals for anything that might prove useful, and posted thousands of leaflets to universities, laboratories, colleges and schools, asking them to notify Babson if anyone ever accidentally discovered how to make things float. Plans for what could be done with the alloy were immense. You could coat artificial wings with it, strap them to people and enable them to fly like birds. You could let people walk on water like Jesus, or be lifted up to Heaven like the Prophet Elijah. You could even screen people's bodies with it and thereby alter their personality. Babson said that when you nodded your head about, gravity pulled on your brain, affecting your emotions. You could test this out yourself, by getting angry then bowing down in prayer. The resulting sense of calm would be gravity's doing, so shielding citizens' skulls from gravity with the alloy would lighten their brains making them better people. So important was this quest that the Foundation's HQ was located in the remote New Hampshire town of New Boston, which Babson deemed far enough away from civilisation for it to survive Soviet nukes come the Third World War. Inevitably, Babson's alloy was never found – had he kept up with Einstein's theories, which showed that gravity was a result of the curvature of space-time, rather than a pure Newtonian force of attraction *per se*, then he would have realised no such material was actually possible.[28]

The Gravity Research Foundation still continues, though its only current function is to run an annual prize awarding $4,000 to the best submitted essay about gravity – past winners include Stephen Hawking! During his lifetime, Babson also donated grants to various American universities with the stipulation they be used to fund anti-gravity research. Babson's money ultimately helped fund the establishment of Massachusetts' Tufts Institute of Cosmology in 1989, where a strange graduation ceremony in honour of the eccentric economist is still held today. One string attached to Babson's money was that big stone monoliths had to be erected on participating institutions' campuses, publicising his aims; the one at Tufts reads 'THIS MONUMENT HAS BEEN ERECTED BY THE GRAVITY RESEARCH FOUNDATION …

IT IS TO REMIND STUDENTS OF THE BLESSINGS FORTHCOMING WHEN A SEMI-INSULATOR IS DISCOVERED IN ORDER TO HARNESS GRAVITY AS A FREE POWER AND REDUCE AIRPLANE ACCIDENTS.' Appropriately enough for such a doomed mission, the slab is shaped like a gravestone – and it is here that Tufts' graduates must kneel in supplication, while an official drops an apple on their head to remind them of mankind's eternal twin debt to Newton and his great twentieth-century disciple.[29]

As for Babson's actual economic theories, some daring renegade investors do still make use of the Action-Reaction model, and a modified variant form of it known as the 'Andrews Pitchfork', under the modern-day rubric of 'swing trading'.[30] Furthermore, in 1962 another economist, Jan Tinbergen (1903–94), proposed a rival financial theory based upon Newton's Laws, known as 'gravity modelling'. This posits the idea that just as how celestial bodies are gravitationally attracted to one another on the basis of their size and proximity, so too are countries' economies in terms of the volume of bilateral trade between one another. The nearby economies of the UK and Ireland, for instance, exert a very strong reciprocal trading-pull, whereas the distant economies of Peru and Ireland do not. There is some controversy about precisely how valid the method is, however. Gravity modelling was actually used by the Treasury in 2016, to estimate what effect a potential Brexit vote would have on the UK economy – and we have already seen how accurate *those* particular calculations turned out to be.[31] Were he still alive today, I'm sure Mr Babson would be delighted to discover that the global stock market, like the reputation of economists themselves, still goes up and down; as all such matters are based upon the natural fluctuations of gravity, how could it ever be otherwise?

Floating on the Stock Exchange: Margaret Storm vs Vampires and Gravity

Surprisingly, Roger W. Babson was not the only American to have developed a pseudo-economic philosophy based partly upon gravity. His long-lost twin was a Theosophist and flying saucer enthusiast named Margaret Storm (b.1902), who in 1959 published an incredibly strange book called *Return of the Dove*, in which she attempted to create the foundational text for a new religion based around the idea that the famous Serbian-American inventor Nikola Tesla (1856–1943), the developer of the alternating current (AC) system, was really a Venusian who had chosen to be incarnated down here upon Earth to save mankind from looming destruction. Tesla was kindly being assisted in his quest by the reincarnated souls of various great men from the past, such as Francis Bacon and an immortal French aristocrat known as the Comte de Saint-Germain (1712–84 – *or perhaps forever*), who were currently travelling across America in disguise demonstrating special self-cleaning tablecloths to housewives. Storm had been a journalist in Paris where, according to her dust-jacket biography, she 'picked up the threads of a previous embodiment during the historic days which led to the French Revolution', an embodiment which had ended with her being sent to the guillotine. Enlightened by her past-life vision, Storm saw through the lies of the material world around her, discovering that death was 'not a natural occurrence' after all, and neither was the current global economic system. Sometime during the Great Depression, Storm pulled herself together, stopped obsessing about the previous forcible divorce of her head and neck, and 'determined to do something about death and taxes on this globe', a programme of bizarre economic resistance which she detailed in *Return of the Dove* – a book whose first edition, it is always worth noting, was printed in green ink.[32]

At the back of her book Storm provided a long 'SUGGESTED READING LIST' which did not restrict itself to books about UFOs, ghosts and spirituality, but also named various tomes that were not really New Age in nature at all, draping a totally deluded occult layer over their contents. Several such books were perfectly ordinary texts demanding monetary reform, with titles such as *Lightning Over the Treasury Building* and *Tomorrow's Money*. Storm praised these treatises as 'providing neophyte armchair economists with a feast beyond compare' while simultaneously denigrating them as being 'already as outmoded as the dinosaur so far as Aquarian Age disciples are concerned'. This was because, as she explained, 'Money as we know it in this year of 1958 is in the museum-piece stage on the Inner Planes' of

Nikola Tesla, history's most famous Venusian. (Courtesy of the Library of Congress)

the universe.[33] So why were we humans still using it? The problem was that Earth had for a long time been under the secret control of a race of financial vampires whom Storm termed 'black magicians', ill-defined evil spirits which floated around within the atmosphere, possessing people's brains and making them do their bidding. Inconveniently, each black magician always had to have a fleshly body hidden away in a remote cave somewhere 'like a hibernating animal' to serve as a sort of 'anchorage for his contaminated energy'. Having stolen some poor chap's body, taken it to his cave and fully established himself in this hidden base for his activities, the black magician then sent out emanations from his astral body to 'thousands of human tools' right across the globe, who had no idea they were being 'played for suckers' in the name of Mammon. This was all 'very unlovely', said Storm, and 'the dear public' had to be told that an 'Invisible Government' made up of magician-possessed 'wise guys and dolls' was running the world from behind the scenes. These vampire-puppets manipulated the entire political and economic system of mankind, said Storm, alleging that every day they:

... hand down directives to their stooges who are active in politics, churchianity, [false religion] diplomacy, banking and economics, education, and in every line of commerce and industry which is in any sense associated with big business. Today they are especially active in connection with newspapers, magazines, television and radio, which they control through advertising. Because books do not carry advertising, the dark forces have never been able to control the book field directly. However, they do control it in subtle ways through various book clubs, and through newspaper advertising, critics and bookshop sales. The dark forces are very active in the field of medicine, and in connection with drugs, pharmaceutical products, vaccines, and even foods – particularly in foods such as candies, ice cream, bottled drinks, and, of course, in cigarettes, liquors and diversions such as movies. But in these commercial fields, their biggest control goes back to advertising. They use the weapon of fear induced through threats of economic boycott. They are also today very, very active in the utilities field, and in all the big industries connected with petroleum, steel, aluminium, and so forth. They are in complete control of all boom-and-bust cycles, even spreading the rumour that these are caused by sun-spots!

Fortunately, Tesla and his Forces of Light had recently brought to an end the reign of the black magicians. It had lasted for as long as nineteen million years, which is quite remarkable when you consider that the human race has existed for only around 200,000 years itself. But what did these black magicians look like? Storm nowhere specifically mentions the word 'vampire', but her descriptions make it clear this is what they were meant to be. Here is her stirring account of how the final black magician upon our planet was at last eliminated by a band of heroic Light-Angels:

> The last black magician who was taken [i.e. killed] had a flesh body hidden away in a cave in Western Europe. The Forces of Light ... closed in on his hibernating flesh form and the angelic legions set to work. They found that [the kidnapped body belonging to] this particular black magician had fangs which extended out from the face, and then far beyond that area the fangs continued in astral matter. This astral line carried a tremendous charge of evil force, and these lines cut deep into the earth, right through soil and rocks, and extended for miles around the globe. In other words, this character had a firm grip on the situation. First the angels had to work from the ends of the astral fangs, and draw back into the body itself all the evil force which had been extended through the earth. When all this evil was drawn back into the flesh body, the whole mass was transmuted with Violet Fire. Then the weary, liberated atoms [of the stolen human body] were carried back to the sun for repolarisation.[34]

A good example of the black magicians' nefarious influence could be seen in the way they had conspired to cover up many of the secret inventions of Nikola Tesla whose unveiling would have proved inconvenient to the abusive form of capitalism the vampires had created. One of the most often-cited myths about Tesla is that he had managed to develop some kind of simple antenna-like device which, if you put it on top of your house or workplace, would draw down limitless reserves of free electricity from the Earth's atmosphere, putting the world's energy companies out of business overnight. Naturally, said Storm, the vampire-possessed financiers, media moguls, politicians and industrialists all joined forces to ensure word of this wonder-invention did not get out. Storm cites one particular occasion when Tesla is alleged to have told J. P. Morgan (1837–1913), the founder of the giant American investment bank of that same name, about his invention, only to be 'told off' by the banker as if he were a naughty child. There would be no way for bloodsucking crooks like him to 'make money off the people' if they could get their power *gratis*, Morgan explained. Tesla argued that because electricity was just there, inherent within our atmosphere, it should be considered 'a free gift from God to His people' like oxygen, but Morgan did not agree, and ensured Tesla's device was smothered at birth. Was this because Morgan was greedy for cash on his own account, or because he was possessed by a vile black magician?[35]

At this point, an awkward question must be asked: when Margaret Storm said 'black magicians', did she really mean 'Jews', in an echo of Frederick Soddy? I do not believe so. If you read her book, it is clear she is very much all 'peace and love', and I doubt that racial prejudice of any kind will have been present within her worldview. Nonetheless, the parallels with Ezra Pound and C. H. Douglas-style conspiracy theories about Jews running the world are clear. Just like the fictional Jews of the *Protocols of the Elders of Zion*, Storm's equally fictional black magicians control the world's media, politics and finance, and enslave whole nations through the parasitic machinations of international capital, manipulating the stock market for their own dire ends. The image of the black magician lying in his cave with his etheric fangs spreading out all across the world is the direct equivalent of the old anti-Semitic propaganda image of the Rothschild Jewish octopus whose tentacles also reach out across our sphere, squeezing and bleeding it dry. There is also the unfortunate fact that, historically, Jews have often been compared to vampires by anti-Semites, playing upon the idea that they suck the blood from ordinary folk via usury. Consider the following rabid passage:

> Since [the Jew] himself never cultivates the soil but regards it only as property to be exploited ... His blood-sucking tyranny becomes so great that excesses against him occur ... The end is not only the end of the freedom of the people oppressed by the Jew, but also the end of this parasite upon the nations. After the death of his victim, the vampire sooner or later dies too.[36]

That's none other than Adolf Hitler, writing in *Mein Kampf* in 1925. Where Hitler led, others followed. Texts such as the 1943 German propaganda pamphlet *The Jewish Vampire Brings Chaos to the World* ranted wildly about how Jewish bloodsuckers had 'propagated political and economic black magic for three millennia', with such sub-humans being nothing but 'evil demons' and 'parasitical apparitions' who feed on people's economic wounds like a 'powerful parasite from dreams' before 'gnawing on all expressions of the Nordic soul'.[37] The conflation of Jews as both vampiric demons and black magicians here is strikingly similar to Margaret Storm's own image of the large-fanged Masters of Finance; but does this really mean she hated Jews? I suspect that the similarity simply lies in the way that people seem to label exploitative financial institutions as bloodsuckers purely because it is an obvious metaphor to deploy – witness the contemporary labelling of the US investment giant Goldman Sachs as being 'The Vampire Squid' by various anti-globalisation activists, for instance. Such critics are not trying to be anti-Semitic towards Goldman Sachs, merely abusive and insulting. Likewise, when the demonstrably nutty Margaret Storm says we are ruled by a secret cabal of vampires, I think she really does mean that we are ruled by *actual vampires*, not by Jews.

However, according to Storm, the final such vampire had been staked through the heart by Light-Angels within its cave in the late 1930s, so why was the global economy still the source of so much inequality? Well, this was only a temporary state of affairs. Even though 'black magicians and their teeming hordes of tools have held money completely captive for millions of years', it was only a matter of time before mankind was finally freed from his economic chains. Ascended Masters like Tesla and Bacon were causing innumerable rays of 'Cosmic Light ... from the heart of the Great Central Sun' to pour down onto Earth every day now, melting the very souls of the Masters of Finance who, as a result, were no longer able to possess any new human bodies. Whereas beforehand, the spirits of these financial vampires would simply 'travel to the periphery of the global atmosphere and back again before striking their fangs' into a new fleshly embodiment, death now really meant death for such entities. The problem was that their power over the minds of men was so strong that some of their dupes continued walking around under the abiding influence of the magicians' original instructions. Because such puppets still held the levers of power, the world's various governments were scheduled to carry on doing evil for a certain time yet, until such people either reached retirement age or died; however, as soon as they did so, that was it, their brainwashed plans would be scuppered forever. This 'cleansing process will sweep through the entire economic system on the planet in a very short time', promised Storm, which was necessary, because the world of money was 'probably the most critical focus of remaining evil' on our globe.[38] Once Tesla's free energy antennae were revealed at last, Storm promised:

> No longer will coal, petroleum and gas hold humanity in enslavement. Existence limited by that kind of primitive power will shortly come to an end and with the changeover to free energy will come an entirely new way of life: an economic system based on unlimited abundance instead of scarcity, maximum leisure and a work schedule devoted only to those constructive creative efforts designed to produce Heaven on Earth in accordance with the Divine Plan for this planet.[39]

On other more evolved planets, which already had such free energy devices, there was no longer any such thing as cash, which helped account for why the Venusian Tesla was not particularly money-wise in terms of earning fortunes from his inventions down here on Earth. According to Storm, Earth was the only planet left that stuck to the primitive notion of money, rather than adopting a more rational economic model based upon obeying God's Divine Laws:

> The solar system operates on a system of spiritual economy in which God's unlimited abundance and supply is accepted as Divine Law. A man-made money system such as exists on this planet is a direct contradiction of that Law. Further, the money system was created here as an instrument to serve

the forces of darkness and has been used for the enslavement of humanity. [St] Paul knew exactly what he was talking about when he stated that love of money was the root of all evil.[40]

Why was money evil? Because there just wasn't enough of it around for people to buy what they wanted or needed with it, as Ezra Pound had also once argued. Storm assures her readers that 'the secret of abundant money' does exist, but it has been 'lost by the race of man on this planet, because man has hidden it from himself in a place he would never remember'. But where could this secret location be? Margaret Storm knew. 'The secret of money lies hidden in the law of gravity,' she proclaimed, but her explanation of quite how so was rather obscure. Storm believed mankind had once possessed the ability to levitate, but that this skill had since been lost. While 'at one time it was as simple for us as raising our hand', now only very rare individuals like Superman and Nikola Tesla (who often clandestinely flew through New York City with flocks of friendly pigeons, under an invisibility-cloak[41]) still had this power. Fortunately, however, 'since the time of Newton we have become quite gravity-conscious', and therefore it should be 'relatively easy' for us to learn how to fly and make objects float again. According to Storm:

> The problem is in the mind, not in gravity itself. We must simply know and prove to ourselves that we can employ gravity at will, and that we can likewise levitate at will. The difficulty now is that we accept appearances. We see everyone around us walking on the earth by lifting only one foot at a time, so we unthinkingly do likewise. We see automobiles rolling along on four wheels and continue to manufacture them to operate in that clumsy, inefficient manner. If we wish to change these things, we must simply refuse to accept appearances. We must then re-focus the beam of our attention. Actually it is much easier to lift two feet off the ground at the same time and levitate. It is easier to design an automobile to go over traffic, than to chug along, bumper-to-bumper, and swing in and out of traffic, mile after weary mile.

Once we had achieved total Newtonian mastery of mind over matter and made our cars able to fly, humanity would then turn its attention towards money and cause it to dematerialise. Money is a fictional concept, it seems, and its current embodiment within dollar bills nothing but a vile con-trick, created by the hypnotism of the undead. By causing coins, notes and gold bars to dematerialise, we can release their atoms back into the Earth's atmosphere and thus allow them to be reconstituted into whatever useful new forms we want, like using a giant invisible 3-D printer. Rather than buying things, in Tesla's wonderful world of tomorrow, people will be able simply to wish them up, like wonders from a genie's lamp:

The change in our money-system will come as soon as we take our attention away from the present diabolically engineered scheming, and follow natural, scientific [*sic*] methods of blessing money. That which is blessed grows and expands. As a race we will unite in freeing money from the imprisoning thought-forms which hold it captive. We will learn to etherealise all forms no longer needed, thus releasing the atoms and restoring them to the universal storehouse.[42]

Atoms were the basis of all things, and were intended to be recycled. To borrow the language of economics, each atom had a very great store of liquidity, being potentially transformable into just about anything. Once upon a time, before the vampires came, mankind had possessed the ability to utilise the high liquidity of atomic capital upon a whim. Should our advanced ancestors have wished to eat a meal, all they had to do was make 'their minds held steady in the Universal Light', whereupon a process of 'instantaneous precipitation' would occur, with atoms falling from the sky and transforming their amorphous liquidity into a 'table bedecked with the finest linens, silver and dishes, and laden with an abundance of food and drink which met the exact nutritive requirements of that particular family.' In this way, the modern stone-age family would 'eat of the body of the God-Substance' and 'drink of the elixir of His circulating energies', the earliest known version of the 'degraded' Holy Communion of present-day Catholicism. However, once the family had cannibalised God, they had no need to keep the dishes or cloths, or even dispose of the leftovers. Instead, 'At the close of the meal the mother performed the next necessary ceremony of etherealisation, or returning to Universal Supply all unused food and drink and all table accessories.' This 'Universal Supply' was some kind of gigantic natural storehouse, in which 'the molecules are broken up and the atoms freed for use elsewhere' – or, in other words, where atomic capital was returned to a state of liquidity within 'a reservoir of unqualified electronic substance ... ready for [further] use by anyone'. It sounds like an idealised version of the recycled natural money of Rudolf Steiner's Threefold Commonwealth, with the added bonus that, in a world of instant plenty, nobody ever had to lift a finger to work: 'In those days, men had never heard of such a preposterous thing as earning a living by the sweat of one's brow. In fact, they were totally unacquainted with sweat.'[43]

Some persons were very sweaty indeed nowadays, however, so what had gone wrong? As Steiner had once warned, the liquidity in the system had got itself stuck, and capital was no longer recycling itself properly into new goods and products. Jesus had tried to show us the correct economic path by conjuring up all those atomic loaves and fishes, but few people had yet proved willing or able to follow his fine example. The trouble was that mankind, under the malign influence of Wall Street, had been conned into thinking that they needed to keep the capital liquidity of the atomic world semi-permanently embodied within consumer goods, thereby allowing vampires to charge us money for things which really should have been free, enslaving us forever. For example, the reader may have a lawnmower stored away inside their shed. If so, the reader is a fool. Instead of continually remaining stuck upon the treadmill of work, enabling you only to buy collections of atoms shaped like lawnmowers with other collections of atoms shaped like banknotes, why not simply pluck a lawnmower from the sky as and when needed? Then you could do without banknotes at all, as the Venusians did. You wouldn't even need a shed. By imprisoning atoms within banknotes and lawnmowers, humanity was cruelly subjecting these tiny shards of the Godhead to 'a long and brutal confinement in matter', causing them to run down in vitality. It was now necessary for these depressed atoms to be freed and 'sent back to the sun for re-charging', like spent batteries. For Storm, the load of mankind's accumulated possessions was quite literally weighing us all down:

> This burden of imprisoned energy constitutes man's karmic burden today. A great part of this confined energy is stored away in attics, cellars, old buildings, slums, abandoned debris, junkyards, crowded clothes closets, the bottom drawer of the dresser, and especially in cemeteries, where burial has replaced the clean, swift, releasing process of cremation. Man will never have access to Universal Supply until he learns to get rid of junk – not just for the sake of getting rid of it – but with the specific mental injunction that it is to be returned to Universal Supply. Then he must get rid of his magpie-like tendency to hoard, hoard, hoard. The person who hoards does not have faith and trust in God, no matter what he may say to the contrary.[44]

She almost sounds like Silvio Gesell ... but mad. This notion of freeing up and then recycling atomic wealth, thought Storm, was the basic message contained within the teachings of the radical American socialist Henry George (1839–97), towards whom Gesell and Steiner had also once been sympathetic. George's major concern was land-reform. He taught that 'we must make land common property' rather than allowing private landowners to make all the profit from it; an equal portion of the wealth derived from land in the form of rent should be shared out unconditionally between all adult citizens for the duration of their lifetimes, in an early Citizens' Wage. Storm claimed that Henry George was yet another Light Worker, one of whose previous incarnations was as an amateur part-time economist at the Court of Versailles during those 'fateful years' leading up to the French Revolution. Together with the immortal Comte de Saint-Germain, George had tried his best to avert the terrors of Revolution, but had clearly failed. While Henry George was 'one of the great men among the spiritual giants who have appeared at opportune times on the American scene', who had 'carried over great memory sequences' from his past lives, he nonetheless had the fatal flaw of being too polite to be terribly persuasive. This led to his soul being withdrawn from global circulation like a dud banknote by his fellow Light Workers, on the grounds that he was 'too valuable a man to waste on ingrates'. This was a shame, because George's economics had been 'solidly rooted in ... the Cosmic Law' which held that, while physical forms such as lawnmowers should be disintegrated into atoms once their period of useful service had concluded, our planet itself was an eternally embodied thing, which should *never* be destroyed and recycled. While it was fine for people to temporarily own enough atoms to build themselves a floating car just by wishing for one, 'man sins against the land' as soon as he tries to lay personal claim to the soil, for the land belongs only to God, being part of 'the universal storehouse of manifested natural resources'. It therefore stood that, in the rapidly approaching Age of Tesla, the private ownership of land would be considered every bit as misguided as the idea of the private ownership of atoms trapped within gold and money. Because of the continued existence of the landlord system, wrote Storm:

> The Good Earth suffers in silence. But on the Inner Planes it is a silence which resounds like thunder. The storm is building up in intensity and will soon break over the usurious muddle which man pridefully calls his economic system. Jesus had something to say about usury two thousand years ago. When he returns ... as a World Teacher [during the Age of Tesla] it is to be hoped He will not have to mention that subject. The least we can do for Him is to clean up the mess ourselves. Usury and private ownership of land are virtually synonymous today, and both must go.

Because of its 'tremendous heart-quality', Storm recommended that Henry George's chief 1879 master-work *Progress and Poverty* be read by everyone who had enough gumption to wish for a copy, this being the only practical means to prevent Jesus from getting angry. Only America could prepare the world for the impending Age of Aquarius, said Storm, as the national figurehead of Uncle Sam was really another of the Comte de Saint-Germain's many cunning disguises, with the USA having been created by him and his Light Worker pals in the first place, to act as a beacon for all humanity. Henry George and Saint-Germain had originally planned to unite Europe into an early version of the EU while working at Versailles, but unfortunately Marie Antoinette (1755–93) had attempted to explain their utopian scheme to the peasants in rather inept terms, leading them to rise up in rebellion. When Marie had (allegedly) responded 'Let them eat cake' to the news that her people did not have enough bread, this was not the callous statement it is so often portrayed as, but an injunction to her subjects to

The American land-reform economist Henry George's excessive politeness caused Nikola Tesla, Francis Bacon, the Comte de Saint-Germain and their fellow Light-Workers to withdraw his soul from Earthly circulation. Mr George's efforts had been more appreciated during the time of the French Revolution. (Courtesy of the Library of Congress)

throw away their stale baguettes and begin materialising lumps of gateaux instead. The proles had misunderstood this garbled statement, however, and failed to perceive that the Light Workers were about to usher in the New Age – a New Age which, after the queen lost her head in 1793, found itself being unavoidably delayed. It still hasn't arrived today.[45]

Kindred Spirits: Green Shirts, White Fox and Social Credit's Special KKK

In June 1934, No. 11 Downing Street, the home of the Chancellor of the Exchequer Neville Chamberlain (1869–1940), came under attack. The chosen method of assault was not gun, knife, arson nor bomb, but a brick, painted bright green, which was hurled through the front window, sending glass flying everywhere. Who could have been responsible for such a senseless crime? The guilty party were the very same band of brothers who were soon also to take the blame for throwing another green brick through the window of No. 10 Downing Street, and for organising a ceremonial Bonfire Night drum-beat march around the premises of the hated Bank of England before ritually burning a guy-like effigy of its then Governor, Montagu Norman (1871–1950), in open condemnation of his financial crimes against humanity – namely, the dreaded Green Shirts, a uniformed paramilitary wing of the Social Credit movement, billed as 'the green-clad shock-troopers of the people's fighting front', once well-known, but now totally forgotten.

Everyone remembers Oswald Mosley (1896–1980) and his Blackshirts in the British Union of Fascists, but the Green Shirts are now obscure. Of confusing ideological cast, the Greens came under assault from the Blackshirts for being Communists, and from the Communists for being fascists. You couldn't get too much of a clue from looking at their uniforms, either. While their green berets, green shirts, black belts and grey flannel trousers made them look like sinister storm-troopers, in fact the green colour of their militaristic outfits was probably a coded reference to the spiritual powers of Nature. This was because, besides its origins in the weird world of Social Credit, the Green Shirt brigade was also a twisted offshoot from an occult wing of the Boy Scout Movement. Their creator was not, as you may expect, Major C. H. Douglas himself, but a deeply eccentric Nature-mystic and cult leader named John Hargrave (1894–1982) – or 'Wa-Whaw-Goosh, White Fox and Head Man of the Kindred of the Kibbo Kift', as he preferred to call himself.

Hargrave was a most extraordinary man. For one thing, he developed his own unique method of curing the sick by exposing them to special psychic paintings of his own devising. Called 'Therapeutic Psychographs', these were abstract daubings infused by Hargrave with his own thought-energy, which he prescribed to patients along with instructions to sit and stare at them for certain set amounts of time, so they could absorb the healing powers locked within the canvas by his magic brush. Considering both magic and science to be equally valid means of manipulating the world around him, Hargrave was also the inventor of a useful gyroscopic means of automatic navigation for aeroplanes. His device was tested by the RAF and found to work, but abandoned due to a wartime lack of available gyroscopes and lenses, and Hargrave failed to patent it. When in 1967 a suspiciously similar piece of equipment was installed in the new Concorde fleet, Hargrave succeeded in having a Public Enquiry take place into whether or not his invention had been plagiarised. In 1976 the Enquiry found against him being owed the £1.8 million he sought, something which may have been influenced by the fact that, despite being virtually deaf, the by-now elderly Hargrave refused to wear a hearing-aid while representing himself in court. Fortunately he had another source of income; a professional cartoonist from the age of seventeen, he contributed commercial illustrations and caricatures to publications as varied as *Vanity Fair* and *The London Evening News,* as well as drawing covers for Mills & Boon titles. A child prodigy, Hargrave began his career aged only twelve, contributing line-drawings to best-selling thrillers by *The Thirty-Nine Steps* author John Buchan (1875–1940). He also wrote a string of popular novels, and was considered such an expert on the sixteenth-century Swiss scientist-cum-alchemist Paracelsus (1493–1541) that he was asked to provide the *Encyclopedia Britannica* entry on him. Given that Paracelsus also successfully straddled the worlds of magic and science, it was little wonder White Fox considered himself the great alchemist's modern-day equal.

Hargrave's Nature-mysticism began during a childhood spent partly amid the glorious setting of the Lake District in the company of his landscape-painter father. In 1908 Hargrave joined the Boy Scouts, adopting the Scout-name of 'White Fox' and rising up through the ranks to become one of the organisation's leading experts on woodcraft. His 1913 book *Lonecraft* established him as a noted writer in this field, but all this was to change following the outbreak of the First World War, in which Hargrave, who had been raised a Quaker pacifist, served not as a soldier but as a stretcher-bearer in the Royal Army Medical Corps (he refused to serve in an Army VD clinic on moral grounds). Appalled by the waste of human life and horrific injuries he saw, following the conflict's end Hargrave moved away from the Boy Scouts, which he saw as increasingly abandoning its roots in Nature and heading towards a rather more militaristic position, a kind of junior cadets corp. Once considered a likely future head of the Scouting movement, Hargrave was now complaining that little boys all across the Empire were being 'taken into the woods by their Wicked Uncle [the Scoutmaster], folded in the Union Jack and smothered' in excessive patriotism. His 1919 book *The Great War Brings It Home* was a call for the nation's youth to be ushered closer to Nature, thereby building their character in a healthy way and so contributing towards the creation of a future utopian society, free of bloodshed and war. Viewing the First World War as the inevitable result of ever-increasing mechanisation and industrialisation, Hargrave wished to move away from old-style Victorian and Edwardian capitalist models of society, and towards something purer and more in touch with the hitherto-repressed human spirit.

Accordingly, in 1920 Hargrave split from the Boy Scouts for good, taking 300 or so equally pacifistic members with him, and set up his Kindred of the Kibbo Kift (KKK, but not *that* one) movement, the name being based upon the supposed magical properties of the letter 'K' and an old English dialect-phrase for 'proof of great strength'. Together with ex-scoutmasters, the KKK also quickly attracted assorted vegetarians, Communists, pacifists, Spiritualists, Theosophists, occultists, and a group of severely deluded persons who claimed to be able to take spirit-photographs of fairies and ghostly Red Indians – as Hargrave himself loved Red Indians too, and modelled his new cult partly on his own inaccurately imagined version of their civilisation, I'm sure this last group were particularly welcome. While the KKK gained open approval from such luminaries as the writer H. G. Wells (1866–1946), those who actually encountered the group during one of their many outings to such numinous countryside locations as Stonehenge, Silbury Hill or the Uffington White Horse might have thought they were hallucinating.

At their most important moots, such as the annual 'Althing' gathering, KKK members were encouraged to dress up in weird costumes, which have been described as some kind of prehistoric version of Art Deco; the men wore wide-shouldered jagged-shaped jerkins that made them look like Fred Flintstone had wandered onto the set of a 1920s German Expressionist film, while the women resembled fairies from the future wearing giant dunces' caps and waving twirlers. As a more standard uniform, they carried sheath-knives and wore odd combinations of cloaks, jerkins, hoods and cowls with tight-fitting shorts, like monks on a monastery Sports Day, these get-ups supposedly being home-made versions of ancient Anglo-Saxon dress such as Hargrave thought Robin Hood had worn. Also home-made were the totem-poles that cultists were encouraged to take with them for use in sacred parades, and the brightly coloured wigwams, covered over in occult slogans, in which they camped out. As the Kibbo Kifters had to adopt their own shamanic animal-names, such as Blue Falcon, Batwing, Sea Otter, Old Mole, Sheepdog, Racoon and Armadillo, and greeted one another by these titles with enthusiastic Hitler salutes, those ordinary country-folk who came across them must have wondered what the hell was going on. Had they concluded that the KKK were Nazis, however, they would have been wrong. Hargrave hated National Socialism, and his Hitler-salutes were based upon an old Native American greeting which, as it involved an outstretched arm and hand, was supposed to indicate you were carrying no weapons. Once he realised that passers-by thought they were Nazis, Hargrave became 'somewhat annoyed' and dropped all use of the Hitler-salute immediately, as the greeting now only 'caused confusion' among the general public.

The point of all this play-acting, said Hargrave, was to enable 'the reintroduction of ritual into modern life', thereby leading to 'the regeneration of urban man and the establishment of a new world civilisation'. Under his tutelage, the Kibbo Kifters would evolve into a new and superior species of humanity, who would return the world back to sanity following the catastrophe of the First World War. 'The time has come when we can control and use that process of natural selection known as Evolution,' Hargrave said – but this was to be an evolution backwards into Eden. Regeneration of the race was necessary, but a return to the primeval state of 'Dawn Men' could not occur in the 'unnatural' modern world of capitalist cities. Therefore, grown-up Boy Scouts and Girl Guides, who were as one with Nature and had the badges to prove it, should be encouraged to mate with one another to produce a new race of bob-a-job *übermensch*. 'We're helping to evolve a New Race of Scout-Men,' Hargrave boasted, 'we're the beginning of a new offshoot of evolution.' Eager to practice what he preached, Hargrave married one of the Merrie Campers, a female Scouting movement of the day. This, Hargrave promised, was 'the natural way'; instead of tying a knot in it,

Kibbo Kifters should now seek to bring new Wonder Men into this world in their tents at night.

By imitating the ways of yesterday at their camps and then falling in love with one another, the KKK would pave the road to tomorrow; the only alternative was for Boy Scouts to marry dirty city-girls who didn't even know how to cook a sausage over a camp-fire, thus leading to a 'less improved bloodline' and severe racial degeneration. Women's main job was to bear evolved Super-Scout children; Hargrave claimed the very idea of sexual equality was 'a form of body contempt' which belonged to 'a dysgenic phase of democratic enfeeblement', and professed utter indifference to the Suffragist campaigns of the day as democracy was rotten to the core and therefore the vote was 'practically useless to either sex' anyway. He also objected to 'homo love', on the grounds that sodomy produced only 'nervous, high-voiced men, who sob on each other's shoulders' and would lead to 'deterioration and racial suicide' in the end. Limp-wristed tent-dwellers like Charles Hawtrey from *Carry On Camping* had no place in Hargrave's world. By freeing the West from the 'mechanical slavery' of industrial capitalism and steering it back towards more traditional, rural ways of life, Hargarve's highly evolved followers would slowly enable the creation of some folkish Green utopia of the kind Sergei Bulgakov might have wished to inhabit, prompting 'a necessary breakaway, a ritualistic exodus, from metropolitan standards of civilisation, from pavements, sky-signs, shops, noise, glitter, smoke'. The engines of industry would still turn on, but automatically, freeing the rest of us from having to work, and facilitating mankind's return to the countryside.

As the hyper-evolved elite of the coming New Age, Kibbo Kifters, who arranged themselves into separate 'Thing-Lodges' given silly names such as Watlingthing and Wandlething, were encouraged to think of themselves as spiritual samurai, which is why their highly evolved children were sometimes made to wear Japanese-style masks and wave around whittled stick-swords under the direction of Hargrave himself, dressed as a giant fox. This, he thought, would prepare KKK members to hold the reins of a future anti-imperialist world-government, once they had reached divine maturity and evolved into god-men, with him as World Leader. The cavalcade of weird costumes was considered by Hargrave to be a kind of 'magical persuasion', intended to bring home the need for global spiritual renewal. Magic was a central part of the KKK, with many early members being Theosophists, and the whole movement was suffused with occult symbols from Rosicrucianism, Freemasonry and the Hermetic Order of the Golden Dawn. White Fox had been advocating the abandonment of Christianity for a 'Universal Religion of the Great Spirit' in which the god of the 'Great Life Force' was worshipped since the end of the First World War, feeling that he was 'an actual organic part of the One Nameless God ... who is Time-Space-Matter' for some time now. Hargrave expected all Kinsmen to educate themselves in things such as Zoroastrianism, Shinto and alchemy, the KKK's equivalent of the Boy Scouts' woodcraft badges, perhaps. Hargrave even had an inner cult-within-a-cult, termed the Ndembo, who would meet within a private 'Taboo Tent', and ... well, no-one knew what they would do, it was private. George Orwell (1903–50) thought the whole thing was little more than dogging in teepees, but the great writer was wrong. We now know that the rituals of the Ndembo involved worshipping a 'Sacred Beetle' during the full moon, casting out evil spirits, and sprinkling the soil and air with water, salt and breadcrumbs, not group-sex.

The real evil spirit Hargrave wished to exorcise was industrial modernity. Like Frederick Soddy, he viewed the contemporary economic world as a kind of black spell cast over the West by malignant sorcerers. As he said: 'It will not be a waste of time to understand mindfully the hunting tribe, its barter economy and its background of homeopathic and contagious magic, for in the long run all politics are closely knit with mindlore and psychology and the New Economics is thwarted not by logic, but by minds and feelings steeped in tribal traditions of the past, hedged about by the ideas of scarcity and taboo.' The hypnotic economic taboos of the modern age could easily be dispelled, however, if people went camping more often: 'A billycan, a blanket and a bivouac – food, warmth, shelter – these are the realisations of all economics, and if you wish a man to know and understand the economic problems of our industrial civilisation, take him first to camp, and he will take himself to textbooks and figures later on.' Not all of White Fox's followers understood this line of thought, though, and during a tour of the standing stones and ancient earthworks of Wiltshire, Hargrave was asked by a puzzled disciple what the hell economics had to do with Stonehenge. Well, he answered, these wonders were built during a pre-economic age, and so 'Those pre-Roman men of the long barrow and the old, straight track [i.e. ley-lines] ... were not fogged with silly notions about Money and Work. Perhaps they knew what they wanted – Food, Warmth and Shelter – and got it. We are in need of the stark common sense of our early forefathers. But ... why talk about it? Let [us hike to] ... the High Places.' As this final comment suggests, rather than rational debate, Hargrave often expected mere exposure to Nature via camping would be enough to subliminally convert people to Social Credit doctrine on its own. 'A whiff of wood-smoke is worth a dozen arguments,' he said.

Going off on hikes to create a new race of Super-Scouts must have been very enjoyable, but the trouble was that Hargrave's slightly over-ambitious plan of instituting 'The Universal and General Reformation of the Whole Wide World' through messing about in woodland areas didn't actually work; for one thing, allowing only spiritual supermen and superwomen to join limited membership somewhat, as it turned out there weren't all that many *übermensch* to go around these days. The Labour Party tried to get Hargrave to turn the KKK into a desired 'Labour Scout Movement', but he refused; after all, disapproving of the very concept of universal suffrage, he would have been something of a hypocrite to ally himself with the prole-loving socialists. In any case, he hated Labour's focus on trade unionism and the working man; in his view, people should be rescued from the very necessity of work, thus allowing them to spend their lives happily in 'Creative Play' of the kind promoted by the Kibbo Kift. You can understand why he loved Major Douglas' idea of a National Dividend; released from wage slavery, maybe a few more Super-Scouts of tomorrow would be freed up to join his band of Nature-warriors. He even proposed lodging such people within a secure and remote KKK Grail-Castle named 'Kin Garth', thereby instituting a 'Noah's Ark policy', in which the cream of the race would be preserved should the twin evils of capitalism and Communism bring about the collapse of civilisation, as expected. His weird beliefs were taken seriously, even if only by his fellow weirdos; on one occasion, Hargrave was invited to the castle of the wealthy Dutch KKK patron Baron van Pallandt (1889–1979), with a young Indian named Krishnamurti (1895–1986), who had also been acclaimed as the future Maitreya-like World Teacher by several prominent Theosophists. The baron intended to leave his fortune to one of the two men, but was unsure which one was the true Messiah. Sadly, the baron chose Krishnamurti; otherwise, Hargrave may never have turned to Social Credit. He originally had plans to buy up every one of Britain's banks and put them right in his own way, reckoning the optimistically low sum of £1 million needed to purchase them all would be easy to muster. In the end, he raised only £150 for the project.

With membership numbers stalling as the 1920s passed into the 1930s and the Great Depression cast its malign shadow across the globe, White Fox began increasingly to focus on more limited economic issues rather than saving the world immediately, wondering what his magic powers could do to alleviate the pressing scourge of mass unemployment. His own financial troubles as head of the Kibbo Kift led him to consider the topic of monetary reform, and his employer at the London advertising agency where he then worked, who knew C. H. Douglas, provided Hargrave with the Major's address, leading to a face-to-face meeting in 1923. In the summer of 1924, White Fox joined up with his disciple Little Lone Wolf and retreated into the Welsh mountains in search of a trial of hardship that would lead to holy illumination about which path it was best to pursue in life; the universe provided Hargrave with the answer that the only way forward was to openly embrace Social Credit. By 1927, KKK meetings involved a lot of talk from White Fox about the need for fiscal reform and the necessity to defeat 'the little band of ghouls who flit noiselessly behind the [account] books and [stock] exchanges of the world' and at that year's Althing gathering, Social Credit was officially adopted into the KKK Covenant.

Come 1928 Hargrave was having articles published in *The New Age* magazine, also home to pieces by C. H. Douglas, Frederick Soddy and Ezra Pound, arguing the need for a revolt of 250,000 Douglasites against the government, to force it into adopting Social Credit policies as 'a matter of biological necessity'. Once they had seized Whitehall and the City, Hargrave's troops 'would not recognise the power of either a Prime Minister or a banker', and would never surrender until 'the Social Credit Decree [had been] proclaimed, printed and posted throughout the land.' Then, they would all go home to their teepees and financial peace would reign forever. In 1931, Hargrave gave a speech commanding his followers to display 'military devotion to duty' in their quest for a new world. The modern age, said White Fox, was the age of 'little gangs of fanatics ... swaying the emotions of the Great Masses ... the day of *Sinn Fein, Bolsheviki, Fascismo, Young Turks ... Ku Klux Klan* and a thousand others'. His idea was that a hard-core of about 1,000 Kibbo Kifters would command the unquestioning loyalty of the larger 250,000 Social Credit army, just as the SS outranked the Wehrmacht, and put an end to democracy in favour of rule by a kind of superior and more qualified technocracy. Mankind's evolution into über-Scouts was not going to happen gradually in an 'even flow', Hargrave now stated, but had need of 'sudden jolts' forwards facilitated by 'use of force', as Chairman Mao was later to preach. In a paramilitary remodelling of the Scouts' 'Be Prepared' motto, Hargrave ordered his followers to be ready to drop everything and come to his side to perform some 'unnamed' secret mission at his behest, if and when society collapsed due to the foolish decisions made by the 'obsolete democratic machinery of the House of Commons'. As Hargrave started pumping out pamphlets with titles such as *Can the Kin Come to Power?* and Nazi agents allegedly made (rebuffed) offers to help fund his schemes, it all started to sound very ominous, especially as mad old conspiracy-nut Nesta Webster had by this point identified the Kibbo Kift as yet another Illuminati-controlled front organisation, bent upon destroying the British Empire in the name of Satan and the Jews. Was a revolution brewing? Not really.

After all, many KKK members were peacenik proto-hippies, so where was this army to come from? In 1931 an unemployed mechanic named George Hickling had created a marching organisation in Coventry called variously the Crusader Legion, Iron Guard or League of the Unemployed, who spent their time heel-clicking their way through the city, demanding jobs. Having been involved in a local 'Workers' Educational Group' which discussed Social Credit ideas, Hickling wrote to Hargrave, asking for advice. Hargrave was attracted by this organised 'Gizza Job' club, and advised the Legion begin wearing a uniform to impress spectators. Anglo-Saxon monk-costumes being expensive to procure, Hickling chose to kit his men out in green shirts and berets, a look which struck Hargrave as impressive, and caused the *Midland Daily Telegraph* to christen them the 'Green Shirts', a name which stuck.

By 1932 White Fox had also started to modernise KKK uniforms along more militaristic lines, aping the Legion's look and phasing out the space-fairies, tight-shorted monks and Art Deco cavemen for something less likely to get them laughed at while out on manoeuvres. The ground was being laid for White Fox to transform his loyal Kindred into what he called 'a megaphone' for Social Credit, an entire army of little green men willing to promote the Douglasite cause.

Viewing the unemployed – or 'new leisured classes', as he had it – as potential allies, Hargrave made serious efforts to woo them from 1928 onwards, setting up a Kibbo Kift Homing Pigeon Club to interest jobless flat-capped miners in the North-East, and touring mining towns affected by the economic slumps of the age, speechifying. It was Hargrave's opinion that mass unemployment should be welcomed, as it would free up people's time and, as it hopefully became increasingly obvious the jobs would not return because of increased automation, create the conditions for widespread demand for a National Dividend. The use of machines meant the employers no longer had to pay their workers, but they should still pay their employees anyway, for doing nothing, according to this viewpoint. In 1932 the Coventry Legion merged with the KKK, leading Hargrave to disband his cult before quickly then re-forming it as the Green Shirt Movement for Social Credit. He tried to persuade those unhappy campers who weren't keen on street-marching that the Green Shirts were not really a private army, but a 'living stream of poetry' whose ultimate triumph would demonstrate 'how all these years of our germinating [in the KKK] has been leading up to this … spiritual and cultural awakening of the British people', but they weren't having it, and numerous original Kibbo Kifters left. However, Hargrave was sending out mixed messages. To some, he promised the Green Shirts would be free of all 'semi-religious slush' in order to attract as many fallen urban sub-humans as was possible, while simultaneously reassuring others that once the Green Shirts had assumed power, it would be safe to reintroduce all the 'fantastic stuff' about worshipping beetles and dressing up as foxes and fairies, so they should keep faith with his plans.

Once formed, the Green Shirts quickly acquired a London HQ in Old Jewry, right next to the very same Bank of England they hoped to destroy. Initially, C. H. Douglas was pleased by all this and gave the group his approval, asking if a Douglas Tartan pattern could be adopted on their uniform as a sign of fraternal unity between the Green Shirts and his own more non-political Social Credit Secretariat. Establishing a new weekly journal, *Attack!* in 1933, Hargrave ostensibly seemed to have moved away from his Quaker pacifist beliefs, but it must be remembered that, deserters notwithstanding, he still brought a lot of his occultist Kibbo Kift followers with him into the Green Shirts, and that KKK doctrine had involved a lot of spiel about members being reincarnations of the Knights of the Round Table, who were engaged in a quest for the modern-day Holy Grail of spiritual unity and peace. Hargrave even advised any pregnant Kibbo Kift females to spend their days thinking calm thoughts about subjects such as Camelot, fairies, Robin Hood and moonlight in order to imprint the babies in their wombs with mystical and valiant Arthurian-type qualities. Therefore, just as the SS were conceived of by Heinrich Himmler as a modern-day brotherhood of black-uniformed Grail-Knights dressed in peaked caps and jack-boots, so Hargrave saw his own troops as benign green-shirted soldiers of Mother Earth or something similar – not fascists, but sacred soldiers nonetheless. Spiritual samurai, they would take the war for men's souls into the heart of the enemy capitalist cities, not simply train themselves up in rural areas like *Dad's Army*.

Whether the majority of White Fox's Green Shirt troops thought this too is another matter, of course. Selling 7,000 copies of *Attack!* per week, they actually had more marchers than Oswald Mosley's Blackshirts at one point, and presumably most of these 2,000–3,000 ordinary urban workers were not themselves Arthurian occultists. Mosley himself began to flirt with Social Credit ideas, and met Hargrave with a proposal that their two groups be merged, but White Fox refused, explaining in a pamphlet that the two street-armies were mutually incompatible as the Blackshirts wanted to transform the *State* along fascist lines, while the Green Shirts wanted to transform the *individual* along hyper-evolved Boy Scout lines. Fascism was not for him. In revenge, a group of Blackshirts smashed up C. H. Douglas' Liverpool HQ in 1936 and put two of Hargrave's Merry Men in hospital; you can see why Hargrave spurned Mosley's offer, especially as White Fox wasn't in any way anti-Semitic, with his mother being part-Jewish. In 1935, following the publicity they had gained from attacking Downing Street with green bricks, Hargrave rejigged his private army once more, renaming them the Social Credit Party of Great Britain and Northern Ireland (SCP), and preparing for another, less violent, assault on democracy via the ballot-box. At this point Major Douglas, who opposed the creation of a specific Social Credit Party and preferred to try to get people to persuade their existing MPs to sign pledges promising to enact his policies instead, began progressively to disown Hargrave and his Green Shirts; their final split came in July 1938. This rivalry even once led to violence when followers of the two men fought a battle during which Hargrave, in full Green Shirt regalia, jumped up on a table in a meeting-hall and denounced his former idol, before being dragged away. More than thirty policemen had to break up the melee.

In the 1935 General Election the Green Shirts put up a single candidate in Leeds South, Wilfred Townshend, who lost but gained 11 per cent of the vote, with 3,642 ballots cast in his name; he gained many celebrity endorsements, ranging from Frederick Soddy to the actress Sybil Thorndike. Many prominent public figures later lent Hargrave their general support, whether open or tacit; the list included T. S. Eliot, the Archbishop of Canterbury William Temple (1881–1944) and, inevitably, Ezra Pound, who donated a banner to the Leeds election campaign and also admired Hargrave's occasional forays into unreadable experimental literature. 'Man's got a mind', Pound said of White Fox. Lord Strabolgi, the future Labour Chief Whip, invited a Green Shirt deputation to the House of Lords in 1934 to discuss the National Dividend, later advising the government to consider implementing it. In 1936 Hargrave even sailed over to Canada to serve in the post of Economic Advisor to the Alberta Social Credit Party, though his time abroad did not last long as he felt his life was under threat there from banker-backed assassins. Thinking William Aberhart a moron, Hargrave suspected that international financiers had been behind Bible Bill's election anyway, hoping to smear Social Credit as nonsense through its new, thoroughly incompetent champion; Hargarve's initial impetus behind renaming the Green Shirts as the SCP was partly so that these same hidden hands could not set up their own idiot-fronted Social Credit Party in Britain and so undermine his message with a brain-dead puppet. The Green Shirts did have some momentum behind them, therefore, with committed paramilitary Grail-Knights frequently interrupting parliamentary proceedings with ritualistic cries of 'Open the National Credit Office! Issue the National Dividend! Apply the Scientific Price!' or 'Social Credit the Only Remedy!' (Green Shirts got given a special Scout-like award named the 'Green Oak Leaf' for doing this), but the government, spooked by them and their rival Blackshirts, passed a new Public Order Act, banning all uniformed organisations and marches, and that was the end of that; the Green Shirts were dead, though for the time being they refused to accept the fact.

Changing tack, the now uniformless Green Shirts began holding weird quasi-religious 'Services of National Regeneration' in the street. 'God's Providence Is Mine Inheritance' became the SCP's new slogan, implying that the National Dividend was backed by Jehovah (this was actually an old Quaker saying, reflecting Hargrave's upbringing). Hargrave designed a logo for the SCP, consisting of two back-to-back letter 'K's, which he termed the 'Double Key'. This was not only a nod to the Kibbo Kift, but also a secret sign that Social Credit was the 'hidden key' which would open the gates of Heaven, allowing God's Paradise to be established down here on Earth, via economic means. However, it seemed that 'Dark Lords' (as Douglas called financiers) were keeping the Pearly Gates firmly locked shut via their control over Parliament. Following the Public Order Act's implementation on 1 January 1937, the term 'Green Shirt' became a total misnomer and public support dissolved, as did sales of *Attack!*, whose publication was suspended. Hargrave's men tried to get around the ban by marching through Hyde Park on May Day with their uniforms carried aloft on coat hangers attached to long poles, but this just made them look stupid. Remembering the free attention they had once gained from lobbing green bricks about, Hargrave now ordered a series of outrageous publicity stunts – which culminated in 1940 when a man dressed as Robin Hood pranced into Downing Street and shot an actual arrow through the open window of No. 10 during a Cabinet meeting. The arrow was painted green, and bore a Social Credit slogan on its shaft; appropriately enough, the man who loosed it was named Ralph Green. Slogans were painted across banks in green paint, too, while yet another effigy of Montagu Norman was hurled at the front door of the Bank of England; the perpetrator got three months' hard labour. Less badly treated was the female Green Shirt who donned an old-fashioned green crinoline dress and approached the Chancellor of the Exchequer in Downing Street, pointing to the motto she had scrawled upon it, namely '[My Dress Is] Out of Date – Like the Money System!' A comical demonstration was also held outside the London HQ of the Wheat Commission, in which sheaves of wheat were set alight as people chanted 'They burn the wheat we want to eat!' in protest at the follies of modern agriculture.

Come the outbreak of the Second World War the Social Crediteers won some brief attention with their excellent proposal to 'Conscript the Bankers First', a slogan they attached to another effigy of Montagu Norman, which was paraded around the City of London, leading to a pitched battle between SCP men, Bank of England clerks defending their boss' honour, and outraged City traders who piled out of stock exchanges to attack them, but as the conflict progressed the Green Shirts faded from view; most of their street-marchers were made to swap green for khaki and fight for King and Country. During the war years, Hargrave tried to create a scandal by writing a scurrilous biography of Montagu Norman, but the Bank of England headed this off by buying up every available copy and destroying them. Following Allied victory, the Green Shirts continued flogging a dead horse, with a few diehard members travelling the country on a 'national eVANgel' mission inside a small van painted with wild messages like 'Would the Maggot Starve if the Apple was Too Big?' while campaigning unsuccessfully to end bread rationing and ban the atom bomb. In 1950 John Hargrave stood as a Social Credit candidate for Hackney North and Stoke Newington but gained only 551 votes, or 0.9 per cent of the ballot, and so wound up his SCP the following year in favour of concentrating upon making magic paintings for sale to invalids.[46]

Hargrave had been moving towards psychic matters for quite some time prior to the 1951 dissolution of the SCP. His idea for an automatic aviation map had come to him fully formed in a dream in 1938 and, during the war years, he was to discover that this was not the only psychic power he possessed. On a visit to Wales to give a speech to mineworkers, while taking tea within one miner's cottage he surprisingly found he had the power of spiritual healing. The miner's grandmother scalded her hand with boiling water from the kettle. Trying to comfort her, Hargrave took the burned hand between his own – whereupon the swelling reduced and the reddened skin became freezing cold, with all pain and blisters vanishing inexplicably. Everyone present was astonished, including Hargrave. Investigating his apparent healing abilities in light of this event, Hargrave concluded he possessed some form of 'radiation from the hand' and after careful experiment decided he could heal people from a distance without even touching them, hence his later magical paintings. Hargrave's sudden detection of his 'healing hands' also led him to form an alliance with Dr Charles Boltwood (1889–1985), a Theosophically inclined Spiritualist and later bishop in a schismatic evangelical Anglican sect, who claimed to be in contact with the ghost of the nineteenth-century clergyman and *Water Babies* author Charles Kingsley (1819–75). Kingsley told Boltwood that it was his job to prepare for the Second Coming of Christ by helping transmute 'human elements into immortal elements' via training people to develop powers of Christ-like healing. Once 'the nucleus of Resurrection-power' had been established among mankind Jesus would then return, Kingsley's ghost told Dr Boltwood. Boltwood wrote a series of books, under the pseudonym 'Crusader', to spread the Good News, establishing his own College of Spiritual Science, where he taught would-be healers of his theories that the 'eating of air' could cure TB, and that sexual intercourse was not absolutely necessary for the production of babies. Naturally, Boltwood was delighted to discover the talented hands of John Hargrave and helped him develop his powers further. By way of recompense, Hargrave taught the future bishop all about Social Credit.

Just as odd, in 1943 Hargrave decided to launch a programme of 'Solar Propaganda', revealing to his dwindling followers that Social Crediteers were now a new race of 'Solar Men' and that henceforth anyone who believed in the true path of monetary reform should be offering up prayers to the sun, each and every day of their lives – a fantastic notion which, apparently, was based upon Hargrave's own deeply aberrant reading of the books of Frederick Soddy. I would guess that White Fox picked up on Soddy's notion of primitive men being closer to the sun in terms of their use of energy, and concluded that, as he was now able to radiate Christ-like healing energy from his hands, just as Soddy said the sun radiated benign energy down to Earth through its rays, he had evolved into one of the *übermensch* predicted in the dogma of the Kibbo Kift. Either way, this focus upon psychic matters and solar energy alike seems to have drawn Britain's first newspaper astrologer R. H. Naylor (1889–1952) into the SCP; Naylor had been responsible for inventing a new form of astrology based on something called 'Sun Signs' himself, so was naturally sucked towards Hargrave's movement. As soon as Archbishop William Temple heard of this news in May 1943, however, he immediately renounced all association with Social Credit in alarm; only fake bishops such as Charles Boltwood could feel truly at home in the SCP, it would appear. Convinced that the power of the sun flowed through his veins, Hargrave now announced that 'the Social Credit mechanism is founded on a SPIRITUAL BASIS'. Major Douglas would have agreed, but would not have said that 'spiritual basis' was some sort of revived solar paganism. In 1943 another prominent Nature-mystic, Quaker and nudist, Aubrey Westlake (1893–1985), joined the SCP and, apparently impressed with its leader's aura of magic, proposed the Party should re-order its hierarchy based upon the legends of Camelot. Westlake suggested he should henceforth be called King Arthur and that the 'magus' Hargrave should adopt the title of Merlin.[47]

Actually, Hargrave would have preferred to adopt the mantle of Paracelsus. From 1948 onwards, he began issuing a monthly 'Solar Message' to his remaining acolytes, and in his 1951 book *The Life and Soul of Paracelsus* implied that he had modelled himself upon the book's inventive occultist-cum-scientist hero, in order to lead humanity into a new era of sun-based plenty:

> It is obvious to anyone … that, but for the few freaks, cranks, originals and odd-men-out, mankind in the mass would still be without fire, without the lever, the wheel … [But thanks to such people – e.g. Hargrave himself] we now stand on the threshold of an Age of Abundance and Leisure, and the failure to pass through the doorway into the New Solar Civilisation, the coming Sun Power Age, is a failure of man's imaginative faculty … The entire structure of the Paracelsian teaching and practice is founded upon one reason-shattering statement: that by his god-like faculty of imagination, and by means of Resolute Imagination, man can accomplish all things.[48]

None of this Solar Madness was calculated to win over the support of the general public, however, rather giving the impression that, in his heart of hearts, Hargrave/Merlin/Paracelsus/White Fox knew full well that the dream of the Green Shirts sitting in the House of Commons was now over for good. Or was it? Not quite, because one of the SCP's fans, a man named Henry Norman Smith (1890–1962), successfully managed to infiltrate the Labour Party, sitting as its MP for Nottingham South between 1945 and 1955. The editor of *The Illustrated Carpenter and Builder*, Smith's readers must have been surprised to be given repeated articles about Social Credit to read when all they really wanted were clear instructions on how to make some fence-panels, but had they also read his 1944 title *The Politics of Plenty*, they may not have been quite so perplexed. Due to his association with the Green Shirts, Smith's home was raided and searched by the police, but they found no tell-tale green bricks and he was free to continue his quest to win a parliamentary seat under the banner of the Labour Party, thereby gaining a platform to preach the Douglasite cause to a wider public. Labour at the time was slightly concerned about the rise of the Social Credit movement, and sought to develop friendly relations with Douglasites by forming a subcommittee to examine the idea; they concluded it was all just 'jugglery with figures' and 'a complete and dangerous delusion', with Smith being labelled a 'currency crank' due to his dogged faithfulness to the notion. Nonetheless, in 1945 Smith was selected by Labour to fight the seat of Nottingham South, which he won after gaining a reputation as an authentic figure who spoke his mind, had original thoughts and was very much his own man, surfing a tide of eccentricity-fuelled popularity of the same kind which has boosted Jacob Rees-Mogg's cult status today. 'He may be relied upon to put South Nottingham on the parliamentary map', declared the *Nottingham Co-Operative Herald* and they were right, he did.

Once in the House of Commons, Smith began repeatedly arguing against Labour policies, believing that America was engaged in a sinister plot to enslave us all with usury, hyper-capitalism and comic-books, recommending we turn down all post-war reconstruction aid and loans from the dreaded Yankees, lest they turn us into whimpering gold-worshippers. He called for a 'war of independence' against the US to free us from capitalism, and made dark mutterings about the looming creation of the nation of Israel, which he saw as a plot by 'fanatical Jews', backed up by 'big money' from the United States. Some people accused Smith of having been placed under some figurative spell by the 'mysterious' John Hargrave, and in his weekly newsletter *The Message From Hargrave*, White Fox praised his alleged puppet to high heaven, dubbing him 'The Mighty Smith' and acclaiming him as a true Solar Man, a 'ray of hope for the future ... penetrat[ing] the world darkness', and curing the Labour Party of its compulsive 'work-complex'. Bemused by his rhetoric, some Labour MPs began to question whether or not Smith understood the subject of economics at all, even though he kept on making obsessive and apparently nonsensical speeches about it. In the grand tradition of Bible Bill Aberhart, Smith admitted he wasn't sure whether he understood Social Credit properly either: 'I happen to be fascinated by the topic of finance, [but] whether I understand it or not, I do not know.' By this stage Smith was becoming an embarrassment, and his former champion Hargrave dropped his support, now labelling him 'The Little Simpleton' and only reporting on his speeches in his new newsletter *Commons Commentary* in order to prove to Smith that, no, he really *didn't* understand Social Credit after all. So useless was Smith that, as he had once suspected with Aberhart, Hargrave began to wonder whether the MP was really a deliberately incompetent stooge, placed in a position of power by bankers to undermine the whole Social Credit philosophy. Having failed to successfully infiltrate Parliament either directly or indirectly, White Fox conceded final defeat in 1951, the year after Henry Norman Smith had been successfully re-elected as the Honourable Member for Nottingham South with a majority of 1,641, thus proving either that the voting public were a bunch of absolute idiots or that the hidden octopus of international finance really did run the world.[49]

Hargrave's influence does still live on, however, albeit in an obscure and low-key way – or so it has been alleged. There appear to have been several historical links between the British Green Party and figures from the weird world of Social Credit down the years; indeed, it would seem that the Party's current much-hyped advocacy of a Citizens' Wage for all is derived partly from such sources. For example, a former Green Shirt named Wilfred Price, who joined the precursor to the Green Party during the 1980s, proved a passionate advocate for Douglas and Hargrave's theories as a form of ecologically sound economics (in 1947, Price had disrupted a Test Match at the Oval cricket ground by invading the pitch and waving around a big SCP banner; sadly, he did this during the teams' lunch-break, thus generating no interest or disruption whatsoever) and the current Chairman of the Social Credit Secretariat, Francis Hutchinson, was once a member of the Association of Socialist Greens, while the Chair of the Green Party Monetary Reform Policy Working Group and long-term editor of the *Sustainable Economics* newsletter/blog, Brian Leslie, had parents who were members of Hargrave's KKK. These people dispute that they are full-blown Social Crediteers – they simply use Douglasite ideas as a starting-point for debate – but they obviously have a close interest in such topics.[50] In a sense, therefore, the Green Shirts still march on, with the current generation of Solar Men now eager to make us all use Solar Panels.

While stepping through the streets, the Green Shirts used to chant the following martial hymn, to the accompaniment of drumming, which was evidently meant to be loud enough to wake the dead:

> *Wake now the Dead!*
> *The Living Dead who stand*
> *Waiting for the Call*
> *That will echo through the land!*
> *Green Shirts advance!*
> *The steadfast and the strong*
> *Rally to the ranks*
> *As the Hosts march on!*
>
> *Dead men arise*
> *From the catacombs of Death!*
> *Rise from the grave*
> *To breathe the Living Breath!*
> *Break, now, the Spell*
> *Cast by numbers over Things,*

False Economies

Fight for your Life,
To which the Spirit clings!

Wake, now, the Dead!
The Spirit-quickened Host,
Resurrected Men,
From the inlands to the coast!
Men of the Green!
Upswing the Shaft of Light
Sweeping like a sword
In the World's Last Fight

Wake, now, the Dead!
By numbers held in thrall;
On this fruitful Earth,
There is Earth-Wealth for all![51]

'The Dead' mentioned here are those inventive persons of the past who gave us what C. H. Douglas had once termed the 'Cultural Inheritance'; that store of inventions and infrastructure also praised by Ezra Pound, which formed the basis of our society's wealth and the future National Dividend, the civilisational riches that were really our birthright, but had been stolen away from us by the quisling bankers and politicians. The 'Earth-Wealth' the inventors had kindly left us were the sort of things listed by Hargrave in his biography of Paracelsus – fire, the lever, the wheel – and it was the job of the Green Shirts to raise the financial spirits of such dead inventors from their graves by demanding that humanity be given their share of the prosperity created by the steam-engine, the train and the automobile as their fair dues in life. The Hell Bankers may have cast a 'spell ... of numbers over things' to trick us out of it, but the divine Excalibur of the Green Shirts could slay these fiends and dispel their vile illusion as if shattering a distorting fairground mirror. It was time at last for Robin Hood to kill King John, ransack his Downing Street Treasury and burn his Inland Revenue castles to the ground, to rob from the rich and give to the poor. Ideas, too, are part of our Cultural Inheritance, however, and, as the Green Party's somewhat accidental resurrection of the shades of men like Douglas and Hargrave shows, ideas never truly die, they just mutate. The wandering corpse of Social Credit has still not been properly staked, with the febrile financial climate caused by the 2007/08 crash allowing the notion of a Citizens' Wage once more to creep from its coffin like Count Dracula reborn; appropriately enough, the distinctly pale and bloodthirsty John McDonnell is another of its contemporary fans. Perhaps the only way to kill it off once and for all is to actually try it out on a large enough scale to demonstrate that it could never actually work? Green Shirts, advance!

A Direct Answer to Your Prayers: Alfred W. Lawson and Economic Equaeverpoise

John Hargrave was odd enough, but surely the very oddest financial quack of the entire Great Depression was the American cult leader, Boston Beaneaters baseball star, author, economic theorist and general all-time nutcase Alfred W. Lawson (1869–1954). From 1922 onwards, Lawson spent much of his time developing a personal system of pseudoscientific philosophy called 'Lawsonomy', which posited that everything in existence was made from tiny living atom-like beings called 'menorgs', thus meaning all of Creation was alive. Lawson proposed the Earth had a secret anus at the South Pole and that, by manipulating the menorgs living within its gut, it would be possible to direct the globe's farts out in whatever direction was required, thus allowing our globe to be become a huge, bum-powered spaceship. Among other bizarre escapades and theories, Lawson also tried to capture solid sunlight in paint in order to eliminate the need for light-bulbs, proposed that animals be eliminated from our Earth forever because they defecated outdoors too much, spoiling the look of the planet, and thought atomic explosions were caused by living atoms farting particularly loudly and unleashing so much destructive rectal energy that they vaporised cities. Amazingly, Lawson was also a genuine aerospace pioneer who, in the one truly impressive achievement of his life, invented the airliner – really, he did! Sadly, his idea of transferring passengers between such vehicles by dropping them out of big interconnected pipes while still in flight did not come to pass, and whenever he actually took the controls of one of his inventions he had an unfortunate tendency to crash them into trees, but nonetheless his main achievement in the field of aviation does still stand.[52]

Nobody is entirely sure where Lawson got his ideas about economics – but then, nobody knows where he got his ideas about *anything*. Surprisingly, though, a close examination of Lawson's financial outlook in fact reveals several similarities with the teachings of other monetary heretics of the day. There is no direct evidence that he read the works of the Social Crediteers, but as we have already seen, ideas, once unleashed, have a tendency to run away from the control of their originators. What we do know is that Lawson tried to link monetary reform notions back to his own brand of Lawsonomy 'science', claiming that his economic theories had a firm prior basis in physics. Lawson's father had once made strenuous efforts to construct a perpetual-motion machine, and when he impregnated his wife with baby Alfred, daddy's sperm had amazingly contained his profound knowledge of

Alfred W. Lawson, cult-leader, inventor of the airliner, discoverer of the Earth's hidden anus, and all-time economic man of destiny. His piercing eyes apparently allowed him to stare directly into his followers' souls. No wonder they liked to sing songs about him. (Courtesy of the Library of Congress)

the science of perpetual-motion physics in concentrated form, meaning that, when he was born, little Alfred was the new Newton. In 1873, aged only four years old, Lawson discovered the secret forces which underlay all of Nature – Suction and Pressure. Noticing some dust swirling about in a chink of light spilling through poorly closed curtains, the tiny genius noticed that he could scatter the dust particles by blowing on them, or else gather them together by sucking inwards; Pressure and Suction in action. As he entered adulthood, Lawson realised that everything in existence was based upon the interaction of these two forces, with the human heart, which pumped blood out into the body, then sucked it back in again, as a prime example. However, by maintaining a kind of equilibrium between the suction and pressure forces within the heart via sublime powers of mental exertion, combined with strict regimes of diet and exercise, Lawson perceived it would be possible to live to be 200 years old, as he explained in his self-published 1923 book *Lawsonpoise and How to Grow Young* (Lawson died aged eighty-five in 1954, thus making him less than 50 per cent successful in this aim).

In subsequent publications, doubtless deeply distressing to Roger W. Babson, Lawson further explained how gravity didn't really exist, and neither did energy – both were mere 'fanciful' notions. Instead, there was no such thing as empty space; any area of space which *seemed* empty was actually full up of things such as light, sound, magnetism and temperature, which were solid substances, all of which had different densities, and so were able to 'penetrate' one another – so, as Lawson believed the entire universe, being made of menorgs, was alive, this meant that when a sinking stone 'penetrated' water, for example, it was in some sense raping it via the force of Pressure. However, as the stone fell off the river-bank into the pond, it temporarily left behind a little vacuum, or 'suction terminal'. This was something the menorgs would not allow, so some other nearby substance, such as cold or heat, quickly rushed in to fill the gap, through Suction. Maybe a bee is buzzing by, and the physical sound of its buzzing jumps in to plug the vacuum. If so, then this solid buzzing noise will then upset the balance of the entire universe, leading to disequilibrium, as every movement that occurs, no matter how tiny, eventually has an impact upon every other particle/menorg in existence, even at the other end of the galaxy, as with the chaos theory idea of a butterfly's flapping wings in Belgium ultimately causing a hurricane in Bermuda. The final aim of all particles in existence was to gain a state of 'equaeverpoise', or ultimate balance. However, as there was always *something* moving, *somewhere* in the universe, this state would never be possible.

Nonetheless, the more equaeverpoise there was in any given natural system, the more calm and ordered it would be. As Lawson put it, 'when a formation [the heart, the sun, whatever] has reached a state of maturity and internal Suction equals external Suction, and internal Pressure equals external Pressure, it is then in a state of EQUAEVERPOISE and as long as it can remain in such condition, it can live.' When equaeverpoise declines, however, natural systems begin to break down and decay, through entropy. Take the Earth. To Lawson, remember, our planet is a living animal, with a mouth at the North Pole, an anus at the South Pole, and a stomach within its underground core. It sucks in space-substances such as meteorites and solid sunlight through its mouth, digests them in its belly, transforming them into a solid gravity-like substance called 'lesether', thus allowing it to float in space, and then farts excess gases out from its bum later on, so it doesn't accumulate too much lesether and float away helplessly into oblivion like a bad balloon. Currently the Earth is in a state of equaeverpoise, allowing it to remain stable, but every time this equilibrium wobbles the planet gets indigestion and lets rip with a huge fart in the form of an earthquake, or a spot of projectile pooing with the eruption of a volcano; it is just like when a human eats too much, then vomits or soils themselves. These surplus substances successfully expelled, the stomach returns to a state of pleasant equaeverpoise. One day, though, the forces of entropy finally win and the Earth dies; our planet will fart itself to death, collapsing inwards and exploding outwards simultaneously after one emission too many shoots apart its stomach, like Elvis Presley dying on his toilet.[53]

Perhaps the reader will be thinking this all has precious little to do with economics – but unlike Alfred W. Lawson the reader, hopefully, is not mad.

Consider Lawson's description of the natural system containing a balance of perfect equaeverpoise between internal and external forces, something it needs to maintain in order to continue to exist. It can be imagined as being a bit like the conditions necessary for a bubble to inflate, prior to ultimately going pop when conditions of equaeverpoise deteriorate ... and bubbles, of course, occur in finance as well as in the world of physics. And, if there was ever too much or too little money available in any given economy for the public to make use of, then wasn't this just another sin against equaeverpoise? Maybe the Treasury should either print more cash, thereby pumping it back out through Pressure, or else withdraw some cash, through Suction, until the nation's finances more approached equilibrium – a truly balanced economy. To do otherwise would be for a country to financially fart itself to death, it might be said. To Lawson, economics was but a 'side partner' of physics, the two being 'like a couple that can't be separated'. According to Lawsonomy, one of the major laws of physics was that because everything in existence was always being moved around and influenced by Suction and Pressure in a never-ending cosmic dance, nothing was ever 'wasted', with each and every physical or mental action living on eternally, as with the butterfly's flapping wings later causing the hurricane. Nature, Lawson said, aimed at 'the utilisation of everything without the loss of anything', but our current system of 'man-made economics' was not like this, with waste and inefficiency everywhere. Thus, a system of 'natural economics' had to be created, thereby leading to a state of economic equaeverpoise, which would burp away the Great Depression.[54] In his strange 1932 editorial column *Something to Think About*, Lawson explained the marriage between economics and Lawsonomic physics thus:

> One of the unchanging laws of the equaeverpoise is economics. Economics, as a factor in the balance of ever-moving material, must be absolutely perfect in its functions and unerring in all of its relations with physics. For if it was not so, then there could be no such thing as the equaeverpoise which causes the eternal balance of all things. So economics plays a most important part in the life and movement of everything physical. Economics must adjust all transformations of matter with such absolute precision and utilisation that nothing is wasted in the change. Every particle must be used over and over again for useful purposes ... That is pure and unadulterated economics.

To illustrate how modern economic actors within a capitalist society do not utilise every particle 'over and over again for useful purposes', Lawson brings in the cautionary example of the slaughterhouse manager who, because he not only sells his pigs' meat for sausages and bacon, but also sells their skin for leather, boasts that 'Our concern is able to find a use for everything about a pig except his squeal.' This sounds like a state of economic equaeverpoise but, because the manager doesn't understand that in Lawsonomy the pig's squeal is not a worthless sound-wave but a potentially useful solid substance that is pulled into people's ears via Suction, thereby aurally raping them, the manager's big-headed remark only goes to prove that he 'is not thoroughly acquainted with the law of natural economics', which 'must find a use for the squeal as well as everything else of a physical nature in connection with the transformation of a pig'. Liking this image, Lawson runs with it, claiming that 'big pigs' rule our economy, duping Joe Public into becoming 'a lot of little pigs' themselves, who seek 'to emulate the example of a few big pigs' by participating in the current corrupt financial system, which blatantly contradicts the laws of Nature. Therefore, instead of wealth being spread out more equally via economic equaeverpoise, everyone had been led 'into a piggish scramble, causing everyone to fight for himself' instead of sharing. This was an oinkonomic world fit only for 'maniacs', which would continue rolling on eternally unless 'our minds are purged of these piggish tendencies' once and for all. The greedy pigs at the top of the financial food-chain had decided to keep all the economic bacon for themselves and let the little pigs fight over only 'the ear-splitting squeal' of the slaughterhouse animal, making the little guy scrabble around to feed on a few scraps of solid sound-rape, rather than swallowing nice plump sausages for their dinner. To teach the big pigs a lesson, Lawson exhorted his readers to sign up to the precepts of a new economic system he had himself now invented, called 'Direct Credits' which, he proclaimed, was 'the most intelligent, scientific, modern and spiritual system ever arranged for the benefit of everybody. It is the hope of mankind.'[55]

This innovative system certainly sounded good, which was unsurprising because its author had 'a greater insight into basic physics than any human being', an insight which came with an official seal of approval from God Himself, who had personally chosen Lawson to spread the news to America. In his 1933 piece *Truth Is Knowledge*, Lawson argued that Direct Credits theory was nothing less than 'Economics as God wants [the people] to know Economics'. Because Direct Credits was a pure expression of Lawsonomic equaeverpoise, it was really akin to 'the First Law of Nature' and 'if you break that law then you break all laws', condemning a person to Hell on Earth. As people participated within a Lawsonomically unbalanced economic system, this rubbed off on their souls and minds too, making them morally and mentally unbalanced, causing them to stab one another.[56] Apparently obsessed with dead babies, Lawson wasted no opportunity to deploy such emotive figures in his writings, here demonstrating how the equaeverpoise of civilisation has now become so skew-whiff that even priests have become naught but modern-day Herods:

There are clergymen who uphold a [financial] system that starves babies because financiers donate money that pays their salaries. They tell with one voice how God loves little children and with another voice that the financial system that robs them of their milk and wrecks their little bodies must be kept in force ... But God knows that everybody who upholds a system that starves babies are as much to blame as if they actually snatched the milk bottles from their little lips.

This was in his 1932 text *The Meaning of Economics*, where the great man fully admitted that overthrowing the 'demoniac system under which we exist' would be difficult because 'people hate to exchange the antiquated notions that clog their mental pipes' as he had once discovered when arguing to a sceptical world that the aeroplane would soon be invented. 'Great Toads!' he wailed. 'How the wise ones giggled' and 'did shake their idealess heads' when he tried to hoover the idea that mechanical flight was impossible from out of their brain-pipes via intense mental Suction, but following the Wright Brothers' famous achievements back in 1903, he had been proved right once before in the face of the world's scorn and would be proved so again. All existing economic systems, whether capitalist or Communist, were 'lopsided' and 'top-heavy', like the poorly designed early proto-planes that wouldn't fly. Neither aeroplanes nor economies which failed to obey the true Lawsonomic laws of physics would ever be able to soar away upwards, so people should heed his word. Lawson was the economic equivalent of both Wright Brothers combined in one towering, Christ-like figure, and was about to make America's economic aeroplane achieve full lift-off at last, a quest which had a moral aspect to it as much as anything. According to Lawson:

> Idiots could do no worse economically than the human lawmakers do with the handling of Nature's bountiful supplies. With maximum opportunities, civilisation gets minimum results. Savages have done much better. Cannibals would not let their food rot while their babies starved. Therefore Civilisation has a lower Economic rating, as well as a lower Spiritual rating, than either Savagery or Cannibalism. A wild beast will not deny another the right to eat after his own stomach has been filled. Even snakes will feed their young. But Civilisation, with machinery capable of producing wealth as cheaply as water is furnished, denies its people wealth and, with food rotting everywhere, allows its babies to starve for the want of it. Could lunatics do any worse? If so, how?[57]

Well, in his pioneering 1931 manifesto-cum-textbook *Direct Credits for Everybody*, Lunatic Lawson took up his own challenge and set out to show how it was that the clinically deranged could do a much better job of running the global economy. Not realising that he himself was profoundly mentally disturbed, in his twin 1933 essays *Greed – Destroyer of Man* and *COME ON PEOPLE*, he warned his potential readers that anybody who did not adopt his Direct Credits creed would literally become insane. Even the 'money-mad' bankers who ran the whole capitalist system would end up killing themselves if they didn't buy his book and follow its instructions. Apparently, in excess of 5,000 non-compliant bankers had already done so, and the number would surely grow with each passing day; this was simply the universe handing out God's justice and restoring moral equaeverpoise by giving baby killers a taste of their own medicine. Arguing like Frederick Soddy that all wealth came ultimately from the sun, and that the natural water-cycle was a kind of equaeverpoise-infused economic system in and of itself, Lawson proposed that his Direct Credits scheme should seek to ape God's natural laws of water-recycling. However, while admitting that 'the Great Being God has done His work well', Lawson thought he could do even better, valuing his book as being 'beyond all estimated value to the human race'. Apparently, 'Of all things that everybody should understand concerning life, liberty and the pursuit of happiness, Direct Credits for Everybody is the most vital and necessary' because only this system could enable mankind to 'develop to a higher plane of usefulness in the universe' instead of murdering babies.[58] This was quite a build-up, so when people actually read *Direct Credits for Everybody*, some might have been a tad disappointed to find that it was basically a weirdly written variation on the ideas of Ezra Pound and C. H. Douglas.

Lawson's chief practical economic insight was summed up in his oft-repeated slogan 'There is as much difference between Capital and Finance as there is between Milk and a Sponge'. You could milk a cow of its healthy white goodness into a pail, via Pressure, but a sponge in a bucket of milk would soak up such lactic liquid loveliness, through Suction. Capital (supplies of money based upon 'real wealth', such as crops or factory products) distributed economic wellbeing throughout the body politic, via Pressure, whereas Finance (fictional debts based upon usurious loans) took all this goodness back out again via Suction. Thus, financial bloodsuckers were really financial milk suckers. Where there was lots of Capital, there was lots of wealth. Where there was lots of Finance, there was lots of poverty. What we had now was a civilisation which resembled 'an enormous body with a half-witted mind that would destroy its hands to soothe its feet', and nobody wanted their hands to be chopped off to soothe their own feet, did they? All usurious sponges in existence had to be squeezed dry, therefore, and the stolen monetary milk spurted back out into dying babies' ever-gaping mouths, largely by the government printing more money and giving out interest-free loans to more-or-less anyone who asked for one. Essentially, Lawson believed in Hell Banks, though he did not label them as such. If money was based on gold, and more money was needed than could legitimately be tied back to gold, then the Hell Bankers conjured it from thin air and lent it out at ridiculous rates before calling it back in again, restricting the money supply as arbitrarily as they had previously increased it, then stole debtors' homes and businesses when they couldn't pay back their debts because the money for them to do so no longer existed. Likewise, by engineering national debts so huge they could never be paid off, the bankers were able to control governments to do their bidding via financial blackmail. In this way, the Great Depression had been intentionally created, by milk-criminals. Nothing new here; Ezra Pound would have nodded sagely at these wise insights into the wicked ways of the milky gombeen-men.

Lawson estimated the true annual Social Credit-like Cultural Inheritance value derived from American products, infrastructure and labour at around $100 billion, but said that, thanks to the sponge-bankers, only $5 billion in cash was currently in circulation, leading to disaster. So, Washington should crank up the printing presses, ban private loans and banking and abolish the Gold Standard, even if gold's glitter did have an appeal to certain silly 'childlike people'. Gold, he said, was 'the most demoralising and death-dealing instrument ever devised' and a 'great bloodsucker .... [which] absorbs everything' like a mega-sponge gone wrong. Instead of being linked falsely back to 'the yellow metal', under Direct Credits rule, money would be set free to become what it truly was, a measure of worth or handy universal ticket, not a tool for the spongy forces of Suction to bleed a mother's milky breasts dry. Insurance (which was scientifically proven to cause people to become lazy murderers) and interest charges would be 100 per cent prohibited, and a kind of Citizens' Wage established – but only for the sick, elderly, students and children. Working-age people would still have to toil, but would have easy access to an infinite series of free $1,000 loans, or even grants, from the Treasury whenever reasonably needed – these were the Direct Credits after which Lawson's system was named. So, if you need any money, just ask and Uncle Sam will kindly open his wallet.

On the other hand, when they died, citizens would no longer be able to leave money or property to their descendants, as inheriting wealth apparently caused people to go mad. Also, sometimes already-mad people left their own wealth to dogs not humans, which was even madder, especially as the dogs could then earn interest on it. Instead of allowing Fido to get rich, therefore, the government would get everything, though Lawson nowhere says what it would do with such freebies. Weirdly, as a consequence of all this, giving to charity would become a crime. If a baby needed milk, then for it to have to rely upon the kindness of strangers to get it was a disgrace, Lawson declared. Charities were evil things, and thirsty babies should be given the money by the State with which to buy their own milk, instead of their parents having to rattle a tin in the street for it like shameless, degraded bums. To spread this message, Lawson had a small ambulance-van painted with the slogan 'CHARITY MUST BE ABOLISHED!' and driven across the Midwest by his followers for propaganda purposes. As he put it: 'To give a bite to a starving baby on Christmas Day may be charity, and some people may derive pleasure from knowing that they are better situated than the tiny neglected starving infant, but that kind of charity must stop. Yes, stop forever. And, by all of the decent instincts within us, it *will* stop.'

Lawsonomic Citizens' Wage payments would not be fixed, but tied directly to recipients' living expenses and cost of care; one invalid might get $50 a month, another $100, depending on how much cash they usually got through, an idea open to obvious abuse. Legal aid would also be made universal, and everyone would have to make twice-yearly sworn public declarations of their earnings, savings and expenditure to ensure they weren't being greedy. If you lied, or tried to hoard your wealth, the White House would employ Suction to claim all your money back as punishment. More pleasingly, taxes would be abolished; when the government needed to buy something, it should just print the necessary dollars to do so. It could even pay itself and all its employees by this means, thus ensuring equaeverpoise in the national finances by abolishing the national debt. Or, Washington could add to the price of all consumer goods, and take their cut from every sale (but this is just VAT ...). If there was ever too much money in circulation, of course, Suction could always be employed to claw the required amount back in again, although Lawson didn't think inflation would be a problem. Full employment could easily be ensured, and a wave of new leisure time released for workers to explore morally and intellectually improving pursuits – like studying Lawsonomy. Being based directly upon physical laws, the scheme could have no possible drawbacks.[59]

One question still remained: who was behind the creation of the current topsy-turvy financial system that had caused the Great Depression? Bankers, obviously, but what kind? And what was their true aim? Lawson's answer was that a shadowy plutocratic cabal of transnationalist 'Alien Financiers' and 'Economic Devil-Men' were to blame for spreading poverty across the globe. These bloodthirsty vampiric forces of Suction didn't just want to make money, via the means outlined above, they had a *Protocols of the Elders of Zion*-like 'Diabolical Ten Year Plan' to enslave us all by engineering ever-worse global slumps, leading to political strife, revolutions and civil wars like those the Aliens had already caused in Russia and Spain, with the aim of getting their dictatorial front-men such as Lenin, Hitler, Mussolini and Franco in charge. These 'two-tailed monkeys', 'wolves' and 'parasites' had played the American populace for fools by secretly gaining control of the Republican and Democrat Parties, and were planning to institute totalitarian rule over everyone, via 'the sword, gun, gas and bayonet'. Plans were already afoot to bring back the public whipping-post, and the armed forces were recruiting unnecessarily large numbers of soldiers who would be paid blood-money to enslave all citizens within a decade. Lawson knew how the bankers operated from his days in the aviation industry, he said, when the Devils and

Aliens had diddled him out of the wealth and investment which, by rights, should have been his own. However, because he was wise to their plans, the plutocratic scum were now 'afraid of Lawson', he boasted, and, to ensure that his ideas could not spread down the generations, ensuring perpetual freedom for mankind, they had hatched another scheme to make most future children illiterate so they couldn't read his books.[60]

As usual, we must ask at this point whether, by 'Alien Financiers' and 'Economic Devil-Men', Lawson really meant Jews. Surprisingly, he didn't. Far from being anti-Semitic, when he later set up an economic cult to spread his word, Lawson was quite happy to let Jews join if they wanted, and the cartoon caricatures of bankers in his various propaganda organs don't have hooked noses and long beards, or resemble Shylock in any way; they are just ordinary white folk, fattened up by years of gluttony, dressed in dinner jackets and smoking fat cigars. Sometimes, they appear as spiders with human faces, spinning their webs around the American people – represented, for no apparent reason, as a giant dumb-looking frog. At other times, they come clothed as Satan, complete with horns. Lawson identified London as the centre of the global financial conspiracy, but nowhere talked of the Rothschild Bank of England.[61] His following description of Alien Financiers is typical:

> Two well-perfumed touts of the financiers sat at a table overloaded with choice viands and imported liquors. They held between their expensive [gold?] teeth special brands of high-priced cigars and blew out of their cunning mouths rings of odoriferous fumes. Their fly-spotless white fronts extended from their double-chins to their waistbands and each supported at the rear of their coat two tails as proof of their superiority to monkeys who have but one tail.[62]

These weren't Jews – just fat men with expensive tastes. Lawson seems to have taken the basic image of the Devil-Jew from the *Protocols* and then recast it so that his plutocrats followed the same methods, but were not actually Jewish. For example, another unpleasant facet of life under the Alien Financiers was the hold they obviously had over academia and the media. Not only had they ruined his aviation career via financial chicanery, these big fat bastards had also refused to publicise or teach Lawson's incredible scientific and economic discoveries in the newspapers and universities that the Devil-Men secretly owned. When he had first fully formulated his Lawsonomy system of alternative physics in 1922, Lawson called a national Press conference in Washington DC to announce the most important discovery of all time to the world – an event to which only three journalists bothered to turn up. When in 1923 the major publishing house G. P. Putnam's & Sons then rejected the chance to publish his genre-defining book about such matters,

Lawson grew confused.[63] He was obviously right in his discoveries, so why was he being ignored? Might there have been a conspiracy afoot to keep the American public trapped in ignorance of all aspects of The Truth? Lawson felt that scientists and economists alike, with their incessant highfalutin talk of abstract things like atoms and exchange rates, rather than more easily understandable things like pigs' solid squeals and hidden polar bumholes, were just trying to pull the wool over people's eyes. In a direct parallel with Ezra Pound, Lawson even thought this conspiracy extended to compilers of dictionaries. His 1932 editorial *The Meaning of Economics* contained the following claims about a mysterious figure who had emerged from Dictionary Corner to provide a deliberately incomprehensible definition of the word 'economics' to publications like the OED:

> The fellow who wrote it must have been one of millions of mystifiers who earn their cheese by putting nonsense into text-books. The fellow who wrote that definition no doubt assumed that those who would read it would know no more about economics than himself and therefore would accept it as scholarly and authoritative if put in the form of a puzzle. It is surprising to what extent lexicographers and also astronomers and College Professors get away with that sort of polished bunk. Now listen everybody, there is nothing mysterious or high-brow about the word Economics. In fact, it can also be summed up in one solitary word – usefulness.[64]

That's also a definition of the word 'utility', though. Therefore, Lawson then expanded this definition to become 'utilisation of everything without loss of anything'. That sounds like the definition of the word 'recycling', but that's what he thought economics was. Also highly Ezra Pound-like was Lawson's assessment of the scam that was university education:

> Are you educated? So is the Organ Grinder's Monkey. The Organ Grinder educates his monkey to tip his hat to those who donate money to him. Isn't that exactly what the Dean of a College does? ... Why do financiers donate such large sums of money to institutions of learning? Isn't it because they want to control them and have students taught just what they want them to know? ... Now what do the financiers [have taught to] you as an education? ECONOMICS? Not if I know anything about it ... They teach you wastefulness, not usefulness. They teach you UNECONOMICS not ECONOMICS [but not the Korendian UnEconomics of Gabriel Green] ... Do the financiers teach you physics? Not if I know anything about Natural Laws. They teach you a lot of bunk that doesn't exist. They make students gulp down idiotic theories that ruin their reasoning functions. They teach them that which ain't, not that which is. As there ain't no ain't, they just create a hyperbolic vacuum in the students' upper storey so when they leave

college they have less sense than when they arrive ... Posterity will consider the theoretical nonsense taught as physics in colleges today as a sort of second spasm of witchery. [Because economics and physics are one and the same thing] they cannot teach basic physics without teaching basic economics and that would upset the financiers' plans to skin the people to a purple hue.[65]

Incredibly, Lawson thought this twisted conspiracy even extended to the symbolic shape of the square mortar-board hats in which students are photographed on Graduation Day:

The financiers laugh at those innocents who graduate from universities. They call them blockheads and have had square hats invented for them to wear and have their pictures taken in so as to prove to the world at large that they are their scholars.[66]

So, the financial and the scientific blockhead conspiracies were indivisible aspects of the same greedy plan. The only hope for mankind was for Lawson to set up a special organisation to promote his discoveries to the world, unmediated. Accordingly in 1931, Lawson made a personal pledge to God to set up a body called the Direct Credits Society (DCS) that, like C. H. Douglas' own Social Credit Secretariat, aimed not for straight election of members to government, but to influence existing movers and shakers to take up Lawson's fiscal teachings and legislate to implement them. With this in mind, Lawson, by this stage so penniless he had to colour in his faded suit with a black pen, bravely fended off imminent starvation to write his *Direct Credits for Everybody* book and somehow managed to set up his DCS initially in Philadelphia, then in Detroit.

He also established a separate arm to handle all the donations and fees he would solicit from members, grandly titled the Humanity Benefactor Foundation (HBF). Because all donated cash and profits from his publications went to the HBF, this meant Lawson could claim to have an empty bank account and be acting purely for the benefit of his followers, even though, because he had sole control over the HBF, it was truly his private piggy-bank. As Lawson, by his own account, ultimately gained some *1.5 million* followers, in reality he must have been well off, though sensibly chose not to live a life of insane luxury. Nonetheless, Lawson declared himself 'Commander-in-Chief' of the DCS, said he alone was in charge and his word was unquestionable law, and began arranging his acolytes into different ranks and telling them to buy naval-type uniforms. They then went on parade, organising expensive pageants in which large floats decorated with slogans like 'THE LAWSON PLAN WILL SAVE OUR CIVILISATION FROM ECONOMIC SLAVERY' were driven down streets, with what looked like fake naval captains at the helm. These events drew thousands of spectators, most of whom weren't there to laugh.[67] What Lawson really wanted was adulation, not money. In 1940 he had a kind of marching-song hymnbook published, *Songs That Will Be Sung Forever*, which acclaimed him as an all-time genius sent to Earth by God to save humanity. As one hymn put it, 'Lawson's plan, [economic] emancipation/'Twas a God-sent inspiration.' These songs were not written by Lawson himself, but by his disciples, whose adulation was frighteningly sincere. Whenever he walked on-stage at a Direct Credits rally, the applause didn't stop for a full fifteen minutes; imagine the reception he may get from clueless student radicals at Glastonbury today.[68]

Lawson was obviously cuckoo, so how did he get so many followers? Even if his estimate of 1.5 million Direct Crediteers should prove an overestimation, he definitely had an army of hundreds of thousands behind him. The obvious answer might be to say 'Well, this was the Great Depression, his members must have been poor and starving and desperate for an easy answer', yet analysis made of Lawson's membership records by his biographer Lyell D. Henry Jr (whose book *Zig-Zag-and-Swirl* comes highly recommended by me) reveals that the majority were actually from the middle classes and better off than the average American was at the time, which makes sense; how could bums, tramps, hobos and Boxcar Willies afford to give Lawson donations, buy marching uniforms, books and pamphlets, or make large, expensive floats for street parades? Of course, once Lawson had finished with you, you might well be a beggar; 1940s journalists dug up horror stories of people who had given Lawson thousands over the years, allegedly having cashed in insurance policies and sold farms and businesses, or foregone buying a home of their own, in the name of Direct Credits. This, however, could simply have been propaganda being spread by the Devil-Men's fatally compromised media interests.

So, why would the middle classes waste good money following Lawson's crusade? According to Lyell D. Henry, Lawsonites gained great satisfaction from hearing, at last, the 'true' nature of America's Depression-era plight explained to them in language they could understand, and felt they were doing their bit to rescue the nation from destruction. Also, the parades, military-style ranks and uniforms gave them a sense of pride and community belonging, something that was only enhanced when their leader told them they were the advance-guard of a future elite, almost a different species from their fellow beings – as we shall see, he ended up teaching his disciples that, by following his ways, they would evolve into intelligent clouds. Furthermore, those of his followers who were poor gained access to a large support network from which free food and cash might be cadged. Then, of course, there was the simple fact that Lawson himself was a highly charismatic and entertaining figure, who claimed to be on a mission from God; such persons always gain their followers, even during normal times, but during the Depression this effect became magnified. In Henry's words, the Direct Credits Society thus became 'a blend of military order, fraternal lodge and church'.[69]

Another element of his appeal was Lawson's genius for speechifying. Speaking without notes, straight from his heart and diseased brain,

Lawson was able to channel the spirits of Ezra Pound and P. T. Barnum simultaneously, pouring out highly amusing abuse in the style of a carnival barker, which was later written down and reprinted verbatim in books and on the front cover of his own slim broadsheet newspaper, *The Benefactor*.[70] Bearing regular slogans including 'Justice for Everybody Harms Nobody' and 'UNLESS YOU KNOW THESE THINGS YOU ARE NOT EDUCATED', *The Benefactor* was a hugely entertaining publication. To give a brief flavour of its contents, here are the edited highlights of one of Lawson's speeches, given to an audience at Kalamazoo, Michigan, as reprinted on the paper's front cover under the typical headline 'FINANCE IS THE BUNK':

You are now living in an age when bunk has reached its zenith. Bunk has reached the inflation of its capacity equal to the circumference of its explosion. Bunk is something that you can hear but you cannot see. You can swallow it, but it doesn't feed you. Bunk is the cud the people of the world have been chewing on for hundreds of years. The smart-alecks call it finance … Now when that right foot of yours gets into that bunk you've got one foot in the grave. And before you come out again you've got both feet in the grave. Your lower extremities are reeking with bunk. What those financiers do to you when you have money or property is a crime for anybody to talk about … Have you been educated in Finance? High Finance? If so you have reached the obscurity of a bottomless pit without walls or ceiling. Finance is the zig-zag-and-swirl of bunk. It is a double-cross running anticlockwise into an abstract vacancy. It operates as a suction clutch without an exhaust valve. Finance is something that isn't, wasn't, nor can't be. It is a bubble without a wrapper. It is a tickle-me-dumb for a donkey without a contact. It is a seven-century itch without a place to scratch. It's a Scourge! Finance … is a self-inflicted hypnosis that makes [people] happy over the success of the rogues who swindle them out of their property … It is the suction power that forces man to give away his soul for the promise of a handful of gold … [Eventually] the people become obfuscated and don't know whether they reside in a palace or in a gas house. Sooner or later they discover that it is a gas house … After living upon this Earth for many years and looking upon life as it is and not as it is pretended to be; and after associating with financiers … for more than a quarter of a century … I am ready to attest as the truth concerning the fact that FINANCE as practiced today on this Earth is the real genuine BUNK. I can truthfully say that there is not the least adulteration about it – it is 100 per cent pure bunk. And, as long as you aid and abet this international game of bunk … then there is absolutely no hope for your future existence in this world or in the next one. If you will not help to stamp out this evil then God considers that you are a part of it. If you stand for this financial game of bunk … then you are a GOLD WORSHIPPER and you can't make God believe otherwise.

I'd certainly go and hear Lawson speak! The comparison of him to a carnival barker is apt, as in such speeches Lawson constantly claimed that there were three main ranks of financial con-men enlisted within the Devil-Men's army, namely the Pee-Wee Slicker, the Second Storey Slicker and the Mastodon Financier, all of whom adopted the disguise of the Three-Shell Trickster, one of those fairground figures who hide a ball under one of three shells and then ask their dupes to guess which one it is under after twisting them around, a well-known con-trick which the customer cannot win. In his speech, Lawson explained how the process worked:

> As you walk around, you run across the Tout of the Three-Shell Trickster. Slippery, slick fellow, with a stiff hat stuck on the apex of his ossified skull. He says to you, 'I know where you can get some money for nothing. Come with me and I'll show you. All you need is good eyesight.' You follow the Tout to the old swindler himself – a Pee-Wee Financier who stands in front of his disappearing table telling the dupes that he's got more money than he knows what to do with and wants somebody to win it from him. This old slicker eyes you up and says 'This is no place for the blind. I'll bet you couldn't see a rhinoceros with a telescope.' You get mad and tell him you can see better than he can ... [Then, you lose] ... You look in your pockets and your money is gone. Then you realise that you have been bunked ... You won't even acknowledge that it was your own fault [and so go on making the same mistakes] ... Now, the Mastodon Financier has a game a million times bigger than that of the Pee-Wee Slicker. He has a game that's a real lullapaloosa ... [He will trick you out of your house] ... Then you go back to Mama with tears in your eyes and say 'Mama, they've stolen the home from us.' Yes, they've stolen the home from Mama and you and all your little children: just because you listened to their bunk. You thought you were going to get something for nothing. You don't get something for nothing in this world.

Except for bunk, presumably. Only Alfred W. Lawson had the mental power to see through these people's schemes, and, he warned his audience, he could peer into their very souls through their faces too, thereby discovering who among them had helped out the Pee-Wees and Mastodons in the past. Even worse, he told them that, if they continued abetting the plans of the Devil-Men, their offspring would become Devil-Children via genetic inevitability, just as he himself had inherited fantastic knowledge of advanced physics from his inventor father's perpetual-motion sperm:

> Now, when you aid and abet a swindling game your face looks like that of a swindler. You can't change your face. It is a map of your thoughts and acts. It talks without words. God has put into your face microscopic muscles that

are connected with your mind, and whenever you think, the muscles write the thoughts on your face. So if you are a swindler, you will always look like a swindler, you can't get away from it. Your children will also look like swindlers because they will inherit all of your weaknesses for cheating ... [Recently] a couple of degraded imps killed a child just for the fun of it. They were put into the penitentiary but their parents were to blame. They had taken the homes of the poor, of the old, and the sick, through the Interest Collecting Swindle. And so, no matter what wealth they gave their children, they had inherited crooked minds ... You must learn that you are paid back for everything you do in this life. Your face proves it ... If you uphold [a crooked system] ... and you look in the glass at midnight by the light of the moon then you will surely see a face that looks like the Devil.

And, if all this didn't work, then Lawson was not above scaring his audience into submission with dire threats about the Alien Financiers' desired world to come:

It will be worked as it has been done in Spain [where General Franco (1892–1975) had recently become dictator following the Spanish Civil War]. One set of Alien Financiers will espouse a fanatical doctrine [fascism] and another set of Alien Financiers will espouse an opposite fanatical doctrine [Communism] and through their different avenues of publicity they will work the people into a frenzy of murderous hatred against each other ... Then whichever side wins, an Alien Financier will put his own bloodthirsty dictator to rule the American people under the direction of the financial master ... It will make no difference which side wins, the people will lose ... They whip you mentally first and physically afterwards ... Remember, people, once the Financier puts in his dictator I am helpless to aid you in any way because martial law will be declared and everybody will be shot.

And that was all just in a single speech![71]

Given his loquacious talents, a question therefore lingers: why did Lawson's Direct Credits movement ultimately fail? Like the Green Shirts, the cult gathered many followers and great attention via its street parades, and yet today is almost unknown. Try to tell most people about Mr Lawson nowadays and they will think you are making it all up. They may even run away. The answer to this conundrum lies, as might be expected, within Lawson's own foibles and eccentricities. As his theories were demonstrably stupid, people's susceptibility to them was based more upon exposure to his weirdly magnetic personality than anything else. Possessing charisma and thinking he had been chosen by God to transform the world, Lawson had genuine self-belief about him, with many of his followers believing his piercing blue eyes literally had the power to see into their souls, thereby allowing him to read their minds (maybe he drew their thoughts in through his eyes, via Suction). In photographs, however, Lawson looks perfectly ordinary, not like the Messiah. Just as Adolf Hitler appeared a bit comical until he got up on a podium and began ranting, perhaps you had to hear Lawson speak in person to get a true impression of his appeal. You can see this in the fact that the vast majority of Lawson's support was concentrated in the Midwestern States of the USA where he had his base, places such as Michigan, Ohio, Indiana and Iowa. Go to Texas, New Mexico, California or New Jersey and they would never have heard of the man.

Even if he didn't like to travel, the Midwest-loving Lawson could always have tried to reach a distant audience through the mass media, talking on the radio like Bible Bill Aberhart up in Canada – but there was a problem with this idea, too. If Lawson was going to maintain that the Economic Devil-Men were barring his access to the media in order to prevent word of his economic panacea getting out, then how would it look if he *did* get his face in the papers? The whole thing was a paradox. Having once railed against 'radio drunks' who get their news via 'the poisonous weapon' of the wireless, something which ruined 'all chances of a human being ever using its reasoning faculties', if he suddenly started using the radio himself he would appear hypocritical. Anyway, Lawson seemed to believe his own conspiracy theories, and so refused to advertise his forthcoming speeches through Press-releases whenever he did occasionally venture away from base-camp, leading to nobody turning up to them – which, of course, was taken as further proof of the Devil-Men's media conspiracy. He had a lot of competitors when it came to Depression-era monetary reform gurus, too, some of whom were not actually mad (this book has largely ignored those dull fellows …) so those who grew disillusioned with Lawson had plenty of options when it came to shifting their economic allegiance.[72]

Most significant of all, however, was the fact Lawson began to get bored with the whole topic. After failing to get Direct Credits taken up in Washington, Lawson decided he wanted to set up his own university and begin building wheel-less cars and solar-powered spaceships there instead, and so gradually started to steer his disciples away from the subject of monetary reform, and urging them to begin reading his books about physics. From about 1936 onwards Lawson made plans to set up a University of Lawsonomy, telling his followers to stop drinking and chewing gum, because, rather like John Hargrave's Kibbo Kifters, they were due to become the basis for an entire new species of humanity, which they would together help create behind closed doors at his pretend seat of learning. Most Direct Crediteers dropped their adulation of Lawson in disgust and disappointment at this rubbish, but it seemed clear that what Lawson truly wanted most of all was a small cult of devoted super-fans, not to change the world through economics, and he managed to convince a number of disciples to follow him on into the next phase of his peculiar career.

Styling himself the 'First Knowledgian' and the 'Wizard of Reason', in 1942 Lawson bought up an abandoned campus in Iowa, fenced it off, and set up his long-desired university, a place where degrees took thirty years to pass and where money was banned, as were all books by anyone other than Lawson himself. Lawson told students that, if they memorised all of his many texts from cover to cover they would become special creatures termed 'Sagemen', passing on Lawsonian knowledge to their babies in the womb, just as Lawson's father had passed on knowledge of advanced physics to Lawson himself, via his special sperm. In order to maintain complete physical health, his followers had to eat salads topped with grass, forgo any dancing or cosmetics, sleep naked, chew every mouthful of food fifty separate times, and dunk their heads in freezing water twice a day before blinking repeatedly in order to keep their superhuman minds sharp. In this way, students would stop being rotten 'pig-bipeds' and split apart from the great mass of humanity, who were doomed one day to become mere 'crab-men', with their lucky Sagemen descendants losing all their teeth and evolving to feed purely upon fresh air, in a floating paradise somewhere above the clouds, controlling the weather, and eventually becoming mists of pure gaseous vapour – yet more hot air from history's strangest-ever fringe economist.[73]

Pies in the Sky: Defeating Communism with Chocolate Coins

An entire nation filled with hot air – and, as we shall soon see, hot air balloons – is the Communist hell-hole of North Korea, whose economy is, for the most part, centrally planned and whose people, therefore, also live in poverty. The DPRK, as it is officially known, suffered particularly badly following the fall of its former sugar-daddy the USSR, with an average annual GDP contraction of 4.1 per cent occurring between the years 1990 and 1998, a time of widespread famine and enforced grass-chewing. Ever since the days of Kim Il-sung (1912–94), the nation's founding father who still technically rules the place even though he is dead, North Korea has pursued a policy of *juche*, or 'self-reliance', which is just another way of saying 'autarky'. The North has failed to publish any official economic data since 1965, which implies that the only people doing well out of the closed command-economy are the military, with it being guesstimated somewhere between 30 and 50 per cent of GDP goes on funding soldiers, sailors, airmen and Kim Jong-un's continuing quest to incinerate the entire peninsular with nuclear missiles (by the time you read this, he may well have succeeded).[74] Because the 'Hermit Kingdom' is about as open to outside penetration as a nun's chastity belt, it seems that most people there don't have a particularly good understanding of the notion of capitalism – which is why attempts have been made over recent years to try and undermine the nightmare dictatorship's economy via the use of chocolate biscuits.

As a result of the catastrophic 1990s famine, the DPRK's top brass allowed some limited economic reforms to take place, the most significant being the creation of the Kaesong Industrial Complex (KIC) in 2002 under the auspices of Kim Jong-il (1941–2011), father of the current chunky little leader, Kim

Jong-un. The KIC was a special economic zone in which sealed-off factories operated by 120 South Korean firms employed 50,000 North Korean workers, getting to pay them lower wages than they would back home while simultaneously opening up the North to outside influences, or so it was hoped. The real reason the DPRK developed the KIC was to increase their foreign currency reserves; workers' wages were paid direct to the North's government, and they then passed back the equivalent sum in North Korean notes to the factory staff – minus some 'necessary deductions', naturally. The KIC is currently closed due to deteriorating relations between North and South, but even while open it proved a source of severe controversy because of one particular product its factories were producing – Choco Pies. Choco Pies are the Far Eastern equivalent of Wagon Wheels, being two little circles of cake filled with marshmallow and covered over in chocolate, manufactured by a South Korean company called Orion. Such items may seem unremarkable in the mouth of a capitalist, but confectionaries of this kind were like miracles to the Communists of the North, to whom buttered cardboard is doubtless considered a culinary luxury. To the downtrodden workers of the DPRK, the KIC's factories contained many hitherto unknown wonders such as toilet paper (and indeed actual toilets) and the Choco Pies were yet another piece of magic from within Aladdin's Capitalist Cave. The South Korean bosses in the KIC factories started paying their workers with free Choco Pies as a non-monetary bonus supplement, hoping to boost morale and increase productivity. The workers seemed pleased with their new bounty, describing them as producing 'ecstasy' upon their very tongues, but inspections of the factory workers' bins revealed something strange – there were no Choco Pie wrappers in them. Why not? Apparently, it was because the workers were taking them home to use as a makeshift currency, deeming them more valuable per unit than many North Korean banknotes were. The chocolate biscuits had become chocolate coins!

At the height of the craze 120,000 Choco Pies were doled out to the biscuit-hungry plebs each day, with even corrupt soldiers guarding the KIC site demanding their customary bribes in Wagon Wheels instead of banknotes. If you believe the highest estimates, some 2.5 million Choco Pies were being used as coins per month, and trading at a value of £6.40 each, compared to their usual price of 16 pence in South Korea. A more realistic estimate of their value was 25 pence, but this was still 1 per cent of the average weekly wage of £25. So valuable did they become that KIC workers started holding sporting contests and placing massive bets in biscuits. This was all quite disturbing to the DPRK authorities because, as well as helping undermine the economy, the mass distribution of Choco Pies was helping undermine the ideological concept of *juche* as well. If capitalists were so bad, then why were their biscuits so tasty? The phenomenon was dubbed an 'invasion of the stomach', and the regime got nervous, remembering the old argument that the Iron Curtain ended up being torn down because the oppressed proletariat of Eastern Europe, jealous of blue Levis, had wanted to get their hands on more Western consumer goods. Several measures were adopted by the DPRK Politburo to stem the crisis, with all Choco Pie bonuses being banned in 2014 in favour of wage top-ups of free sausages instead. Another tactic was to spread fake news about the Choco Pies; according to North Korean media, the biscuits had been infected with unspecified 'weird substances' by the South, intended to 'shake our national defence' or cause illness. In some sense the Choco Pies were really undercover secret agents, which were 'spying and scheming' upon behalf of their capitalist masters, hoping to create a situation where 'the ideology of the people could wither at any moment'. These 'sweet symbols of capitalism' were then replaced by the North with cheap forged knock-off versions, a breed of pirated pies which just didn't taste as nice, thereby undermining the pseudo-currency's value.

To fight back, in 2014 activists in the South began dressing as paramilitaries and tying tens of thousands of real Choco Pies to helium balloons before sending them drifting over the border. They could go a bit crumbly at high-altitude, but kept their taste well enough to still be worth collecting, especially as they came packaged complete with amusing cartoon posters and propaganda leaflets depicting Kim Jong-un as a big fat warmonger. In particular, they implied he had stolen money intended to buy food-aid and used it to fund his missile-programme instead, with cartoons of giant nuclear-tipped corncobs undergoing blast-off intended to ram this message home to the starving millions. This invasion of the DPRK's sovereignty was considered so serious that Red soldiers were ordered to shoot any stray balloons on sight, and the launch-sites were threatened with artillery bombardment. Alternatively, DPRK officials warned their subjects that the leaflets and Wagon Wheels contained miniature bombs or highly powerful biological agents, which would immediately give you cancer 'and make your body suffer' if you so much as touched one. Foreign food, it was said, 'contains material that is harmful to socialism', so had to be prodded away into a designated safe area with a long stick. The balloons mirrored the Cold War phenomenon of *mauerseglers*, or 'wall sailors', balloons bearing gifts that were launched over the Berlin Wall by generous West Berliners to show their Eastern cousins what capitalist goodies they were missing out on. According to one South Korean academic, 'When North Koreans see high quality consumer goods [like Choco Pies] produced overseas, they begin to understand that their economic system doesn't really deliver.' If it can so easily be undermined by generic marshmallow treats, then the North Korean economy really must be in trouble; should all the currency within the DPRK's Treasury come one day to be made entirely from confectionary, there is a severe danger Fat Boy Kim might just eat it.[75]

Conclusion
The Penny Drops?

History doesn't repeat itself, but it does rhyme.
Mark Twain, author

Wouldn't it be nice if you didn't have to do any work and still got paid? If money quite literally rained down on you from nowhere? If only you had been wise enough to invest in a small shitting man, then such a dream could once have come true. The 'Money-Shitter', or *Geldschîsser* (also known as 'The Little Money Man' for those with more sensitive ears), was a type of Germanic fairy believed in during medieval times. Those possessed of one were fortunate indeed, as the being would constantly produce from within its anus a veritable shower of what must have looked like chocolate coins in reverse; brown on the outside, gold on the inside. Described as being a little grey man with light eyes, wearing a green cap and red jacket, and able to magically transform into an owl, toad or beetle, you could come across one by digging beneath a clump of three hazel trees found near a crossroads at midnight. Maintenance of the Money-Shitter was relatively simple. All you had to do was feed it, let it live in your attic, cellar or dung-pile (you do have a big pile of dung lying around your home, right?), and bathe it every day in a spoon. If you could manage all this, then you would be made for life – literally, because it was virtually impossible to get rid of a *Geldschîsser* once you had one, even by chucking it into a fire.[1] Medieval coin-shitting goblins have now gone right out of fashion, though.

Throughout this book we have seen many bizarre and clearly quite silly financial ideas make an appearance, from shrinking banknotes to economic equaeverpoise. Why is it that so many persons, many of whom appear well-educated and perfectly sane, can fall for such obvious fairy tale *Geldschîssers*? In answering this question, I can do no better than reproduce the conclusions of Hugh Gaitskell, a much more sensible man of the Left than some of those active in British politics today. Writing in a 1933 essay called *Four Monetary Heretics*, which discussed the likes of Major C. H. Douglas and Silvio Gesell, the former Labour leader had the following to say about such eccentrics:

> The ideas of monetary heretics are frequently vague or complicated and not as a rule expressed in the clearest possible manner ... [However] vagueness and complexity are not really limitations but, on the contrary, advantages, for they make the task of criticism difficult and tedious and enable the heretic to say with perfect truth that his views have never been refuted. At the same time, the support of the plain man is not in any way forfeited. For the most part he will not bother his head on the complicated details. He will be content to accept the broad conclusions largely on irrational grounds. As a rule the heretic can claim that he is a practical man, in touch with the realities of economic life and vitally interested in its reform, not content to toy with abstractions behind the shelter of a professorial salary ... It is in keeping with this outlook that every monetary heretic offers a single complete solution. The *one* thing alone has to be done. A unique masterstroke is required. There is to be no painful waiting, no lowering of standards, no difficult compromises, no social upheaval, but simply the adoption of one perfectly simple, perfectly feasible PLAN. Finally, the heretic is able to enlist support just because he is not an expert, just because he represents and expresses the common dislike and revolt against the expert. He is a plain practical man, proving to other plain practical men that the mysteries which these exalted intellects are alone suffered to understand are matters which can be made perfectly intelligible to the rest of the community. Thus he restores the public's self-respect.[2]

This may sound like a total rebuff to Michael Gove's now-celebrated jibe about experts, but in fact Gaitskell's opinion was more nuanced; he might have thought Gove was in some ways correct in his brusque assessment. Gaitskell's ultimate conclusion was thus: 'Economic experts can never be wholly trusted, and only with the utmost possible freedom for criticism ... can rapid ... progress be made.'[3] Disturbingly, therefore, when it comes to economics, we may well be in a situation in which neither acknowledged experts nor outright non-experts are entirely to be relied upon, given that either could easily be prone towards making genuine mistakes of interpretation, or else harbouring hidden agendas. Economics is no more an exact science than is Lawsonomy, and if economics really is more art than science, then perhaps nobody truly has all the answers. Some problems don't have solutions, at least not any complete or easy ones. No perfect economic system exists, I would venture to say; the flawed one we have in the West now may be just about the best humanity can do, although doubtless tinkering around its edges is always possible. Sadly, the poor will always be with us – especially under the aegis of certain economic 'gurus' like Hugo Chávez.

Being Economical with the Truth

The fact that Hugh Gaitskell was talking about the public's exasperation with the pronouncements of conventional economic experts way back in 1933 – the year Hitler came to power – speaks volumes. We will recall that people like Ezra Pound, confused by the financial abstractions of his day, blamed them all upon a giant Jewish conspiracy. Now that the world of finance has once more become bemusingly abstract and divorced from reality, surely there is a risk certain individuals might choose to follow similarly unpleasant and destructive paths yet again? If economic and political affairs go on being mismanaged as they are in the wake of the 2007/08 financial crash, and political and economic elites continue to try to frustrate the will of the people over issues such as Brexit, unwanted mass immigration, crony capitalism and hyper-globalisation, then the number of disillusioned people who ask themselves why this is happening and, hearing the siren-song of the economic conspiracy-theorists, conclude 'It's because of the Jews!', or something equally stupid, is only going to grow. Either that, or one day some loopy ideologue like Jeremy Corbyn will end up getting elected somewhere in the Western world, or some impractical lunacy like the Citizens' Wage be adopted, making national Treasuries dissolve away rather faster than even Silvio Gesell might have liked them to do. Instead of just ignoring all this as the Ship of State steams steadily on towards the looming iceberg, why do our politicians not act and take more account of people's reasonable concerns about such things, thereby popping the extremist bubbles of both Left and Right?

Support for capitalism across the West appears to be falling,[4] which, given that it is the greatest engine for wealth-creation the world has ever seen, is a terrible thing. In failing to sensibly temper its more unreasonable excesses, politicians and economists are in danger of seeing its core beneficial tenets assaulted in a far more unreasonable fashion, perhaps even by self-confessed Marxists like John McDonnell who by rights should have been consigned to their coffins long ago. Are our jelly-brained, jelly-spined leaders really so self-absorbed, sneering and tin-eared as to be unable to see that they are at severe risk of unleashing a new generation of Ezra Pounds upon the world if things carry on the way they are? Maybe someone should forge a book called *The Protocols of the Elders of Islington* and give these arrogant metropolitan fools a taste of their own medicine; either that or the Estate of Roger W. Babson should lend them his desired time-tube and collection of old newspapers and let them learn the lessons of history for once.

The Sick Men of Europe

Times may change, but human nature never does. The world's economy, being a financial expression of the activities, ideas, opinions, fears, hopes and follies of the human race, will always fluctuate; there never will be a complete end to intermittent periods of bubble and burst, no matter what Gordon 'No More Tory Boom and Bust' Brown may once have said.[5] There will always be economic winners and economic losers – except under systems like Communism, where everybody loses. Panics, downturns and declines will always appear, and so will hucksters offering utopian panaceas to a depressed and desperate public. No matter how illogical, dubious or outright poisonous their content, if they come coated all over in enough sugar, and the economic and social pain which they profess to eliminate is severe and distressing enough, such fake medicines will always have their willing takers; if a man as obviously mentally ill as Alfred W. Lawson can get 1.5 million followers for his peculiar daydreams about the forces of economic Suction and the potential financial benefits to be derived from a pig's solid squeal, so can anyone.

Such quack doctors' patients should be made aware, however, that the 'cure' being offered up by the Jeremy Corbyns, Ezra Pounds, Chesterbellocs, Benito Mussolinis, Karl Marxes, C. H. Douglases, Bible Bills, Adolf Hitlers, John McDonnells and Hugo Chávezes of this world is very often far worse than the original ailment ever was. Voters who, at this moment in time, are tempted to lend their votes to those politicians of whatever ideological cast who claim to be able to offer them paradise on a plate at zero cost, should be extremely careful they don't walk into the doctor's surgery complaining of a headache and then stagger out again sometime later suffering from a fatal dose of financial ebola. A headache is a personal problem; ebola becomes epidemic, and fast. Marx may have been wrong about most things, but was worth listening to when he said that 'History repeats itself, first as tragedy, then as farce' – in economic terms, especially. When will the head-buriers who rule us finally realise? Perhaps not until Europe's neo-Marxists begin confiscating their homes and property … a fate which, in many ways, they might actually deserve. If and when the Titanic does start to go down, let's hope the blind captains who steered us all here get the privilege of being drowned first.

Notes

NOTE: *All websites accessed between March 2017 and September 2017.*
ACKNOWLEDGEMENT: Earlier, shorter versions of sections in this book regarding the economic ideas of Roger W. Babson, Hugo Chávez and Master Okawa's Happiness Realisation Party previously appeared in *Fortean Times* magazine and are reprinted here with permission in edited and altered form. Many thanks to the magazine's editor, David Sutton, for allowing this to happen.

Introduction: An Expert Dismissal

1. https://www.ft.com/content/3be49734-29cb-11e6-83e4-abc22d5d108c?mhq5j=e1
2. https://www.spectator.co.uk/2017/01/michael-gove-was-accidentally-right-about-experts/
3. https://www.theguardian.com/business/2016/oct/04/imf-peak-pessimism-brexit-eu-referendum-european-union-international-monetary-fund; https://www.theguardian.com/business/2016/jun/18/imf-says-brexit-would-trigger-uk-recession-eu-referendum; https://www.theguardian.com/business/2016/may/13/imf-warns-stock-market-crash-house-price-fall-eu-referendum-brexit; *Daily Mail*, 25 July 2017, pp.2, 16; *The Times*, 25 July 2017, p.12
4. http://www.bbc.co.uk/news/uk-politics-38525924; https://blogs.spectator.co.uk/2017/01/economists-didnt-call-brexit-wrong-andy-bank-england/; http://www.independent.co.uk/voices/economy-brexit-bank-of-england-forecasts-spending-outlooks-a7386181.html
5. http://uk.businessinsider.com/morgan-stanley-brexit-economic-forecasts-2017-1?r=US&IR=T
6. Bregman, 2017, pp.109–16

1. Unsound as a Pound: Ezra Pound, Vegetable-Money, Social Credit and Other Great Follies of the Great Depression

1. *The Paris Review* issue 28, Summer-Fall 1962, online at https://www.theparisreview.org/interviews/4598/ezra-pound-the-art-of-poetry-no-5-ezra-pound
2. Marsh, 2011, pp.14–15; Sehgal, 2015, p.150
3. Marsh, 2011, p.137
4. *An Introduction to the Economic Nature of the United States* in Pound, 1951
5. Hyde, 2006, pp.234-7, 245
6. Hyde, 2006, pp.262-4, 245
7. Marsh, 2011, pp.121, 125–6; Hyde, 2006, pp.245-7

8. Sieburth, 1987
9. *The Paris Review* issue 28, Summer-Fall 1962
10. Hyde, 2006, p.221; Marsh, 2011, p.51
11. Marsh, 2011, pp.61–6
12. Pound cited in Hyde, 2006, p.221
13. Cited in Marsh, 2011, p.144
14. Pound, 1933, pp.94–5
15. Sieburth, 1987
16. Marsh, 2011, p.132
17. *America, Roosevelt and the Causes of the Present War* in Pound, 1951
18. Hyde, 2006, p.262; Marsh, 2011, p.133
19. *Social Credit: An Impact* in Pound, 1951; Hyde, 2006, pp.261–2; Marsh, 2011, p.132
20. https://en.wikipedia.org/wiki/Banca_Monte_dei_Paschi_di_Siena
21. Cox, 2016, p.92
22. *Social Credit: An Impact* in Pound, 1951
23. Hyde, 2006, p.262
24. Pound, 1970, p.27
25. *Gold and Work* in Pound, 1951; I have conflated and re-ordered several different but related quotes here.
26. Marsh, 2011, p.91
27. Hyde, 2006, pp.242–3
28. Marsh, 2011, p.133
29. Ferguson, 2009, pp.56–7
30. *Social Credit: An Impact* in Pound, 1951
31. Sehgal, 2015, pp.168, 288
32. Hyde, 2006, pp.253–4
33. Ferguson, 2009, pp.36–7; Cox, 2016, pp.38–9, 72, 77–8
34. Marsh, 2011, pp.135–6
35. Ezra Pound, *On the Protocols*, available online at https://archive.org/details/OnTheProtocols
36. Sieburth, 1987
37. *Gold and Work* in Pound, 1951; Hyde, 2006, p.267
38. *What Is Money For?* in Pound, 1951; Hyde, 2006, p.264
39. *What Is Money For?* in Pound, 1951
40. *Social Credit: An Impact* in Pound, 1951
41. Sehgal, 2015, p.131
42. Ferguson, 2009, pp.79–98
43. *America, Roosevelt and the Causes of the Present War* in Pound, 1951
44. Hyde, 2006, p.249
45. *Gold and Work* in Pound, 1951
46. Hyde, 2006, p.268
47. *Gold and Work* in Pound, 1951
48. *What Is Money For?* in Pound, 1951
49. Hyde, 2006, p.246
50. Pound, 1933, p.14
51. Pound, 1933, p.20
52. Pound, 1933, p.42
53. Pound, 1933, pp.101–2
54. Pound, 1933, p.56
55. Pound, 1933, p.55
56. Pound, 1933, p.17
57. Pound, 1933, p.23
58. Pound, 1933, p.83
59. Sieburth, 1987

60. Pound, 1933, pp.114, 122, 123
61. Pound, 1933, p.125
62. Pound, 1933, p.109
63. Pound, 1933, p.93
64. https://mises.org/library/myth-just-price; https://en.wikipedia.org/wiki/Canon_law; https://en.wikipedia.org/wiki/Just_price
65. *Rerum novarum* online at http://w2.vatican.va/content/leo-xiii/en/encyclicals/documents/hf_l-xiii_enc_15051891_rerum-novarum.html
66. *Quadragesimo anno* online at https://web.archive.org/web/20060902085107/http://www.vatican.va/holy_father/pius_xi/encyclicals/documents/hf_p-xi_enc_19310515_quadragesimo-anno_en.html
67. Chesterton, 1910, p.59
68. Information and quotes about Distributism derived from http://www.theimaginativeconservative.org/2014/06/what-is-distributism.html; https://mises.org/library/whats-wrong-distributism; http://www.theamericanconservative.com/articles/distributism-is-the-future/; http://distributistreview.com/g-k-chestertons-distributism/; http://distributist.blogspot.co.uk/2007/01/distributivism-of-hilaire-belloc.html; https://en.wikipedia.org/wiki/Distributism
69. http://distributistreview.com/g-k-chestertons-distributism/
70. Goldberg, 2009, p.297
71. *America, Roosevelt and the Causes of the Present War* in Pound, 1951
72. Goldberg, 2009, pp.31–6, 44–5
73. Welk, 1938, pp.23–39; 43–72
74. Cited in Welk, 1938, p.33
75. Goldberg, 2009, pp.207–9
76. Goldberg, 2009, pp.14, 52
77. http://www.washingtontimes.com/news/2015/nov/15/editorial-a-lttle-history-of-politically-correct/
78. *Social Credit: An Impact* in Pound, 1951
79. Sieburth, 1987
80. Goldberg, 2009, p.33; http://archives.chicagotribune.com/1935/12/19/page/3/article/queen-of-italy-gives-treasury-wedding-rings
81. Gaitskell in Cole, 1934, pp.282–9
82. All quotes and details here taken from Douglas, 1935
83. All quotes and details here taken from Marsh, 2011, pp.118–20; Martin-Nielsen, 2007; http://en.wikipedia.org/wiki/Social_credit
84. Stingel, 1997, pp.12, 13, 45–51
85. *The Social Crediter*, 6 May 1939
86. Douglas, 1937b
87. Douglas, 1936a
88. Sehgal, 2015, p.102
89. Douglas, 1936c
90. Douglas, 1936b; Douglas, 1937a
91. http://en.wikipedia.org/wiki/Social_credit
92. Douglas, 1936a
93. All quotes and details here taken from Douglas, 1947; http://en.wikipedia.org/wiki/Social_credit
94. All quotes and details here taken from Stingel, 1997, pp.41–3, 51–5, 97
95. Cox, 2016, p.72
96. All quotes and details here taken from Stingel, 1997, pp.1, 57–8, 61–3, 65–8, 101–4, 108, 109–10, 118–19, 128, 129–30, 132, 137–9, 140, 149
97. Hugh Gaitskell, *Four Monetary Heretics* in Cole, 1934, pp.311–24; Werner Onken, 2000; https://en.wikipedia.org/wiki/Silvio_Gesell; http://historum.com/european-history.19444-how-war-declared-against-switzerland-1919-a.html; http://spartacus-educational.com/GERbavarian.htm; *New York Times*, 14 April

1919; https://en.wikipedia.org/wiki/Bavarian_Soviet_Republic; http://www.ic.org/wiki/eden/

98. Keynes, 1936, pp.353–8
99. Gaitskell in Cole, 1934, pp.311, 35–16
100. Cited in Gaitskell in Cole, 1934, p.315
101. Hyde, 2006, pp.263–4; Gaitskell in Cole, 1934, p.317–18
102. *Gold and Work* in Pound, 1951
103. Gaitskell in Cole, 1934, pp.321–3; Keynes, 1936, pp.357–8
104. Marsh, 2011, p.14
105. http://www.oocities.org/vienna/5373/notgeld.htm; http://en.wikipedia.org/wiki/Notgeld
106. Fisher, 1933, Ch.IV
107. Cited in Fisher, 1933, Ch.IV
108. Fisher, 1933, Ch.IV; Gaitskell in Cole, 1934, pp.323–4; http://www.litaer.com/2010/03/the-worgl-experiment/; https://mises.org/library/free-money-miracle; some of the precise figures about the Wörgl experiment differ from account to account.
109. Onken, 2000, pp.609–22; http://www.ic.org/wiki/eden/
110. Gatch, 2009
111. All quotes and details here taken from Fisher, 1933, Ch.II
112. Fisher, 1933, Ch.V
113. Fisher, 1933, Ch.V
114. Fisher, 1933, Appendix I
115. Douglas, 1936a; Marsh, 2011, pp.120–2

2. Pennies from Heaven: Buddhist Economics, the Economy of Eden and Talking High Finance with the Ghost of Mrs Thatcher

1. Moss, 2010, pp.4–13
2. Wood, 1984, pp.220–2
3. Schumacher cited in Wood, 1984, p.223
4. *Daily Mail*, 12 June 2017, p.23
5. Lachman, 2006; Barrett, 2011, pp.34–6; http://www.bbc.co.uk/news/education-28646118
6. Preparata, 2003; http://www.rsarchive.org/RelAuthors/BarfieldOwen/barfield_economics.php
7. http://social-ecology.org/wp/2009/01/rudolf-steiner%E2%80%99s-threefold-commonwealth-and-alternative-economic-thought/; https://www.rudolfsteinerweb.com/Rudolf_Steiner_and_Economics.php
8. Steiner, 1972; Preparata, 2003
9. Onken, 2000
10. Paull, 2011; Lectures One and Two of Rudolf Steiner's Agriculture Course, accessed online at http://wn.rsarchive.org/Lectures/GA327/English/BDA1958/19240607p01.html;http://wn.rsarchive.org/Lectures/GA327/English/BDA1958/19240610p01.html; https://en.wikipedia.org/wiki/Byodynamic_agriculture
11. Kurlander, 2017, pp.19, 55–6, 146–50, 233–6, 239–40; http://social-ecology.org/wp/2009/01/anthroposophy-and-ecofascism-2/
12. More-Collyer, 2004; https://en.wikipedia.org/wiki/Soil_Association
13. Wood, 1984, pp.236–7
14. Schumacher cited in Wood, 1984, p.229
15. Wood, 1984, pp.230–1; http://www.duversity.org/institute_2.htm
16. http://www.duversity.org/institute_2.htm; https://en.wikipedia.org/wiki/John_G._Bennett
17. Wilson, 2006, pp.502–4, 506–11; https://www.gurdjieff.org/driscoll5.htm

18. Cited in Moss, 2010, p.23
19. Wood, 1984, pp.234–6
20. Schumacher cited in Wood, 1984, p.238
21. Wood, 1984, pp.240–2
22. Wood, 1984, pp.242–4
23. https://en.wikipedia.org/wiki/Flag_of_India
24. http://www.mkgandhi.org/articles/gandhian_economics.htm; https://en.wikipedia.org/wiki/Gandhian_economics
25. Kumarappa, 1984, pp.119–20; https://archive.org/details/AGandhianEconomistAheadOfHisTime-J.C.Kumarappa; https://en.wikipedia.org/wiki/J._C._Kumarappa
26. Kumarappa, 1984, pp.10–11
27. Cited in Cox, 2016, p.145
28. Kumarappa, 1984, pp.12–14
29. Kumarappa, 1984, p.22
30. Kumarappa, 1984, pp.117–18
31. Kumarappa, 1984, pp.110–14
32. Kumarappa, 1984, p.9
33. Wood, 1984, pp.314–15, 317–18, 320
34. Wood, 1984, pp.244–5
35. Wood, 1984, pp.250, 252
36. Cited in Wood, 1984, pp.312–13
37. Wood, 1984, pp.246–7, 317
38. Wood, 1984, pp.248–9
39. http://wn.rsarchive.org/Lectures/GA327/English/BDA1958/19240610p01.html
40. Sedgwick, 2009, pp.23–4, 25–6, 28, 212–13; Wood, 1984, pp.255–6
41. http://www.centerforneweconomics.org/content/small-beautiful-quotes
42. Guénon, 2001, pp.49, 51–2
43. Kumarappa, 1984, pp.3, 56–60, 78–82, 89–91
44. Guénon, 2001, pp.55–61
45. All quotes and details here taken from Guénon, 2001, pp.105–112
46. Cited in Moss, 2010, p.48
47. Moss, 2010, p.24
48. Cited in Moss, 2010, p.36
49. All quotes and details here taken from Rudolf Steiner, *The Ahrimanic Deception* (1919), accessed online at http://wn.rsarchive.org/Lectures/19191027p01.html
50. Wood, 1984, p.237
51. Schumacher, 1989, pp.33–4
52. http://www.wisebrain.org/RightLivelihood.pdf
53. Schumacher, 1989, pp.57–9
54. Schumacher, 1989, pp.60–1
55. Cited in Moss, 2010, p.46
56. Schumacher, 1989, p.66
57. http://www.centerforneweconomics.org/content/small-beautiful-quotes
58. Sedgwick, 2009, p.213
59. http://www.centerforneweconomics.org/content/small-beautiful-quotes
60. Schumacher, 1989, pp.63–4
61. *The Times*, 24 January 2015, p.17
62. Compiled from *Daily Mail*, 26 January 2015; *The Times*, 23 January 2015; *The Times*, 3 February 2015
63. Biography of Bulgakov compiled from Young, 2011, pp.108–9; Stanchev, 2008, pp.152–5; Evtuhov, 'Introduction' in Bulgakov, 2000, pp.1–7; https://en.wikipedia.org/wiki/Sergei_Bulgakov

64. Biography of Solovyov compiled from Young, 2011, pp.92–4; Judith Deutsch Kornblatt, *Russian Religious Thought and the Jewish Kabbalah* in Rosenthal, 1997, pp.75–6
65. Kornblatt in Rosenthal, 1997, pp.79–80; https://en.wikipedia.org/wiki/Sophia_(wisdom)
66. Poem online at http://www.poetry-chaikhana.com/Poets/S/SolovyovVlad/ThreeMeeting/index.html
67. Young, 2011, p.107
68. Kornblatt in Rosenthal, 1997, pp.79–85
69. All quotes and details here taken from Young, 2011, pp.99, 101–5; Kornblatt in Rosenthal, pp.79–80, 85
70. Bulgakov, 2008, pp.157–8
71. Bulgakov, 2008, p.160
72. Bulgakov, 2008, pp.166–7
73. Young, 2011, p.110; Cox, 2016, p.69; https://en.wikipedia.org/wiki/Economy
74. Tawney, 1926, pp.31–2
75. Bulgakov, 2008, pp.169, 171–2
76. Bulgakov, 2008, p.172
77. Weber cited in Bulgakov, 2008, p.173
78. Bulgakov, 2000, p.18
79. Bulgakov, 2000, pp.95–103
80. Bulgakov, 2000, p.103
81. Bulgakov, 2000, p.103
82. Young, 2011, p.117
83. Bulgakov, 2000, pp.110–11
84. Bulgakov, 2000, p.108
85. Bulgakov, 2000, pp.114–15
86. Bulgakov, 2000, pp.72–3
87. Bulgakov, 2008, p.142
88. Bulgakov, 2008, pp.134–5
89. Bulgakov, 2008, p.136
90. Bulgakov, 2008, pp.139, 141
91. All quotes and details here taken from Bulgakov, 2008, pp.145–7
92. Bulgakov, 2008, pp.151, 152
93. Bulgakov, 2008, p.154
94. Wood, 1984, p.312
95. Wood, 1984, pp.265–6
96. Cited in Moss, 2010, p.46
97. Schumacher, 1989, p.297
98. http://www.smallisbeautiful.org/library.html
99. http://www.centerforneweconomics.org/content/small-beautiful-quotes; Moss, 2010, p.57
100. http://earthjournalism.net/stories/6468; http://www.gnhcentrebhutan.org/what-is-gnh/the-story-of-gnh/; https://www.theguardian.com/world/2012/dec/01/bhutan-wealth-happiness-counts
101. https://www.theguardian.com/lifeandstyle/2010/nov/14/happiness-index-britain-national-mood; https://www.theguardian.com/politics/2011/mar/27/schumacher-david-cameron-small-beautiful; https://www.greenparty.org.uk/archive/news-archive/2358.html; https://www.theguardian.com/society/2006/jul/02/voluntarysector.conservativeparty; http://www.fwi.co.uk/business/camerons-pledge-for-the-future.htm; https://www.theguardian.com/politics/2011/mar/27/small-beautiful-david-cameron-big-society
102. http://happy-science.org/ryuho-okawa/; http://happy-science.org/el-cantare/
103. http://happy-science.org/activities/

104. http://eng.the-liberty.com/about-us/

105. http://eng.the-liberty.com/2013/4397/; http://eng.the-liberty.com/2013/4400/; http://eng.the-liberty.com/2012/995/

106. http://eng.the-liberty.com/2015/5527/

107. http://eng.the-liberty.com/2015/6030/

108. http://eng.the-liberty.com/2016/6121/; http://eng.the-liberty.com/2016/6323/

109. http://eng.the-liberty.com/2015/5649/; http://www.bbc.co.uk/news/business-35436187

110. http://eng.the-liberty.com/2015/6030/

111. http://dailysignal.com/2015/09/15/heres-how-religion-shaped-margaret-thatchers-politics/

112. Kintz, 1997, pp.217–29; https://www.washingtonpost.com/national/religion/michael-novak-theologian-who-made-a-spiritual-case-for-capitalism-dies-at-83/2017/02/17/fa38989c-f212-11e6-8d7a; https://acton.org/pub/commentary/2017/02/22/michael-novak-book-that-changed-reality; https://www.nytimes.com/2017/02/19/us/michael-novak-dead-catholic-scholar.html?mcubz=0

113. Haigh, 1994

114. All quotes and details here taken from http://www.share-international.org/maitreya/Ma_prior.htm; http://www.xan.co.uk/wordpress/tag/bartering/

115. Barrett, 2010; Barrett, 2011, p.43

3. Taxing Credulity: Gabriel Green and the Interplanetary Campaign to Abolish Income-Tax

1. Sources used here and throughout this chapter for general information about Green's life: http://www.ourcampaigns.com/CandidateDetail.html?CandidateID=48068; http://gabe-green.blogspot.co.uk/2013/09/interview-at-august-1960-afsca.html; http://gabe-green.blogspot.co.uk/2013/09/america-needs-space-age-president.html; http://gabe-green.blogspot.co.uk/2015/11/green-at-57-saucer-convention.html; https://hatch.kookscience.com/wiki/Gabriel_Green; https://hatch.kookscience.com/wiki/Amalgamated_Flying_Saucer_Clubs_of_America_(AFSCA); https://en.wikipedia.org/wiki/Gabriel_Green

2. Clark, 2010, pp.160–1; Clark, 2000, pp.177–8; http://science.howstuffworks.com/space/aliens-ufos/monka-mars.htm

3. *Los Angeles Mirror-News*, 11 July 1959 & 10 August 1960; *Houston Post*, 15 May 1966; http://rsparlourtricks.blogspot.co.uk/2005/11/lets-face-facts-about-flying-saucers.html

4. An extensive archive of Green's variously-titled magazines, newsletters and pamphlets, including all those numbered issues from which I state in the main text that I have taken information, both above and below, is available online at http://www.afu.se/Downloads/Magazines/United%20States/

5. The full text of *UFO Contact from Planet Iarga*, together with an introduction from Wendelle Stevens, is online at http://www.galactic.no/rune/iarga.html; other info taken from http://www.exopaedia.org/Korendor; Tucker, 2017, pp.141–4

6. http://exonews.org/true-exopolitics-space-people-warn-dangers-social-divide/

7. Sehgal, 2015, pp.190–1

8. http://ourcampaigns.com/CandidateDetail.html?CandidateID=48078; http://www.modbee.com/living/article3118424.html; http://ulcnetwork.blogspot.co.uk/2010/07/truth-about-kirby-hensley-ulc-modesto.html; http://kernelmag.dailydot.com/issue-titles/religion/11097/universal-life-church-ordained/; http://community.beliefnet.com/cauleys/blog/2011/03/07/the_history_of_the_universal_life_churh; *Weekly World News*, 27 October 1981, p.34; http://www.nytimes.com/1976/09/19/archives/half-of-towns-residents-ordained-to-qualify-for-taxexempt-status.html?mcubz=0; https://en.wikipedia.org/wiki/Kirby_J._Hensley; https://en.wikipedia.org/wiki/Universal_Life_Church; http://www.ourcampaigns.

com/CandidateDetail.html?CandidateID=48068; https://hatch.kookscience.com/wiki/Gabriel_Green

9. See *AFSCA Information Sheet Number Three*, online at http://www.afu.se/Downloads/Magazines/United%20States/

10. http://web.archive.org/web/20050206145820/http://friendpages.com/p/pages/cover.cgi?pageid=flyingsaucers11

11. The website from which all this information was gleaned, though no longer online, was once located at http://members.shaw.ca/akwu

12. http://www.unecfreedom.com/; http://www.unecfreedom.com/universal; http://www.unecfreedom.com/bio; http://www.unecfreedom.com/video.html; https://grahamhancock.com/bournewp1/

4. Going Caracas: Hugo Chávez and the Economic Murder of Venezuela

1. *The Times*, 30 May 2017, p.31, 18 September 2017, p.36; https://www.theguardian.com/commentisfree/2016/may/22/radical-leftwing-tourists-pimps-dictatorship-hugo-chavez-venezuela-sex-tourism

2. All figures compiled from *The Times*, 13 May 2017, p.48, 7 Aug 2017, pp.26, 32, 9 September 2017, p.46, 16 September 2017, p.47; *Sunday Times*, 6 August 2017, p.15; *Daily Mail*, 7 August 2017, p.16; http://www.bbc.co.uk/news/world-latin-america-38646464; https://www.bloomberg.com/news/articles/2016-04-27/venezuela-faces-its-strangest-shortage-yet-as-inflation-explodes

3. http://theweek.com/article/index/241250/3-conspiracy-theories-about-hugo-chavezs-death; http://www.theguardian.com/world/2011/dec/29/hugo-chavez-us-cancer-plot; http://www.theguardian.com/world/2013/mar/07/maduro-alleges-chavez-cancer-plot

4. Carroll, 2013, pp. 136–8, 182–3; http://www.reuters.com/article/us-venezuela-chavez-mars/chavez-says-capitalism-may-have-ended-life-on-mars-idUSTRE72L61D20110322

5. Carroll, 2013, pp.211–15; http://www.venezuelasolidarity.co.uk/tony-benn-vsc-statement/

6. Carroll, 2013, pp.47, 59–61

7. Carroll, 2013, pp.101–3

8. Carroll, 2013, pp.65–6, 217–18; *The Times*, 7 August 2017, p.26

9. *The Times*, 30 May 2017, p.31, 7 August 2017, p.26; https://www.theguardian.com/world/2017/jul/31/us-venezuela-sanctions-nicolas-maduro

10. Carroll, 2013, pp.21–2, 160

11. *The Times*, 23 July 2015, p.37, 10 July 2017, p.36; 7 August 2017, p.33; *Daily Mail*, 8 August 2017, p.9

12. Carroll, 2013, pp.216–7, 281–2; *The Times*, 26 August 2014, p.32, 25 July 2017, p.38

13. *The Times*, 9 January 2014, p.30

14. Carroll, 2013, pp.57, 133, 216–17

15. Carroll, 2013, pp.121–2, 162–7; *The Times*, 7 August 2017, p.26; http://www.reuters.com/article/us-venezuela-giordani/venezuela-becoming-laughing-stock-ex-chavez-economic-guru-says-idUSKBN0L71KV20150203; https://www.thguardian.com/world/2017/feb/17/venezuelan-vice-president-just-latest-to-be-called-drug-traffickers

16. Carroll, 2013, p.178; https://www.theguardian.com/world/2017/jul/31/us-venezuela-sanctions-nicolas-maduro

17. https://en.wikipedia.org/wiki/Antisemitism_in_Venezuela; https://www.theguardian.com/world/2017/may/17/venezuela-president-nicolas-maduro-hitler-jews; http://www.radiojai.com.ar/OnLine/notiDetalle.asp?id_Noticia=64998

18. *Daily Mail*, 7 August 2017, p.16

19. http://en.wikipedia.org/wiki/Nicol%C3%A1s_Maduro
20. *The Times*, 13 August 2013, p.33, 31 July 2014, p.27
21. *The Times*, 6 November 2013, p.39
22. *The Times*, 13 November 2014, p.45
23. http://www.reuters.com/article/2013/11/09/us-venezuela-economy-idUSBRE9A808C20131109
24. http://www.dailymail.co.uk/news/article-2481553/Hugo-Chavezs-face-mysteriously-appears-tunnel-wall-diggers-drill-Venezuela.html
25. http://www.economist.com/blogs/americasview/2013/12/venezuelas-local-elections
26. Carroll, 2013, pp.14, 16–17, 23–4, 73, 136
27. http://en.wikipedia.org/wiki/Hugo_Ch%C3%A1vez
28. *The Times*, 31 July 2014, p.27
29. *The Times*, 3 February 2015, p.31
30. *The Times*, 3 September 2014, p.33
31. *The Times*, 17 April 2014, p.30
32. *The Times*, 5 August 2017, p.39
33. Carroll, 2013, pp.220–1; Kozloff, 2008; *Sunday Times*, 6 August 2017, p.15, 13 August 2017, p.16; *The Times*, 19 September 2014, p.43, 13 May 2017, p.48; http://foreignpolicy.com/2014/09/16/dont-get-sick-in-venezuela/; http://www.reuters.com/article/us-venezuela-health/venezuelas-maduro-asks-u-n-to-help-ease-medicine-shortages-idUSKBN16W063; https://www.nytimes.com/2016/09/28/world/americas/venezuela-refuses-us-aid.html; http://venezuelatoday.net/venezuelan-government-continues-to-block-humanitarian-aid-efforts-that-could-save-lives-during-crisis/
34. *The Times*, 3 August 2017, p.14; *Daily Mail*, 8 August 2017, p.8
35. *Daily Mail*, 8 August 2017, p.8, 9 August 2017, p.10
36. *Daily Mail*, 1 August 2017, p.12
37. *The Times*, 2 August 2017, p.27
38. https://www.handsoffvenezuela.org/mcdonnell-pushes-pm-chavez-choice.htm
39. *The Times*, 3 August 2017, pp.14, 30, 7 August 2017, p.9; *Daily Mail*, 11 August 2017, p.18
40. *The Times*, 3 August 2017, pp.14, 25, 5 August 2017, p.15; https://www.theguardian.com/uk-news/2017/sep/12/unite-boss-len-mccluskey-we-could-break-law-to-strike
41. https://www.theguardian.com/world/2014/apr/08/venezuela-protests-sign-us-wants-oil-says-nicolas-maduro; https://www.theguardian.com/world/2014/apr/08/maduro-hippy-love-led-zeppelin-john-lennon; https://www.theguardian.com/commentisfree/2014/apr/09/venezuela-protest-defence-privilege-maduro-elites
42. *The Times*, 3 August 2017, p.14
43. *Daily Mail*, 3 August 2017, p.5, 19 September 2017, p.35
44. *The Times*, 4 August 2017, p2; *Daily Mail*, 9 August 2017, p.10; https://www.theguardian.com/politics/2017/aug/03/ken-livingstone-venezuela-crisis-hugo-chavez-oligarchs; http://www.washingtonexaminer.com/the-british-left-doubles-down-on-venezuelas-nicolas-maduro/article/2630549; http://www.bbc.co.uk/news/uk-politics-40810341
45. *The Times*, 1 August 2017, p.13; *Daily Mail*, 4 August 2017, p.8; http://news.bbc.co.uk/1/hi/england/london/6377867.stm; https://www.theguardian.com/politics/2017/aug/03/ken-livingstone-venezuela-crisis-hugo-chavez-oligarchs; https://www.marxist.com/chavez-historic-visit-london180506.htm
46. *Daily Mail*, 3 August 2017, p.5
47. Carroll, 2013, pp.93–6
48. *Daily Mail*, 20 September 2017, p.10
49. *The Times*, 3 August 2017, p.14
50. *Daily Mail*, 3 August 2017, p.19

51. https://www.theguardian.com/commentisfree/2012/oct/09/chavez-victory-beyond-latin-america

52. https://www.theguardian.com/commentisfree/2013/feb/19/no-alternative-latin-america-has-a-few

53. http://www.theguardian.com/world/2017/mar/17/bakers-arrested-illegal-brownies-venezuela-bread-war

54. https://www.theguardian.com/world/2017/sep/14/Venezuela-president-maduro-rabbit-plan

55. *Times*, 12 July 2014, p.37

5. Loose Change: A Pocketful of Fool's Gold and Bad Pennies

1. Sehgal, 2015, pp.42–55

2. Gaitskell in Cole, 1934, pp.325–34; https://blog.supplysideliberal.com/post/77041501112/robert-eisler-stable-money-the-remedy-for-the; https://en.wikipedia.org/wiki/Man_into_Wolf

3. Compiled from Kossy, 1994, pp.145–7; http://telekon.org/kook/brainbeau.html

4. Gaitskell in Cole, 1934, pp.304–11; http://www.cadmusjournal.org/node/146; https://en.wikipedia.org/wiki/Frederick_Soddy

5. http://www.nytimes.com/2009/04/12/opinion/12zencey.html?_r=1&ref=opinion

6. Soddy, 1933, Ch. I

7. Soddy, 1933, Chs. II, III, VI; http://www.nytimes.com/2009/04/12/opinion/12zencey.html?_r=1&ref=opinion

8. Soddy, 1933, Ch. VI

9. Soddy, 1933, Ch. V

10. Soddy, 1934, p.207

11. Soddy, 1934, p.214

12. Soddy, 1934, pp.213, 215; Webb, 1976, pp.131–5

13. Soddy, 1934, pp.218–20

14. http://longstreet.typepad.com/thesciencebookstore/2012/07/frederick-soddys-economics-and-the-protocols-of-the-elders-of-zion-1939-.html

15. Soddy, 1933, Ch. XIV

16. Roger W. Babson, 1948, *Gravity: Our Enemy Number One*, reprinted in Collins, 2004, pp.828-831

17. Mulkern, 1995, pp.3–16; Gardner, 1957, pp.92–100; http://www.babson.edu/about-babson/at-a-glance/babsons-history/Pages/biography-of-roger-babson.aspx

18. Babson, 1950, pp.266–73

19. Babson, 1930, p.49

20. Babson, 1950, pp.266–73; Babson, 1932, pp.49–50

21. Babson, 1950, pp.245–56

22. Babson, 1950, p.248

23. http://www.babson.edu/about-babson/at-a-glance/babsons-history/Pages/biography-of-roger-babson.aspx

24. All quotes and details here taken from Babson, 1950, pp.257–65

25. Babson, 1950, pp.307–8

26. http://www.prohibitionists.org/history/roger_babson_bio.htm; https://en.wikipedia.org/wiki/Prohibition_Party

27. All quotes and details here taken from Babson, 1950, pp.299–316, 327–8

28. Gardner, 1957, pp.92–100; Babson, 1950, pp.340–4

29. http://www.popsci.com/science/article/2011-03/gravitys-sworn-enemy-roger-babson-and-gravity-research-foundation; http://www.gravityresearchfoundation.org/origins.html

30. http://tradersnetwork.com/educational/swing-trading-with-market-timing-intelligence-using-action-reaction-and-median-lines-to-improve-your-timing-for-entry-and-exits/

31. http://www.economicsonline.co.uk/Global_economics/Gravity_theory_of_trade. html; https://www.theguardian.com/business/economics-blog/2017/jan/08/ economic-forecasts-hardwired-get-things-wrong
32. Tucker, 2016, pp.201–4; http://hello-earth.com/margaretstorm/margaretstorm.html
33. Storm, 1959, p.272
34. All quotes and details here taken from Storm, 1959, pp.216–19
35. Storm, 1959, pp.132–3
36. Cited in Kurlander, 2017, p.231
37. Kurlander, 2017, pp.252–4, 256–7
38. Storm, 1959, p.272–4
39. Storm, 1959, p.184
40. Storm, 1959, p.108
41. Storm, 1959, p.85
42. All quotes and details here taken from Storm, 1959, pp.274–6
43. Storm, 1959, pp.139–40
44. All quotes and details here taken from Storm, 1959, pp.147–8
45. All quotes and details here taken from Storm, 1959, pp.276–80
46. All information about Hargrave compiled from Webb, 1976, pp.86–93, 119–36, 512–13; Craven, 1998, pp.181–97,251–306; Barberis, McHugh & Tyldesley, 2000, pp.226–30; *New Scientist*, 10 June 1976; http://www.historyextra.com/ article/premium/march-green-shirts-history; https://www.theguardian.com/ artanddesign/2015/nov/02/kindred-of-the-kibbo-kift-1920s-youth-movement; https:// web.archive.org/web/20160305104722/http://kibbokift.org/jhbio.htm; https:// web.archive.org/web/20160304174253/http://kibbokift.org/chronolo.htm; https:// web.archive.org/web/20160315142213/http://kibbokift.org/kkkhist.htm; https:// www.newcriterion.com/print/article/8702; https://thejohnfleming.wordpress. com/2012/03/20/the-eccentric-uk-cult-of-the-kibbo-kift-kindred-the-greenshirts-of- the-1930s; https://en.wikipedia.org/wiki/John_Hargrave
47. Webb, pp.123–4; Craven, 1998, pp285–6, 304–5; http://www. anglicanfreecommunion.org.uk/Boltwood.htm; https://web.archive.org/ web/20160305104722/http://kibbokift.org/jhbio.htm
48. Hargrave cited in Webb, 1976, pp.512–13
49. Gildart, Howell & Kirk, 2003, pp.254–60
50. Wall, 2003; Craven, 1998, p.286; http://archive.sustecweb.co.uk/past/sustec15-3/ why_i_am_not_a_social_crediter.htm; http://www.douglassocialcredit.com/; http:// www.spunk.org/texts/pubs/freedom/raven/sp001749.html
51. https://web.archive.org/web/20160421224812/http://kibbokift.org/wakenow.htm
52. Tucker, 2016, pp.247–50, 277–81
53. Henry, 2009, pp.114–27
54. Henry, 2009, pp.128–9
55. All quotes and details here taken from Lawson, 1935, pp.1–5
56. Lawson, 1935, pp.6–8
57. All quotes and details here taken from Lawson, 1935, pp.12–19
58. Lawson, 1935, pp.23–9
59. All quotes and details here taken from Lawson, 1931; Henry, 2009, pp.129–37
60. Henry, 2009, pp.168–71
61. Henry, 2009, pp.154–5
62. *The Benefactor* Vol.1, No.4
63. Henry, 2009, pp.117–18
64. Lawson, 1935, pp.12–13
65. *The Benefactor* Vol.1, No.5
66. *The Benefactor* Vol.1, No.4
67. Henry, 2009, pp.143–51
68. Henry, 2009, pp.162–4
69. Henry, 2009, pp.156–62

70. Henry, 2009, p.167
71. All quotes taken from *The Benefactor* Vol.1, No.5
72. Henry, 2009, pp.152–3, 165; *The Benefactor* Vol.1, No.4
73. Henry, 2009, pp.180–2, Tucker, 2016, pp.279–81
74. http://www.investopedia.com/articles/investing/013015/how-north-korea-economy-works.asp
75. Compiled from *The Times*, 9 April 2016, p.41; *Daily Mail*, 3 July 2014, p.32; https://www.lrb.co.uk/v35/no9/richard-lloydparry/advantage-pyongyang; https://www.washingtonpost.com/news/morning-mix/wp/2014/07/01/north-korea-has-reportedly-banned-choco-pies/?utm_term=.57dea2d58921; http://www.atimes.com/atimes/Korea/KE21Dg01.html; http://edition.cnn.com/2014/01/27/world/asia/choco-pie-koreas/; http://www.bbc.co.uk/news/world-asia-29751650; http://www.telegraph.co.uk/news/worldnews/asia/northkorea/8909888/Chocopie-inflation-in-North-Koreas-Kaesong-Industrial-Park.html; http://www.telegraph.co.uk/news/worldnews/asia/northkorea/10999802/South-Korea-sends-chocolate-snacks-into-North-Korea-via-balloon.html; http://www.telegraph.co.uk/news/worldnews/asia/northkorea/11666825/North-Korea-launches-Choco-Pie-counter-strike.html; http://english.chosun.com/site/data/html_dir/2010/01/12/2010011200624.html; http://english.chosun.com/site/data/html_dir/2014/06/30/2014063001853.html; https://www.theguardian.com/world/2014/may/08/choco-pies-disappear-pyongyang-north-korea; http://www.dailynk.com/english/read.php?cataId=nk01500&num=11124; http://www.dailynk.com/english/read.php?cataId=nk00100&num=11439; http://www.dailynk.com/english/read.php?num=11785&cataId=nk01500

Conclusion: The Penny Drops?

1. Lecouteux, 2013, pp.155–8
2. Gaitskell in Cole, 1934, pp.334–5
3. Gaitskell in Cole, 1934, p.335
4. *The Times*, 29 September 2017, p.8
5. http://www.channel4.com/news/articles/politics/domestic_politics/factcheck+no+more+boom+and+bust/2564157.html; http://www.telegraph.co.uk/finance/recession/4322033/UK-recession-Gordon-Brown-refuses-to-admit-return-of-boom-and-bust.html

Bibliography

NOTE: *When it comes to books, the dates of publication given below are for the editions I personally made use of while writing this book, and do not necessarily correspond with each title's first printing.*

Babson, Roger W., *Easy Street* (New York: Fleming H. Revell Company, 1930)

Babson, Roger W., *Cheer Up! Better Times Ahead* (New York: Fleming H. Revell Company, 1932)

Babson, Roger W., *Actions and Reactions: An Autobiography of Roger W. Babson* (New York: Harper & Bros, 1950)

Barberis, Peter, McHugh, John & Tyldesley, Mike, *Encyclopedia of British and Irish Political Organisations: Parties, Groups and Movements of the Twentieth Century* (London: Continuum, 2000)

Barrett, David V., 'I'm Not the Messiah' in *Fortean Times* 260, April 2010, p.8

Barrett, David V., *Secret Religions: A Complete Guide to Hermetic, Pagan and Esoteric Beliefs* (London: Robinson, 2011)

Bregman, Rutger, *Utopia for Realists: And How We Can Get There* (London: Bloomsbury, 2017)

Bulgakov, Sergei, *Philosophy of Economy: The World as Household* (New Haven, Connecticut & London: Yale University Press, 2000)

Bulgakov, Sergei, *The National Economy and the Religious Personality* in *Journal of Markets and Morality*, Vol.11, No.1, Spring 2008, pp.157–79

Carroll, Rory, *Comandante: The Life and Legacy of Hugo Chávez* (Edinburgh: Canongate, 2013)

Chesterton, G. K., *What's Wrong With the World* (London: Cassell, 1920)

Clark, Jerome, *Extraordinary Encounters: An Encyclopedia of Extraterrestrials and Otherworldly Beings* (Santa Barbara, California: ABC-Clio, 2000)

Clark, Jerome, *Hidden Realms, Lost Civilisations and Beings from Other Worlds* (Detroit, Illinois: Visible Ink Press, 2010)

Clover, Charles, *Black Wind, White Snow: The Rise of Russia's New Nationalism* (New Haven, Connecticut: Yale University Press, 2016)

Cole, G. D. H., *What Everybody Wants to Know About Money* (New York: Alfred A. Knopf, 1934)

Collins, Harry, *Gravity's Shadow* (Chicago, Illinois: University of Chicago Press, 2004)

Cox, Harvey, *The Market as God* (Cambridge, Massachusetts: Harvard University Press, 2016)

Craven, Joseph Francis Charles, *Redskins in Epping Forest: John Hargrave, the Kibbo Kift and the Woodcraft Experience*, academic thesis submitted to University College London, 1998

Douglas, C. H., *The Pyramid of Power* in *The English Review* issue 28, 1919, pp.49–58

Douglas, C. H., *Money and the Price System* (London: Social Credit Press, 1935)

Douglas, C. H., *The Approach to Reality* (London: KPP Publications, 1936) [Douglas, 1936a]

Douglas, C. H., *The Tragedy of Human Effort* [Douglas, 1936b] – accessed online at www.socred.org/index.php/pages/the-douglas-internet-archive

Douglas, C. H., *Money: An Historical Survey* in *The Fig Tree*, No.2, September 1936, pp.139–47 [Douglas, 1936c]

Douglas, C. H., *Dictatorship by Taxation* [Douglas, 1937a] – accessed online at www.socred.org/index.php/pages/the-douglas-internet-archive

Douglas, C. H., *The Policy of a Philosophy* (London: Social Credit Press, 1937) [Douglas, 1937b]

Douglas, C. H., *Realistic Constitutionalism* (1947) – accessed online at www.socred.org/index.php/pages/the-douglas-internet-archive

Ferguson, Niall, *The Ascent of Money: A Financial History of the World* (London: Penguin, 2009)

Fisher, Irving, *Stamp Scrip* (New York: Adelphi Company, 1933)

Gardner, Martin, *Fads and Fallacies in the Name of Science* (New York: Dover Books, 1957)

Gatch, Loren, *The Professor and a Paper Panacea: Irving Fisher and the Stamp-Scrip Movement of 1932–1934* in *Paper Money* No.260, March-April 2009, pp.125–42

Gildart, K., Howell, D. & Kirk, N., *Dictionary of Labour Biography, Volume XI* (Basingstoke: Palgrave Macmillan, 2003)

Goldberg, Jonah, *Liberal Fascism: The Secret History of the Left from Mussolini to the Politics of Meaning* (London: Penguin, 2009)

Guénon, René, *The Reign of Quantity and the Signs of the Times* (Hillsdale, New York: Sophia Perennis, 2001)

Haigh, Tim, *Is Creme Crackers?* in *Fortean Times* issue 74, April/May 1994, pp.39–42

Henry Jr, Lyell D., *Zig-Zag-and-Swirl: Alfred W. Lawson's Quest for Greatness* (Iowa City, Iowa: University of Iowa Press, 2009)

Hyde, Lewis, *The Gift* (Edinburgh: Canongate, 2006)

Keynes, J. M., *The General Theory of Employment, Interest and Money* (London: Macmillan, 1936)

Kintz, Linda, *Between Jesus and the Market* (Durham, North Carolina: Duke University Press, 1997)

Kossy, Donna, *Kooks: A Guide to the Outer Limits of Human Belief* (Portland, Oregon: Feral House, 1994)

Kozloff, Nikolas, *Revolution!: South America and the Rise of the New Left* (New York: Palgrave Macmillan, 2008)

Kumarappa, J. C., *Economy of Permanence: A Quest for a Social Order Based on Non-Violence* (Rajghat, India: Sarva Seva Sangh Prakashan, 1984)

Kurlander, Eric, *Hitler's Monsters: A Supernatural History of the Third Reich* (New Haven, Connecticut & London: Yale University Press, 2017)

Lachman, Gary, *Dweller on the Threshold* in *Fortean Times* 205, January 2006, pp.44–51

Lawson, Alfred W., *Direct Credits for Everybody* (Detroit, Michigan: Humanity Publishing Company, 1931)

Lawson, Alfred W., *Powerful Editorials* (Detroit, Michigan: Humanity Publishing Company, 1935)

Lecouteux, Claude, *The Tradition of Household Spirits* (Rochester, Vermont: Inner Traditions, 2013)

Marsh, Alec, *Critical Lives: Ezra Pound* (London: Reaktion, 2011)

Martin-Nielsen, Janet, *An Engineer's View of an Ideal Society: The Economic Reforms of C. H. Douglas, 1916–1920* in *Spontaneous Generations*, Vol.1, No.1, 2007, pp.95–109

Marx, Karl, *Capital* (Oxford: Oxford World's Classics, 1999)

More-Collyer, R., *Towards Mother Earth: Jorian Jenks, Organicism, the Right and the British Union of Fascists* in *Journal of Contemporary History*, Vol.39, No.3, pp.353–71, 2004

Moss, Walter G., *The Wisdom of E. F. Schumacher*, 2010; essay online at www.wisdompage.com/SchumacherEssay.pdf

Bibliography

Mulkern, John R., *Continuity and Change: Babson College, 1919–1994* (Massachusetts: Babson College Press, 1995)

Onken, Werner, *The Political Economy of Silvio Gesell: A Century of Activism* in *The American Journal of Economics and Sociology* Vol.59, No.4, October 2000, pp.609–22

Paull, John, *Attending the First Organic Agriculture Course: Rudolf Steiner's Agriculture Course at Koberwitz, 1924* in *European Journal of Social Sciences*, Vol.21, No.1, 2011

Pollen, Annebella, *The Kindred of the Kibbo Kift* in *Fortean Times* 336, January 2016, pp.34–9

Pound, Ezra, *ABC of Economics* (London: Faber & Faber, 1933)

Pound, Ezra, *Money Pamphlets* (London: Peter Russell, 1951)

Pound, Ezra, *Guide to Kulchur* (New York: New Directions, 1970)

Preparata, Guido Giacomo, *Perishable Money in a Threefold Commonwealth: Rudolf Steiner and the Economics of German Anarchism*, 2003 academic paper online at http://www.tripartizione.it/articoli/GGPreparata_Perishable_Money_in_a_Threefold_Commonwealth.pdf

Rosenthal, Bernice Glatzer (Ed.), *The Occult in Russian and Soviet Culture* (Ithaca, New York: Cornell University Press, 1997)

Schumacher, E. F., *Small Is Beautiful: Economics As If People Mattered* (New York: Harper Perennial, 1989)

Sedgwick, Mark, *Against the Modern World: Traditionalism and the Secret Intellectual History of the Twentieth Century* (Oxford: Oxford University Press, 2009)

Sehgal, Kabir, *Coined: The Rich Life of Money and How Its History Has Shaped Us* (London: John Murray, 2015)

Sieburth, Richard, *In Pound We Trust: The Economy of Poetry/The Poetry of Economics* in *Critical Inquiry* Vol. 14, No.1, Autumn 1987, pp.142–72

Smith, Adam, *An Inquiry Into the Nature and Causes of the Wealth of Nations* (London: W. Stratham & T. Cadell, 1776)

Soddy, Frederick, *Wealth, Virtual Wealth and Debt: The Solution of the Economic Paradox* (London: Britons Publishing Company, 1933)

Soddy, Frederick, *The Role of Money: What It Should Be, Contrasted With What It Has Become* (London: Routledge, 1934)

Stanchev, Krassen, *Sergei Bulgakov and the Spirit of Capitalism* in *Journal of Markets and Morality*, Vol.11, No.1, Spring 2008, pp.149–56

Steiner, Rudolf, *World Economy: The Formation of a Science of World Economics* (London: The Rudolf Steiner Press, 1972)

Stingel, Janine, *Social Credit and the Jews: Anti-Semitism in the Alberta Social Credit Movement and the Response of the Canadian Jewish Congress, 1935–1949*, academic thesis submitted to McGill University, Montreal, 1997

Storm, Margaret, *Return of the Dove* (Baltimore, Maryland: Millennium Publications, 1959)

Tawney, R. H., *Religion and the Rise of Capitalism* (New York: Harcourt & Brace, 1926)

Tucker, S. D., *Forgotten Science: Strange Ideas from the Scrapheap of History* (Stroud: Amberley, 2016)

Tucker, S. D., *Space Oddities: Our Strange Attempts to Explain the Universe* (Stroud: Amberley, 2017)

Wall, Derek, *Social Credit: The Ecosocialism of Fools* in *Capitalism, Nature, Socialism*, Vol.14, No.3, 2003, pp.99–122

Webb, James, *The Occult Establishment* (La Salle, Illinois: Open Court, 1976)

Welk, William G., *Fascist Economic Policy: An Analysis of Italy's Economic Experiment* (Cambridge, Massachusetts: Harvard University Press, 1938)

Wilson, Colin, *The Occult* (London: Watkins, 2006)

Wood, Barbara, *E. F. Schumacher: His Life and Thought* (New York: Harper & Row, 1984)

Young, George M., *The Russian Cosmists: The Esoteric Futurism of Nikolai Fedorov and His Followers* (New York: OUP, 2012)

Index